City of 201 Gods

City of 201 Gods

Ilé-Ifè in Time, Space, and the Imagination

———

Jacob K. Olúpònà

UNIVERSITY OF CALIFORNIA PRESS

Berkeley   Los Angeles   London

University of California Press, one of the most distinguished university presses in the United States, enriches lives around the world by advancing scholarship in the humanities, social sciences, and natural sciences. Its activities are supported by the UC Press Foundation and by philanthropic contributions from individuals and institutions. For more information, visit www.ucpress.edu.

University of California Press
Berkeley and Los Angeles, California

University of California Press, Ltd.
London, England

Library of Congress Cataloging-in-Publication Data

Olúpònà, Jacob K. (Jacob Kéhìndé), 1951–.
    City of 201 gods : ilé-ifè in time, space, and the imagination / Jacob K. Olúpònà.
        p.   cm.
    Includes bibliographical references and index.
    ISBN 978-0-520-26555-4 (cloth : alk. paper)
    ISBN 978-0-520-26556-1 (pbk. : alk. paper)
    1. Ife (Nigeria)—Religion.   2. Yoruba (African people)—Nigeria—Ife—Religion.   I. Title.   II. Title: City of two hundred one gods.
III. Title: City of two hundred and one gods.
    BL2470.N5O48   2011
    299.6'83330966926—dc22   2010021799

19   18   17   16   15   14   13   12   11
10   9   8   7   6   5   4   3   2   1

For Learned kings, scholars, and teachers
H. R. H. Ọba Dr. Solomon Babáyẹmí, the Olúfì of Gbọ̀ngán (1929–1997)
H. R. H. Ọba Dr. Timothy Olúwọlé Fáṣawè, the Olúòkè of Òkè-Igbó (1935–2007)
and
my other mother,
Oròníkẹ́ (Mama Kẹ́hìndé) of Òkè-Ìjege Quarters, Òkè-Igbó (c. 1919–1980),
who raised me as a twin
. . . in love and appreciation

CONTENTS

ILLUSTRATIONS

MAPS

FIGURES

My desire to carry out long-term ethnographic research in Ilé-Ifẹ̀ was first conceived in 1976, when I was employed as a Research Fellow by the University of Ifẹ̀ (renamed Ọbáfẹ́mi Awólọ́wọ̀ University) Ilé-Ifẹ̀. I began researching the city out of a profound sense of mission and curiosity. During that year, I lived with my parents at St. Philip's Vicarage, Aiyétòrò, Ilé-Ifẹ̀, a fair distance from the university campus, and I took a route that passed through the city center. I began to notice as I drove back and forth from the campus that I was always running into groups of people celebrating one form of festival or another. I also noticed that as one ceremony would end another would begin. It dawned on me that what I had thought was simply a common figure of speech—that there is only one day in an entire year when a festival is not performed in Ilé-Ifẹ̀—was literally true. As I returned home late one evening in December, I noticed that the city was not as bustling as usual in the late evening. Indeed, the city center was quiet and almost deserted. My parents were on the balcony anxiously waiting for me to come home. As I parked and walked up the stairway, my mother scolded me for being out so late, which was not unusual as I normally held evening classes on campus.

The difference this time around was that it was rumored that the king had joined his ancestors. As an Òkè-Igbó native of Ifẹ̀ extraction, my mother knew better than I that it was not safe to drive around the streets at night in those days, especially at such an auspicious time when the king-god was rumored to have ascended to the heavens of his ancestors. Rumors abounded about the rituals of burial of the deceased Ọ̀ọ̀ni and the investiture of a new Ọ̀ọ̀ni. One Ifẹ̀ chief who visited my father the next day told me that when an Ọ̀ọ̀ni died his body would be covered with smallpox and that traditional rituals were required to remove this impurity from the corpse before his burial. This ritual, according to the chief, was necessary before any mortal being could touch the deceased Ọ̀ọ̀ni. For the chief this was a sign that the king was indeed a living deity, but for me it was a reconfirmation of the mysteriousness that surrounded the city and its inhabitants. This event, which occurred almost seven years before I began my research, would spark my idea of authoring a work on the sacred Ilé-Ifẹ̀, a city of numerous, uncountable gods. The incident also made my parents ask one of the parishioners in the Ifẹ̀ law faculty, Mr. Awóyọdé, to find an apartment for me close to the campus and far from the city center. I lived there for the rest of the academic year before traveling to Boston for my graduate work.

It is, therefore, exceedingly important to begin by thanking my late parents, Michael and Henrietta Olúpọ̀nà, for supporting my early research and for taking a keen interest in my professional life. In addition, I benefited immensely from their hard work and good home they provided as missionaries in the Ilé-Ifẹ̀ Anglican community. Everywhere I went in Ilé-Ifẹ̀ to conduct research, when I introduced myself as the son of the Venerable Olúpọ̀nà, the response was always "Ọmọ Bàbá daadaa (the son of a good man)." The respect and affection Ifẹ̀ people had for my parents opened many doors and provided significant support and cooperation from the Ifẹ̀ elders, even those who were not Christians. This experience confirmed for me the popular Yorùbá adage that orúkọ rere saǹ ju wúrà àti fàdákà lọ (a good name is more precious than silver and gold)! Yet I did not feel ready enough to begin serious field research until after my doctoral work in Oǹdó, which culminated in my book Kingship, Religion and Rituals in a Nigeria Community. After returning to Ilé-Ifẹ̀ from Boston in 1983 I developed a second postdoctoral research interest and began to conduct occasional fieldwork in the city where I then lived. I thank most gratefully my sister and brother-in-law Sole and Laoye Jaiyeola for their support.

My other reason in embarking on this work comes from a disciplinary perspective and training in the comparative history of religions. My desire is to place on record at a crucial time in Yorùbá and Nigerian history, a time when the old traditional worldview and spiritualities are fast disappearing, deprived of institutional recognition and rejected as an unimportant source of contributions to moral and epistemological culture and the public sphere. Hence, my concern is to produce as much work as possible, through ethnographic description of Ilé-Ifẹ̀ religions and rituals, as well as phenomenological interpretation of events, so that the work becomes accessible to scholars, literate indigenes, and future scholars. It is hoped that through this work researchers may see clearly the religious changes taking place within the tradition. Perhaps if my research and interest in comparative religion had not taken me to such distant places as Japan, India, South Korea, and Hawaii, where I observed forms of Asian and indigenous spirituality very similar to those found in Ilé-Ifẹ̀, my passion for studying and interpreting Ilé-Ifẹ̀ tradition would have been less developed. I am still puzzled as to why indigenous religious cultures in those societies are still central to the local worldview even though their societies have also embraced Western modernity. God forbid that Yorùbá religious tradition becomes shuffled off the face of the earth, for it is certain that in a century or less from now, future generations will begin to ask what was there before Christianity and Islam took over! Scholarship on neo-Confucianism and neo-Hinduism has led to the reinvention of these various traditions, and Yorùbá religion may face a similar destiny. My work and the work of others like me such as William Bascom may then appear in the genealogy of Ifẹ̀ traditions as veritable accounts and testimonies of the Yorùbá ancient tradition in transition.

I am immensely grateful to several individuals, students, friends, colleagues, and relations in Nigeria and America whose assistance have gone a long way in making it possible to complete this work. The following persons at the University of California, Davis, supported me immensely during my sixteen-year sojourn in Davis: Moradewun Adejunmobi, Patricia Turner, John Stewart, Clarence Walker, Adela de la Torres, Bobbie Bolden, Aram Yengoyam, Akili Bekele, Connie Zeiller, and John Ortis. Barbara Ceptus was my faithful research assistant, while Marilu Carter worked tirelessly as my reader and editor. While my students constantly engaged me in serious conversations about several of the issues I raised in this book, my colleagues in the departments of religion and ethnic studies at Hart Hall and the Davis Humanities Institute provided the much-needed collaboration that was necessary to focus on our research. I would also like to thank all the individuals at the popular coffee shop near my house on Zarogoza Street, Davis, for their friendship. I often went there to focus and concentrate on my writing. I owe the friends I made there and particularly, its owners, a big thank-you.

I am grateful to the various grant-making institutions who supported several parts of this work: the Guggenheim Foundation, the Getty Foundation in Santa Monica, California, and the University of California Humanities Research Office in Oakland. Their generous support enabled me to take time off to do field research in Ilé-Ifẹ̀ and to conduct archival research in Ìbàdàn, Nigeria, and Birmingham, U.K. A Rockefeller Fellowship in Bellagio, Italy, provided the opportunity for a one-month sojourn in the serenity of a beautiful villa in southern Italy.

The several honors I garnered in the course of my career provided significant impetus to continue to work hard, especially in important moments of accomplishment but also in the moments of disappointment and despair that academic politics can occasionally cause. I take solace in the Yorùbá saying *Tibi tire ni a dá ilé ayé!* I thank colleagues, friends, and the University Council of Edinburgh University, Scotland, and the University of Abuja, Nigeria, for each awarding me honorary doctorates. The Nigerian National Order of Merit (NNOM), presented by the late President Yar'Adua, I regard as my most treasured honor because it was given to me by my people, my colleagues and my nation. I pray that Allah grant the late president peaceful rest.

I am always amazed at how my entire career has been marked by a deep friend-ship with the Yorùbá kings, and I have been wondering if this relates to the *oríkì* (praise song) of my lineage, which describes us as the protectors of the sacred king-ship and the children of the king of Ute, my hometown. So it is important that I pay homage to several of these royal fathers who have always supported my research and my career in general: the Ọòni of Ifẹ̀, Ọba Ọkùnadé Ṣíjúadé Olúbùṣe II; the Ọlọwọ of Ọ̀wọ̀, Ọba Fọlágbadé Ọlátérù-Ólágbègí; the Ọwá of Ìdànrè, Ọba Fredrick Arọ̀lóyè; and the Olute of Ute, Ọba Akínrọ̀gbà. To all I say *Kádé pẹ́ lórí, kí bàtà pẹ́ lẹ́sẹ̀, Àṣẹ!* I must also express my gratitude to the following people, friends and col-leagues at Ọbáfẹ́mi Awólọ́wọ̀ University, Ilé-Ifẹ̀, who played important roles in my research and career: Kẹ́mi Rótìmi, Tony Akíntọ̀mídé, David Ògúngbilé, Fred Alọba, Dr. and Mrs Adékilè, Mrs Tanwa Adébiyi and Professor Adéodù. I must especially thank Dr. Kẹ́mi Rótìmi, Professor Funnmi Togonu-Bickersteth, and her husband, Chief Lanre Togonu-Bickersteth for their generosity, kindness, and assistance—especially during my many summers of research in Ilé-Ifẹ̀. They always took care of the logistics of my stay during those years. I must thank my uncle in-law: Chief and Mrs. Àkànwó, and of course my brother Babátunde Olupona in Ibadan.

I offer special gratitude to the people of Ilé-Ifẹ̀, especially the priests, chiefs, and other individuals who contributed so much to my research in the city. The Ìṣòrò chiefs, too many to list here, were very enthusiastic about this project, and I learned much from them about the rituals and ceremonial life of the ancient place; this work would not have been possible without their assistance. I must, however, mention the late Chief Fáṣọgbọ́n, the Lódọkọ̀ of Ifẹ̀, and Chief Òrìṣàkúadé for the deep in-terest they took in this work. In the palace of the Ọòni, the late Bàbá Ẹmẹsẹ̀ Èkeje took me to many places and told me when we met last shortly before he died that I should hurry up and finish this work because the end was near for him! I am glad he introduced me to his son, who has now replaced him in the palace. I also express my profound appreciation to my former student and research assistant Kẹ́hìndé Elújùlọ, who was with me throughout my fieldwork in Ilé-Ifẹ̀.

I specially thank the Ọòni of Ilé-Ifẹ̀, Ọba Ọkùnadé Síjúadé Olúbùṣe, and the Yèyélúwa of Ifẹ̀, both of whom granted me several interviews that enabled me to write the concluding chapters to this book. My interviews with the Olorì Morísádé Ṣíjúadé enabled me to focus on the changing role of religion in the city. Ms. Tólá Bamigboye, the Ọòni's personal assistant, facilitated my contact with some palace chiefs, while my former student and the then provost of the Anglican Church, Very Reverend Adétunbí, provided the first links to the Ọòni and the Olorì.

At Harvard, my new home, several individuals and colleagues contributed to the success of this work: Kimberly Patton and David Carrasco in the Divinity School and Biodun Jeyifo in the Department of African and African American Studies. My research assistants, Lisanne Norman, Venise Battle, and Brown Roantree, have been particularly helpful in completing the work. Outside Harvard, Lindsey Reed and Marilu Carter gracefully edited earlier versions of the manuscript.

I thank Rowland Abíọ́dún, Barry Hallen, Charles Long, Anthonia Kalu, and Henry Drewal for the very helpful suggestions they gave me in reading various chapters of this book. Professor Abíọ́dún is a mentor to me, and I thank him and his wife, Leah Abíọ́dún, for their unalloyed support. Babaláwo Bàbálọla Ifátóògùn, one of the most knowledgeable diviners of our time, spent many sessions with me working on Ifá divination texts. His demise last year left a major vacuum in Yorùbá studies.

To my wife, Modúpẹ́, and our lovely children, Tolúlọpẹ́, Bùsáyọ̀, Bọ́lánlé, and Babájídé, I reserve the last but not the least appreciation. Thank you for your support, love, and kindness and for always being there for me.

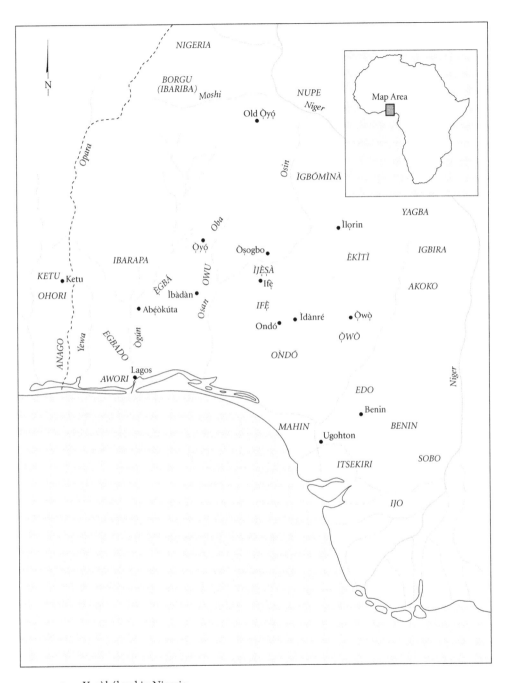

MAP 1. Yorùbáland in Nigeria

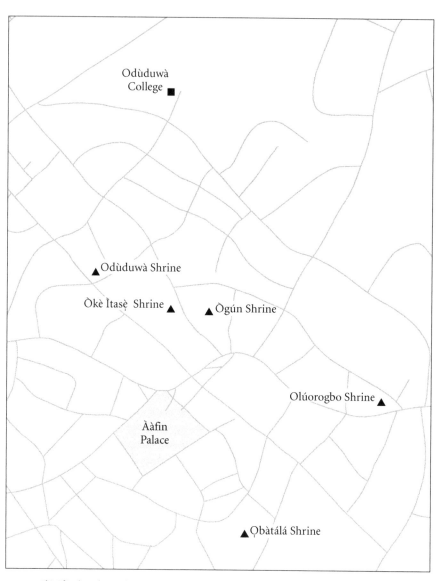

MAP 2. Ilé-Ifẹ̀, detailing places of interest

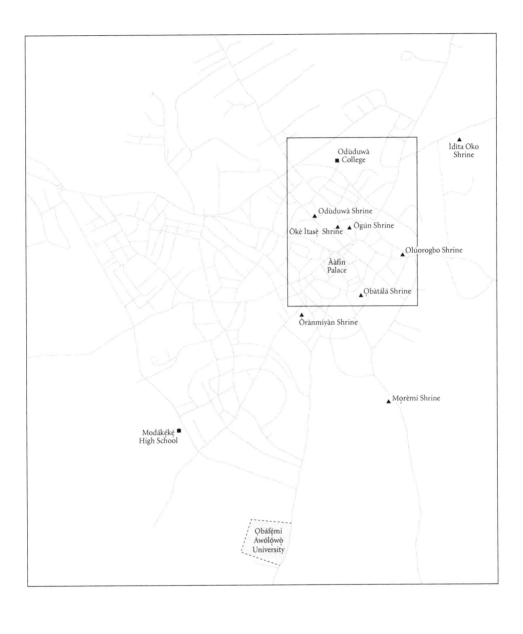

Many African and religious studies scholars who, like myself, have grown up in indigenous traditions and have been educated in the West are undertaking a journey to define the realities of African culture.[1] This is in reaction to a number of works that do not take seriously or interpret adequately the depth of the African experience. In our reading of these works, we have encountered serious problems, including mistranslation and distortions of meaning. To avoid such problems, scholars must agree to go beyond phenomenology by privileging what I refer to as "indigenous hermeneutics": that is, exploring paradigms and modes of interpretation that are explicitly embedded in the traditions we study. Because these traditions are interpretive, our understanding of them should take into consideration how they provide meaning to those who encounter them. It is our role as scholars to highlight the interpretive meanings within these traditions and to incorporate them into the larger discussion of African religion.

In this new quest, few topics deserve more in-depth study today than the sacred Yorùbá city of Ilé-Ifè. Located in central southwest Nigeria, the city has served as an archetype sparking numerous discourses in the history of religion touching on cultural identity, ritual, historical myth, and memory. In this study, I will problematize the discourse surrounding sacred cities by incorporating relevant discussions of the phenomenology and history of religions, cultural studies, and geography. I will examine pioneering works of various scholars engaging in discourses on postcolonialism, cultural studies, and community studies that are pivotal both to this project and to other studies of sacred cities and indigenous religious traditions.

The title of this book, *City of 201 Gods,* refers to the idea that in the Yorùbá cosmology there are 201 deities, although the number is at times reckoned as 401.[2] The exact number is not fixed, but the extra numeral 1 may not be omitted; according to some informants, it stands for the sacred king, the only deity who speaks in a human voice, while according to others it stands for the additional deity the Yorùbá people may create to add to the existing pantheon.

I chose this book title partly as a result of an early encounter with a great-aunt whose late husband bore the name Igba Imọlẹ̀ (201 gods). Imagine my surprise when she gave the full meaning of my uncle's name by using an Ọ̀wọ̀ proverb: *Igba imọlẹ̀ kò lè pa ẹni tí kò bá ṣẹ̀* (Two hundred and one gods cannot kill someone who has not offended the gods). This powerful proverb has always resonated with me, so it seemed only fitting to pay attention to those 201 deities.

In seeking to understand Ilé-Ifẹ̀ as a source for connection to the ancient Yorùbá religion devoted to the *òrìṣà*, or gods, we must explore the diverse dimensions of orality, divination, festivals, and socio-spatial identity as part of the Yorùbá world-view, thought system, and society. This holistic approach will combine the theoretical and methodological perspectives of the history of religion and cultural studies to create an interdisciplinary focus that transcends both hermeneutical phenomenology and traditional anthropological studies of religion.

The Yorùbá religion in Nigeria and the cultural complex within which the sacred city originates are not monolithic. The Yorùbá people can be divided into several cultural subgroups recognized as such by the groups themselves. Within this mosaic are numerous political and subethnic entities associated with various *òrìṣà* who represent concepts and manifestations of war, the sky, rain, and wisdom. Numerous literary, linguistic, philosophical, sociological, archaeological, and ethnohistorical studies document such regional variations fairly well, including the work of Wándé Abímbọ́lá, Rowland Abíọ́dún, John Pemberton, Barry Hallen, Ọmọ́tọ́ṣọ̀ Elúyẹmí, Andrew Apter, Oyèérónkẹ́ Ọlájubù, Karin Barber, Ọlábíyìí Yai, Babátúndé Lawal, J. D. Y. Peel, Kamari Clarke, J. Lorand Matory, Oyèérónkẹ́ Oyèèwùmí, and Henry and Margaret Drewal. Throughout the global African diaspora, the Yorùbá hold fast to a common orientation that integrates these ethnic variations, which all remain anchored in Ilé-Ifẹ̀, the city of origin and the sacred center of the Yorùbá world.

The vibrancy of the Yorùbá culture originating from the city of Ilé-Ifẹ̀ attracts numerous scholars in African and diaspora studies. Yet few have examined the conceptual spheres that encapsulate this sacred center. A lack of significant archival materials on Ilé-Ifẹ̀ compared to the very rich Church Missionary Society materials in Birmingham, England, concerning other cities in Yorùbáland may have discouraged scholars from investigating Ilé-Ifẹ̀'s sacred cosmos.

To conceptualize Yorùbá traditions and the Yorùbá sacred center, one must be able to view them from the perspectives of both "insider" and "outsider," applying the tools of comparative analysis. However, this task is especially difficult not only because of the complexity of Yorùbá cultural variations, religion, and histories but also because of developments in the study of religion. Retreating from the possible pitfalls of studying religion as an extension of theological studies, recent comparative studies of Yorùbá religious traditions by scholars such as Abímbólá, Drewal and Drewal, Oyèéwùmí, Olajubu, Fẹ́mi Taíwò, Pemberton, Fúnṣo Afọláyan, Abíọ́-dún, David Laitin, Matory, Apter, Hallen, and myself have adopted interdisciplinary approaches.[3] Whether perceived as overemphasizing liturgical meanings or fundamentalist theological debates over the orthodoxies and schisms of faith, the former methodologies of theological exploration have been abandoned.

Recently, scholars have made remarkable advances in archaeology, social scientific methodologies, and cognitive psychology that have contributed significantly to the comparative study of religion but at the same time have created fundamental problems, especially in grasping the essence and history of the phenomenon. I agree with Mircea Eliade that "before making the history of anything, one must have a proper understanding of what it is, in and for itself."[4] However, for the comparative study of religion, understanding historical myth is more important than postulating or simplifying theories of cultural or conceptual evolution that often underestimate the significance of religion. Furthermore, an overemphasis on cognition and rationality in ritual undercuts the importance of the ritual act itself to the "participant-insider," as defined within the religion.[5]

The most intellectually valuable benefit that can be gained from the study of religion is an understanding of what a religion means to the participant-insider. Thus it is important to allow ourselves to develop modalities, methodologies, and theories that emanate from the insider's perspective. As Charles Long, whose influential works have shaped some of my recent thinking, has repeatedly stated, "the search for origins"—that is, "the archaic in objective history"—must begin with a search for "the archaism of the subject," or primordial elements in the structure of consciousness.[6]

This perspective requires the development of a new and responsible hermeneutics that focuses on a culture's orientation to the transcendent and the sacred and on what religious culture means to the people within that culture. This task may challenge the Western construction of religion and those who do not often pursue the ethnographic archaeology of indigenous religions such as the Yorùbá tradition. At its root it requires a willingness to go outside Western conceptions of rationality. In this indigenous African context, we see the development of logical ways to account for events that may nevertheless be perceived by "outside" observers as illogical. These forms of expression are not solely the product of self-interest, nor are they universal in that they can be applied arbitrarily to other cultures. Instead, they derive from a core of ontological beliefs developed over the collective experience of a people and represented in historical myth, ritual, and orality.

Unfortunately, instead of attempting to modify entrenched ways of thinking in order to understand a culture's multiple identities as expressed in religion, some scholars have taken a largely oppositional approach to the study of sacred cities and human cultural centers. Long comments on Western notions of "irrationality" in analyses of "exotic" or "early" cultures:

> One of the dominant ways in which scholars of Western cultures tried during the modern period to formulate a science of the human was to turn to an examination of foreign and exotic cultures (the primitives) and discuss and analyze these cultures in terms of their religions. Furthermore, they tended in their work to emphasize the irrational nature of religion in these cultures. The unexamined assumption contained in these investigations was that primitive cultures represented an early stage of human development, an irrational stage gradually being supplanted by the rationality of modern thought and life. What they failed to grasp was that their ideals of rationality and objectivity, rather than being the self-evident properties of critical method, reflected an ideological bias which prevented them from seeing and understanding the phenomena they were studying.[7]

We can try to avoid the ideological bias that Long describes by focusing upon the culture of the participant-insider, emphasizing indigenous values and developing an overall appreciation of religion *qua* religion in a particular culture. We can better comprehend the phenomena of religion by including the social forces and economic units that support religious cultures. In other words, we can begin to develop a sense of the ontological nature of value and of cultural lineage. No work on Yorùbá religion can include its full diversity, and this work makes no attempt to do so. However, we can begin by examining Ilé-Ifè as the core of Yorùbá life and existence and its relationship to the global community in which Yorùbá traditions infuse the culture and define the identity of millions of black and white people in Brazil, Cuba, Puerto Rico, Trinidad, and the United States. One can begin to grasp the meaning of this holy city, Ilé-Ifè, as the spiritual, cultural, and historical center of the Yorùbá world. If the question of the origin of culture and tradition is important to our scholarship—as Peter Berger and Long clearly claim it is—for the Yorùbá people the study must begin in the realm of the imagination of Ilé-Ifè, their sacred city.

This effort requires developing new research modalities and overcoming the simplified, romantic assumptions inherent in many previous efforts to understand the Yorùbá world.[8] It is a curious irony that many pioneers of Yorùbá studies, such as Leo Frobenius, began studying the sacred centers of the Yorùbá people in the fields of world arts and archaeology, even though they could not accept the fact that Africans had founded and created these great cities.[9] The limited imagination of the West shaped the domain of images and symbols attributed to indigenous cultures. Long describes the psychological process by which a culture is defined from the outside by another: "These imaginative configurations [Westerners' images and symbols of indigenous cultures outside the West] are not derived from concrete relationships; they are not the result of observation, experience, or perceptible reality, but rather have their origin in a psychological urge. The intricate mixture of these two tendencies in the origin and formation of the West enables us to understand how, in the search for new lands—lost utopias and paradises—empirical lands and peoples are symbolized and brought within the political and imaginative orbit of the West."[10]

In responding to Long's concerns and in the context of a new hermeneutics for Yorùbá religious studies, it is imperative that I address a set of questions on the sacred center, Ilé-Ifè. How does the city influence Ilé-Ifè's religion, and how does Ilé-Ifè's religion influence the city? How does the mystique of Ilé-Ifè define the historical and social system of the Yorùbá peoples in southwestern Nigeria? Building upon critical theory and the deconstruction of Western approaches to non-Western religions, this work is part of a scholarly effort to preserve for posterity the values, teachings, and practices of this religion and its way of life as expressed in Ilé-Ifè's traditions. Perhaps in the distant future scholars will rely on this work, along with other similar works, as they seek to recollect, construct, and preserve the legacy of Yorùbá tradition. It is part of an effort to write down ancient oral traditions fundamental to African values and ethics before these traditions are lost forever. As indigenous religions throughout the world and especially in Africa face the onslaught of Islamic and Christian evangelism, an issue I will examine thoroughly in the last two chapters of this book, it is likely that by the end of this century only remnants of West Africa's Yorùbá religion will survive.

The absence, until very recently, of scholarship on pre-Christian "pagan" religions in Great Britain may serve as a lesson to indigenous scholars: scant oral and material culture survives to document these cultural traditions. This book may assume a certain authority in documenting a transitional religious period, much as the classic Book of Idols documented religious traditions of pre-Islamic Arabia, even for orthodox Muslim scholars who despised the conditions of the Jahiliyya era, which Islam and the Prophet Muhammad had sought to destroy.[11] But I must warn my readers that I am not working from the vantage point that tradition and culture are static. Far from it, for as this work will show, Ilé-Ifè traditions are constantly being recast, even by those who claim to be devout adherents of òrìṣà tradition. Ilé-Ifè is constantly given new meaning and interpretation as it interacts with Christianity, Islam, and the forces of Western modernity.

To the Yorùbá people, Ilé-Ifè is the place where the Yorùbá connect to a historical and mythic lineage that defines, creates, and promotes an understanding of the world and a source of identity throughout West Africa and the diaspora. This book, then, is a discourse on civilization that explores the source (orísun) of Yorùbá society and culture.

APPROACHING THE STUDY OF YORÙBÁ RELIGION: ILÉ-IFẸ̀'S SACRED CENTER

A Westerner visiting Yorùbáland for the first time would quickly notice that in many respects the Yorùbá embrace a religious system quite distinct from the visitor's own. If this visitor were to take time to investigate what this religious conviction was all about, she would soon notice, among other things, references to belief in a supreme deity called Ọlọ́run or Olódùmarè and, at the same time, to belief in a multitude of deities, òrìṣà and imọlẹ̀, presumed to be lesser in authority than the supreme deity. If such a visitor was educated in religious or theological studies, she might ask to see published materials to help clarify this apparent pantheonic complexity, and it is most likely that she would skim through the pages expecting to read material that would confirm her beliefs in concepts as monotheism, polytheism, and even henotheism.[12] But she would probably find that the books instead challenged the use and validity of these concepts for discussion of non-Western religions, and she would come away more confused than ever.

The theistic beliefs of the Yorùbá people have generated much controversy and debate among scholars, European and African alike. These debates reached their climax in the nineteenth century, an era of intense theological argument in Europe pitting the religions practiced by traditionally oriented cultures against the so-called "higher" religions.

Two primary approaches characterize studies of Yorùbá religion. First, the Christian missionary enterprise tends to portray Christianity as a consummation or completion of an incomplete African religion. From this viewpoint, the missionaries are a sort of collective European Paul, introducing the knowledge of the living God into an African shrine dedicated to an Unknown God. Second, there is what one can call, for lack of a better word, a "nationalist" approach taken mainly by African scholars themselves. In their rush to defend their religions against European detractors, these Africans attempt to place what European scholars have labeled the "little tradition" within a framework equal to that established by scholars of "great" religions. The result of both endeavors is that Yorùbá religions have been characterized as monotheistic, despite their lack of resemblance to religions that emerged from the Near East, and are considered part of what is coming to be known as "Semitic monotheism."

In their attempts to maintain academic rigor, such scholars force traditional religious data into conceptual frameworks that are extraneous to the religions themselves. Perhaps the most startling example is the unqualified use of concepts such as "redemption," "salvation," and "sin." Derived mainly from Western Christian theological thinking, these concepts in no way fit the data emanating from non-Christian theologies, any more than concepts emanating from non-Christian religions would be suitable for describing Christian sects.

Perhaps at the core of these debates is the failure to recognize that religion is essentially "pretheoretical." In the first encounter, religion is not an "intellectual" enterprise. Before they were codified as written or oral corpora, the religious doctrines of various cultures all over the world occurred to their "founders" primarily on the basis of a series of unique spiritual experiences, each particular to a specific geographic and cultural region. Canonical authorities for devotees of various religions came into being long after the deaths of their founders. Consequently, there is confusion between religion as a unique phenomenon and religion as an intellectual exercise.

In any meaningful study of Yorùbá religious traditions, for example, a scholar or curious individual should begin with a basic question: "How do the Yorùbá themselves experience their world in a fashion that can be called religious?" The Yorùbá experience a world in which the sacred and the profane are symmetrical counterparts. Ordinary human experience mirrors what we might call the world of the supernatural or the sacred. At the core of the experience for the Yorùbá devotee is the sacred center located within the city of Ilé-Ifè, one of the vital sacred centers in the world.[13] Within the Yorùbá historical tradition, Ilé-Ifè is the first city in the world: the birthplace of the gods and the place where the principal deities, or òrìṣà, first came to the world and became associated with all that came to exist. The palace of the Ọ̀ọ̀ni, the sacred king and ruler of the city, stands in the exact center of all that has existed, all that exists, and all that will exist. Like the sacred city centers of Jerusalem, Mecca, Banaras, and Rome, Ilé-Ifè signifies and forms the core of Yorùbá identity. Although Ifè historians' comparisons of Ilé-Ifè and its religiously meaningful sites to places mentioned in the Bible may sound strange to Western ears, in the imagination of the Yorùbá such parallel religious motifs are quite natural. Sacred cities exist under diverse circumstances, encapsulating for a given people the totality of historical myth, identity, gender, and ritual.

To the Yorùbá, Ilé-Ifè is the City of 201 Gods, gods associated with powers of divination, war, rainmaking, and farming. Together, the òrìṣà personify an array of concepts ranging from wisdom, represented by the god Ọ̀rúnmìlà, to the sanctity of iron and other extraordinary materials, represented by the god Ògún. Ilé-Ifè represents the earthly site to which the sixteen spirit forces, odù, descended from heaven to establish social order, as well as the site where humans first appeared and where social and industrial economies, including agriculture, trade, and metallurgy, originated. Ilé-Ifè is the site where Ọ̀rúnmìlà, the god of divination, established his trade and built a center of divination practice, called Ifá, the global geomancy now practiced in lands as distant as Japan, Cuba, the United States, and the Netherlands. From this ritual center, the great city of Ilé-Ifè, the Yorùbá world opens out in the four directions of the universe.

To understand its living religious history with its complex and intricate teachings of morality and traditions of healing and divination, the Western reader must make a conscientious effort to expand the dimensions of Western thought, reaching beyond the limitations of secular humanism, modernity, and skepticism. One must be willing to develop an awareness of Yorùbá and African worldviews, imagination, and hermeneutics that allow for a culture that is remarkably adaptable, profound, and open to creative meanings and interpretation. One cannot allow Western discourse to dictate the meaning and function of religion. All useful heuristic concepts and ideas must be reexamined and relocated within their indigenous hermeneutical traditions for their proper application. This book will reexamine ritual, myth, memory, history, space, and gender. Through a creative imagination and expansion of restrictive models of thought inherited from Western tradition, we can come to a fuller and deeper understanding of the nature of this city and its culture.

THEORIZING SACRED SPACE AND CEREMONIAL CENTERS

As previously noted, Ilé-Ifẹ̀ is one of the world's principal sacred centers. Since the publication of Paul Wheatley's *The Pivot of the Four Quarters,* Ilé-Ifẹ̀'s complexity and continuing significance to Yorùbá polity and culture have caught the attention of scholars worldwide. Wheatley's groundbreaking work on ancient centers of the world included Ilé-Ifẹ̀ as a focal point in which the divine meets the corporeal.[14] In much the same way, scholars such as Eliade and Long have described sites that serve as junctions between separate and multiple planes of existence.[15] Throughout the world, these sacred centers are considered to be points where symbolic and historic myths intersect. In the case of the Yorùbá city of Ilé-Ifẹ̀, the city gates mark a boundary between this place of symbolic juncture and the ordinary physical world.

As Long has noted, Thorkild Jacobsen's study of Mesopotamian culture and Wheatley's work on six cultures show urban communities to be based upon a ceremonial center that represents the genesis of human habitation within the urban form.[16] Correspondingly, in investigating Aztec civilization, David Carrasco emphasized the importance of Tenochtitlan as one of the few historical examples of a city that emerged out of a ritual center based upon religious violence integral to urbanization.[17] Carrasco analyzed the Aztec city as a public sphere that became possible only because of ceremonially cultivated cruelty and institutionalized hatred. As urban centers continued to expand outward from their ceremonial cores, a civilization emerged that used institutionalized human sacrifice as a means to construct both warrior and urban identities based on a series of myths, hierophanies, sacred centers, and rituals. This identity established individuals' specific orientation to their immediate world.

For Long, "The ceremonial center is the site of the revelation of sacrality; it sets forth the possibility for the effective use of space. One might say that it is the archetypal meaning of space as a human container. The ceremonial center allows for the 'domestication' of space. The urban community may occupy the site of the ceremonial center or be founded at some distance from it; in any case, the ceremonial center is the power that generates the creation and sustenance of every other form of the space of the urban environment."[18] The urban community relies upon this sacred center as a means of defining itself and projecting an identity to the world at large. As Long describes, "A particular urban form identified with the ceremonial center becomes the locus of power and thus creates all the areas around it as peripheries, dependent upon the power of the center. The relationship between the center and the periphery fluctuates between the centrifugal and the centripetal dynamics of power. Power moves from the center to the periphery and then returns to the center. Power is authenticated to the extent that it participates within the center and all powers and meanings at the periphery must seek their legitimating through their participation in the center."[19] A sacred center such as Ilé-Ifẹ̀ similarly organizes human consciousness by domesticating both conceptual and physical space.[20] The sacred center serves as a bulwark between an inhabited microcosm and a multifaceted zone of chaos and death. It is a source of stability, order, and continuity that encapsulates and transcends the individual.

In his classic work *Images and Symbols,* Eliade comments on the plausible origins of fortifications in urban ceremonial centers: "It is very probable that the defenses of inhabited areas and cities began by being magical defenses; for these defenses—ditches, labyrinths, ramparts, etc.—were set up to prevent the incursions of evil spirits rather than attacks from human beings. Even fairly late in history, in the Middle Ages for instance, the walls of cities were ritually consecrated as a defense against the Devil, sickness, and death."[21] As in many other early urban cultures, the city walls, barriers, and gates of Ilé-Ifẹ̀ are not just physical boundaries. They mark a conceptual transition between the sacred and the profane, what Eliade terms a boundary situation in which individuals discover their place in the universe.[22] This place is sacred because it represents a point of intersection between heaven, earth, and the underworld.[23] The symbolic union of these three cosmic regions is identified through ritual, magic, and historical myth.[24]

This identity of residents of the sacred city requires that people be ordered and stratified according to patterns described by sacred myth and set at the city's genesis. What Long calls an urban genesis is an ontological dimension of sacred reality, expressed in interrelated cultural modes of experience and behavior.[25] Long comments on the events that define such social structures and relationships: "The experience of the sacred reveals the social structure as an arena in which intimacy and obligation, actualities and potentials, and habits and conduct are defined and clarified. It is within the social structure that the dynamic relationships between groups and persons express a generality of conduct and behavior that becomes normative for the society, thus defining the events of social life."[26] The need for such definitions explains the genesis of oral texts, mythologies, and belief systems that bring order, ethics, and a system of morality to a multidimensional center. The center is determined, not solely by the specific geometrical dimensions imagined in Western scientific thought, but instead by several microcosms collectively consisting of sacred space.[27] As Eliade notes, this space is consecrated by a hierophany through ritually constructed means constituting a plurality of centers of the world that may operate on different planes of existence.[28] It is space that expands from such places as the ritual drum, which expresses the energy of the divine and which only the drummer can truly hear. It is the space that the pilgrim hopes to enter by breaking through the membrane of the profane. It is a form of reality, a mode of being that exists before and separate from other cultural categories.[29]

In Yorùbá culture, the center consists of the sacred city as a physical entity, as well as the beliefs, ritual practices, mythology, and arts of the inhabitants who make direct claim to residency and citizenship there. Although the Yorùbá of today may have difficulty conceiving of their ancient past, citizenship bestows on the indigene of Ifè a sacredness respected by the entire Yorùbá-speaking world: Ẹ́ f 'Onúfẹ̀ ṣẹbọ (We never offer the life of an Ifè indigene as a sacrifice). These lyrics are sung in the Igogo ceremony performed in the far distant eastern Yorùbá city of Ọ̀wọ̀, in the state of Oǹdó. The Yorùbá believe that the essence and reality of Ilé-Ifè is constituted in a world created by Olódùmarè, the Supreme God, and his agent Odùduwà, who is their ancestor. As descendants of Odùduwà, residents of the sacred center trace their lineage to dynasties represented by kings and kingdoms, some of which historically predated modern Ilé-Ifè. These political lineages participate in a hierarchy of spiritual forces. The leaders and highest-ranking priests of these ancient lineages, shrines, temples, and gods organize religious ceremonies. Today the devotees of the lineage gods and their subjects still regard the heads of religious ceremonies as Ọba (kings). Historically, in the time of primordial origins in the city of Ilé-Ifè, there were many Ọba. The Ifè people refer to these numerous Ọba in Ìdìta, one of the larger Ilé-Ifè lineages and the home of Ọbàtálá (Odùduwàʼs adversary), as Ọba kékèkè ní Ìdìta (the lesser kings of Ìdìta). As in the Yorùbá pantheon itself, today each of these spiritual-political leaders reveres the king of kings, known as the Ọ̀ọ̀ni, who represents the nexus of the spiritual and the political within the divine center.

RELIGION AND POSTCOLONIAL DISCOURSE

These relationships with the divine define the historical and mythic identities of the Yorùbá people, as well as their emerging identities in the postcolonial era. Today their religious identities are profoundly influenced by three legacies: secular modernism, colonial Christianity, and Islam. From the vantage point of the Yorùbá religion and its sacred centers, we can see much of what Long refers to as postcolonial discourse, in which the definition of "indigenous" religion reveals the fusion of several traditions throughout Africa. To understand indigenous traditions today, we must recognize the context for these emerging dynamics. The postcolonial experience concerns the way people understand, interpret, analyze, and give meaning to indigenous traditions. Thus the challenge to understanding the significance of Ilé-Ifẹ̀ in the Yorùbá experience lies in using a methodology that allows us to conceptualize data through simultaneous indigenous, Islamic, Christian, and even "secular religious" perspectives. By including "secular religious" perspectives here, I am postulating that part of the Yorùbá worldview has evolved into a form of civil religion in which traditional beliefs may have faded away, although traditional actions, rituals, and mythologies remain part of the Yorùbá psyche and cultural identity.

I am motivated to incorporate multiple layers of religious traditions into this study because most of my informants claim multiple religious identities. Consider, for example, my encounters with Chief Erédùmí, a priest of the Ọ̀rànmíyàn tradition and one of the most knowledgeable Ilé-Ifẹ̀ holy men. On more than two occasions, when I went in search of him, Chief Erédùmí was in the mosque praying, for he was a Muslim as much as he was the chief priest of Ògún and the sacrificer in the Odùduwà shrine. I first observed Erédùmí performing the sacrificial ritual of Odùduwà. At midnight, just before he raised the sword to perform the sacrifice, the lyrics reminded him that the task of severing the ram's neck with just one stroke was exceedingly difficult: *Erédùmí ó mà múdà le, ọrùn àgbò mà yi* (Erédùmí, hold the sacrificial sword tightly, because the neck of the ram is tough). Tradition warns that failure to perform this onerous task correctly is seen as having drastic consequences.

In another historical context illustrating multiple layers of religious traditions, we can examine the experiences of the Ọ̀ọ̀ni and the British colonial governor in 1903, which I will consider in detail later in this book. The British colonial governor requested that the Ọ̀ọ̀ni travel from the sacred city of Ilé-Ifẹ̀ to the city of Lagos to settle a dispute as to whether a Yorùbá king in Ẹ̀pẹ́, now part of the state of Ògún, was a legitimate descendant of Odùduwà and therefore entitled to wear the sacred crown. The governor's request was unprecedented. From the beginning of time, the Ọ̀ọ̀ni had never vacated the sacred city of Ilé-Ifẹ̀. The Ọ̀ọ̀ni embodies the sacred center that radiates out from Ilé-Ifẹ̀ on physical, temporal, and spiritual planes. In the new era, however, the Ọ̀ọ̀ni opted for a radical break with tradition by lending his traditional authority to British rule. To the great dismay of many Yorùbá Ọba in cities as diverse as Ọ̀yọ́, Ìjẹ̀bú, Abẹòkúta, Ọ̀wọ̀, and Oǹdó, the Ọ̀ọ̀ni granted the request of the colonial governor and made the astonishing trip to Lagos. After settling the dispute, the Ọ̀ọ̀ni shrewdly asked the British for reciprocal assistance in restoring the badly deteriorating Ilé-Ifẹ̀ palace. The British complied.

The Ọ̀ọ̀ni's earth-shattering trip brought about unintended, unsettling consequences among many practitioners of the Yorùbá faith because it challenged their conceptual paradigm of the sacred center. It jarred their notions of sacred boundaries as bulwarks against the profane, for it seemed as if their god-king had capitulated to British rule. These shocking experiences under colonial rule, and more importantly in postcolonial settings, raised fundamental questions about the nature of the Yorùbá sacred center, its ritual and social roles. In attempting to clarify these questions, I propose that the forces of Islam, Christianity, and modernity make up an essential part of indigenous tradition and that they are linked through almost unconscious mechanisms of ideology.

This ideological framework has become increasingly relevant to my research as I examine the practices of religion within the city of Ilé-Ifẹ̀. Although indigenous òrìṣà traditions have vigorously infiltrated Islam and Christianity, the òrìṣà traditions have co-opted Islamic and Christian frameworks and interpretive models to make sense of their own plausible structures. Although unacknowledged, these religious worldviews and belief systems have benefited from each other. Though not necessarily through conscious borrowing, the language, rituals, or actions of roving cultures such as Christianity or Islam can express African beliefs and ideas through popular modalities of global cultures.

Increasingly, exogenous cultural elements are used to convey indigenous beliefs. Africans have little control over the process; it is a pattern occurring largely without premeditation or overt loyalties to the forces of modernity. For example, during my return to Ilé-Ifẹ̀ in the final phase of my research, I developed a strong friendship with a priest of Ọbàtálá. Suddenly, upon seeing me, he jumped up from his table to greet me, shouting several times the Christian word "Hallelujah!" I would expect this joyous outburst from an Aládúrà Christian but not from a priest of Ọbàtálá.[30]

In other more radical examples of conversion or borrowing from other cultures, Yorùbá children attend evangelical schools while at the same time they are obligated to join their families in propitiating their lineage deity. The youth do not hesitate to rehearse Christian lyrics under their breath while performing for the òrìṣà.[31] They bear Christian and Muslim names while using indigenous terms, phrases, concepts, and expressions. Thus, even though indigenous religion continues to bestow meaning, purpose, and life to the sacred city, the forces of Christianity, Islam, and modernity influence Yorùbá social and personal identity.

I will also discuss the conceptual frameworks and analytic structures that provide evidence for the description and interpretation of the city of Ilé-Ifẹ̀ as a sacred center. This book is concerned with many recurrent themes: lineage and clan identity, ritual, mythic history, sacred kingship, the sacred center, and gender relations, sacrifice, and redemptive suffering. These themes are essential to an understanding of actions, beliefs, and institutions that inform the sacredness of Ilé-Ifẹ̀. Although the book explores the interrelationships of these themes from diverse theoretical perspectives, I focus primarily on the mythic worldview, the imaginative constructions of sacredness in travelogues and works on human ecology by European scholars traveling and working in Ilé-Ifẹ̀, and ritual performances in Ilé-Ifẹ̀. These cultural tropes are the source of Ilé-Ifẹ̀'s status as the sacred city of the Yorùbá people.

PLAN OF THIS BOOK

This book is a historically and culturally grounded ethnography of the Yorùbá sacred ceremonial center. Based on a wealth of data collected over fifteen years and my intimate knowledge of the city, the project affirms the indispensable linkages between religion, cosmology, migration, and sacred kingship as espoused in the power of the royal lineages, hegemonic state structure, gender, and the Yorùbá sense of place.

Regarded as a sacred center of Yorùbá antiquity, the southwestern Nigerian city of Ilé-Ifẹ̀ today still invokes religious fervor among the Yorùbá in West Africa and their diaspora throughout the Americas. The shared cultural symbols of the city—expressed in the arts, language, cosmology, creation myths, music, dance, festivals, and ritual—provide the context for the production of meaning and understanding of the city that has infused a widespread collective religious identity among the Yorùbá. The work explicates the complex imagination and ambiguous identity emanating from Ilé-Ifẹ̀ and radiating across the Atlantic Ocean. Despite the collective religious identity that the city provides to forty million Yorùbá, Ilé-Ifẹ̀'s often violent history of conflict and war situates it in a league with other holy pilgrimage sites such as Mecca, Banaras, and Jerusalem—world religious centers similarly beleaguered by hegemonic ethnic and religious factionalism. This study offers ample evidence of the resilience of the Yorùbá religion over time, despite the transatlantic interchange of its devotees, the influences of the organized religious ideologies of Islam and Christianity, and conditions of modernity that weigh heavily upon the expression of its ancient cosmology and ritual practices.

Throughout this book, the reader will encounter stories of the Yorùbá—their heroes, goddesses, gods, kings, god-kings, and other supernatural beings. The book describes Yorùbá religious culture, myth, and cosmos through time and space—all centered in the most sacred city of Ilé-Ifẹ̀, the center of the universe.

The book contains stories of Yorùbá òrìṣà (gods and goddesses) and supernatural beings that appear to possess the human characteristics of anger and compassion: Ajé, the goddess renowned for inventing money as well as savings and banking systems; Ògún, the god who prefers to bathe in blood but who, if propitiated in the Ọlọ́jọ́ Festival, ensures the Ọ̀ọ̀ni, the great king of kings, a peaceful reign over his kingdom; Mọrèmi, a culture heroine who offered up her own body as a secret weapon to defeat an enemy invasion but as a consequence had to sacrifice her only son and thus remains to this day an icon and a goddess for the modern age; and the chief priest of Ifá (or Àràbà), who, after undergoing special medicinal preparations, becomes the "Leopard King" and is believed to be in danger of crossing the tenuous line between human and animal and turning completely and uncontrollably into leopard-man.

At the center of the Yorùbá religious universe is Ifá, the sacred practice of div-

ination that aids people on earth and specifically the client through the interces-
sion of a priest-diviner, who uses his sacred instruments of divination and his power
to call a particular god to be present at the divination session. As the present-day
priest-diviner communes with Ọrúnmìlà, god of divination, on behalf of his client,
the ancient diviner of long ago joins in the communion and makes present the ancient energy for therapeutic healing of the diviner's client. Traditional Yorùbá culture continues to believe strongly in the regular and obligatory practice of sacrifice
to and communion with the gods, as well as in the amazing chemical properties of
certain herbal medicines harvested from local plants that have proved useful, if infused with the power of the *òrìṣà*, as antidotes against poison, pain, and ill will.

The City of 201 Gods guides the reader through narratives of supernatural beings, medicine men, and medicine women called "Our Mothers," whom nineteenth-
century Western missionaries, colonialists, anthropologists, and religious scholars,
applying their culture's own biased term, have superficially imagined as "witches."
In this text, readers will learn about socioreligious traditions that have ordered the
lives of the Yorùbá for centuries, such as the belief that all newborns, as they wade
through Heaven's River to enter the world, receive an individual "destiny" that resides within their "inner being" or "inner head." They will also learn that for many
Yorùbá the sacred center of Ilé-Ifẹ̀ is surrounded by the cosmos, which includes
the layers of heaven and earth and the underworld, and that the divine authority of
the center is maintained through the power of the sacred *àṣẹ* (a strong magical
force) infusing the *arè* or crown that elevates the Ọ̀ọ̀ni, or king of kings, to the status
of a god.

The City of 201 Gods corrects assertions that Ilé-Ifẹ̀ is the "lost city of Atlantis,"
stories claiming that Ilé-Ifẹ̀ was settled by migrants from the holy city of Mecca,
and claims that exquisite Yorùbá bronzes and terra-cotta sculptures, all rendered
in splendid naturalistic style—the only such lifelike finds in all of Africa—were actually produced by a preexisting "non-Negro" race. The book calls attention to the
pioneering work of a German archaeologist (Leo Frobenius) and an American anthropologist (William Bascom) and to archaeological finds that predate the era of
Islam and Christianity as well as many other ancient kingdoms in the region of West
Africa.

The book consists of ten chapters and is divided into three parts. Part One concerns the cosmology, history, and ethnography of the sacred city of Ilé-Ifẹ̀. Chapter 1 provides a panorama of ancient Ilé-Ifẹ̀ as a ceremonial center of the Yorùbá
cosmos and recounts its mythic history. The chapter situates Ilé-Ifẹ̀ within the comparative study of sacred cities among world religions. Chapter 2 establishes Ilé-Ifẹ̀
as a sacred center. Founded by the cultural hero and ancestor of the Yorùbá, Odùduwà, Ilé-Ifẹ̀ (or Ifẹ̀) represents the place where the principal deities Odùduwà
and Ọbàtálá began to create the primordial universe. In corroborating Ilé-Ifẹ̀'s preeminent mythic status as legendary birthplace of the Yorùbá, chapter 2 examines

the triangulated evidence of written and oral historical accounts, archaeological material culture, and semiotic indicators of art history. Chapter 3 offers a brief overview of the religious philosophy and culture, sacred values, and cosmology of Ilé-Ifẹ̀. The chapter describes religious life and the meaning of the term *religion* to the people of Ilé-Ifẹ̀ as the divine in everyday life—in mythic history, sayings, song lyrics, poetry, and performance arts, as well as continuous year-round celebrations of the supernatural and the Supreme Being.

Part Two examines rituals and festivals in detail. Chapter 4 describes the spectacular Ọlọ́jọ́ Festival of Ògún. Leader among the gods (Ọsìn Imọlẹ̀), the quintessential Ògún is the powerful Yorùbá god of iron and war. The Ọlọ́jọ́ Festival, the core civil ritual of Ilé-Ifẹ̀, renews the people's belief in their sacred king and their understanding of the cosmos in which their god-king (the Ọọ̀ni, the descendant of Odùduwà) rules Ilé-Ifẹ̀, just as, to a lesser extent, their goddess Ajé (goddess of wealth and the market economy) regulates wealth and the marketplace economy. Chapter 5 describes the festival of Ọbàtálá and his counterpart Yemòó, a couple both divine and human. Ọbàtálá, the highest-ranking god (below the Supreme God, Olódùmarè) in the Yorùbá pantheon, is the creator god, the divine sculptor who collaborates with Olódùmarè. Ideologically, the Ọbàtálá Festival offers an excellent illustration of how a marginalized subgroup can maintain social control using the status symbols of religious ritual. Chapter 6 tells the story of Ifá (also named Ọ̀rúnmìlà), the Yorùbá deity of divination, and the divination process itself. Ifá regulates the Yorùbá universe, the spiritual and social affairs of Ilé-Ifẹ̀, and the city's divinatory practices, as well as its religious and moral systems of thought. The Ifá Festival demonstrates Ifá's power to legitimize the authority of the king, the Ifá lineage identity, and the Àràbà, chief priest of the Ifá divination priests. Similarly, the sacred king legitimizes Ifá's authority as envoy of the 201 Yorùbá deities.

Chapter 7 deals with the goddess Mọrèmi, at times referred to as a princess. She is the most celebrated savior in Ilé-Ifẹ̀ legends and in the Yorùbá imagination. Over generations, stories of Mọrèmi emerge from mythic and sometimes faded memory, but the quarrel over land rights between the Ilé-Ifẹ̀ and the Modákéké, an Ọ̀yọ́-Yorùbá people, has persisted through the Yorùbá civil wars from around 1877 to 1893 and to the present day. The story of Mọrèmi suggests an elevated status for women in legendary Ifẹ̀. However, as is often characteristic in a patriarchy, despite the esteem given to female supernatural beings in stories that have been retold for generations as mythic history, festivals in Ilé-Ifẹ̀'s public space far more often celebrate male deities and heroes. In this chapter I examine the role of women within the ceremonies and rituals of the sacred city. I concern myself principally with scholarship on religion and gender and adopt an interdisciplinary, phenomenological, and hermeneutic approach. Although the question of gender is not central to my work, much recent research has foregrounded the crucial role of women in Ilé-Ifẹ̀ religious and ritual practices. R. M. Gross's statement that "rituals for and devotions to goddesses and other female personifications of sacred power are often extremely popular, especially with ordinary believers, both male and female," is very applicable to the history of Ilé-Ifẹ̀ religion.[32]

Chapter 8 is the story of Odùduwà. According to Ifá divination texts, the comprehensive source of Yorùbá epistemology, Odùduwà is at once warrior, founder, creator, and god-king of the Yorùbá civilization. He is the mythic ancestor of Ilé-Ifẹ̀ who provides an eternal sacred canopy for his descendants, the Yorùbá people. The Yorùbá as we know them today define themselves as his children. The Odùduwà Festival reinforces the social separation of genders and of the Odùduwà group from other lineages; reinforces the civil authority of the eight powerful civil chiefs (Ọ̀tún Ifẹ̀), strengthening the authority of the ancestral deity over the territory placed under their control; redefines the city's economic base and redistributes wealth in the form of gifts to Odùduwà; and establishes a strong relationship between Ilé-Ifẹ̀'s religious ideology and the city's socioeconomic and political structures.

Chapters 9 and 10 are based on research conducted a year after the rest of the book was completed. Chapter 9 recounts the unusual face-to-face interviews I conducted with the Ọ̀ọ̀ni, the king, in 2004 in his grand palace in Ilé-Ifẹ̀. Crowned in 1980, the king transformed the palace into an enviable public space. He used his immense wealth, power, and prestige to improve the palace, construct additional structures, and renovate his residences. This chapter includes the king's story of his encounter with imminent violent death and his miraculous rescue from armed murderers—a rescue that he attributes to the power of the Christian God. Also included are interviews with the king's most senior wife. A native of Ifẹ̀ who was raised as a staunch Aládúrà "born-again" Christian, she introduced Christian meetings and rituals into the palace as she took the unprecedented step of constructing a palace chapel for daily Christian fellowship and "ardent" prayer.

Chapter 10, on the struggle currently taking place between traditional Yorùbá religion and new evangelical movements, examines how power is defined in theory and practice in Western academic discourse and how this definition differs from the conception of power and authority in Ilé-Ifẹ̀'s public space. It explores how religion constitutes a source of power in contemporary Ilé-Ifẹ̀ that defines how the city space is controlled and governed; how contemporary narratives of the ancient city express newly introduced Christian ideologies of Pentecostal-Charismatic evangelicism and to a lesser extent radical Islam; how the new quest for religious influence in the public space of the palace is playing out; and how Ilé-Ifẹ̀ identity is being reimagined in the city today. In so doing, the chapter examines the indigenous religious community, its worldview, and its practices as emblematic of the sacred space and site, as well as its religious agents, especially priests, diviners, and leaders, and their roles in the modern sphere. It addresses the challenges to indigenous Yorùbá society that have changed understandings of social class within Ilé-Ifẹ̀ in the contemporary era.

Currently, new religious movements active in Ilé-Ifẹ̀ are engaging in a second wave of missionary efforts (begun in the 1970s and 1980s) to achieve the people's radical and total conversion to Christianity (or Islam), to create a new worldview based on Euro-American conservative Christian values (or conservative Islamic values), and to sow intolerance of indigenous cultures and traditions.[33] These efforts threaten the destruction of indigenous culture, values, and even language. Indeed, in a number of churches it is forbidden to speak the Yorùbá language! There is also an attempt to create a new space in which these new religions will increasingly challenge the authority and privilege of òrìṣà indigenous culture at the center of Ilé-Ifẹ̀ city life. Although there is ample evidence that òrìṣà traditions are in retreat, there is also significant evidence of their renewal. Throughout the world, Yorùbá diaspora communities of the Caribbean and the Americas are repositioning Yorùbá-derived traditions—Santería in Cuba and the United States, Candomblé in Brazil, and new òrìṣà traditions among African Americans in the United States and Trinidad—as global religious traditions whose influence and constituency extend far beyond the home base in Ilé-Ifẹ̀.

Local òrìṣà devotees in Ilé-Ifẹ̀ are re-energized and empowered, not only to see themselves as the center of a venerable worldwide movement and tradition, but also to see the need for "holding down the fort," as the Christian lyrics put it. How long the tradition will survive is, however, unclear. It is my hope that this book will contribute both to the understanding of African religion and to a wider discussion of contested sacred spaces.

PART ONE

1

Ilé-Ifè in Time and Space

For a variety of reasons, some traceable to colonialism and Western missionary campaigns, the study of religion that developed in nineteenth- and twentieth-century America and Europe had no significant impact on the study of religion in Africa. As a result, Africa lacks a comparative history of its religions such as those pioneered by Mircea Eliade, Charles Long, and other scholars of the Chicago School.

Heavily influenced by Christian theological perspectives, many Africanist scholars, including Geoffrey Parrinder, Bọ́lájí Ìdòwú, John Mbiti, and Placid Temple, side-stepped the comparative history of religions and adopted a spurious approach to African indigenous religions, refracting them through a Judeo-Christian prism or clothing indigenous religious experiences in foreign concepts. In so doing, the founders of this discipline in African universities incurred the wrath of scholars outside the African religious studies circle, including the British anthropologist and philosopher Robin Horton and the Kenyan agnostic Okot p'Bitek. Indeed, Robin Horton labeled these founders "members of the devout opposition." Horton and p'Bitek believed that scholars of African religions should abandon models that continued to pose irrelevant questions to African religious traditions. A discourse on African religions that asks whether Africans are monotheistic or polytheistic, for instance, entirely misses the point. Rather, scholars should focus on conceptual and analytical issues that are implicit within a tradition.

Unfortunately, religious studies in Africa have been dominated by clerics and theologians. More importantly, the few Africanist scholars engaging in religious studies have tended to study religious traditions in isolation, without paying attention to the comprehensive, complex structures of space, time, and imagination that produce an all-embracing sacred cosmology of ritual and festival cycles. But even as the debate between clerical and nonclerical scholars was going on in the 1960s, some scholars of human geography were analyzing African cultural traditions and religions through structuralism, spatialized schemes, and metaphor. However, because cross-disciplinary study was unfashionable then, scholars of African religions paid little if any attention to studies in what we now know as cultural geography and the geography of religion. Pioneering scholars like the geographers G. J. Afọlábí Òjó and Paul Wheatley used the same ethnographic data available to religious studies scholars to arrive at more creative, African-centered interpretations. Their work on the Yorùbá of western Nigeria was the first to analyze the significance of spatial dimensions in Yorùbá religious traditions and culture.

In this chapter, I will use general observations of Wheatley, Òjó, Eliade, Long, and other scholars as a lens for examining the significance of place and space in Ilé-Ifè and Yorùbá religious experience and imagination. The Yorùbá of southwestern Nigeria, who now number forty million, commonly claim that their world was created in Ilé-Ifè, and they regard Ilé-Ifè City as the original home place *(ilé)* from which they all moved to the various places they live today. My aim is to correlate the history of religious scholarship linked to place with special metaphors in the study of Yorùbá religion and Ilé-Ifè City. This requires, first, an examination of how scholars of comparative history and religions theorize about sacred places crossculturally.

SACRED PLACE IN THE COMPARATIVE HISTORY OF RELIGIONS: THEORETICAL CONSIDERATIONS

Few have attributed more significance to place and space in the understanding and interpretation of religion than Eliade. His works, though much criticized by his colleagues, are classics in the history of religions. Eliade attempted to develop a structural theory that described religion as something experienced primarily in spatial terms. He observed that human cultures create special places symbolizing centers of the universe. In agreement with Eliade, the ecological anthropologist Roy A. Rappaport theorizes that these are sacred places designed to allow humans to communicate with the ultimate being; they function as cosmic navels "through which the divine enters the material world, and from which that world is oriented."[1] The center gives humans a fixed point by which to orient: according to Eliade, "If the world is to be lived in, it must be founded—and no world can come to birth in the chaos of the homogeneity and relativity of profane space. The discovery or projection of a fixed point—the center—is equivalent to the creation of the world."[2] Eliade's belief that this spatial metaphor in religion is normative and applicable to all cultures has been called into question, with Jonathan Z. Smith criticizing Eliade for "overemphasizing the significance of centers" and Rappaport observing that Eliade "seriously overvalued the case for the priority of space in the religious experience."[3]

But despite these critiques, Eliade's work on the sacred, like that of Emile Durkheim, has significantly influenced the perception and understanding of place among historians of religion.

For Eliade, the sacred is that which is set apart from the profane or "the non-enchanted world." However, this oppositional definition may be inconsistent with the traditions of certain cultures and societies such as the Yorùbá, the Maori, and many Native American groups, which do not draw sharp distinctions between the sacred and the profane but rather view them as dialectical.[4] Further, Jonathan Smith has pointed out that not all religions are "locative"; some are "utopian" (placeless). In the Yorùbá imagination, home is, as Smith aptly observes, a home place, a center where one locates one's self and being. It is at the same time a place of memory and nostalgia for the past, conveying deep meanings for both individuals and the collective.[5] On the other hand, religions that take root in a new place and land (such as some diasporic religions) may refer to no home place in the existing world. Nevertheless, Eliade's spatial metaphors provide a starting point for interpreting African religious experiences.

In *God's Place in the World: Sacred Space and Sacred Place in Judaism,* Seth Kunin suggests two models of sacred space: the dynamic and the static.[6] Dynamic sacred space, like the moving camp, remains untied to any particular location, while static space is fixed to a unique location. Jerusalem's Temple of Solomon is an excellent example of sacred static space, whereas dynamic sacred space is often tied directly to sacred peoples: that is, sacred space is considered to be any space that a particular people inhabits. As Kunin notes, "Dynamic sacred place is temporary and disassociated from physical space"; it is "fluid," for "any place can become contextually sacred."[7] The reference to the sacred here, as the term is often used in the history and phenomenology of religion, implies the recognition that something (an object, site, or person) is "placed apart from everyday things or places, so that its special significance can be recognized and rules regarding it obeyed."[8] Sacred places occupy a significant category in the phenomenology of African religion because they are sites of origins and endings for individuals, peoples, customs, and traditions. They have metaphorical and ontological significance for both the individual and the collective. In the context of Yorùbá religion, sacred place and sacred space normally are static and centralized and are associated with a "historical and mythological experience of the divine."[9]

In recent years, Eliade's theory has been reinvigorated, especially among scholars of the Chicago School who are applying the method and theory of the history of religions and their interpretive orientations of land, space, and territory. David Carrasco, Charles Long, Lawrence Sullivan, Mary MacDonald, and Belden C. Lane, to mention a few, are engaged in new interpretations of place and space. These scholars have revived the study of what we may call, for lack of better terminology, the "spatiality of religion" or the "materiality of religion."

I would like to apply these new interpretations to the sacredness of place in Yorùbá religious traditions, especially to the sacred city of Ilé-Ifè, examining both their universality and specificity in the many cultural regions of southwestern Nigeria where the various Yorùbá peoples live. I will also question the significance of spatial concepts developed in the field of the history of religion. The sacredness of place is often defined in opposition to outsiders to the place, who are considered incapable of recognizing the territory's sacred qualities, its significance to mythic history, and the very *being* of its inhabitants.

The Yorùbá philosophical concept of place may best be understood by the ancestral proverb *Ọmọ onílè tè é jéjé, àjòjì tè é wùrù wùrù* (While the indigenes of a place tread very gently on it, the stranger treads very roughly). Although "outsiders" may see indigenes enacting in certain ways the recognition that a place is sacred, they do not fully understand the numerous signs and symbols that mark a place as sacred territory and may be unwilling to accept its sacredness because it stands beyond the location of their own sacred place and space. However, for indigenes, the place invokes certain qualities, special meanings, and memories. It is their experience, and their reality is lived, adored, and held holy.

An ancestral home and rights of ownership over it play important roles in the Ilé-Ifè ethos. For "tread very gently" the proverb quoted above uses the metaphor of doing a "slow dance" *(tè é jéjé)*, which may refer to the drumbeat for the ancestral masquerade that is performed, for example, in the Egúngún Festival in Òkè-Igbó, a Yorùbá town of Ilé-Ifè origin in Oǹdó State and my mother's home place. In another example of differentiation between insiders and outsiders, the New Yam Festival, known as Owé, celebrates the autochthonous spirit and owner of the lands and territory of Ilè-Olúji, a nearby town in Oǹdó State and my wife's hometown in Nigeria. At the height of the festival, the natives are led by their king (Jẹgun) toward a place of high ritual. Loudly shouting, *ògbèrì kúrò!* (Outsiders, leave!), the insiders drive away all nonindigenes to prevent outsiders from viewing the sacred symbol and earthly propitiation of their deity and culture hero, Ọlófin.

Still deeper levels are invoked by sacred place in the Yorùbá imagination. Sacred place encompasses not only easily recognizable sites but also a larger space, often unmarked in Yorùbá cities. I have noticed that in a procession—either a carnival, a parade, or any ceremony commemorating funeral rites or rites of passage—suddenly the drummers may stop drumming at a certain place, such as the burial place of a cultural hero or a mythic personality, or the site of certain sacred events believed to have occurred in the beginning of time. When viewed in their historical context, the land and space considered sacred remain part of the identity and spiritual self-definition of the people who claim the place. This claim is especially relevant when a group or an individual is defined in relationship to a place, space, or territory.

PROLEGOMENA TO THE STUDY OF PLACE:
YORÙBÁ RELIGIOUS EXPERIENCE IN ILÉ-IFẸ̀

Ilé-Ifẹ̀, sacred city of the Yorùbá people of West Africa, is obviously quite familiar to Africanists, especially archaeologists and historians; I do not know of any other ancient African city whose artistic traditions and archaeological findings have been more thoroughly studied. Yet despite all the pioneering works, we know very little about the religious and ritual life, the moral order, and the thought systems that give the city its historical significance and its cultural identity as the ceremonial center of the Yorùbá people. We look in vain for works that put Ilé-Ifẹ̀ on a par with other sacred centers such as the Mesoamerican sacred city of Teotihuacán in Mexico, the Hindu city of Benares in India, or the ancient cities of Jerusalem, Mecca, and Rome. The reason for this lack of knowledge is that art historians and archaeologists have focused primarily on the artifacts of material culture. Knowledge of material culture without its essential counterpart of knowledge regarding religious metaphors, symbols, and mythic traditions cannot adequately reconstruct Ilé-Ifẹ̀'s religious culture. We know that the history of religions—the discipline dealing with the scientific study of religions whose primary concerns are myth, ritual, and signs—is perhaps the least developed scholarly tradition in African studies, for reasons that I have addressed elsewhere.[10]

This chapter provides a panoramic picture of the ancient city of Ilé-Ifẹ̀ as a ceremonial center. By examining aspects of its legends, myths, ethnohistory, and oral texts, as well as the archaeological and iconographic evidence of the contemporary city, I reconstruct the meaning and significance of Ilé-Ifẹ̀ sacredness in the Yorùbá imagination, social structure, and philosophical systems. My initial claim is that the city is a classic model of a sacred center that the inhabitants of Ilé-Ifẹ̀ and the Yorùbá people across the globe construct partly in the imagination, according to a mental map. While the construction and memory of ancient Ilé-Ifẹ̀ continue to provide a strong political and religious ideology for Yorùbá nationalism today, paradoxically, the city's encounter with modernity, especially with secular culture and globalization, has turned it into a highly contested space in Nigeria. I will argue that this unfolding of historical events has created for Ilé-Ifẹ̀ a pattern of paradox common to sacred cities the world over.

There is no better starting point for raising contextual issues regarding the significance of Ilé-Ifẹ̀ in Yorùbá religious experience than Wheatley's scholarship. Wheatley claims that civilization is based on the growth of the city-state. In *The Pivot of the Four Quarters,* he develops an analysis of the cross-cultural significance of urbanism. He identifies seven primary regions of world civilizations, including the Yorùbá of southwestern Nigeria, and categorizes these civilizations in a typology that serves as a framework of analysis. For Wheatley, ritual and religious ceremonies help define complex systems of defense, commercial relations, and emerging market economies. In any society, as ceremonial centers grow in importance they become public ceremonial structures, symbolic of cosmic, social, and moral order. Similarly, they operate as institutions that control developing political economies, regulating the distribution of resources and creating social hierarchies.[11]

Wheatley wrote at a time when the role of religious ideology in the development of urban centers and civil societies was hardly recognized. Perhaps more than anyone else, he took seriously the significance and role of religion in the development of urban cities cross-culturally and demonstrated to a great extent what David Carrasco has described as the "interplay between the religious imagination and urban centers."[12] Wheatley's ideas and concepts about the ceremonial complex have provided useful points of reference and a cross-cultural model for several anthropologists and historians of religion interested in studying ceremonial centers from various perspectives. Carrasco, for example, writes that "the story of Mesoamerican religion is the story of cities and symbols of cities."[13] He observes that "the earliest and most influential institutions contributing to the organization of peoples into urban centers were sacred ceremonial precincts. Therefore, it is useful to approach the study of Mesoamerican religions through the central patterns and presence of cosmovision and ritual action created and celebrated within these ceremonial centers and their city states."[14] His own studies of sacred ceremonial precincts such as Tenochtitlan draw on mythical, cosmological, ethnohistorical, and iconographic sources to demonstrate these places' centrality to Mesoamerican religions and cultures.

Such city-centered religiosity is by no means limited to so-called indigenous civilizations. In her study of Banaras, Diana Eck observes, "Some of the world's cities have generated entire civilizations and seem to condense the culture and values of these civilizations in one place. . . . Their names became virtually synonymous with that culture, for they have gathered together the energy of a wider civilization and converted that energy into culture."[15] Eck calls such sacred cities "orthogenetic," following Milton Gorger and Robert Redfield's use of the term, because such cities give birth to whole civilizations and define the social and moral order with which the culture identifies. "[The] primary self-image is that they reproduce a cosmological order and make it accessible on the human plane. They are centers of pilgrimage and centers of the world-ordering rites and ceremonies of the gods, or of the kings." In contrast, "heterogenetic" cities are bureaucratic and commercial centers whose "technical order" and "primary self-image is that of action and work. They hum and produce; they order power, production, and wealth."[16]

Belden C. Lane's fascinating work on American sacred landscapes reminds us of the need for a new orientation to the study of sacred space and religion, one that seeks to understand more than the "individual human appropriation of sacred places" and to focus less "on the spiritualized significance that people attribute to a place than on the place itself as a cultural and phenomenological reality."[17] I understand the latter to be an appreciation of a sacred place as having an intrinsic quality that demarcates it as special and sets it apart from ordinary secular space. Ilé-Ifẹ̀'s complex geographical configuration and sacred oral narratives—especially the numerous mythic narratives in the Ifá divination corpus pertaining to the city as well as its ancient architectural and artistic traditions—are some of the tools that will enable us to discuss and project those cultural and phenomenological realities that according to Lane constitute "the enduring identity of a sacred place."[18] In the Yorùbá imagination, the above-mentioned Ifá narratives, which are examined in greater detail in chapter 4, are considered to be the definitive utterance of the Yorùbá gods. The 256 chapters of Ifá oral poetry are provided by Ifá, also known as Ọ̀rúnmìlà, the god of divination, who is often described as the "master storyteller" (Bàbá Ọ̀pìtàn) or the "great Ifẹ̀ historian" (Ọ̀pìtàn Ifẹ̀). These numerous powerful legends of the 201 gods in the city of Ilé-Ifẹ̀ confirm Lane's argument that the "role of the story-teller is essential in grasping the power that place exerts on the religious imagination."[19] My many informants in Ilé-Ifẹ̀ hold ritual positions that give them the authority to explicate the stories of the 201 Ilé-Ifẹ̀ gods to scholars, students, and tourists. The "cultured despisers" (to adopt Friedrich D. E. Schleiermacher's phrase)—such as Christian and Islamic missionaries and Yorùbá modernists and transnationalists—have all focused on destroying what they consider to be the last vestiges of paganism in a city that is the nexus of origin for forty million Yorùbá the world over.[20] But the perspectives provided by my informants provide a more well-rounded picture of the power, essence, and persona of Ilé-Ifẹ̀.

As Gabriel Cooney and Eoin Grogan remark, a sacred city is not necessarily constructed by the objective reality of a place that underpins people's actions; rather, a "mental map" or social consciousness shaped by a culture dictates how they view it.[21] This book reflects on the feelings and perceptions that people from diverse cultures, including European and African, indigenous and nonindigenous, as well as inside and outside the city today, hold about this ceremonial center. By providing what Jonathan Smith calls "the social configuration of the ideal cultic place," I hope to explain how the sacred city rose to preeminence in Yorùbá religion, culture, and society.[22]

The study of Yorùbá religious life in Ilé-Ifẹ̀ requires a vast number of sources and, obviously, an interdisciplinary focus. Students of Yorùbá religion can no longer depend on traditional ways of carrying out ethnographic studies, such as fieldwork based on interviews, to document traditional myth, ritual, and festivals. Interdisciplinary documentation based on archaeological, art-historical, and ethnohistorical studies—as well as oral and literary sources—is as important as conventional fieldwork. Both Ilé-Ifẹ̀'s definition of itself and outsiders' views of it as a sacred ceremonial center depend to a large extent on sets of myths and rituals and on architectural and archaeological evidence that point to its preeminence.

LOCATION

There is a historical, political, and pragmatic reason why Wheatley's model of a ceremonial center is important to this case study of Ilé-Ifẹ̀. Almost twenty years ago, a new state called Ọ̀ṣun was carved out of the former Ọ̀yọ́ State of southwestern Nigeria to which Ilé-Ifẹ̀ belongs. Ilé-Ifẹ̀ indigenes wanted their city to become the capital of the newly created state. However, instead of the exalted sacred city of antiquity, the state selected the city of Òṣogbo, a commercial, technocratic city rife with political turmoil but home to the world-famous goddess Ọ̀ṣun. Though Ilé-Ifẹ̀ indigenes thought that their city, as the center of Yorùbá civilization, would be a natural choice, it lost this bid, to their bitter disappointment. But one Yorùbá elder remarked about Ilé-Ifẹ̀'s failure to become the capital: "When we introduce Ilé-Ifẹ̀ City into the frailty of Nigerian politics and the filthy lure of its commerce, it will lose its sanctity and its tradition will diminish in importance. What it lost in politics, power, and wealth, the city gained in authority, status, and reverence." The elder certainly had not read Wheatley, nor did he know the difference between orthogenetic and heterogenetic types of cities, but his comments aptly illustrate what ethnographic scholars have theorized about sacred cities in their own ethnographic work. For reasons that will become evident further on in this chapter, Ilé-Ifẹ̀ as a traditional ceremonial center continues to play a pivotal role in the life of Yorùbá society and culture that other cities far larger do not.

The phenomenology of Ilé-Ifẹ̀ religious experience and expression, the focus of this work, should recognize Yorùbá sacred geography. Central to sacred geography is the experience of place and space identities. Topographical features and important geographic landmarks are endowed with religious meanings and associated with events that embody a people's cosmology and worldview. These events confer meaning and distinction on the Yorùbá people and places. We can argue that the entire Ilé-Ifẹ̀ religious system is a record of places, activities, and peoples in experiences of religious significance.

Yorùbá construction of place emanates from a perception of space, imagination, mythology, and history. Such perception may differ from what we call the secular perception of place. As Dorothea Theodoratus and Frank La Pena note about the sacred geography of the Northern California Wintu, "The qualities of a place or a region which make them sacred, as well as the concomitant reverence and spiritual activities of the native practitioners, are profoundly different from mainstream perceptions of these places, attitudes and actions."[23]

I will begin my analysis and description of the Ilé-Ifẹ̀ experience of place with the Yorùbá creation myth, rather than with an inventory of the city's sacred geography, because it is primarily the sacred story that gives this city its legitimacy and identity. I will touch on the primary expressions of the Ifẹ̀ world—the people, the

place, ritual sacrifice, and institutions of sacred kingship, as well as the gods, ancestors, and spirits who have their origin in the experience of place.

YORÙBÁ COSMOLOGY AND THE NATURAL WORLD

The power of the natural world is prominently featured in creation myths of Yorùbá
society and in the Yorùbá conception of the universe in general. In the most cited
Yorùbá myth of origin, Olódùmarè, the Supreme Being, decided to create the world
in the sacred city of Ilé-Ifẹ̀. He gave Ọbàtálá, one of the gods, a mythical five-toed
guinea fowl, along with a quantity of earth in a small shell and a chain, with instructions to descend into the universe and perform the ritual of creation. On his
way to carry out Olódùmarè's assignment, Ọbàtálá met other divinities who were
drinking. He joined them, got drunk, and fell asleep. Another divinity, named Odùduwà, overheard Olódùmarè's message and saw Ọbàtálá fast asleep. Odùduwà
picked up the materials for performing the tasks to create the world and descended
from the sky into the world with the aid of the chain. Reaching the earth, Odùduwà
poured out the soil from the shell onto the primal water and placed the guinea fowl
upon it. The bird scattered the earth around, creating dry land on the water. Afọlábí
Òjó, a cultural geographer, graphically describes the extraordinary primordial phenomenon that the "earth spreader" performed: "The mighty bird, a special giant
bird, descended on the sand and used its huge claws to dig, and spread out the sand.
Where the claws dug deep, valleys were formed. Hills, uplands, and mountains were
left within the interstices of the claws."[24] The place where Odùduwà accomplished
this task was named Ilé-Ifẹ̀, the place where the earth spreads. The "earth spreader"
symbol represented by the bird is a significant motif in African religion and art.

The Yorùbá creation story, like most cosmogonies, presents many themes and
motifs familiar to the historian of religions. It begins by describing primordial waters out of which the universe emerged. It recalls a theogony, an epiphany of the
òrìṣà and divine human beings in the created world. Through creation the worlds
of the divinities and of humans merged, and a horizontal relationship, a passage up
and down, was established between gods and humans, creative forces, and creation
itself. The universe thus created was not an empty one. Through the activities of the
divine being, Odùduwà, the basic elements of the universe and the earth's mor-
phology became established. Dry land and wetlands and animal and plant life were
firmly entrenched.[25] The palm nut, which Odùduwà planted, became the tree of life
that gave birth to the plant world. It is also an important element in the Ifá divination process employed to discern the wishes of heaven.

Moreover, the creation myth suggests that at the time of creation Olódùmarè's
creative and spiritual power were transformed into the created space—its plants,
dry land, rivers, valleys, and trees. Through the dissemination of this potent force,

special places were infused with sacred power. As the primordial gods and spirits, sixteen in number, descended into the world, they made these special places their homes, and from then on miraculous occurrences began to take place there. I cannot describe here the numerous myths associated with the descendants of these gods, referred to as òrìṣà afẹ̀wọ̀nrọ̀—those who descended the primordial chain—the cosmos, and the experience of space and place. However, I will present some aspects of their role in making Ilé-Ifẹ̀ in chapter 3 when I examine the religious ethnography of the sacred city.

THE COSMOS AND THE EXPERIENCE OF SPACE AND PLACE

In the Ifẹ̀-Yorùbá imagination, the cosmos is often described and explained in metaphors of place, structure, spatial dimensions, and orientation. Ilé-Ifẹ̀, the city where creation took place, means literally "an expansive land." It is also described as "the place where the day dawns" *(níbi ojú ti mọ́ wá):* Ilé-Ifẹ̀ is the center from which the inhabitants of the world first viewed daylight. The earth was conceived as highly expansive, in no way spatially confined.

The Yorùbá universe consists of three concentric spherical layers. The highest and first layer is ọ̀run, the sky (heaven), the inhabited realm of Olódùmarè, the supreme god, and some of the lesser gods, or òrìṣà, and other spirits *(imọlẹ̀* or *ẹbọra)*. No human is directly concerned with the affairs of heaven *(iṣe ọ̀run)*. The second and middle layer *(ayé)* is the center of the cosmos and the inhabited place of the living and of some divinities and spirits. It is the vitalizing center of the world and the point at which all the cosmic forces and power in the three layers intersect.[26] The third layer, *ilẹ̀,* the underworld, is the opposite of the sky; it is the place of the dead. *Ilẹ̀* is personified by the female earth deity, Onílẹ̀, regarded as the source of creative and generative power of fecundity, exemplifying moral aptitude and justice, and acting as the ultimate judge in human affairs. This deity also represents the idea of death as the product of human life. When we die, she takes us into her body.[27]

Each of the three concentric layers of the cosmos: sky, world, and underworld. contains its own inhabitants, gods, mortals, and demons *(alájogun)*. Where they live determines the extent of sacred powers entrusted to them. For example, in addition to being the habitat of Olódùmarè and some divinities, ọ̀run, the sky, is the space in which the sun, moon, and stars live and act. The Yorùbá draw heavily on celestial metaphors to convey the experiences of humans and to effect potent action through sacred words and images. The sun and the moon are viewed as two opposing but necessary pairs. The rising sun signals the dawn of a new day *(àtiwáyé ojọ́)* and is portrayed as the arrival into the world of new beings. The invocation *Àtiwáyé ojọ́* simultaneously carries the divine command that the moon must disappear before the arrival of the new day, represented by the sun *(ojọ́ kì í mọ́lẹ̀ rí òṣùpá).* Observations of the movement of the sun and the moon are often rendered in proverbs. A more elaborate ritual invocation precedes an Ifá divination and is made by the diviner. It reads:

> *Iwájú ọpọ́n*
> *Èyìn ọpọ́n*
> *Olùbùlótùn-ún*
> *Olùmọ̀ràn lósì*
> *Àárín ọpọ́n*
> *Òde òrun*
> *Àtiwáyé ọjọ́*
> *Àtiwọ̀ oòrun*
> *M'áfi ibi pe're*
> *M'áfi ire pe'bi*
> *Máfòlòlò fọhùn.*

> The front of Ifá
> The back of Ifá
> The right side of Ifá
> The all-knowing on the left
> The center of Ifá
> The center of heaven
> From the dawn of the day,
> To the setting of the sun,
> Do not say it is good when indeed the message is evil.
> Do not say it is evil when the message is good.
> Do not speak in a deceitful voice.

Here the invocation is a request to Ifá to guide the diviner's consultation in the right path so that unequivocal truth may emerge. The prayer-poem symbolically dramatizes the creation of the cosmos. The metaphor for the first setting of the sun is particularly significant. At the center of the divination technique is the idea that the universe and its events are guarded by spiritual and temporal analogies to life. Ifá is thus the regulator of events in the universe (Agbáyégún). Note also that the divination performance refers to the four cardinal points of the universe, plus the center—the fifth and focal point. The five important axes of powers are replicated on the Ifá divination tray *(ọpọ́n Ifá).* This circular tray, usually a carved wooden structure, is a replica or, in James Livingston's words, a "reproduction, on the human scale, of the cosmos or of creation itself. It is an *imago mundi,* an image of the original world order."[28]

At times in the course of divination, the Babaláwo (the Ifá priest) may draw the axes in the yellow powder on the tray, indicating the connection between the four cardinal points and the center. The center of the divining tray *(àárín ọpọ́n)* is the link to the center of heaven *(ita òrun),* the abode of Olódùmarè and the storehouse of

FIGURE 1. Ifá divination trays. Photo by W. Bascom (1950s).

sacred knowledge required to unravel the secret surrounding the client's inquiry, especially in case of sickness, when the Babaláwo assumes that hidden spiritual forces are behind his client's ailment. The gesture of touching the tray at the four directional points and the center with the divination chain, or ọ̀pẹ̀lẹ̀, is an act of religious symbolism. By this act, the tray becomes the earthly sacred center from which the diviner makes a connection with the heavenly center *(ìta ọ̀run),* the ultimate place of Ifá's àṣe (healing power), and the individual client's orí (personal destiny). Although the Yorùbá recognize that Ifá inhabits the earthly cosmos, his ability to commune with the beings of heaven *(ará ọ̀run)* makes divination practice possible. Hence, Ifá also is called Agbáyé Mọ̀ṣe ọ̀run (He Who Lives on the Earth and Knows the Feats of Heaven).

A GEOGRAPHY OF YORÙBÁ SACRED SPACE: CREATION AND THE COSMOS

Within each layer of the cosmic sphere, several activities take place to connect the layers vertically. The creation process that begins in the first sphere (heaven, the abode of the Supreme God) and forms the other two spheres (the world and the underworld) also establishes vertical relationships between the three spheres. Ọlọrun, or

FIGURE 2. Divination session with the former Àràbà, Chief Awosǫpé.

Olódùmarè (the Supreme Being), controls events in the first sphere, which is also
the place of the creation of humans. There Ọbàtálá, the most senior deity, fashions
physical human forms from heaven's clay. Once fashioned and provided with the
breath of life, humans depart to take their destiny *(orí inú)* from the home of Àjàlá,
the custodian of destiny. The spirit of a person carries the calabash of fate *(igbá ìwà),*
which he or she drops at the threshold of heaven. The spirit then crosses the river
of forgetfulness and enters the world of the living, where the individual is born as
an infant.

   Except for the Supreme Being, who maintains a relative silence after the world
has been created, the gods and spirits dwelling in heaven are actively connected with
the living on earth. After creation, the first sixteen immortal gods came down from
ọrun to take charge of different realms on earth. Ògún, god of iron and war, led the
way with his cutlass, clearing a path in the world. Ọ̀ṣun, goddess of cool water and
the only female deity of the original sixteen, followed, as did Ṣàngó, god of thunder and lightning, and Ifá, or Ọ̀rúnmìlà, god of divination and counselor of the gods
and humans. Other deities in charge of various human activities and of geographic
and physical features followed the original sixteen until all agricultural fields, rivers,
mountains, and forests were inhabited by one deity or another. There are deities associated with specific functions, such as Ajé, the goddess of wealth and prosperity.
Ajé takes charge of the market economy, working closely with the sacred king to
ensure success in trade and commerce in Ilé-Ifè. Ọ̀sanyìn takes charge of herbal

medicine. Of the 201 or 401 deities, almost all have a department to control or a function to perform in the world.

No natural phenomena lack signifiers of the sacred in the Yorùbá imagination: rain, rainbow, thunder, storm, and wind are interpreted as heavenly forces. When I was growing up in a traditional Yorùbá town, children were encouraged to reflect on these natural phenomena in riddles. For example, an elder might ask, "What is a long thin rod that touches heaven and earth?" *(Ọ̀pá tẹ́ẹ́rẹ́ ó kan ilẹ̀, ó kan ọ̀run lọ?)*. We answered, "Rain." The appearance of the rainbow on a wet rainy but sunny day indicated that Òṣùmàrè, a deity of multiple colors, was drinking water from a riverbank close by. The appearance of a new moon was always welcomed as a fa- vorable time to say a prayer for the good luck and blessings that it might bestow *(oṣù kó lé ìre sími lára o)*. The new moon was also a sign that the mentally ill might become more agitated than usual and a warning to avoid them. We all saw how un- usually bright the moon was in December 1999, an indication that a new millen- nium was about to begin.

Several places in Yorùbáland became imbued with sacred qualities either because the descending gods made these places their abode or because certain "miraculous" events occurred there. While some gods and spirits found their abodes on moun- tains and hills, others preferred the deep sea and large rivers. The world *(ilé-ayé),* the second sphere, is a complex universe encompassing both space and habitat. The Yorùbá worldview emphasizes that the central prayer or request from *òrìṣà* is for a devotee to have a peaceful existence in his or her space and abode *(kí a wà láyé, kí a wà láàyè wa)*. Within this second sphere lie cultivated lands, towns and cities, and forests.

Yorùbá towns and cities are regarded as sacred enclaves for inhabitants of the world *(ayé)*. Since early times, most cities and towns, of which Ilé-Ifẹ̀ has been the principal place, have been walled off to protect inhabitants from intruders and evil spirits. City gates and entrances are not mere passages but thresholds distinguish- ing people of the city from those of the forest outside. City gates are sites of magi- cal objects and shrines, where Èṣù, gatekeeper god and divine police officer, filters out evil spirits and neutralizes the power of malevolent magic and medicine. Èṣù's protective role is very important for the community, earning him the honorific of Ọlá Ìlú (prosperity or honor of the city). Paradoxically, the *oníbodè* or gatekeepers who operate city gates are often notorious ex-convicts on parole, whose immense physical presence repels intruders.[29]

The city gate in the olden days was a transitional point between the city and the outside forest. The forest was the abode of spirits, demons, ghosts, dangerous ani- mals, wild plants, and trees. One need only read D. O. Fágúnwà's novel *Ògbójú Ọdẹ Nínú Igbó Irúnmọlẹ̀ (Forest of a Thousand Demons: A Hunter's Saga)* to appreciate the significance of the forest in the Yorùbá imagination.[30] Only ghosts, medicine men, and brave hunters who were fortified to withstand the possible dangers of the forest's spiritual powers dared to enter the forest. Stories of encounters with spirits disguised as humans and human and animal ghosts with messages to loved ones abound in Yorùbá narratives.

A sizable forest near a city is often designated as a sacred forest (Igbó Orò), a place where various cult groups occasionally meet. The Òṣùgbó and Ògbóni secret societies perform religious activities such as masked rites in such forests. In the past, the sacred forest served as the place of public executions. A section of the forest may be demarcated for burial of victims of a horrific death, such as smallpox.

THE CITY AS PLACE AND HOME

I would like now to examine the meaning, images, and spatial orientation of Ilé-Ifè, the place where the world was created. Generally, names of Yorùbá cities and towns are prefaced by the prefix *ilé* (home, house) or *ilẹ̀* (land, earth). Thus home, land, and territory are one. In Yorùbá ontology, *ilẹ̀* also signifies the final place of rest: in the context of funeral rites after death, to go home is to join one's ancestors in the afterlife and to return to one's place of origin.

Life in this world is symbolized as a journey that ends with a return to one's home—*Ayé làjò, bi ó tilẹ̀ pẹ́ pẹ́, a ó relé* (The world is a journey, and no matter how long we stay abroad we will return home). As Jonathan Smith remarked, there is a logical connection and a relationship between "home place" and "land."[31] In addition, there is a sense in which, for the Yorùbá, the city is both a place and a people; indeed, Ray Laurence's comment on the ancient Romans, that "it was impossible to speak of a city as a place without a people," applies to them as well.[32] The people of the city sustain the ancestors, gods, and land, and the land in return bestows manifold blessings on the people.

In the history of religions, one of the most studied aspects of sacred place is the sacred city. Three types are noticeable in world religions. According to R. J. Zwi Werblowsky, a place may acquire sacredness for any of three reasons: because of historical or mythical circumstances or events, "because either in theory or in actual fact [it was] constructed so as to reflect cosmic reality—a kind of microcosmic reflection of the macrocosm and its divine ground," or because it is the home of a shrine, tomb, or holy object.[33] Ilé-Ifè is sacred for all three of these reasons.

The Yorùbá regard Ilé-Ifè as the most central and potent place. It is seen as the mother of all cities, the place where the structure and meaning of the sacred cosmos first unfolded. I would like to explore the meaning of Ilé-Ifè in the Yorùbá religious experience and the role this city has played in constructing Yorùbá religious identity and a sense of place in contemporary Yorùbá politics.

In his classic work *Olódùmarè: God in Yorùbá Belief,* the father of Yorùbá religious studies, Bọ́lájí Ìdòwú, recalls his experience of Ilé-Ifè and describes it for younger generations: "A young person who was lucky enough in those days to be taken by his parents to Ilé-Ifẹ̀ would approach the city with feelings which baffled analysis. He was bound to be assailed on entering the city with successive waves of emotions. He would be almost afraid to look; for at every turn might be walking or lurking, for all he knew, some divinities or ghosts!"[34] Ìdòwú further remarks, "It is clear, then, that a modern and new study of the religion of the Yorùbá should center around Ilé-Ifẹ̀ although the investigator must take account of all the other important religious and civic centers of Yorùbá life."[35] He confirms Wheatley's earlier discovery of the significance of Ilé-Ifẹ̀ as an urban center and as the model for the foundation of the other Yorùbá city-states.

THE PLACE MOST HALLOWED:
THE SACRED CITY OF ILÉ-IFẸ̀

In *The Pivot of the Four Quarters,* Wheatley indicates that no place in sub-Saharan Africa has such cosmic significance as the Yorùbá city of Ilé-Ifẹ̀. Known as the City of 201 (or 401) Gods, Ilé-Ifẹ̀ is the base of the entire Yorùbá civilization and culture, and its significance goes far beyond the immediate geographical and national boundaries of Nigeria. The religious culture of Ilé-Ifẹ̀ has influenced the development and growth of new African religious movements as far off as Brazil, the Caribbean, and the United States.

Ilé-Ifẹ̀, a city of about half a million, is situated at the geographical center of the Yorùbá city-states. To the west lies Ìbàdàn, the largest city in sub-Saharan Africa, and to the east lies Oǹdó, gateway to the eastern Yorùbá city-states. Ilé-Ifẹ̀ is about two hundred kilometers from Lagos, which was Nigeria's coastal capital city for over a century. Unlike the political, commercial, and administrative cities of Ìbàdàn and Lagos, contemporary Ilé-Ifẹ̀ is a ceremonial city par excellence; like the cities of Banaras, Jerusalem, and Mecca, in the people's imagination it is the preeminent sacred place, beyond the secular and profane.

I begin with Ilé-Ifẹ̀'s various sacred place names, because epithets vividly show the significance of sacred cities. Stephen Scully argues in his book *Homer and the Sacred City* that "human centers such as Troy are richly and complexly described through the epithets attached to them."[36] Citing an earlier study by Paolo Vivante, Scully contends that "city epithets, whenever they occur, bring out the essential aesthetics and contextual quality of place names." These epithets serve "as a resource of power and a medium of signification in their own right." They are "visual and concrete in nature, and thereby evocative of an essential and generic quality" of whatever they qualify.[37]

Ilé-Ifẹ̀'s inhabitants have conferred numerous sacred Yorùbá names on their city. It has been called Ifẹ̀ Oòdáyé, "The Expansive Space Where the World Was Created," referring to the cosmogonic myth asserting that ritual creation occurred in this very place, and as Ibi Ojú Ti Mọ́ Wá (Where the Day Dawns). In Yorùbá creation myth, Ilé-Ifẹ̀ is conceived of as the place where the sun rises and sets, the center of origin of the universe. Ilé-Ifẹ̀ is also called Ifẹ̀ Oòyè, the place of survival or the city of life, because, like Noah's ark, it was a place of refuge from a primordial deluge that destroyed earlier settlements and left survivors to establish a new era. Various oral sources refer to the Ilé-Ifẹ̀ as the place where the 201 gods came down from heaven to live and interact with humans on earth.

Though Ilé-Ifẹ̀ is the city of the source of life, it is, paradoxically, also the city of the dead. The Yorùbá believe that those who die immediately return to Ilé-Ifẹ̀, the starting point for their pilgrimage to the other world. Several years ago, I was in my own hometown, Uté, in Ọ̀wọ̀ District, a town located at the extreme eastern end of the eastern Yorùbá territory, to conduct research on death in Yorùbá thought. In an important song sung in the Ọ̀wọ̀ tradition during the burial, the deceased is enjoined to "go on the straight road that leads to Ilé-Ifẹ̀ and not stray by the wayside" (Ọ̀nà yó r'ufẹ̀ má yà o). Ilé-Ifẹ̀ is regarded as the only stopping place before the dead pass into the underworld, so the rite of passage must ensure that the deceased not tarry on the way to the ancient city. In ancient times, it was the practice of those who had lost a loved one to travel to Ilé-Ifẹ̀ to see if they could find the deceased person and learn from him or her about the cause of the death so that they could avenge a wrongful death or hear about unfinished business on earth that the deceased wanted living relatives to see completed if possible.

Ilé-Ifẹ̀ attained primacy on the basis of its hallowed status as the source for all the crowned cities (ìlú-aládé). An important Yorùbá myth refers to the dispersal of Odùduwà's sixteen royal children, who went out from Ilé-Ifẹ̀ to found new kingdoms. Each was assigned a sacred crown, or adé, a symbol of authority. (In 1903 the colonial administration determined that the Ọọ̀ni of Ifẹ̀ was the most qualified to say who ought to own and wear this crown.) Each was assigned a sacred sword representing the divine power to take possession of new territories. Stories of the origin of several Yorùbá kingdoms are filled with anecdotes about the royal princes' and princesses' encounters as they conquered aboriginal groups in their newfound lands and ruled with the sacred insignia of office: the crown and the sword.

I should add that in several cities the Ifẹ̀ cosmovision serves as a model for other lesser but equally significant sacred centers in the Yorùbá world. A case in point is Ìdànrè, an important city in the eastern Yorùbá region of Oǹdó State, Nigeria, where I have also carried out field research. Ìdànrè's inhabitants lived for a long time on an isolated mountain, Òkè-Ìdànrè, and they have always maintained a connection with Ilé-Ifẹ̀. The ancient name for the present-day city of Ìdànrè was Ufẹ̀kè (Ifẹ̀ on the Mountain). Legends of Ìdànrè migration argue that their founders, Ọlọ́fin and his followers, were immigrants from the ancient city of Ilé-Ifẹ̀.[38] The founders claimed that they possessed the ancient crown of Odùduwà and other royal garments. They hid on a mountain, where they were constantly assailed by other Yorùbá groups who wanted to seize these royal treasures.

FIGURE 3. The Ọwá of Ìdànrè, Ọba Arọ̀lóyè, during the Idẹn Festival in Ìdànrè, similar to the Ọlọ́jọ́ Festival in Ilé-Ifẹ̀.

During the annual Idẹn, or King's Festival, the Ọwá of Ìdànrè dons the ancient crown of Ọlọ́fin (also regarded as Odùduwà) in the dark of night. Putting on the ancient crown signifies renewal of his kingship and celebrates his valor and military strength in conquering all intruders who pursued the Ìdànrè to steal his crown. Indeed, Ìdànrè is one of the most revered cities of southwestern Nigeria. Its inhabitants are particularly famous for their control over and use of traditional medicine and the spoken word *(ohùn),* the magical or sacred formulas to make things happen. The Idẹn Festival that bears the signature of Ìdànrè sacred kingship is similar to the Ọlọ́jọ́ Festival in Ilé-Ifẹ̀, the festival of sacred kingship and of Ògún, the god of war, in which the Ọ̀ọ̀ni wears his own sacred *arè* crown. Thus the legend signifies that the Ifẹ̀ cosmovision is duplicated by other Yorùbá cities whose inhabitants share in Ilé-Ifẹ̀'s sacred myth and history.

SYMBOLIC CITY STRUCTURE

The structural organization of Ilé-Ifẹ̀ and its special religious, political, and spatial form symbolize the sacred cosmology behind the city's origins. The most important section is the center, the Ọ̀ọ̀ni's palace, or *ààfin,* often called *òkè-ilé* (the high or big house), located on an elevated site, and the five principal quarters that constitute the old city of Ilé-Ifẹ̀ radiate out from it. Three major roads leading from these sections converge in front of the palace at an intersection called Ẹnu Ọwá, literally, "Mouth of the King."[39] They function as an *oríta* (crossroads), an important phenomenon in Yorùbá religious life. *Oríta* are not mere crossroads; they are ritually potent spaces where sacrifices may be offered to spirits or evil forces *(alájogun)* and messages may be conveyed to witches, wizards, and spirits of the underworld or heaven. The royal palace is protected by the city's concentric layout around its center. As one moves from outermost to innermost circles, degrees of power and sacredness increase. Located close to the palace are the sacred precincts that cradle the three most important ritual centers in the city: the grove, the shrine, and the temple.

The grove belongs to Odùduwà, cultural hero and founder of the city; Òkè-M'ògún is the shrine and hill of Ògún, warrior god, patron deity of the sacred kingship; and Òkè Ìtasẹ̀, Ifá hill and temple, is the abode of Àràbà Àgbáyé, chief diviner of the universe. Sacred sites of Yorùbá cities are determined by the divination process. Each principal city underwent a divination ritual to determine the best site for its origin and growth *(odù tí ó tẹ Ìlú dó).* When I asked one of my consultants to name the *odù* (chapter of the corpus of oral texts on divination) on which Ilé-Ifẹ̀ was founded, he exclaimed in surprise, saying that all sixteen principal *odù* talked about the city's origin, an indication that this city was greater than any other city in Yorùbá territory.

SACRED SPACE AND SOCIAL ORDER:
IDENTITY, NATIONALISM, AND PLACE

I turn now to the significance of place for nationalism and identity construction in contemporary Yorùbá society. One lacuna in the history of religions is the general lack of in-depth analysis of the relationship between religious phenomena and the social order within which these phenomena exist. The danger of overemphasizing the social context of religion at the expense of the phenomenon itself has encouraged many to avoid exploring the possible social consequences of religious behavior. If historians of religions were to take more seriously Peter Berger's suggestion for analyzing religious phenomena, that we should view religion in terms of its origin, functions, and intrinsic and substantive value, we would produce a more rounded interpretation of religion that did not privilege one aspect at the expense of the others. Recently, Roger Friedland and Richard Hecht have contended that there is a strong connection "between the construction of sacred space and the social organization of power" and that "ultimately, an adequate theory of sacred places must take cognizance of the political dynamics that play a key role in how it is appreciated, controlled, interpreted, and contested."[40] According to these two authors, "Because they undergird identities and ethical commitments, because they galvanize the deepest emotions and attachments, material and symbolic control over the most central sacred places are sources of enormous social power."[41] Ilé-Ifè is a prime example of how this social power shapes notions of identity, nationalism, and place.

I will examine the role of the Ilé-Ifè homeland and territoriality in the construction of ethnic nationalism, patriotism, and community identity among the Yorùbá. By *nationalism,* I refer not to the contemporary nation-state context (Nigeria) but to the Yorùbá nation as a cultural group with a homeland, a language, a religion, and a shared culture.[42]

Three related themes should be considered as a template for understanding how sacred cities function in the context of modern nationalism. First, Ilé-Ifè, as a hallowed land of religious and cultural traditions, was used to mobilize the Yorùbá as a unified patriotic and nationalist group. Second, symbols of sacred place were used in the development of a homeland of subcultural identities and to galvanize the Yorùbá community into a patriotic and national group. Third, the Yorùbá mark their boundaries of sacred space in what have been called rituals of "hallowing the land."[43]

The study of sacred places in Yorùbá religious experience may help answer puzzling questions about Yorùbá identity and the role the Yorùbá religion plays in modern Nigerian politics. Why are the ethnicity and ethnic identity of forty million Yorùbá people so strong that their cultural and political lives are difficult for outsiders to penetrate? Part of the answer lies in the role of place, and particularly the role of Ilé-Ifè as a centralized sacred place, in "creating a religious, communal, and political identity" and mobilizing people politically.[44] A second relevant issue, borrowed from Kunin's argument, is that a centralized model of sacred place not only constructs identities but also creates boundaries that establish the relationship of "insiders" and "outsiders" to the sacred center.[45]

The Yorùbá origin myth discussed above is normally followed by another equally powerful myth: that of the dispersion, migration, and odyssey of the children of Odùduwà, who left the sacred city of Ilé-Ifẹ̀ to conquer, inhabit, and establish new dynasties and new cities and towns. With this odyssey, new city-states similar to Ilé-Ifẹ̀, such as Oǹdó, Ọ̀wọ̀, Benin, Adó-Èkìtì, Ìjẹ̀bú-Òde, Ketu, and Ọ̀yọ́, were created. In the context of space and land, the migration myth from Ilé-Ifẹ̀ "provides for a plan of cosmological *relatedness.*"[46] The Yorùbá historian Adéagbo Akínjọ́gbìn describes this relationship between the Ilé-Ifẹ̀ center and the new city-states as one based on *ẹbí* (lineage) ideology: semiautonomous kinship groups with defined territorial boundaries are joined in a sacred pact.[47] The sociologist Akínṣọlá Akìwọwo has described their alliance as being based on what the Yorùbá call *àjọbí* (principles of kinship and religious association).[48] Though Ilé-Ifẹ̀ provides a unifying myth, an equal element of decentralization of sacred space is evident in Yorùbá mythology. Multiplicity of sacred space does not negate our thesis of a centralized sacred space.

The significance of Ilé-Ifẹ̀ in Yorùbá political life is especially revealed by two incidents: the visit of the Ọ̀ọ̀ni, paramount ruler of Ilé-Ifẹ̀, to Lagos in 1903; and the formation, in the 1940s and 1950s, of a centralized pan-Yorùbá cultural and quasi-political association based on the Odùduwà myth, Ẹgbẹ́ Ọmọ Odùduwà (Society of the Descendants of Odùduwà) and its political successor, the Action Group Party.

The unprecedented visit of an Ọ̀ọ̀ni to Lagos was chilling to all the other Yorùbá Ọba, including the Aláàfin of Ọ̀yọ́. Before this visit, it had been taboo for an Ọ̀ọ̀ni to leave the city of Ilé-Ifẹ̀. The other Yorùbá Ọba viewed the announcement of his journey with such great alarm and seriousness that they decided to vacate their palaces and stay outside their city for the duration of his visit until they could confirm his safe return. Although the Ọ̀ọ̀ni's visit can be interpreted as a sign of the capitulation of the traditional center and society of Ilé-Ifẹ̀ to the new colonial center in Lagos, the visit also signaled a reinvention of tradition.

Under the British system of indirect rule, the colonial government had created a new city legislative council in charge of the affairs of the new region. In 1903, a dispute between two Yorùbá rulers, the Ẹlẹ́pẹ́ of Èpẹ́ in Ìjẹ̀bú Rẹ́mọ and the Àkàrìgbò of Ìjẹ̀bú Rẹ́mọ, was referred to the state legislative council for adjudication. The Àkàrìgbò protested the Ẹlẹ́pẹ́'s wearing a beaded crown, which by tradition could be worn only by an Ọba claiming direct descent from Odùduwà, who had been authorized to wear the crown by the Ọ̀ọ̀ni of Ilé-Ifẹ̀. The reigning Ọ̀ọ̀ni was Adélẹ́kàn Olúbùṣe I, the grandfather of the incumbent Ọ̀ọ̀ni. At the suggestion of council members, the Ọ̀ọ̀ni was invited to Lagos in February 1903 to rule on the matter.

Hidden behind a screen (since it was forbidden to behold the face of the Ọ̀ọni), the Ọ̀ọni answered all the questions the council put to him. He denounced the Ẹlẹ́pẹ́, lamenting that if it were the old days, the Ọ̀ọni would have summoned the Ẹlẹ́pẹ́ to Ilé-Ifẹ̀ and had him beheaded. What happened between the Ọ̀ọni and the British governor after the meeting must be the subject of another work. In short, the Ọ̀ọni was entertained by the governor in a private meeting, and upon the Ọ̀ọni's safe re-turn to Ilé-Ifẹ̀, the Yorùbá Ọba returned to their palaces. By reinventing the tradi-tional power, the British colonial government was able to wend its way through tur-bulent issues such as this dispute between the two rulers. Ilé-Ifẹ̀, the Yorùbá place of origin, played a significant role in this process.

The second incident is from the preindependence era of Yorùbá politics, when new colonial dispensations of power in Nigeria reinforced old ethnic fault lines. The seeds of Yorùbá nationalism were planted in Britain when Yorùbá students abroad, led by Ọbáfẹ́mi Awóḷọ́wọ̀, a lawyer in training, formed the pan-Yorùbá group called Ẹgbẹ́ Ọmọ Odùduwà (Society of the Descendants of Odùduwà). Chief Ọbáfẹ́mi Awóḷọ́wọ̀ a member of the new educated elite, became engaged in politics on his return to Nigeria, founding a new political party, the Action Group Party, and gath-ering the Yorùbá under its banner. He appealed to the sensibilities of the Yorùbá, urging them to identify with the already existing Ẹgbẹ́ Ọmọ Odùduwà. Ilé-Ifẹ̀ be-came a powerful symbol used by the Ẹgbẹ́ Ọmọ Odùduwà to mobilize the Yorùbá into a new sociocultural and political order. In the Yorùbá imagination, Awóḷọ́wọ̀ gradually became the reincarnation of Odùduwà, a transformation reflected in the chieftaincy title he bore, Aṣíwájú (leader) of the Yorùbá. A popular song in praise of Awóḷọ́wọ̀, composed by Herbert Ògúnde, a celebrated Yorùbá musician, aptly describes the roles of Ilé-Ifẹ̀ and Awóḷọ́wọ̀ in this pan-Yorùbá nationalism:

Kíni ǹbá sìn
Bíkòṣe Olúwo wa
Awóḷọ́wọ̀, Ìwọ ni mojírí lónìí, ire ńbámi bọ̀,
ire owó, ire ọmọ, ire Àlàáfíà.

To whom shall I pay homage [literally, worship] if not to Awóḷọ́wọ̀?
Our great high priest [Olúwo].
You are the one to whom I have come to give praise [as in propitiation of a deity]
When I pay homage to you, I will receive the blessings of children, wealth, and long
    life.[49]

Implicit in this song of praise is the essence of the Yorùbá religious quest for a full life as promised by the *òrìṣà*. The subtext is that those who associate themselves with the great Yorùbá political priest will receive from the deity the threefold bless-ings of life. Awóḷọ́wọ̀ is referred to as the Ifá high priest and senior diviner (Olúwo), who is powerful enough to discover the secrets of heaven and provide to his people the promise of a good life. It is very interesting that this new modern political party, the Action Group Party headed by Chief Awólọ́wọ̀, was anchored in Odùduwà's myth of creation. When, several years later, a renegade group attempted to challenge the hegemony of the Action Group by setting up a counterpart Yorùbá political group, the NNDP, its own cultural and ideological base was expressed in its name, Ẹgbẹ́ Ọmọ Ọlọ́fin (Society of the Descendants of Ọlọ́fin). Ọlọ́fin is a synonym for Odùduwà, an indication that there was no way of getting out of the matrix of the Odùduwà/Ọlọ́fin myth of Yorùbá origin that had taken place in the sacred city of Ilé-Ifẹ̀.

While Ilé-Ifẹ̀ provides the basis for a pan-Yorùbá ideology of natural unity, other cities and towns that claim their origin from the sacred source have developed subethnic identities for their inhabitants. Since the 1990s, following several years of military misrule and neglect, Yorùbá towns and cities have succeeded in spurring their communities' social and economic development. The absence of any meaningful improvement in the welfare of the people has made community projects even more important today.[50] The strongest instrument of mobilization is the appeal to symbols of religion and culture, such as myths of the sacred home place and the totemic symbols associated with natural phenomena such as rivers, mountains, forest, and trees.

In the construction of the subethnic Yorùbá identity and invocation of city nationalism, the most vital symbols invoked are represented by geographical elements connected to the city origin, totemic objects regarded as the spiritual source connected to Ilé-Ifẹ̀: the Ọ̀ṣun River goddess in Òṣogbo; Òrósùn Hill in Ìdànrè; Òkè-Ìbàdàn Hill in Ìbàdàn; and Olúmọ Rock in Abẹ́òkúta, the basis of Ẹ̀gbá-Yorùbá unity.

The history and geography of religion provide ample evidence of the ways religious myths, rituals, and symbols sacralize places and territories. Through their religious experiences and expressions, the Yorùbá people of southwestern Nigeria have elaborated a special metaphor from their experience of place as originating in the sacred city of Ilé-Ifẹ̀. This concept or significance of place is not limited to traditional life but continues to influence their activities in present-day Nigeria, as is demonstrated by its role in politics and nationalist movements.

VIOLENCE IN THE SACRED CITY

So far, we have examined Ilé-Ifẹ̀ in the context of its myth and history and have showed how the city assumed its character as a place of origin and the epicenter of Yorùbá culture and religion. Paradoxically, if Ilé-Ifẹ̀ is the City of Life (Ifẹ̀ Oòyé), it is also a highly contested place in which communal violence frequently surfaces.

In the history of religion worldwide, virtually no sacred city has managed to escape from occasional skirmishes. Indeed, one can postulate that violence and bloodshed are intrinsic to the nature of sacred cities. The ancient and modern history of Rome, Mecca, and Jerusalem, three classic city centers in human civilization and religious traditions, is emblematic of the intrinsic connection between violence and the sacred. Ilé-Ifẹ̀ has not escaped this fate and has from its very foundation been seen and imagined as a violent place marked by intermittent communal feuds. Ironically, when compared with similar Yorùbá people from cities such as Ilẹ́sà, Ìbàdàn, and Oǹdó, Ifẹ̀ indigenes are considered very peaceful people. This characterization even extends to popular parlance. Though in other towns locals' envy of "foreign" entrepreneurs has led to crises, Ilé-Ifẹ̀ is a place where foreigners are uninhibited in trade and commerce and prosper without being molested by locals. I remember that at the celebration of 1998 Ọlọ́jọ́ Festival, the Oṣògún—the chief priest of Ògún—greeted the Ọ̀ọ̀ni as "an enviable king, who takes care of both natives and foreigners" (ó tọ́jú onílé, tọ́jú àlejò).

Like other sacred cities, Ilé-Ifẹ̀ has been caught up in violence from its mythic beginnings up to the present. The story of the creation of Ilé-Ifẹ̀ unfolds in battles of conquest. Odùduwà and Ọbàtálá were engaged in a war that ultimately led to Ọbàtálá's defeat. Scholars who support the thesis that Odùduwà was a foreign invader who came and conquered the pre-Odùduwà aboriginals also agree that numerous wars of conquest were waged before the Odùduwà finally established their dynasty. Powerful warlords arose during this unsettled period, such as Ọbamerì and Bàbá Ṣìgìdì, described as Odùduwà's war general who, immediately on hearing rumors of war, was ready to fight (a gbọ́ ọjọ́ ogun fẹsẹ̀ janlẹ̀ janjan). Ifẹ̀ rituals and festivals today refer to these violent conflicts. One tradition informs us that as the primordial battle over establishing the city became fierce, a boy god, Olúorogbo—also called Oníwe Ọ̀run or "Holy Scribe" because of his ability to write and draw images—was sent quickly to Olódùmarè to report on events on earth and to solicit his immediate intervention. Hence, the Ifẹ̀ people derive the proverb Ó kù dẹ̀dẹ̀ kí ayé Onúfẹ̀ bàjẹ́, ni Olúorogbo wá tún ayé ṣe (At this point the world of Ifẹ̀ was close to collapse; thus Olúorogbo intervened to remake the world).

In ancient times, Ilé-Ifẹ̀ was a city of sacrifice, like Tenochtitlan as David Carrasco describes it. Maintenance of established kingdoms required regular sacrifices to the 201 or 401 gods who made up the Ilé-Ifẹ̀ pantheon. These prehistoric violent conflicts, conquests, and sacrifices helped to demarcate the various groups that make up indigenous Ilé-Ifẹ̀ and that define its religious and civil life today; they also provide the ultimate legitimacy for the sacred kingship of the Ọ̀ọ̀ni.

IFẸ̀ ORÍKÌ POETIC TRADITION

The following oríkì (praise poem) reveals Ilé-Ifẹ̀'s image in the ancient Yorùbá kingdom as a center for ritual sacrifice.

> Àbú Ìtẹ́ní, son of Ifẹ̀, the Eternal City,
> Àbú, king of Ifẹ̀, the landowner, who wears velvet costumes,
> The king who wears the white coral beads.

Àdìmúlà [the Ọọ̀ni] who would offer human sacrifices, cutting open the chests
    of victims and exposing their livers.
Such violent [human] sacrifice makes me dislike the Olufẹ̀'s palace.

Àbú, the king of Ifẹ̀, the Ọọ̀ni
He who turns his face away from the incision knife.
He is forbidden to have facial scarification.
The Ọọ̀ni's presence invokes fear and trembling.
One never remains standing to greet the [important] people of Ilé-Ifẹ̀.
Also, one never stoops to greet them in Ilé-Ifẹ̀.
If one does not greet them in Ifẹ̀, one is asking for trouble.
If one greets them in Ifẹ̀, one will be looked down upon.
If one does not greet them in Ifẹ̀, one will be despised.
After having greeted them, one will become a sacrificial offering.
They are the natives of the East from the place where the daylight shines forth,
At the place where doors are made of kolanut tree trunks.
The son of the owner of the forest of kolanut trees, where it is very dark.
They are the children of certain drum that is beaten at Ifẹ̀,
A certain drum made of leopard skin
And of the thick strong hide of the forelegs of the elephant.
The slaves in the palace must not dance to its rhythms.
The indentured servants must not even move to its rhythm.
People with no tribal marks [the free people of Ifẹ̀] have the privilege to dance
    to its rhythm.
The children of the king are the only ones allowed to beat the skinned drum
    for the king.
Non-natives must not beat the royal drum called *alùkan*.
It is the children of Olufẹ̀ who must beat the drum called *ikin*.
That is why the royals beat the *ikin* drum for the king.

The Ọọ̀ni evokes fear and trembling.
For the fear provoked by a drum
Was the cause of their dispersal at one time.
That was when six principal elders left Ilé-Ifẹ̀.
The day the *ikin* drum was beaten was the day all of them were driven away.
To behold the Ọọ̀ni is terrifying indeed.[51]

It has been suggested that this poem about Ilé-Ifẹ̀ was created by the Arókin (palace
balladeers) of Ọ̀yọ́, the rival city of Ilé-Ifẹ̀. Nevertheless, it points to the popular belief that Ilé-Ifẹ̀ was the central sacrificial center of the Yorùbá people and confirms
the traditional belief that the people of Ilé-Ifẹ̀ abhor the permanent markings created by facial scarification, unlike the Ọ̀yọ́ Yorùbá, who consider them beautiful.
The war and the crises that led the Ifẹ̀ people into exile are also mentioned. More
importantly, arrogance was considered a customary trait of the Ifẹ̀, based on a sense
of superiority due to their privileged connection to the Yorùbá place of origin, and

was often marveled at by their enemies. The poem says that whether or not you greet an Ifẹ̀ person, he or she looks down on you as an inferior being. Although the contemporary Ifẹ̀ people whom I lived with are far from unsociable, the poem nevertheless recalls the pride of an ancient people who perceived themselves as the guardians of the Odùduwà crown and their city as the place of origin of the Yorùbá people.

THE ILÉ-IFẸ̀ AND THE MODÁKẸ́KẸ́

Violence between Ilé-Ifẹ̀ and the Modákẹ́kẹ́ people has a long history: It escalated over 150 years and came to a climax in the last two decades of the twentieth century. There are many scholarly accounts, from Samuel Johnson's somewhat partisan but detailed exploration of the causes of conflict to more recent works by Olufẹ́mi Ọmọ́sini, Adéagbo Akínjógbìn, Ọmọ́tọ́ṣọ̀ọ́ Elúyẹmí, and Richard Ọláníyan. The impact of these violent encounters has been excellently described by Ọláníyan and Peyi Ṣóyínká-Airewele.[52]

In this section, I will offer some cultural and religious interpretations of this violence, especially as it relates to the notion of the sacred center to which Ilé-Ifẹ̀ lays claim. I will argue that rather than viewing it as an aberration, we should view it as part of a long history of claims that groups make to sacred centers.

The Modákẹ́kẹ́ people were descendants of the Ọ̀yọ́. Because of the Yorùbá civil wars during the early nineteenth century, they became refugees and sought asylum in Ilé-Ifẹ̀. In their favor was their appeal to tradition and the image of Ilé-Ifẹ̀ as the ancestral home of the Yorùbá people. By the beginning of the nineteenth century, the Modákẹ́kẹ́ people settled among the Ilé-Ifẹ̀ people and in surrounding smaller towns. With successive rulers on the throne of Ilé-Ifẹ̀ came different attitudes and responses to the settlers. Some favored the presence of the Modákẹ́kẹ́, whereas others rejected them. By 1830, Ọ̀yọ́ refugees in Ilé-Ifẹ̀ were experiencing intense hostility from their hosts. Ọọ̀ni Abewéelá accommodated the Modákẹ́kẹ́ in large numbers, to the displeasure of the Ilé-Ifẹ̀ people, so that by his death in 1849, Ifẹ̀ and Modákẹ́kẹ́ were engulfed in civil war.[53] Two major wars were fought between 1849 and 1886; in 1849 the Modákẹ́kẹ́ sacked Ilé-Ifẹ̀ and took thousands of its citizens prisoner, then held the city for the next five years.[54] Later clashes enabled the Ifẹ̀ to regain their city. At last, a peace treaty initiated by the colonial government and signed in 1886 recommended that the Modákẹ́kẹ́ be relocated outside Ifẹ̀ territory. After much delay, in accordance with the terms of the peace agreement, in June 1908 the Modákẹ́kẹ́ were relocated to a new site in Ọdẹòmu. This resettlement took place during the reign of Ọọ̀ni Adélẹ́kàn Olúbùṣe I (1894–1910), grandfather of the present Ọọ̀ni, Okùnadé Olúbùṣe II.

The *oríkì* of Olúbùṣe's royal lineage reflects the provisional victory of Ifẹ̀ over the Modákẹ́kẹ́. It is recited largely in reference to the Modákẹ́kẹ́ defeat:

Olúbùṣe ẹ̀rí ogun
Èbìtì kimọ pìrì yinmọ nù
Ò súnmọ sílẹ̀ súnmọ ṣẹ́ní
Ò kumọ lósùn kunmọ láta

Olúbùṣe, the great warrior
The trap that suddenly catches the prey and releases it
He that chases away the disobedient child and draws closer the favoured one
He who pets the obedient child and punishes the erring one

The *oríkì* provides a traditional counterpart to written accounts of family history. Both are embedded in the collective memories of groups of people, which strengthen group identity and determination. In the imagination of Ifẹ̀, the memory of Olúbùṣe I includes his great sacrifice and redemptive suffering.

During my fieldwork, I heard a remarkable reference to the temporary evacuation of the Modákẹ́kẹ́ from Ilé-Ifẹ̀ in 1897, a measure effective partly because of the diplomacy and zeal of Olúbùṣe I. For a long time before this exodus, the Modákẹ́kẹ́ had vowed publicly to stay in their homes. One of my informants told me that when the disputants were deadlocked, Ọ̀ọ̀ni Olúbùṣe called his medicine men together to inquire what course could be taken to resolve the conflict. The medicine men warned that perhaps they would have to perform a major sacrifice that could involve loss of the king's life *(á bá ẹ̀mí lọ)*. The king pondered this, but his love for Ilé-Ifẹ̀ was foremost in his mind. Finally, he agreed to order his own sacrifice. His medicine men began preparations, and at night, the king was made to carry the sacrificial rituals on his head while walking naked to the quarters of the Modákẹ́kẹ́. As the Modákẹ́kẹ́ saw the unclothed king of Ifẹ̀ approaching them, they were terrified. It was an absolute abomination to behold the king unclothed. At this point, they hurriedly packed their belongings and fled from Ilé-Ifẹ̀. I recount this story to show that collective cultural memories of imagined or true events are used in reconstructing mythic history. The memory of an Ọba's redemptive suffering and his willingness to sacrifice himself to save his city from humiliation will resurface as we examine Ifẹ̀ ritual and festivals, especially the legend of Mọrèmi, the daring goddess of Ilé-Ifẹ̀.

Ifẹ̀ historians usually juxtapose this event and the deeds of Olúbùṣe I with events during the reign of the successive Ọ̀ọ̀ni. The reign of Ọ̀ọ̀ni Adémilúyì Ajagun from 1910 to 1930 ushered in a different era. With the exception of the Ọ̀ọ̀ni currently reigning in 2009, the successive Ọ̀ọ̀ni stood in great contrast to Ọ̀ọ̀ni Olúbùṣe I in their handling of Modákẹ́kẹ́ affairs.

Sympathizing deeply with Modákẹ́kẹ́ refugees, Ọ̀ọ̀ni Adémilúyì Ajagun ordered them to return to Ilé-Ifẹ̀ in 1922, an act that brought on regular clashes with his own people until his death in 1930, when Ọ̀ọ̀ni Adérèmí (1930–80) ascended the throne. As Ọláníyan has noted, several skirmishes between Ilé-Ifẹ̀ indigenes and their Modákéké tenants triggered violent conflict.[55] The most infamous were the reparations the Modákéké demanded from the local government secretariat over payment of ìṣákólè, the annual tribute that tenants customarily paid to property owners. Tragedy also ensued over the appointment of a separate chief imam for the Modákéké, which signified their de facto religious independence from Ilé-Ifè. During the reign of Ọòni Adérèmí, there were occasional outbreaks of fighting between the two groups, but Adérèmí used diplomatic tactics to prevent the all-out violence that had characterized the reign of his predecessors. For example, he instituted trends of intermarriage and friendly alliances. His favorite wife, Sègi, was from the Modákéké, and consequently many Ifè and Modákéké elite intermarried.[56]

The Modákéké's demands for a local government and their resistance to the payment of ìṣákólè are issues of dispute over land and territorial independence. Perhaps correctly from their perspective, the Modákéké argued that it was absurd to continue to pay ìṣákólè to Ilé-Ifè because the Modákéké were descendants of Odùduwà from the sacred city of Ilé-Ifè. However, Ifè claimed superiority over the rest of the Yorùbá city-states, asserting that the Modákéké had no political autonomy outside the Ifè boundary and that the Modákéké expansion had deprived them of prime land and territory. From 1984 to 2004, renewed conflicts and intense hostilities between the two communities led to wanton destruction of property and life.

Central to the violent conflict between the Ilé-Ifè and the Modákéké have been several intricately linked social and cultural issues: the autonomous nature of land and its role in constructing identity in the Yorùbá geographical realm, the collective memory of violence and revenge, and external factors such as the failure of the nation-state to control its regional provinces. Ifè people assert that historically and culturally, the Modákéké have no traditional claim to the space and land they currently occupy other than their status as settlers, refugees, or a marginalized group. Robert Thornton has underscored the importance, especially in times of social crisis, of the power that autochthony can claim on sacred lands: "If politics is the art of the possible, then possibilities for legitimacy include the appeal to the earth itself, to the aesthetics of landscapes, to the native (in the sense 'one born in'), and to autochthony."[57] During my fieldwork, the Ilé-Ifè people I interviewed often recalled their nostalgia for a time when the land of the Ifè people was indisputably theirs. They claimed that by waging war against Ilé-Ifè the Modákéké had violated a sacred trust, the relationship between tenants (the Modákéké) and property owners (onílé), the aboriginal owners of the land (the people of Ifè).

More than a century of social, religious, economic, and familial interactions between the two communities has not eliminated this tension as a cause of chronic violence in the sacred city and has allowed for no meaningful integration of the two peoples. After renewed conflict in 1996, reports of killing on both sides defied imagination. Spouses and children of "mixed" marriages were caught up in the conflict, some being killed by their own blood relatives. In these instances, conjugal and familial love offered no protection to family members; the collective love for one's land—ancestral land for the Ifè, inhabited land for their Modákéké antagonists—took on a more central role.

Collective memory in social and cultural guise plays a significant role in the continuing dissension between the people of Ilé-Ifè and Modákéké. Richard Werbner has aptly pointed out that the public practice of memory plays a role in disruption and terrorism in postcolonial Africa generally: "The challenge in everyday life, in major public occasions and in disruptive events of terror and civil unrest is to the very means and social models of remembrance."[58] Social memory is invoked not only as a tool of political power and manipulation but also as a moral force in communal relations. Both Ifè and Modákéké appealed to memory of past mythic history. Memory played a central role in the unfolding of the crisis and at the same time served as a tool for possible reconciliation between the two warring communities. Both the Ifè and the Modákéké recognized Ilé-Ifè as the Yorùbá ancestral home, thus legitimizing Ọòni Abewéelá's decision to absorb a group of wandering Yorùbá refugees into his fold. However, the Ifè insisted that Modákéké rights to tenancy failed to denote rights of ownership of land.

In conversations with me, the Ifè frequently mentioned the Modákéké's long-ago successful attack on Ilé-Ifè as evidence of their continuing hostile intentions against landowners. As one might expect, the Modákéké appealed to Ifè's mythic history, citing the Odùduwà story in which the Ifè were to act as protectors of all those who claimed to be of Ilé-Ifè origin. Memories of past oppression under Ilé-Ifè's rule also remained strong. One Modákéké elder told me, "We were like the children of Israel in the land of the pharaoh in Egypt." Successful leaders of the Modákéké were often compared to Moses leading the oppressed children of Israel out of the house of bondage into the Promised Land. As descendants of Odùduwà, the Modákéké insisted it was unethical to be made to pay endless iṣákọ́lẹ to Ilé-Ifè.[59] In no other situation did the reconciliation of two deep-rooted opposing social codes require more potent political and moral leadership (supplied by the current Ọba, the grandson of Olúbùṣe I) than in the renewed outbreak of civil war between the two groups that began in 1990, a crisis whose foundation had been laid a century earlier.

Understanding the Ifè-Modákéké crisis requires looking at forces outside the nationalist and indigenous paradigm just discussed. As much as the invocation of collective memory was an impetus for reviving previous animosity between the two groups, the conflict was equally exacerbated by social and economic problems. In 1999, the Bode George Commission, engaged by the federal government of Nigeria to resolve the Ifè-Modákéké crisis permanently, mentioned particularly the restless youth on both sides of the conflict as impediments to the peace process. The commission invoked the time-honored saying that "the devil finds work for idle hands." The postindependence Nigerian state has failed woefully to provide economic and social development in the region, and as a result youth unemployment, communal violence, and lawlessness prevail. The latest developments over the past two years are that the Modákékế have been granted a local government office named the Ifẹ̀ East Area Office and that the Modákékế king has been given permission to wear the beaded crown.[60]

In an essay on modernity in Papua New Guinea, Deborah Gewertz and Frederick Errington criticize a particular method of ethnography in Papua New Guinea that has often failed to recognize changes in ostensibly traditional societies.[61] Ethnographers may emphasize narrow observations in the ethnographic present without accounting for the broader encounters that subjects experience under the influence of modernity. Some aspects of modernity are revealed during ethnographic field research. Subjects and informants not only encounter forces such as globalization, consumerism, capitalism, evangelical Christianity and Islam, tourism, and the electronic media but also often negotiate these encounters. In the modern period beginning in 1980s, inhabitants of indigenous Ifẹ̀ have responded to powerful waves of ideological and cultural encroachment on the city, but they have succeeded in negotiating modern influences in ways that have altered the character and identity of the city.

This chapter provides a panoramic view of the ancient city of Ilé-Ifẹ̀ as a ceremonial center of the Yorùbá cosmos. Its legends, myths, ethnographic history, and oral texts, as well as its archaeology and iconography, offer symbols signifying Ilé-Ifẹ̀'s sacredness in the Yorùbá imagination, social structure, and philosophical systems. The city is a classic model of a sacred center whose inhabitants across the globe apply the same imaginative geography. No matter where they are, the Yorùbá claim Ilé-Ifẹ̀ as their original home place *(ilé)*. When viewed in their historical context, the land and sacred spaces remain part of the identity and spiritual self-definition of a people, especially when groups or individuals define themselves in terms of their relationship to a place, space, or territory.

Discourse inquiring whether Africans are monotheistic or polytheistic is misguided. Rather, our investigation should explore conceptual and analytical questions about the significance of spatial dimensions in religious traditions. Religious traditions usually arise from a particular site or geographical region. Human cultures create extraordinary places as sacred centers of the universe where humans can communicate with the Ultimate Being. Sacred places function in mythic narratives of the divine and exist to orient and elevate the material world from profane chaos. Although the Yorùbá, the Maori, and many Native American groups see little separation between the sacred and the profane, they still sanctify an originary center as a place to experience the divine within the habitable world.

2

The Imagined Sacred City

Ilé-Ifẹ̀ in the History of Exploration and Discovery

This chapter will describe Ilé-Ifẹ̀ as imagined and portrayed by both Europeans and Africans in travelers' reports, legends, and myth. It will examine the archaeological and iconographic evidence for Ilé-Ifẹ̀'s preeminent status among Yorùbá and African states and will analyze the symbolic significance of the city as a ceremonial center in cosmological, mythical, and ritual contexts.

THE PORTUGUESE IMAGE OF ILÉ-IFẸ̀

The Europeans saw Ilé-Ifẹ̀ as the preeminent city-state and as an important ceremonial center in what was then often referred to as "the Negro world." The seafaring Portuguese, the first Europeans to explore the coast of West Africa, arrived in the fifteenth century. Although they had heard much about the city of Ilé-Ifẹ̀, their inability to access interior forested regions made contact very difficult. However, the Portuguese recorded their impressions of the importance of this ancient city, especially of its artistic and historical relationship and connection to the kingdom of Benin, with which the Portuguese had earlier contact. Writing in his navigational guidebook *Esmeraldo de Situ Orbis,* the well-known Portuguese explorer Duarte Pacheco Pereira noted that to the east of the Benin Kingdom, about one hundred leagues (four hundred miles) inland, was a country with a king named Licasaguou, who was said to be lord of many people and to possess great power. Close by, Pereira explained, another great lord, Hooguanee, "is considered among the Negroes as the Pope is among us."[1] Although the identity of the first king, Licasaguou, remains unknown, the "Pope of the Negroes" may refer to the Ọ̀ọni of Ilé-Ifẹ̀, since the neighboring Benin people commonly referred to this king as Hooguanee (Ogene).

Some of the earliest written records about Ilé-Ifè come from the Portuguese sea-farers who traded with the Benin Kingdom. One such record was *Da Asia,* by João de Barros, which provided a detailed discussion of the political and ritual kinship of Benin and Ilé-Ifè in the precolonial period.[2] According to this interesting account, the king of Portugal, Don João, learned from the ambassador of the king of Beny (Benin) and also from Joa Alfonso d'Aveiro that to the east of the Benin Kingdom, about a twenty moons' journey (about 250 leagues), "there lived the most power-ful monarch of these parts called Igane. Among the pagan chiefs of the territo-ries of Beny [Benin], he was held in as great veneration as is the Supreme Pontiff with us."[3] The informant also described a ritual link between Benin and Ilé-Ifè. In compliance with an ancient tradition, whenever a new king ascended the throne of Benin, the Benin sent ambassadors to the monarch to the east with many gifts to inform him that the new king of Benin had succeeded his deceased father and to request confirmation of his new status. As a sign of consent, Prince Ogene sent the new Benin king a "staff and a headpiece of shining brass, fashioned like a Spanish helmet in place of crown and scepter." He sent a brass cross to be worn around the neck, "a holy and religious emblem similar to that worn by the *commendadores* as of the Order of Saint John," for, "without these emblems, the people do not recog-nize him as the lawful ruler, nor can he call himself truly king."[4] De Barros reported that the ambassadors from Benin never saw the king himself, since he was always secluded behind a "curtain of silk." However, to authenticate the mission, just be-fore the ambassadors departed from Ilé-Ifè, the king showed "a foot behind the cur-tains," indicating that he agreed to Benin's request. The ambassadors were bestowed with gifts as compensation for the great journey to Ilé-Ifè. The gift to each ambas-sador consisted of a "small cross similar to that sent to the king, which is thrown round his neck to signify that he is free and exempt from all servitudes and is priv-ileged in his native country, as the *Commendadores* are with us."[5]

This is one of the most detailed descriptions we have of Benin's connection with Ilé-Ifè, illustrating the perception of Ilé-Ifè and the sacred kingship in Benin. There have been several discussions about the historicity of this passage, especially re-garding the authenticity of the Benin ambassadors and the gift of the cross.[6] The passage supports the account of the modern Benin monarchy's origin in Ifè and the role of Òrànmíyàn (also named Òrányàn), the son of Odùduwà, in the establish-ment of Benin's modern rule. It also establishes the ritual relationship between the two kingdoms in rites of coronation and burial. Although some traditional rituals have been modified or have disappeared in the contemporary Nigerian state, the coronation ceremony performed today for the Ọba of Benin, whereby the Ọọni of Ilé-Ifè sends a traditional gift to the new Ọba, confirms the ancient connection be-tween the two kingdoms described in the Portuguese sources. Moreover, archaeo-logical investigation in Ilé-Ifè reveals an ancient burial ground, called Òrun Ọba Àdó (literally, "the heaven of Benin kings") that holds only certain parts of the dead bodies of kings brought from Benin. Some scholars suggest that the Ilé-Ifẹ̀ burial site reserved for the Benin kings shows their ancestral connection with the city of Ilé-Ifẹ̀.

Because rituals are constantly reinvented in response to the contemporary social and political contexts in which they are performed, such customs often disappear gradually from practice. In my view, the significance of the Portuguese story does not lie in whether it is absolutely true. Even if it occurred only in the realm of the imagination, without the archaeological and ritual evidence that lends it credence, the story would still enable us to comprehend the enigma that lies behind Ilé-Ifẹ̀'s preeminence in the fifteenth- and sixteenth-century Portuguese accounts of explorations in the land of the "Negroes." I will return to these sources later in the chapter.

ILÉ-IFẹ̀ IN THE ANNALS OF WESTERN EXPLORATION: LEO FROBENIUS REVISITED

Ilé-Ifẹ̀'s preeminent status is based on archaeological and iconographic evidence that confirms its significance as a ceremonial center in cosmological, mythical, and ritual contexts.

The best-known European visitor to Ilé-Ifẹ̀ was Leo Frobenius (1873–1973), a German ethnologist and researcher who visited the city between 1910 and 1912. Frobenius was the head of the German Inner African Exploration. At the time of his visit, the city's population was over twenty-five thousand.[7] His contribution to the West's knowledge of Ilé-Ifẹ̀ and of Africa in general was so significant that President Leopard Senghor wrote in a foreword to a book marking the centenary of Frobenius's birth: "No one did more than Frobenius to reveal Africa to the world and the Africans to themselves."[8] An essential part of this "revelation" consisted of the ancient Ifẹ̀ bronzes and terra-cotta pieces that Frobenius brought to the attention of the world. In spite of Senghor's warm comments, Frobenius's pioneering works are little read and appreciated.

Why has Frobenius not achieved a status similar to that of William Bascom, the American anthropologist who worked thirty years in Ilé-Ifẹ̀ after Leo Frobenius? The answer lies in Frobenius's Eurocentric views and his racist remarks about the Ilé-Ifẹ̀ people throughout his sojourn there. Frobenius was convinced of the superiority of the German race over other European groups in Africa, especially the British, and he frequently referred to German thoroughness, which for him far surpassed that of the British, as exemplified in their colonizing efforts in Ilé-Ifẹ̀. Frobenius's goal was to discover artifacts more genuine in form and style than the "inferior" arts hitherto discovered by his English predecessors.[9] Frobenius was both amazed by and envious of the British looting of Benin artifacts during the so-called punitive expedition against the Ọba of Benin Kingdom in 1885. He reasoned that since Ilé-Ifẹ̀ was older than Benin and, indeed, gave birth to Benin, the art objects "from Benin were nothing but the products of degenerate times, mere imitations of an older, more genuine and sincere art."[10] This was a point of contention that caused the British to work against the success of his mission. Frobenius's ideas and theories represented the best in the European imagination of the African people during this period. Having read or heard of Ilé-Ifẹ̀ in Europe, he concluded that it must be "the lost city of Atlantis" in black Africa, where remnants of the Greek culture that worshipped Poseidon lived.[11] When Frobenius first saw two pieces of reddish-brown terra-cotta pottery in the sacred shrine of Olókun, he observed: "Here were the remains of a very ancient and fine type of art, infinitely nobler than the comparatively coarse stone images, not even well-preserved. These meagre relics were eloquent of a symmetry, a vitality, a delicacy of form directly reminiscent of ancient Greece and a proof that, once upon a time, a race, far superior in strain to the Negro, had been settled here."[12] Frobenius acquired many terra-cotta heads, including the famous Olókun sculpture. He was convinced that the religion and culture of the ancient Greeks had been extensively disseminated, reaching even to Ilé-Ifẹ̀, and that the "Yorùbá religion was not unique to the African people, that it is definitely linked to the perfected system of a primeval age."[13]

Frobenius, in his desperation to provide scientific evidence to support his thesis, resorted to unconventional methods of fieldwork, employing all manner of blackmail and intimidation to collect information about hidden Ifẹ̀ artifacts. But despite his often questionable methods, he also used great skill and intelligence to discover significant bronzes and terra-cottas that have given Ilé-Ifẹ̀ its renown in global art today. These discoveries included numerous extremely "noteworthy objects," including such archaeological artifacts as vessels, sculptured stone tools, and stone crocodiles. Frobenius requested that members of his party, in particular Carl Arriens, draw oil sketches of these finds.

To his credit, Frobenius learned how the Ifẹ̀ people had preserved their sculpture and thus shrewdly deduced the probable location of the icons. The people of Ilé-Ifẹ̀, aware of traditional folklore, believed that the terra-cotta heads were buried because their legends spoke of the "disappearance" of the gods into the earth's crust. These legends were passed down from one generation to another. In all probability, their shrines were, therefore, the hierophanies of the gods and the places where ritual objects were buried. Having discovered this, Frobenius employed the Ifẹ̀ people to dig in locations where their legends said "that an ancestral god had gone below."[14] His instructions produced several valuable artifacts, including the famous granite head, the Ìdènà, which a young boy brought to sell him one early morning.[15]

Frobenius requested and was granted permission to search for the abandoned bead industry in a place that he had heard was Ilé-Ifẹ̀'s treasure island, located on the outskirts of the sacred city. After much meandering through an impassable forest, his expedition arrived at the goddess Olókun's sacred grove (Ebolokun), where beads coated with multicolored glazes lay about.[16] At the Olókun Shrine, some of the most precious works were discovered: "broken glazed pottery, terra cotta foot, trunk, and head ornaments."[17]

Astounded by the remarkable finds, Frobenius remarked: "They must be reckoned among the most precious of the things we had so far uncovered, because they all went to prove the pre-existence of a race possessing nothing in common with Ifẹ̀, one usually ticketed 'Negro.' " Frobenius was convinced that this was indeed a remnant of an ancient civilization, unlike any culture produced before by the "Negro" race. He remarked of the great discovery, "Slowly but surely the sublime grandeur of the city of an erstwhile civilization was rearing its front above the dusk of Negro life which envelops Ilefe [Ilé-Ifẹ̀] as it stands today." He further rhapsodized, "Yea—even the holy lord of the sacred grove by Ebolokun [Olókun], of Atlantic Africa's great Poseidon himself, rose from a world which had forsaken him and now again revealed him, wrathful maybe with us, the strangers who had dared to call him forth from the dawn of his existence before the gloom of negrodom had overshadowed it, wrath with us who had dragged him to the daylight."[18]

After much persuasion, the priest of Olókun, who was in charge of this ancient shrine, agreed to show Frobenius the location of another precious bronze hidden in the marshes. On seeing it, and believing it to be the Poseidon he was searching for, Frobenius remarked, "Before us stood a head of marvelous beauty, wonderfully cast in antique bronze, true to the life, incrusted with a patina of a glorious dark green. This was, in very deed, the Olokun Atlantic Africa's Poseidon." Frobenius envied the sub-Saharan African forest civilization that harbored this marvelous find, unexplored before his own encounter. He declared: "Profoundly stirred, I stood for many minutes before this remnant of the erstwhile Lord and Ruler of the Empire of Atlantis. . . . I was moved to silent melancholy at the thought that this assembly of degenerate and feeble-minded posterity should be the legitimate guardians of so much classic loveliness."[19]

I have quoted extensively from Frobenius for two reasons: first, to engage scholars of Yorùbá studies in a deeper discussion of and greater appreciation for the relevance of this work, especially in view of the light it sheds on our understanding of Ilé-Ifẹ̀ archaeology and religion, and on the city in particular at the turn of the twentieth century; and second, to put into context the passion and polemical attention that Frobenius gave to the artifacts of Ilé-Ifẹ̀, which he regarded as vestiges of the lost civilization of Atlantis.

Frobenius did not set out to undertake a systematic study of Ifẹ̀ ritual places, and his tendency to exaggerate means that we should take his evidence with a grain of salt. Even so, he provided some of the most detailed descriptions of the religious and ritual life of the Yorùbá people that we possess today, including an account of the Ògbóni secret society and its rigorous initiation rite. He also collected visual evidence of the last remnant of human sacrifice in the holy city. He established the relationship (at times incorrect) between art and religion, noting that the sculptures were elevated to the status of divinities: "All the reports to hand, even in my early Hamburg days, made it clear that the good Ilifians [people of Ilé-Ifẹ̀] had raised a good many of the treasures of antiquity to the dignity of the Gods they still revered, still obeyed, and to whom they largely offered sacrifice."[20] Frobenius described the Ifẹ̀ sacred priesthood, which he erroneously called shamanism.[21] Ifẹ̀ priests were independent and regarded as belonging to the nobility. The people held them in awe and very much feared them, yet their friendship was widely courted. He described them as "the actual wielders of an omnipotent magic on which every manifestation of Divine Power in general and the power of each God in particular depends: No single God can make himself known, no dead man express his desires, no sick person recover health, without the strength and central magic might which [they] grant."[22]

Another significant aspect of Frobenius's work was his comparison of Ilé-Ifẹ̀ art and symbolism with that of other cultures, including the Etruscan and "lost" Atlantis civilizations. He was preoccupied with showing that the art and general sophistication of ancient Ifẹ̀ tradition were comparable with those of other ancient civilizations the world over, and he brought his comparative ethnographic method to bear on the Ilé-Ifẹ̀ materials. For example, he compared the significance of the numbers four and sixteen in Ifá divination, specifically the four cardinal points of Ifá and the sixteen principal *odù* (chapters of the unwritten book of Yorùbá divination), to their use in ancient Rome for ordering the layout of sacred architecture; to the four cardinal points of the heavens in Korean and Pueblo Indian divination systems; and to the sixteen cardinal points of the Etruscan divination system. Such striking correspondences were for Frobenius more than mere coincidences. His comparative study, crude as it may seem, was the first of such references to Yorùbá religious studies.

Finally, Frobenius cultivated a strong friendship with the Ọ̀ọ̀ni (king of Ifẹ̀). He never made derogatory remarks about the king; indeed, he held him in high esteem and ensured that he was always in the king's good favor. A similar relationship began thirty years later when the American anthropologist William Bascom entered Ilé-Ifẹ̀ to carry out a major ethnographic study of the city.

ILÉ-IFẸ̀ IN THE YORÙBÁ IMAGINATION:
LEGEND, MYTH, AND HISTORY

I would now like to examine the legends and myths of the origin of Yorùbá Ilé-Ifẹ̀ to elucidate the meanings embedded in these oral and written sources. Whether these narratives are true accounts of what actually happened or products of human imagination, they provide support for the primacy of Ilé-Ifẹ̀ among the Yorùbá people.

The Ọ̀yọ́ Yorùbá historian Samuel Johnson—the Herodotus of the Yorùbá nation—published the earliest written account of the origin of the Yorùbá. Johnson was born in 1846; at the age of eleven, he moved from Sierra Leone to Lagos in 1857. He worked as a schoolmaster in Ìbàdàn and was a pastor of the Church Missionary Society (CMS) in Ọ̀yọ́. Johnson presented what may now be called the Ọ̀yọ́ version of the Yorùbá myth of origin. He depended solely on traditions collected from the Arọ́kin, the professional singers, griots, and court storytellers at the Ọ̀yọ́ royal palace.

According to the Ọ̀yọ́ version, the Yorùbá are the children of Lámúrúdu, who was at one time king of Mecca in Saudi Arabia, the most holy city of Islam.[23] Odùduwà, the crown prince of Mecca, "lapsed into idolatry during his father's reign," but because of his great influence he had many followers. Odùduwà turned the great mosque of Mecca into a pagan temple, and his priest Asara became the fashioner of the temple images. Asara had a son named Braima (Buraimoh) who was himself a Muslim but was responsible for marketing his father's idolatrous images to the public—a job he did reluctantly, as he abhorred "pagan" worship. Odùduwà, who was bent on making "pagan" worship the state religion, sent out a decree to all males born in Mecca to hunt for three days before the annual celebration of the "Festival of Images."

Before one such annual ceremony, the able-bodied men went out to hunt, and Braima, who was by then a grown man, took advantage of the absence of the people in the city to attack the images in the great mosque. He succeeded in destroying most of them and left the ax with which he had hewn the "idols" into pieces lodged in the neck of the "chief image," a huge life-sized human image. When the people returned from the hunting expedition, they were appalled at the sight of the destroyed images and went in search of the perpetrator of this evil. When Braima was asked if he knew who had committed the deed, his response was simply, "Ask the image who did it."[24] When the people responded, "Can he speak?" Braima replied, "Then, why do you worship things which cannot speak?" Braima was seized and condemned to be burnt alive for his apostasy.

The people fetched a thousand loads of firewood and brought several pots of oil to carry out the punishment. Almost immediately, civil strife broke out between the Muslim supporters of Braima and the idolaters. In the end, the Muslims were victorious. Lámúrúdu, the king, was assassinated by the Muslims, and his children were expelled from Mecca. Some of the princes who managed to escape became the kings of Gogobin and Kukuwa, regions to the west. The legend says that Odùduwà traveled eastward for ninety days until he reached Ilé-Ifẹ̀, where he then settled. Upon his arrival there, he met a man named Àgbọnìrègún (also known as Ṣẹ̀tílù) who founded Ifá divination. Odùduwà had brought with him two of the "idols" from Mecca, but meanwhile a party was sent from Mecca to pursue him, kill him, and destroy the idols he carried. Odùduwà's followers, however, defeated the Muslims, and a copy of the Qur'an was seized from them. This copy of the Qur'an, known as *idì*, preserved in the Ifá temple, was venerated and worshipped by succeeding generations, who regarded it as a sacred relic.

Commenting on this "commonly received account" of the origin of Ilé-Ifẹ̀, Samuel Johnson noted, "The people being unlettered, and the language unwritten, all that is known is from traditions carefully handed down."[25] This is perhaps a reference to the Arọkin storytellers and the Yorùbá intelligentsia of the time, who were well aware of this story during the period of Johnson's research. Johnson, however, was right to say that the Yorùbá, in general, refute the story because they know that they are not of Arab origin and did not migrate from Mecca. Further, no such record exists in the annals of the Arab chronicles of kings of Mecca. If, indeed, the story were true, Arab historians, usually diligent and meticulous record keepers, would have noted it down and commented on it in detail. T. L. Hodgkin observes that the legend does, however, contain some facts: "That the Yorùbás came originally from the East there cannot be the slightest doubt as their habits, manners and customs, etc., all go to prove. With them the East is Mecca and Mecca is the East. Having strong affinities with the East, and Mecca in the East looming so largely in their imagination, everything that comes from the East, with them, comes from Mecca; and hence it is natural to represent themselves as having hailed originally from that city."[26]

I began the account of the origins of Ifẹ̀ and the Yorùbá civilization with this example from the oral tradition for three reasons. First, it is often erroneously assumed that oral traditions that are collected from native informants are accounts and pure descriptions of what actually took place. Second, this particular story has often been presented as an attempt by the Yorùbá to justify their connection to the Islamic religion, as in political legend.[27] Third, we have here an accumulation of three traditions—Yorùbá, Islamic, and Old Testament—as Johnson himself recognized and noted. Even though the story is presented as purely indigenous, it fuses three separate traditions into one.

I propose that the story, with its more dominant Islamic motif, represents the Ọ̀yọ́-Yorùbá account of Islam in the Hijaz and, indeed, the story of the Prophet Ibrahim (Abraham). Lámúrúdu, Crown Prince Odùduwà, and the other princes in the story represent the political and social order in the Hijaz at the time of Muhammad's boyhood, in an era that Muslim historians often called the Jahiliyya period. It was then that the Kabbah, the central Mecca shrine, was dedicated to the worship of the pre-Islamic goddesses regarded as the daughters of Allah. The pre-Islamic Kabbah was the abode of several images—including those of the three daughters of Allah—some of whom Odùduwà must have taken with him in his flight from Mecca. Braima metaphorically stands for the Prophet Muhammad, who shared the dilemma of being born into the Quraish tribe that was supposed to take charge of the "idolatrous" temples of Mecca. The story presents the familiar dilemma of the prophet who, though born into a noble family, was a "Hanif" believer in the monotheistic God and hence rebelled against the long-standing family tradition. We know that before his conversion Muhammad visited the cave to meditate. The story's tradition of an annual hunting season before the Festival of the Images represents the annual bazaar and pilgrimage in pre-Islamic Mecca. This was the occasion when people gathered in Mecca to trade, celebrate, and worship "idols." In the story, Braima seized the opportunity to strike at idolatry in Mecca. We are reminded here of the Prophet Muhammad's own rebellion against Mecca's polytheism, an issue that divided the city just as in Braima's case. The battle against the people of Mecca ultimately led to the triumph of Islam, the destruction of the Kabbah idols, and purification of Islam's holy shrine. Moreover, Muhammad's triumph signaled the beginning of a series of battles and the expansion of Islam from its Hijaz origin into outside territories.

What can we make of Odùduwà's victory over the Muslims who pursued him and the triumph of indigenous religion over Islam in Ilé-Ifẹ̀, or, rather, the incorporation of the latter into the traditional Yorùbá pantheon? To some extent, the story may reflect the fortunes of Islam in the land of the Yorùbá, for, with the exception of the city of Ìlọrin, where Islam gained a stronghold, no other Yorùbá city has an overwhelming Muslim population (80 percent and above), and the indigenous religion still remains strong.

The ability of the Yorùbá to domesticate Islam is evident in the *odù Ifá*, the corpus of oral texts that is used for divination. Some of its 256 chapters *(odù)*, called *odù Ìmàle* (Muslim divination texts), are filled with adulterated Arabic idioms and verses. In addition, many Ifá myths refer to Odùduwà's visit and pilgrimage to Mecca.[28] More significantly, however, the Ifá cult was already firmly in place when Muslim invaders arrived. It seized upon the Qur'an, incorporating it into the Yorùbá *òrìṣà* tradition as a symbol of reverence and an indication of Yorùbá religious pluralism today. *Ìdì* is the Yorùbá word for the suras, the chapters in the Qur'an. The Yorùbá encounter with Islam reflects the peace of the fifteenth to seventeenth centuries, compared to the more militant encounter with the jihadists and bearers of Uthman Dan Fodio's flag in the eighteenth and nineteenth centuries. The story may represent a metaphor for the Yorùbá encounter with the more militant form of Islam in the eighteenth century, as Uthman Dan Fodio's Islam swept the northeastern Yorùbá cities of Ìlọrin and Ọ̀yọ́, Ọ̀ffà, Ògbómọ̀ṣọ́, and the region before the incursion was stopped in Òṣogbo.

The storytellers, though largely Muslim, were not impervious to the new Christian faith, which arrived much later than Islam. Samuel Johnson embarked on a rigorous missionary campaign against both the perceived Yorùbá idolatry and the presence of Islam. Hence, we have Johnson's reference to and comment on the Old

Testament story of Gideon, who destroyed the Abiezrite idols, and Gideon's father, Josiah, who sarcastically questioned the idols' power, just as Braima did the idols of the Mecca.

At the time that the "Meccan legend," as I prefer to call this tradition, was in circulation, a substantial part of the population was already Muslim. Given the pattern of Islamic penetration into West Africa, it is likely that the itinerant Sufi preachers and traders were the propagators of this story and that the Arókin learned it from them. The story may therefore explain the attempt to link the Yorùbá people with the Middle East and thus to indicate their continuity with the Islamic past. However, while presenting the ostensible Muslim origins of Yorùbá ancestry, the legend casts the Muslim heritage in a negative light: the Yorùbá were Muslim idolaters, expelled from the holy city and forced to resort to Ifá divination, which was considered "inferior" to Islam in their new home. The legend therefore represents a Muslim clerical explanation of the continuity of indigenous Yorùbá traditions. Akínwùmí Ìṣòlá, in revisiting the Ṣàngó origin story in Ọ̀yọ́, has made a similar point about the Christian representation (or, rather, misrepresentation) of the Ṣàngó king and deity in Ọ̀yọ́ society as propaganda and as a metaphor for the eventual triumph of Christianity over the indigenous religion.[29] Finally, the story presents the situation of conflict in which Odùduwà established the Ilé-Ifẹ̀ dynasty, a point related to the classic Yorùbá myth of origin to be considered below.

ILÉ-IFẸ̀ AND THE ANCIENT KINGDOM OF BENIN

Ilé-Ifẹ̀ gains further credibility as a sacred center because of its connection with the ancient kingdom of Benin. According to the Benin historian Jacob U. Egharevba, following a series of unsettled crises in Benin, the Owòdo, the last of the Ogiso kings of the first dynasty, was deposed. The Edo (Benin) people then sent emissaries to Ilé-Ifẹ̀ (Uhe), asking for a "wise prince" who would reign over them. Odùduwà, the Ọba of Ifẹ̀ at that time, decided to test the sincerity and endurance of the Edo (Benin). In response to their request, he sent lice to the chiefs of Benin with instructions that they were to care for the lice and return them to him after three years. The Benin chiefs took great care of these lice and returned them after three years to the Ọba of Ifẹ̀, who was impressed. Convinced that people who could, without question, take care of such minute pests as lice, could undoubtedly take good care of his son, he sent the Ifẹ̀ prince Ọ̀rànmíyàn, accompanied by palace servants, courtiers, and a native medicine man (ogiefa).

Ọ̀rànmíyàn and his entourage reached Benin after an arduous journey that included a hazardous crossing of the Obie River. Upon his arrival in Benin, Ọ̀rànmíyàn met with resistance from one Ogiamwen, the son of Evinan, who had temporarily taken charge of Benin affairs during the interregnum, after the termination of the first dynasty. Ọ̀rànmíyàn triumphed over Ogiamwen, settled in Usama Palace, which had been built by the Benin chiefs, and married a woman named Erinmwinde, with whom he had a son. After a few years, he grew tired of Benin and the many crises with which he had to contend there. He called an assembly of the Benin people and relinquished the throne, after naming the city Ilẹ̀-Ìbínú, "the land of anger," from which Benin, the current name of the city, comes. He decreed that only someone born and brought up in Benin and properly schooled in its traditions and mysteries should be its king. Ọ̀rànmíyàn then installed his son Eweka as king in his stead and returned to Ilé-Ifẹ̀, his own native place, leaving the palace chiefs and medicine people to take care of the new king. On his way back to Ilé-Ifẹ̀, Ọ̀rànmíyàn stopped in Ugba (Okha) and Obboh, for three and two years, respectively, to ensure that his son reached maturity before he finally returned to Ilé-Ifẹ̀. Eweka was crowned at Usama, his father's palace. When Eweka died, his remains were returned to Ilé-Ifẹ̀ for burial. This tradition, in which "the remains of the Ọba of Benin were taken to Ilé-Ifẹ̀ in every third reign," was continued until very recently.[30]

I am not concerned here with the historicity of the story or with its claim to truth. Rather, I regard it as an origin myth believed to be true by those who hold onto it as a part of their tradition. The story establishes the sacred origin of Benin kingship, projecting it as an extension of the Ifẹ̀ sacred kingship that was certainly in existence long before this period. It establishes a kinship relationship between the Ifẹ̀ and Benin kingdoms, although Benin later took on a more radical form of sacred kingship than that which exists in Ilé-Ifẹ̀. Benin became an absolute monarchy, with the first son of the reigning Ọba named as the heir apparent, whereas in Ilé-Ifẹ̀ the kingship rotates among four ruling lineages, so that the first son of a reigning king does not succeed his father and there is a strong system of checks and balances on the power of the reigning king.

Ọ̀rànmíyàn's role is an important one in this story, especially in the spread of religious ideas and political values, presumably from Ilé-Ifẹ̀ to Benin. Several traditions concerning Ọ̀rànmíyàn exist in Ilé-Ifẹ̀. One tradition refers to him as the son of Odùduwà, which is consistent with the Benin story. Another tradition refers to him as a great Ifẹ̀ warrior who left his mark permanently on the Ifẹ̀ landscape in the mystery of the Staff of Ọ̀rànmíyàn (Ọ̀pá Ọ̀rànmíyàn), a stone staff with iron marks that has become a tourist attraction, if not a pilgrimage site, in Ilé-Ifẹ̀.

Several other traditions support this warrior ethos and connection, and Ọ̀rànmíyàn features prominently in the annual ritual of Ògún, also known as Ọlọ́jọ́ (the festival and ritual of kingship). Ògún, the Yorùbá warrior god and god of iron, is equally important in Benin society and cosmology and possesses the same characteristics and features attributed to the deity by the Yorùbá people in general.

The tradition of returning the body of the Benin Ọba to Ilé-Ifẹ̀ for interment symbolizes the return of the "stranger king" to his autochthonous place for burial, in keeping with the Yorùbá and Benin tradition of burying kings and commoners in their ancestral place of origin. Why did Ọ̀rànmíyàn call the city Ilẹ̀-Ìbínú, the "land of anger," which then became Benin's permanent name? Part of Benin's continuing enigma is that the city's secret cannot be unfolded, especially by outsiders, a dilemma that caused Ọ̀rànmíyàn (an outsider) to vacate the throne and replace himself with a son born of a Benin woman (an insider). The inherent tension in the "insider-outsider" conflict remains part of Benin's identity today.

Three other significant cultural factors are alluded to in the Ọ̀rànmíyàn story: the mystical power of the Benin king; the importance of magic and medicine in sustaining the king's power; and the burden of preserving, at all cost, the institution of kingship to ensure the survival and well-being of Benin society. The story places the burden of preserving kingship on the community. According to Egharevba, Ọ̀rànmíyàn was not sent until Odùduwà had confirmed that the Benin people would take good care of their king and the institution of kingship. Those who had demonstrated their ability to preserve lice would certainly guard very jealously the institution of sacred kingship, an equally delicate and onerous task, to which the Benin have devoted their full resources up to the modern era. The institution of kingship needed to be guarded by powerful medicine and magical rituals. Odùduwà sent with Ọ̀rànmíyàn a medicine man to make potent magic for the sustenance of the king. This tradition remains part of the royal cult of Benin mysticism; indeed, more than any other kingship system in Nigeria, Benin rituals, arts, and ideology of kingship demonstrate the importance of sacred power for the preservation of kingship.

Despite revisionist theories, especially in the last ten years, aimed at disconnecting the linkages between Benin and Ilé-Ifẹ̀, suggested by Egharevba and Robert Bradbury, the above story supports the origin of Benin kingship in Ifẹ̀ tradition.[31] As Kees Bolle points out, the central issue in myth is not "what is true" in the story but "What have societies, civilizations, communities found necessary to point to and preserve as centrally valued for their entire existence?"[32] The story thus permanently establishes the sacredness and significance of Ilé-Ifẹ̀ as an important ceremonial center and as an ancestral city to an equally powerful kingdom that lies to its east.

ILÉ-IFẸ̀ IN THE CHURCH MISSIONARY SOCIETY'S IMAGINATION

Most scholars of Yorùbá colonial history view the Church Missionary Society archives now in Birmingham, England, as the foremost resource for reconstructing nineteenth- and early twentieth-century Yorùbá life.[33] This is because the CMS mission compelled their missionaries, both Europeans and Africans, to write copious reports about events in the field. These reports and memoirs form the core of CMS archives, affording many historians abundant research sources. But the CMS archives contain little or nothing about Ilé-Ifẹ̀—at least compared with numerous records on Oǹdó, Ìbàdàn, and Ilésà.

Although Ilé-Ifẹ̀ was the sacred city of the Yorùbá city-states and geographically central to the region, it was no favored place of the CMS, for reasons that will soon become clear. Consequently, Ilé-Ifẹ̀ lacked the kind of verifiable historical data that helped reconstruct the history of other cities, such as J. D. Y. Peel's significant study of Ìjẹ̀ṣà. Even though we seek in vain for similar copious ethnographic materials, the available evidence suggests that Ilé-Ifẹ̀ and the CMS missionaries forged a mutually hostile relationship. Those missionaries who ventured near the city were very fearful and seized every opportunity to show their contempt for it. In the imagination of the missionaries, what were the city and its inhabitants like? What did they represent from the perspective of a missionary? In practical terms, what happened between the missionaries and people of Ilé-Ifẹ̀?

Sifting through the CMS archives, I spent four weeks examining the Yorùbá Mission papers collected from 1854 to 1936, especially materials on Ilé-Ifẹ̀. Aided by Peel's prior correspondence with me, I was able to locate the few meager references to Ilé-Ifẹ̀ in CMS archives. Despite a dearth of materials on Ilé-Ifẹ̀, those available are significant. They confirm Ilé-Ifẹ̀'s primacy and significance among the Yorùbá states and then little-known aspects of Yorùbá religious practices, such as the reference to the òrìṣà Ọ̀rànmíyàn, in Ilé-Ifẹ̀, which I will discuss later on. These materials also provide information about how the Europeans and Africans who became missionaries in Africa tried to make sense of the world they observed. Although the materials reflect both the missionaries' own ideological stance and the world of Yorùbá that they observed, the materials also illustrate the significance of Ilé-Ifẹ̀ in nineteenth-century Yorùbá society and the mystique the city held for Western missionaries in the Yorùbá societies of West Africa.

Reverend David Hinderer, the most visible European missionary of the nineteenth-century Anglican CMS and the most important missionary visitor to the Ifẹ̀ people, became a central figure in attempts to evangelize the Yorùbá. All missionary observers in the region accepted Ilé-Ifẹ̀ as the center of Yorùbá civilization, and several of them collected stories and myths of creation featuring Odùduwà and Ọbàtálá—the two most visible deities in Yorùbá cosmogony. However, the missionaries avoided Ilé-Ifẹ̀ because of its tenacious embrace of Yorùbá indigenous religion, which the missionaries maligned and labeled "idolatry." Hinderer called Ifẹ̀ "the seat of all Yorùbá idolatry and the origin of all creation."[34] At the time, in 1875, Hinderer was paying his second visit to Ilé-Ifẹ̀, which was in ruins as a result of the Yorùbá civil war and Ifẹ̀'s quarrel with the Modákẹ́kẹ́ people, whom he later called Ifẹ̀'s slaves and neighbors.

Hinderer asserted that the Christian missionary post established earlier in Ilé-Ifẹ̀ had been a total failure, even though a Sierra Leonean missionary named Thomas had been stationed there, because of the people's continuous involvement in traditional òrìṣà practices. Hinderer stated in his report: "Things went well for a while until the faithful man [Thomas] would no longer bear the continued human sacrifices which the king had promised to stop."[35] His remark indicates how strongly the people of Ifẹ̀ were attached to traditional beliefs and practices. In the nineteenth century Ifẹ̀ remained a major center of the Yorùbá religion but lost to its neighbors, such as the Ìjẹ̀ṣà and Oǹdó peoples, the "benefit" of becoming a principal Christian post in the region.[36]

In another context, Hinderer claimed that Thomas's evangelical zeal had caused him prolonged sickness and ultimately death: "Thomas spoke strongly against the admonitions, which had been the ruin of their farm, a few years ago and which would surely bring down God's righteous judgment again. This was too much for the haughty aristocrats of Ifẹ̀, in a few weeks Thomas sickened and died. It was said by foul means."[37]

At the time of Hinderer's third visit sixteen years later, Ilé-Ifẹ̀ had recovered from the destructive civil war with its Modákẹ́kẹ́ neighbors, and Hinderer wanted to congratulate the Ọ̀ọ̀ni of Ifẹ̀, but not without reminding him of the need to stop the practice of human sacrifice. According to Hinderer, he could not reach the king because the king was "invisible." Most likely, the Ọ̀ọ̀ni was in ritual seclusion connected with one of the principal Ilé-Ifẹ̀ ceremonies honoring the deities Ọlọ́jọ́, Mọrèmi, or Odùduwà. Hinderer's visit highlights the "Ifẹ̀ mystique"—the notion of "Ifẹ̀, the mysterious city" in the European imagination.

Western visitors like Hinderer and Leo Frobenius had similar perceptions of Ilé-Ifẹ̀ as a sacred precinct devoted to the òrìṣà. It was common at the time for outsiders to condemn òrìṣà traditions and any form of "pagan" religion. Following this tradition, missionaries, explorers such as Leo Frobenius, and other ethnographers of Ilé-Ifẹ̀ condemned it as a pagan enclave.[38] Encounters between the missionaries and Ilé-Ifẹ̀ elders and chiefs often resulted in calculated maneuvering—with Ilé-Ifẹ̀ people appearing to be the victors at the end of the conversation. These encounters portrayed a clash of worldviews: the Yorùbá religion against Western evangelical theology.

In an example of this kind of hostile relationship, Hinderer met with Ifẹ̀ chiefs, chastised them for what he called "their daily human sacrifices," and "begged them to do away with these admonitions, for God would severely visit them."[39] After Hinderer's reprimand, the Ifẹ̀ people promised to take the message to the Ọ̀ọ̀ni and return with an answer.

The Ifẹ̀ people came back with a proverb that shocked Hinderer: "Ifẹ̀ was the fountain of all things for all creation but as people spread to other places from there, we (white people included) had corrupted the stream." Hinderer angrily responded that he regarded the Ifẹ̀ people to be "mean, to be as heady and as evil as they had ever been." The people of Ifẹ̀ boasted of the power of their òrìṣà, telling Hinderer, "No Christian missionary could live in the City. The òrìṣà would kill him."[40]

These conversations illustrate that Ilé-Ifẹ̀ remained solidly an òrìṣà city: although missionaries attempted to proselytize its citizens, conversion to Christianity was minimal. Even in villages outside the city, where Christianity had made better inroads, missionaries could not escape the religious influence of Ifẹ̀.

In the clash of worldviews and cultures, Hinderer's evangelical zeal prevented him from seeing the importance of ancestral veneration, especially because it involved human sacrifice. He described an idyllic world "beyond" that "would stand judgment against them,"[41] according to the biblical ideal described by St. Paul. The Ifẹ̀ people, of course, disagreed. Unlike other cities in which CMS missionaries were already having a field day harvesting "lost" souls, Ilé-Ifẹ̀ remained steadfastly resistant to missionary propaganda. The Ifẹ̀ aristocrats, as Hinderer called them, believed completely in the òrìṣà system and felt that the missionaries were foolish. Seeing the world around them gradually being turned upside down by a new empire of Christian privilege, the Ifẹ̀ were in no hurry to exchange their ways for the so-called "civilized" culture of European invaders. They were convinced of the rightness of their own course.

The missionaries did not hesitate to write about Ilé-Ifẹ̀'s religious exploits, especially in surrounding towns and cities, such as Oǹdó, that had the advantage of missionary stations. When the people of Ilé-Ifẹ̀ displayed the magical powers given to them by the òrìṣà in exchange for money, the highly valued òrìṣà acted as "commodities" to outsiders beyond Ilé-Ifẹ̀. In one instance, a man and a woman from Ilé-Ifẹ̀, devotees of the god Ògún, visited Oǹdó brandishing live snakes that symbolized Ògún and blessing the people of Oǹdó in Ògún's name. This blessing brought them large numbers of cowries. However, an Oǹdó chief charged the couple with unlawful conduct, and the Lisa, second in command to the king, ordered them to leave Oǹdó. Similarly, on hearing the Reverend Charles Phillips, a Yorùbá missionary stationed in Oǹdó, preach a sermon against the gods, an Ifẹ̀ indigene and a devotee of Ṣàngó became enraged, presented a countersermon to the audience, and at the end of it persuaded the audience that Phillips "was too ignorant to speak with him." According to Phillips's account, the indigene of Ifẹ̀ ended his sermon extolling Ṣàngó and saying, "[Ṣàngó] can convert me and all my companions to corpses within several days."[42]

Several questions may be asked here. What gave the people of Ilé-Ifẹ̀ the confidence in the power of the òrìṣà to challenge and confront these interlopers, the reverend gentlemen of the CMS? We have no record of such strong resistance in the peripheral Yorùbá towns, where quite often òrìṣà devotees capitulated to missionary proselytizing. Despite their zeal and confidence in the Christian gospel, why were missionaries frightened of Ilé-Ifẹ̀? Given their movements into other towns and cities, were the Ilé-Ifẹ̀ people engaged in similar "missionary" enterprise for the òrìṣà? Why did missionaries single out the Ifẹ̀ people for castigation?

Despite the Western missionaries' antagonism toward Ilé-Ifẹ̀ religious life, they provided valuable information on hitherto obscure aspects of Ifẹ̀ traditions and on the role of religion in the conduct of the Yorùbá civil war. A classic example was an episode that illustrates the role and status of Òrànmíyàn in the Yorùbá pantheon. Although we know from most oral sources that Òrànmíyàn was a mythic-historical figure and son of Odùduwà in Ilé-Ifè, and that he probably founded the Òyó and Benin kingdoms, Òrànmíyàn could hardly be portrayed as a deity. He was generally seen as a cultural hero. In this particular instance, Òrànmíyàn, described as the god of war, "was offered a human sacrifice to prepare for the war between Ìbàdàn and Adó-Èkìtì." According to this record, the people of Ilé-Ifè were in possession of the òrìṣà. They held the sacrificial performance despite the objection of Ìbàdàn's general, Arè Ònà Kakanfò, who was described also as a devout Muslim. Although Àrè Ònà Kakanfò offered to sacrifice cows and horses, his chiefs and the Ifè people refused to accept them, insisting on the traditional sacrifice of human beings. Àrè Ònà Kakanfò then offered a Hausa (Gàmbàrí) slave as the human sacrifice. Why did Àrè Ònà Kakanfò succumb to Ifè's pressure for traditional sacrifice? Why did the Ifè retain a veto in the conduct of a war that was not directly theirs? Were they the de facto group in charge of ritual affairs of Yorùbáland at this time? One probable explanation was that Ilé-Ifè played a critical role in the war between Ìbàdàn and Adó-Èkìtì, and indeed Ilé-Ifè warriors enjoyed much respect from other Yorùbá soldiers.

This narrative offers us information about the relationship between Òrànmíyàn and Ògún in nineteenth-century Ilé-Ifè and helps to answer a much larger question: why the quintessential Ògún was not mentioned. We can speculate about the fact that Ògún later became a universal Yorùbá deity of war. Was Ògún a relatively remote deity, whose popularity spread only in the aftermath of the nineteenth-century Yorùbá civil war? Indeed, Ògún was a universal Yorùbá deity of war and, like Ifá, benefited from the popularity of being a pathfinder deity who originally led the descent of the gods from heaven to the sacred center, the city of Ilé-Ifè. But the episode narrated above points toward a salient feature of Yorùbá religious traditions. Each city features a homegrown cultural hero, local god, or patron deity who enjoys a more proximate, existential function in the local affairs of the people. Òrànmíyàn took on such a role in Ilé-Ifè, a role that will resonate again in the great Olójó Festival of Ilé-Ifè, which is discussed in chapter 4.

The state of affairs in Ondó seems to support the above thesis, as do the most detailed missionary accounts from this Yorùbá region. In virtually all records, Ògún, the quintessential deity, was hardly mentioned, though if an Ògún performance had been held during the missionary era the missionaries would not be likely to have missed it. The two most important festivals in Ondó were the Òràmfè Festival, named for an "immigrant" deity borrowed from Ilé-Ifè, for whom human sacrifice was compulsory, and Odún Oba, the Festival of the King. However, Ògún enjoys great popularity in Ondó today. In the 1980s during my early fieldwork in Ondó City, Ògún's festival was more popular than the festival of Òràmfè or Odún Oba. Similarly, the propitiation of Èṣù, a festival that involved human sacrifice, had almost vanished by the missionary era. In all likelihood, Ògún emerged as the quintessential universal Yorùbá deity in response to the Yorùbá civil war, while Òrànmíyàn still functioned as Ifẹ̀'s de facto deity of war. Ilé-Ifẹ̀'s imperial relationships with other Yorùbá kingdoms are often mentioned to show that the new kings of those places, including Ọ̀yọ́, upon their investitures, sought the sword of victory (Idà Òrànmíyàn) from the sacred city of Ilé-Ifẹ̀. Clearly, the authority of the new kings to govern new territory derived from Ilé-Ifẹ̀.

The missionary records for other Yorùbá monarchies occasionally refer to immigrants from Ifẹ̀ and the primary places they hold in the ritual and civil life of other Yorùbá cities and city-states. In November 1887, the Reverend Phillips, the Oǹdó missionary, wrote that one week before the Òràmfẹ̀ Festival (dedicated to the god Òràmfẹ̀, who originated in Ilé-Ifẹ̀ and spread to Oǹdó), all foreigners in the city—excluding Ifẹ̀ settlers—were asked to leave, perhaps to maintain secrecy about the ritual of human sacrifice. The Ifẹ̀ people were exempt from banishment because they were considered worshippers, and perhaps also as a sign of respect for a people who had originated from the center of Yorùbá universe, home to this powerful deity, Òràmfẹ̀.[43]

Other documents in the missionary archives deal with speculations about the gender of Odùduwà, which continue to play a role in Yorùbá history and ethnography. Conventional wisdom assumes he is male, a position that is widely supported by numerous myths in Ifá divination texts. However, to complicate matters, in eastern Yorùbá kingdoms each town often worshipped its own version of Odùduwà. In many eastern towns, such as Ìdànrè, the local Ọlọ́fin was believed to be the personification of Odùduwà or the "Son of Odùduwà." On August 26, 1889, the Reverend E. J. Elliot recorded that in Adó-Èkìtì Odùduwà was worshipped as a goddess and that the priestess of Odùduwà held more power than local civic leaders. Adored with "the same honor as given to the king himself," she was called "Ọbabìnrin, the Queen." Similarly, the woman-king, called Lóbùn in Oǹdó, was loved much as the priestess of Odùduwà was adored in Adó Èkìtì.[44] Although the woman-king was not associated with the adoration of Odùduwà, she was regarded as the mythic descendant of Púpùpú, daughter of Odùduwà, and the first Ọba of Oǹdó. Lóbùn controlled Ajé, the deity of wealth and fertility, and presided over the installation of any king ascending to the throne. As I argued in my previous work on Oǹdó, *Kingship, Religion, and Rituals in a Nigerian Community,* the state of affairs in Oǹdó may reflect a change from original female rule to male rule: Airo, the Oǹdó king who followed the rule of Púpùpú, the woman-king, is regarded as a usurper who displaced her. Thus, according to some missionary records, there is ambiguity in the perceived gender of Odùduwà.

Archival documents also include Reverend Matthew J. Luke's description of the shrines of Ifẹ̀. Arriving on November 21, 1888, Luke was the first indigenous missionary to visit Ilé-Ifẹ̀. Luke took an interest in the religious geography and arts of the city, and his commentary is very helpful to scholars of Ifè art. On this tour of Ilé-Ifè, the Ifè people showed Luke the Ọ̀pá Ọ̀rànmíyàn, known as the Staff of Ọ̀rànmíyàn, and the Idió Moon or Òṣùpá Idió—a shimmering granite stone that appears to glisten like moonlight. As Luke described the experience, "They showed me the sacred spots with which are connected many fabulous stories—such as the Idió where the moon is said to shine during the day because stones of brilliant beauty are plentifully scattered below three natural pillars of white stone, the middle measuring about seven feet high, and two remaining, one on each side and measuring about four feet."[45] Undoubtedly, the Reverend Luke was amazed at this local explanation of the Idió granite, but he reported local accounts faithfully in his diary.

To what extent are Ifè's sacredness and Ifè indigenes' beliefs concerning the *òrìṣà* determined by Ifè artistic traditions, in which the images of the gods and their devotees stand as constant reminders of the power of Ifè religious traditions and the inviolability of the ancient city? To answer this question, we will now turn to archaeological excavations that have uncovered the artistic traditions of the sacred city.

ARCHAEOLOGICAL FINDINGS IN ILÉ-IFÈ

Scholars generally agree that Ifè civilization spanned the period from 800 CE to 1700 CE, which can be further subdivided into three subperiods: the period of the Ọba civilization, from 850 to 1050, during which the two prominent deities, Òrìṣà-Ńlá and Ògún, began to be featured; the classical period, from 1050 to 1500, when terra-cotta and bronze sculptures were made; and the postclassical period, from 1500 to 1700, when Ifè influenced many of the eastern Yorùbá regions and when the Ọ̀wọ̀ and Benin artistic tradition developed and flourished. After this third phase, Ilé-Ifè declined as the political and cultural center of Yorùbá civilization, overtaken by the expanding the Ọ̀yọ́ Empire. Not until the coming of the British in the late nineteenth century did Ilé-Ifè begin to re-assert itself as the cultural and spiritual center of Yorùbá civilization. This period of Ilé-Ifè's reemergence coincided with the colonial and postcolonial era of the Nigerian nation.

The excavations of artifacts in Ilé-Ifè spanned almost ninety years, from Leo Frobenius's first major discovery in November 1910 and the first major reports published of Ifè finds to the more recent work of the indigenous archaeologist Ọmótọ́-ṣọ̀ọ́ Elúyẹmí. Archaeologists and art historians alike have documented and analyzed Ilé-Ifè artifacts more than any other artifacts in sub-Saharan Africa. The key figures have been Frank Willett, William Fagg, and, to a lesser extent, Elúyẹmí. The iconography of the materials has received equally serious attention from several art historians, including Suzanne Blier, John Pemberton, Henry Drewal, Rowland Abíọ́-dún, Ekpo Eyo, and Babátúndé Lawal.[46] Several archaeological investigators have been concerned with preserving the artifacts, dating them, establishing their historical periods and linkages with artifacts from other civilizations, interpreting their overall continual relevance, and preserving them. Studies by art historians, of course, overlap with the archaeological studies, but in general these have been concerned primarily with the forms, functions, and materials of the objects; with their aesthetic significance within historical, visual, verbal, and cultural contexts; and with their relationship to the Yorùbá cosmology, kingship system, and worldview. Rather than elaborating on the archaeological and architectural elements in these Ifè works, which the scholars in these two disciplines have long pursued with much success, I will be concerned here with the light this scholarship may throw on the ancient or prehistoric religious life, rituals, and cosmology of Yorùbá civilization in Ilé-Ifè and how this may lead to a deeper understanding of Ilé-Ifè as a ceremonial center.

The prehistoric religious elements of Yorùbá traditions have often been overlooked in Yorùbá religious scholarship. But, if carefully interpreted, these works may help elucidate Yorùbá prehistoric religious traditions and ritual life. For one thing, excavations have occurred primarily in locations that are connected with religious and ritual precincts and sacred groves: shrines, temples, cult compounds, streets, and quarters named after deities. Their analysis and interpretation should, therefore, provide an overview of the city's Yorùbá religious history and thus further establish its preeminence as a ceremonial center. Ultimately, we hope to provide answers to several crucial questions. What was the role of the technocrats of the sacred (sacred king, priests, chiefs)? What religious and ceremonial functions and meanings do the artifacts provide? What light can they shed on the ritual customs and beliefs of the Ifè people who lived during this period? Can our findings throw more light on the religious configuration of the city?

Since the first formal excavation of Ilé-Ifè (1910–12) by Leo Frobenius, several other excavations have been carried out and numerous discoveries have been made. Although the original Olókun brass head (Orí Olókun) found by Frobenius in the Olókun Sacred Grove later vanished, its replica is safeguarded in the Ifè Museum in Ilé-Ifè. Of greatest interest to the archaeological community is the naturalism that the head manifests, since no other naturalistic portrait sculptures are found in any other part of Africa.[47] For scholars of religion, the Olókun discovery provides remarkable information about this goddess of the ocean and earth, who had almost become forgotten in modern Ilé-Ifè but was still quite actively celebrated in Benin. The prized brass sculpture—or its replica—thus provides a further link with the Benin Kingdom and tentatively confirms the religious and artistic relationship with Ifè.

At a subsidiary shrine to this major grove, in the Wálóde Compound, owned by the Wálóde family, a further discovery was made several years after Frobenius's first discovery: numerous fragments of terra-cotta sculpture right at the center of the shrine. Two unique pieces were among the finds: one in a natural style, described as one of the finest examples of the Ifè arts to be discovered; and the other a sculpture of a "small head with enormous ears." Several other fragments in this find, including "the leg of a bushcow, the left thighs of two different kneeling figures, two hands holding a bowl, a right hand holding a matchet, . . . and a dozen other pieces," suggest that they are connected with the worship of Olókun and that the entire as-semblage of terra-cotta indicates a ritual spot with all the essential paraphernalia of a major sacrifice.[48]

A team led in 1953 by William Fagg also excavated the Olókun Grove, which Frobenius had originally visited in 1910. During the 1953 excavation, the team dis-covered that the grove "covered an extensive area to the north of Ilé-Ifẹ̀."[49] Some bell-shaped chambers found there probably represent burial places for the priests of the deity, which is consistent with Ifẹ̀ tradition, according to which the high priest is buried in the outer compound of the grove of his òrìṣà.

By mere accident, in 1938 a foundation digging at Wúnmọníjẹ́ Compound led to the discovery of thirteen life-sized bronze heads not far from the palace, and, in the following year an additional four heads were found, along with a male figure thought to be an Ọ̀ọni, wearing "a beaded crown, an elaborate beaded neck-ring, armlets, and necklaces."[50] William Bascom, the young American anthropologist who was later to write extensively on Yorùbá religion, culture, and society, and in par-ticular on the Ifá divination system in Ilé-Ifẹ̀, played a leading role in analyzing these important findings. Commenting on the significance of this discovery, Willett wrote: "The primary impact of this discovery was felt in the art world which was aston-ished to find what was evidently a significant tradition of naturalistic art in Africa. Since the naturalism of these works was comparable to anything that ancient Egypt, Classical Greece and Rome, or Renaissance Europe had produced, it was assumed that they must have been made in one of these traditions."[51] It was further assumed that if, indeed, these artifacts had been crafted in Africa, since Africans were por-trayed in these bronzes, then Europeans working in these traditions must have made them rather than African artisans. The possible African origin of these discoveries was not even considered.

A few comments on the religious significance of the Ifẹ̀ bronzes are appropriate here. Some of the heads have crowns and depict the sacred kings or Ọ̀ọni of Ifẹ̀. The crowns resemble the insignia of contemporary Yorùbá Ọba: the beaded veil that "hides" the face of the king. It has been suggested that these bronze heads were used as commemorative figures in the second burial ceremonies of the Ọ̀ọni, cor-responding to the Yorùbá burial tradition of commemorative effigies.[52] They were, therefore, meant to showcase the power and dignity of kingship. One unique bronze mask has drawn the attention of scholars and even of the previous Ọba himself, Ọ̀ọni Adésọjí Adérẹ̀mí. The mask is the so-called Ọbalùfọ̀n mask, associated with one of the earlier Ọ̀ọni of Ifẹ̀, Ọbalùfọ̀n II, named after Ọ̀ọni Ọbalùfọ̀n, to indicate this Ọ̀ọni's connection with the beginning of bronze casting in Ilé-Ifẹ̀. Unlike others, this mask was set aside in the Òmìrìn chamber inside the palace and featured promi-nently in the royal coronation ceremony.[53]

In 1957, construction workers leveling ground for a building discovered another major bronze in Ìta Yemòó, the quarters of the goddess Yemòó, wife of Ọbàtálá. The discovery included seven objects that Willett describes: an Ọ̀ọni figure about eighteen inches in height; a royal pair with arms and legs interlocked (over eleven inches high); a vessel placed on a road stool and "the figure of a queen curled round the pot holding a staff in her hand"; two similar staffs "topped with human heads (one of them is gagged)"; and finally "two ovoid mace-heads, each bearing two gagged heads." Although these objects were all naturalistic in style, the heads were disproportionately large—a quarter of the entire size of the figures—and the legs were considerably less than half the height.[54] Willett has pointed out the contrast with the European sculptural tradition, in which the heads of figures are much smaller. The oversized heads indicate the importance of the *orí*, the inner head, in Yorùbá thought and artistic culture. Orí, often depicted as a god and personification of one's inner head, is the controller of destiny, on which one's position and status depends.

According to Ifẹ̀ informants, the rope-gagged heads were victims of sacrificial offerings; this is in keeping with the tradition whereby the victims are prevented from making a speech, since this might put a curse on their executioner (in Ifẹ̀ belief curses were potent).[55] The regalia of the Ọ̀ọni correspond closely to that worn by the male figure found during the dig in Ìta Wúnmọníjẹ́ (described above). The Ọ̀ọni holds the insignia of his authority, objects with magical power *(àṣẹ)*, with which he utters prayers or curses as he deems fit. Furthermore, excavations around Ìta Yemòó have enabled archaeologists to conclude that this was a ritual site active between 10 BCE and 10 CE and that the "classical period of naturalistic Ifẹ̀ sculpture is thus confirmed as being earlier than the first European contacts."[56]

Evidence of Ifẹ̀'s ancient origin and religious and ceremonial significance also abounds in the numerous terra-cotta objects excavated in Ilé-Ifẹ̀. Fagg excavated several votive and cultic instruments and religious objects, ranging from headless Luna figures of sacrificial victims to an official staff of the Ògbóni secret society, an ax, a drum, a ritual staff, and animal sculptures, including a snake. In general, there was a preponderance of animal figurines among the Ifẹ̀ terra-cotta sculptures, including ram's heads, several representing the sacrificial offerings at the various shrines located throughout Ilé-Ifẹ̀. Some may represent animal icons that belong to a specific deity or to the divine royal kingship, such as a leopard, elephant, owl, chameleon, and bird.

Unlike bronzes and terra-cotta pieces, stone sculptures are relatively rare in Ilé-Ifẹ̀, although several excavated or discovered in groves are of magnificent quality and significance. One of the wonders of Ilé-Ifẹ̀ is Ọ̀pá Ọ̀rànmíyàn (the Ọ̀rànmíyàn Staff), a tall granite column about seventeen feet high, decorated with iron nails. In the popular imagination, the Ifẹ̀ legends of the Ọ̀rànmíyàn adventure regard this as the walking stick of the Ifẹ̀ cultural hero, warrior, and founder of the modern Benin dynasty, referred to earlier in this chapter. Staffs of a similar style, though

FIGURE 4. The Ògún Ladìn Shrine.

much shorter, are found in several other shrines, including Ògún's shrine at Òkè-Mògún (the main shrine of Ògún) near the palace, and another at Orè Grove. Inside the palace stands a shrine to Ògún accompanied by similar objects: a granite mudfish, a large wrought-iron pointed conical shape, and a quartz cylinder. These objects are overlaid by earthenware shards. During my recent fieldwork in the palace of Ilé-Ifè, the palace messengers revealed the mythological origin of the ritual objects that belong to Ògún Ladìn, whose shrine is marked by the objects. This mythical figure was Odùduwà's blacksmith, who descended from heaven to work as a smith but later was turned into a large laterite stone. In the recent past, the Ògún Ladìn Shrine served as a place where people came to swear to Ògún to prove their innocence. The palace messenger reminded me that more recently it has become a place where prayers are offered. Here again is evidence of foreign religious influence on an indigenous culture. The messenger remarked, "In the past people came here to curse or request [the deity] to adjudicate in disputes, but today they come to offer prayer for long life, many children, and to be prosperous." Evidence of such prayer offerings abounds in the coins and palm oil that litter the shrine.

These excavations and discoveries in Ilé-Ifè took place almost entirely in compounds, shrines, groves, and occasionally abandoned sacred sites, which are abundant in this truly sacred and ceremonial city. Streets, quarters, and compounds have names connected with the sacred elements in Ifè cosmology. For example, in Ògbọ́n Ọya (Ọya Street), named after the Yorùbá goddess of the River Niger, one of the most formidable rivers in Nigeria, archaeologists have found an abundance of potsherd pavements, quite uncommon in the city, as well as terra-cotta human heads, both naturalistic and stylized in form.

In addition, archaeological discoveries have led to further confirmation of the strong ties between Benin and Ilé-Ifẹ̀ discussed earlier. According to information supplied by R. E. Bradbury, Benin kings were returned to Ilé-Ifẹ̀ for interment at the site called Ọ̀run Ọba Àdó as recently as 1888. Eleven burial pits were discovered and excavated in this area between 1960 and 1961, and "several potteries" and animal bones were recovered, although there was no trace of the heads of the Benin kings, as the tradition has maintained. It has since been suggested that perhaps "only nail parings and hair clippings from the corpses" were taken to Ifẹ̀ for burial and that the animal bones may be remnants of sacrificial offerings made to the deceased kings.

WILLIAM RUSSELL BASCOM (1912–81): AMERICAN ANTHROPOLOGIST IN ILÉ-IFẸ̀

William Bascom's sojourn in Ilé-Ifẹ̀ and his pioneering scholarship on Ifẹ̀ festivals and Ifá divination practices could be seen as a chapter in American anthropological research. Bascom's premature death prevented him from securing the fame accorded his teacher and mentor, Melville Herskovits. Any study of Ilé-Ifẹ̀ City requires an interrogation of Bascom's research methods, findings, and interpretations, as well as the global politics that have influenced his contribution to African and Yorùbá studies. If Frobenius inadvertently placed Ifẹ̀ on the world map, Bascom has carried out one of the most scholarly, in-depth studies of Ifẹ̀'s traditions to date, especially regarding the Ifá divination system in Ilé-Ifẹ̀. Bascom carried out the first modern study of Ilé-Ifẹ̀ City. In many ways, his writings contradicted those of Frobenius; however, like Frobenius, Bascom cultivated the friendship of the Ọ̀ọ̀ni of Ifẹ̀, Ọ̀ọ̀ni Adérẹ̀mí, and likewise was caught up in the international furor surrounding Britain's continued desire to dominate African arts. Ifẹ̀ became the arena for such international rivalry.

Whereas Frobenius opened up Yorùbá studies to European scholars, Bascom brought Yorùbá studies to the attention of Americanists. Born May 23, 1912, Bascom was educated between 1937 and 1938 at the University of Wisconsin and Northwestern University. He put to good use a Social Science Research Council fellowship to finance his work among the Yorùbá people. Between 1942 and 1946 he worked with the U.S. government in the Office of Strategic Services as special assistant to Nigeria, and between 1943 and 1946 he was in the Foreign Economic Administration as special representative to British West Africa with headquarters in Accra, Gold Coast (now Ghana). Bascom first visited Ilé-Ifẹ̀ in 1938–39, when he was involved in the excavation of Ifẹ̀. He was awarded a Fulbright research fellow-ship to work again among the Yorùbá between 1950 and 1951 and a Wenner Gren Foundation grant for research in Cuba on Afro-Cuban religion derived from Yorùbá religious traditions.

In examining William Bascom's encounter with Yorùbá traditions in Ilé-Ifẹ̀, one may ask several relevant questions. How does Bascom's picture of the city, its people, and their religious traditions reflect on the image of the city today? How will Bas-com's research and field experience enable us to understand Ilé-Ifẹ̀ religious life in the early part of the twentieth century? How will a reconstruction of his work en-able us see the continuity and changes in Ilé-Ifẹ̀ religious life over the centuries? On the basis of his years of interviews and research among Ilé-Ifẹ̀ diviners, Bascom doc-umented Ilé-Ifẹ̀ social and commercial life in his most weighty works: *Ifá Divina-tion: Communication between Gods and Men in West Africa* and *The Yoruba of South-western Nigeria.* These two works have become durable classics in the ethnography of Nigeria's southwestern Yorùbá.

Drawing primarily on the earlier work of Frobenius, and thus accepting in prin-ciple the primacy of Ilé-Ifẹ̀, Bascom availed himself of its artistic, historical, and ethnographic materials, especially his study of festivals, bringing the city to the at-tention of the world, but especially North American scholars. Although Bascom was unaware of Wheatley's pivotal work cited above, he seems to have been the first to consider Ilé-Ifẹ̀ in the spirit of Wheatley's thesis, as a ceremonial city par excel-lence. In June 1951, Bascom wrote Herskovits: "Tomorrow, we [including his wife] are leaving for a week at Ifẹ̀. Aside from the previous points I want to check up on, I will be interested to go over the religious picture in terms of what I have learned this time. The question of religion as you know, is an endless one and everywhere we go, we come across a new set of Orishas."[57] Though Bascom felt overwhelmed by his encounter with a multitude of Ifẹ̀ *òrìṣà,* his anthropological training enabled him to carry out an in-depth study of the gods and festivals of Ilé-Ifẹ̀. He did not chart the Ifẹ̀ festival calendar or see the larger picture of the geography and land-scape of Ifẹ̀ tradition; nor did he engage in in-depth interpretation of the materials he otherwise faithfully collected. However, his book on Ifá divination gave him the honor and prestige he still enjoys in African studies today. His painstaking effort in gathering data on Yorùbá traditions is reflected in his comment: "I did manage to complete *Ifá Divination* in thirty-one years (1938–1969), and *Sixteen Cowries* in twenty-nine years (1951–1980)."[58]

Bascom's research on the Ifẹ̀ socio-religious system enables us to understand not only the transition that Ifẹ̀ was undergoing at the time of his fieldwork but also the impact of foreign influences on the ancient city. Although he was not interested in providing a fully developed ethnography of Ifẹ̀ religion or pursuing a central the-sis, he provided useful glimpses of religious life.

Perhaps one of the most fascinating social innovations in Ifẹ̀ was the traders' guild or Ìpàǹpá, a highly organized group of importers who enjoyed a monopoly over all imported goods. The imports were mainly European trade goods and merchandise from neighboring towns and from other ethnic groups. The guild usually resold these items to local traders or directly to consumers. According to Bascom, the Pàràkòyí (supervisors of trade) managed the Ìpàǹpá, although Ìpàǹpá representatives remained in charge of the traditional wards of Ilé-Ifẹ̀ and the Pàràkòyí served as executive directors. The position of the Ìpàǹpá was undoubtedly powerful; Bascom claimed that "half of the daily profits [of each member of the Ìpàǹpá] was turned over to the Pakoyi."⁵⁹ When guild members met to share a meal in the house of the Pàràkòyí, part of the proceeds went to the Ọ̀ọni.

Commenting on the political economy of the city, Bascom observed that local traders he interviewed failed to recognize "any of their numbers as head or chief of the market." That is, there was no title called Ìyálójà or Ìyálájé at that time, as was the custom in most Ọ̀yọ́ Yorùbá cities in the western Yorùbá region. Only the Ọ̀ọni was regarded as worthy of the title "Owner of the Market" or Ọlójà. Bascom claimed that "the title, Ìyálóde (literally, mother of the streets), a female chief and the city women's leader, was borrowed only recently from the Ọ̀yọ́ district."⁶⁰

Two other issues are significant here. First, it was evident that foreign trade and external cultural elements were being introduced into the religious, social, and economic life of traditional Ilé-Ifẹ̀. Because modernization brought about expanded trade and introduced new worldviews, it was quite plausible for "foreign elements" to slip into the life of the city. Bascom reported that although the Pàràkòyí could not control the entire trade, they were especially unable to control the female traders and retailers, often called Aláróbò or Alájàpá. The Pàràkòyí were responsible for the annual sacrifice to the deity Odùduwà, the ceremony to which all traders contributed. This responsibility was understandable, given that the cult of Odùduwà claimed authority in the land and that its festival was at the end of the festival calendar. To buttress Bascom's position here, I observed that in the celebration of Odùduwà during the parched harmattan season from 1986 until 1990, a large number of traders brought their offerings to the deity to pray for prosperous trade the following year.

Bascom reported some of the changes in modern life. In 1910–12, he claimed, the Ìpàǹpá guild disintegrated because European merchants successfully broke its guild's monopoly to establish stores in Ilé-Ifẹ̀ City that sold directly to consumers without the intervention of intermediaries. Bascom reported that at the time of his field research only about ten members remained out of the 210 who he heard had formerly been members of the Ìpàǹpá. In addition, the Pàràkòyí became mere figureheads, lacking their previously enormous economic power. Indeed, the incumbent Pàràkòyí complained to Bascom that although the Pàràkòyí of Ìbàdàn, Abẹ̀òkúta, and Ìjẹ̀bú-Òde were officially recognized, Ilé-Ifẹ̀'s Pàràkòyí was not recognized. The significance of Bascom's research was that he showed how Ilé-Ifẹ̀'s economy—especially modern commerce—was organized and how a nontraditional,

modern economy was supporting traditional ritual and religions through the spon-
soring of traditional festivals.

Bascom's most influential work was a monograph describing the Yorùbá of southwestern Nigeria that was based almost entirely on Ilé-Ifẹ̀. There Bascom acknowledged that "in economics, government, and in particular in art and religion, they [the
Yorùbá] rank with those other West African groups which represent the highest
level of cultural achievement in sub-Saharan Africa."[61] He set forth a framework
for appreciating Yorùbá religious traditions, especially with regard to their emphasis on obtaining earthly blessings *(ire),* as opposed to the otherworldly spirituality of Islam and Christianity.[62] He wrote that the Yorùbá desire five "good" things—
marriage, children, wealth, long life, and defeat of their enemies—and seek to avoid
above all the misfortunes of early death, illness, fights, loss of property, and poverty.

Bascom's research in Ilé-Ifẹ̀ provided him with significant ethnographic material that enabled him to define larger theoretical and thematic issues in folklore and
anthropology, especially as these disciplines related to Yorùbá religion. He was one
of the first American ethnologists to give myth the definition and identity it now
bears. He characterized this task as "an attempt at definitions of myth, legend, and
folklore that are applicable cross-culturally; with the hope that the folklorists, at least
will use those terms consistently." Bascom concluded that myths about the *òrìṣà* are
stories believed to be true and that the stories about how the *òrìṣà* arrived on earth
in Ilé-Ifẹ̀ differ from lineage to lineage. He observed that each man in Ilé-Ifẹ̀ tended
to present an event in terms favorable to his lineage. Each lineage claimed "seniority because its own progenitor came from heaven earlier than others."[63] Similarly,
each lineage portrayed itself as the most prestigious and significant in the pantheon.

Bascom's observation underscores the significance of the kinship group as the
most important religious and ritual unit in Ilé-Ifẹ̀. It is the pivotal point and the
point of reference for Ifẹ̀ religious sensibility. When I asked Odùduwà devotees why
their group was not as popular as the Ọbàtálá group, they responded that their own
lineage forbade outsiders to participate in the cult, whereas the Ọbàtálá group welcomed outsiders. One chief informed me: "As you are now, you can become a chief
in Ọbàtálá's lineage tradition. We do not do so here."

In his detailed study of Ifẹ̀ religious life and Yorùbá mythology, Bascom cited
numerous metaphoric references to the sacred and the profane, including the sexual escapades of cultural heroes and divine beings, which he called the "salacious and
even pornographic and seemingly sacrilegious myths about the gods." Bascom later
cited a "myth about the *ọba*'s ears" that was popular among Yorùbá diaspora communities in Cuba and Brazil. Actually, the myth—which is similar to numerous narratives and folk tales that were transported from Africa to the Americas—originated
in Ifá divination texts collected from Ilé-Ifẹ̀. Bascom observed that this myth "provoked gales of laughter from the Yorùbá listeners who translated the text for him."
To assuage Western prudishness and cultural bias in discussing sexual matters,

Bascom prefaced his essay with a request for tolerance: "I have no intention of disparaging Yorùbá religion."[64] Elsewhere he commented, "It seems to be a serious problem for Western scholars to deal with such stories heavily laden with sexual imagery and those that could provoke jokes and laughter. Yorùbá mythology is infused with sacred and profane images of the gods and culture heroes are often portrayed in human metaphors and images. The gods and goddesses are metaphors for human conduct, and lived experiences."[65] As this book will further show, Bascom's ethnography of Ilé-Ifẹ̀ enables us to account for some of the changes that have occurred in the last fifty years in Ilé-Ifẹ̀'s religious life since publication of his own work and the current study.

IFẸ̀ ENCOUNTERS MODERNITY:
THE "GREAT CROWN" CASE

In the history of Ilé-Ifẹ̀, 1903 was an earth-shattering year for the Yorùbá people. It was the year that the Ọ̀ọ̀ni, the god-king of the Yorùbá, encountered directly the full impact of British modern colonial rule. From the perspective of the Ọ̀ọ̀ni and from the perspective of the colonial governor in Lagos, the year ended the preceding era and opened a new investiture for Ilé-Ifẹ̀ City and the Yorùbá states of southwestern Nigeria. Although the governor, Sir William Macgregor, referred cursorily to the occasion as the "Great Crown" case, to Ọ̀ọ̀ni Adélẹ́kàn Olúbùṣe I (1894–1910) and to the Yorùbá people, it was a precedent-setting "Great Journey" because it marked the first time in the history of Ilé-Ifẹ̀ that an Ọ̀ọ̀ni would venture out of his palace and beyond the center of the universe.[66] For Westerners, the occasion would have been tantamount to asking God to leave heaven to answer the call of a mere mortal.

The Ọ̀ọ̀ni traveled to Lagos, then the center of British regional administration. For the Yorùbá, news of the unprecedented journey provoked fear, anxiety, and uncertainty because it was a great taboo for the Ọ̀ọ̀ni to vacate the sacred city of Ilé-Ifẹ̀ to travel to another seat of power, however that power might be defined. Therefore, symbolically, the journey of the Ọ̀ọ̀ni signified the capitulation of tradition to modernity and of religious authority to secular authority. However, the events for which the Ọ̀ọ̀ni was invited to Lagos were as remarkable as the journey itself, for they symbolized the colonial government's attempt to impose traditional rule as a mechanism of the British indirect rule system. Most importantly, these events symbolized the Yorùbá attempt to co-opt the British notion of colonial rule by reinventing and re-establishing their sacred city as the symbolic center of Yorùbá custom and tradition. Thus, while the British attempted to manipulate the Yorùbá, the Yorùbá simultaneously attempted to manipulate the British under the auspices of acceding to colonial rule and legitimacy.

In a letter dated April 18, 1902, the governor of Lagos ordered the clerk of the

Central Native Authority in Lagos to write to the Ọ̀ọ̀ni, asking that the Ọ̀ọ̀ni provide at his earliest convenience a list of "*ọbas* and chiefs who have the right to wear
the crowns originally when leaving Ifẹ̀." The governor sent the request because of a
dispute between the Ẹlẹ́pẹ́ of Èpẹ́ (a town in the Ṣágámù district) and the Àkàrìgbò
of Ṣágámù (now Ìjẹ̀bú Rẹ́mọ) over who had the right to wear the sacred beaded
crown that originated in Ilé-Ifẹ̀, and thus the legitimacy to rule. The Àkàrìgbò of
Ṣágámù claimed primacy over the entire Ìjẹ̀bú Rẹ́mọ district and refuted the right
of the Ẹlẹ́pẹ́ of Èpẹ́ to wear the crown. Although the Ọ̀ọ̀ni compiled and sent to the
colonial office in Lagos a handwritten list of about fifty-four titles, the governor "invited" the Ọ̀ọ̀ni to visit Lagos to help resolve the dispute over which of the two Ọba
was sovereign.

In 1903, the importance of the Ọ̀ọ̀ni's visit and the ancient authority of Ilé-Ifẹ̀
as the sacred center were underscored in the governor's note to him: "As the question is engaging presently the attention of the Central Native Council and to enable them to arrive at a definite conclusion in the matter, it is important that they
be placed in possession of your report on this important question, as the recognized head of Yorùbáland, who has the right of issuing crowns, at an early date."

In describing his journey to Lagos, the Ọ̀ọ̀ni emphasized only religious and political aspects of the trip, although he observed great apprehension in the people of
Ilé-Ifẹ̀, indeed in the people throughout the entire land of the Yorùbá. Many of his
subjects accompanied him to the distant River Aṣẹ̀jìrẹ́ that forms the boundary between Ilé-Ifẹ̀ and the land of the Ìbàdàn people, and many vowed to remain there
until he returned unharmed to Ilé-Ifẹ̀.

All across the land, including the region of the Aláàfin of Ọ̀yọ́, the Ọ̀ọ̀ni observed
that the Yorùbá Ọba began to vacate their thrones. Astonishingly, they remained
outside the gates of their cities, waiting until the Ọ̀ọ̀ni's safe return. A time of great
dread fell upon the land, as the Ọba feared that the Ọ̀ọ̀ni's departure could bring
devastation. Clearly, the Yorùbá held their Ọ̀ọ̀ni in great esteem. The British governor confirmed that he had received a telegram from the Aláké of Abẹ̀òkúta, one
of the principal Ọba in Yorùbáland, inquiring about the time that the Ọ̀ọ̀ni would
return home so that the Aláké could meet him "outside the walls of Abẹ̀òkúta in
order to pay his respect to the Ọ̀ọ̀ni." To ensure a successful journey to Lagos, the
Ọ̀ọ̀ni performed sacrifices "all along the journey." Accompanied by a large entourage
of wives, musicians, chiefs, and servants, the Ọ̀ọ̀ni arrived in Lagos on February
23, 1903. He was lodged at Tinubu Square, and he held his first meeting with Governor Macgregor on February 24. The historic meeting between the governor and
the Ọ̀ọ̀ni indicated that both were exploring mutual benefit. Discreetly, the Ọ̀ọ̀ni
expressed great admiration for a governor who caused such a break with the ancient custom that forbade the Ọ̀ọ̀ni to leave Ilé-Ifẹ̀, the spiritual home of the Yorùbá,
to travel to Lagos.

Thanking the Ọ̀ọ̀ni for the admiration shown to him, Governor Macgregor expressed the desire that "the Ọ̀ọni would keep a quiet mind as regards the ancient tradition of Ifẹ̀." Acting from an entirely different worldview that accorded no significance to the Ọ̀ọni's spiritual beliefs or sacrificial practices, Governor Macgregor remarked: "There was nothing in the national tradition to forbid the Ọ̀ọni traveling in the governor's special hammock and riding to Lagos from Ibadan in the train. If the tradition of Ifẹ̀ forbade the Ọ̀ọni traveling in a hammock, the Ọ̀ọni felt that the reference must have been to an ordinary hammock . . . and not to the governor's own hammock." He further commented, "I could not conceive that traveling in the train was forbidden by the tradition of Ifẹ̀." Governor Macgregor valued his hammock and the train as symbols of the modern transportation system in the new era and could not imagine why an indigenous tradition should reject or forbid an offer to travel.

The meeting between Governor Macgregor and the Ọ̀ọni demonstrated that the two men imbued their exchange with different meanings and manipulated each other to maximize their gains. The governor recognized that "tradition"—properly modified and modernized—could very well serve the political purpose of the British rule in Lagos and the region. On the other hand, the Ọ̀ọni recognized that changes were inevitable and that "modern" changes could serve tradition. By performing sacrifices throughout his journey, the Ọ̀ọni could ameliorate the damage of breaking the ancient taboo. He was mindful of the new British power and of the means by which he could tap into the new resources to enhance his own status to bring honors to his empire and the Sacred City.

With the collapse of the previous Ọ̀yọ́ Empire, with the disintegration of the central political structure of the Yorùbá, and with the institution of British colonial rule, the British knew very well that invoking the prestige and myth of the Yorùbá ceremonial center and its wide-ranging symbols could augur well for British rule. However, according similar power to Ọ̀yọ́ and the Aláàfin would create political power that could one day rise up to challenge British authority. Thus it was expedient for the British to invoke Ilé-Ifẹ̀'s mythic tradition as a spiritual ceremonial center.

It is significant that Governor Macgregor did not hesitate to invoke the Aláàfin's name in underscoring with the Ọ̀ọni the propriety or taboo of visiting Lagos. After all, the governor was aware of the deep division among the Yorùbá people over Ilé-Ifẹ̀ and Ọ̀yọ́ traditions and the sporadic rivalry between their two rulers. The governor reminded the Ọ̀ọni that the Aláàfin had done the governor a great favor when the governor visited the interior by venturing out of the city to see him. The governor emphasized that he had not asked the Aláàfin to do so but that the Aláàfin had honored the governor of his own volition. The governor was glad "the Ọ̀ọni had conferred a more distinguished honor upon him." The reference to the Aláàfin made great sense to the Ọ̀ọni, especially because the Aláàfin was often his rival. The governor was quick to capitalize on the rivalry between the two.

Moreover, Governor Macgregor was following his own British traditions, in which his queen—seen as the spiritual and ceremonial head of the British Empire—provided a much-needed sacred canopy for a myriad of diverse nationalities in Britain. He was acting out of his own familiar history and cultural traditions, while at the same time playing down aspects of Ilé-Ifè tradition that he believed could impede modernization and the "civilizing" mission of British rule.

Who Shall Wear the Crown?

At their initial meeting, Governor Macgregor recounted to the Ọ̀ọ̀ni the reason for requesting his extraordinary visit to Lagos. The Ọ̀ọ̀ni was invited to "instruct the Lagos chiefs and the native council on the great question" of who was entitled to wear the crown. For the British government, Macgregor claimed, it was a question of justice and entitlement—significant ethical values imposed by British rule. It was important for the British authority in Lagos to uphold "the rights, position, dignity and authority of the kings, chiefs and traditional rulers of the country" and to "uphold and strengthen the ancient authority and power of the Ọ̀ọ̀ni of Ifè" in particular.

One significant issue here is that even though Ifè's status as the ceremonial center of the Yorùbá people was already established, the transfer of such power to a more central place was carried out partly in the colonial and postcolonial era by British colonial rule. Ifè's role was reinvented based on an already existing tradition, but it achieved its pan-Yorùbá influence only after the British began to rule. British rule acted as a catalyst that made the postcolonial dispensation and pivotal role of Ilé-Ifè possible. It is therefore not surprising that Ifè indigenes and historians often cite the Ọ̀ọ̀ni's visit as a proof of both Ifè's and the Ọ̀ọ̀ni's authority over the Aláàfin of Ọ̀yọ́.

As the governor began to inform the Ọ̀ọ̀ni about the events planned for the following day, the issue of traditional kingship authority came up once again. Each of the plaintiffs—the Àkàrìgbò and the Ẹlẹ́pẹ́ —was to bring ten elders, men who knew the tradition very well, to testify on his behalf to his claims of authority, and the Ọ̀ọ̀ni would have the final say on the matter. The Ọ̀ọ̀ni reminded the governor that tradition forbade him to meet face to face with the two Ọba and with the members of the council. It was then agreed that the Ọ̀ọ̀ni would wear his veiled crown, which completely obscured his face, and that the Ọ̀ọ̀ni would be seated facing away from the two plaintiffs and members of the Central Native Council.

The meeting convened in the evening of December 24, 1903. The governor reminded all the parties why he had invited the Ọ̀ọ̀ni to Lagos: to obtain "trustworthy information" about the great question that was before the council. The governor commented on the influence of the house of Ifè: "There was no chief in Yorùbáland who did not know who the Ọ̀ọ̀ni was. The greatest chiefs, including the Aláàfin of Ọ̀yọ́, traced their descent from Ifè. Because of its antiquity, the house of Ifè was the most ancient in Yorùbá until the present day." Ifè remained the only place where the highest distinctions were conferred on the great chiefs of Yorùbá. The greatest authority on questions connected with the wearing of crowns therefore centered on the Ọọni of Ifẹ̀.

Governor Macgregor's opening remarks once again underscored the British colonial government's agenda, policy, and system of indirect rule. It was designed to see the chiefs and Ọba as "allies" in administrating the colonies, to support traditional institutions that the British considered advantageous to colonial rule and to the British agenda. More significantly, the governor supported the status of Ifẹ̀ as the most significant city in the Yorùbá geopolitics—and the Ọọni as the king of all kings. Rather than being directly involved in governance, the British exploited the Ọba, chiefs, and emirs as tools in providing British governance. The governor and the educated elite of Lagos had ostensibly invited the Ọọni to "enlighten" them, but their real agenda was to maintain order and peace in the colony.

The governor continued that what was important was not so much the wearing of the sacred crown by the Ẹlẹ́pẹ́ as the two pertinent principles upholding the great crown. The first was that the crown signified distinction intended only for titled royalty who were the Ọba. If the governor failed to establish an authentic list of those entitled to wear the crown, the authority and privilege of the Ọba would be devalued. The second principle focused on the British administration of justice, fairness, and human rights. "It would be a serious thing not to allow a chief to wear a crown if he was entitled to do so by birth and position."

After the Àkàrìgbò and the Ẹlẹ́pẹ́ asserted that they were both sons of the Ọọni, the Ọọni spoke through an interpreter and pronounced that throughout the entire realm of the Ìjẹbú only the Awùjalẹ̀ of Ìjẹbú-Òde and the Àkàrìgbò of Ṣágámù were entitled to wear the sacred crown. "No one on the face of the earth has power to give the Ẹlẹ́pẹ́ of Èpẹ́ a crown except the Ọọni of Ifẹ̀," the Ọọni asserted. "Even the Aláké of Abẹòkúta and the Aláàfin of Ọ̀yọ́ had their crowns originally from Ifẹ̀."

The Ẹlẹ́pẹ́ insisted that his predecessors had come from Ilé-Ifẹ̀ and that consequently he was clearly entitled to wear the crown. At a certain moment in the meeting, he asked the Ọọni if he was not the Ọọni's son. The Ọọni's prolonged, solemn silence signified his decision—the Ẹlẹ́pẹ́ was not entitled to wear the crown. Thus ultimately the council took the cue from the Ọọni to rule against the Ẹlẹ́pẹ́.

It is instructive to read the astonishing concurrence of the members of the elite Native Council of Lagos in their response to the Ọọni's decision. "If a crown does not come from Ilé-Ifẹ̀, it is a worthless thing," remarked Sufiano, one member. Another, Súlè Giwa, declared, "The Ọọni has issued crowns to all the members of Yorùbá from the Aláàfin of Ọ̀yọ́ downward. If the Ẹlẹ́pẹ́ did not receive his crown from the Ọọni, that crown has not come from Ilé-Ifẹ̀." One Alli Balògún stated, "We also pray for long life for the Ọọni, we beg the Ọọni to forgive the Ẹlẹ́pẹ́. The Ẹlẹ́pẹ́ has sinned; he has no right to wear a crown." And Ogbògún stated, "We are very much thankful to the Ọọni. This sort of matter brings trouble. The strongman crowns himself and brings on war. This matter is in such a case. It is well known that only the Ọ̀ọ̀ni can issue crowns. Ifẹ̀ is the cradle of our race. All power and authority come from Ifẹ̀."

At the end of the meeting, the governor thanked the Ọ̀ọ̀ni for granting them his presence. The Ọ̀ọ̀ni returned to the place where he was lodged. This very carefully choreographed meeting succeeded in reinvigorating the understanding of the primal place of Ilé-Ifẹ̀ in Yorùbá politics and culture. As a place of origin, Ifẹ̀ served as a sacred canopy under which various subethnic groups converged to claim a common identity and a central ideology. Thus the ground was prepared for the future polity of the region and the Nigerian nation when the Yorùbá would provide the strongest unifying group in the nation's political history. Unity was based not on religion, which Islam provided in the northern region of the country, but on an ethnic myth of origin.

As their history amply demonstrated, if the Yorùbá were to claim any other compelling myth or ideology outside this space, it would be seen as completely absurd. The meeting helped the British colonial dispensation immensely, and its work of governing a large territory was aided by constant appeal to the Ifẹ̀ myth. Governor Macgregor's claim that he wanted to show the Ọ̀ọ̀ni how in "earnest the governments were in their endeavors to safeguard the rights, the position, dignity, and authority of the leading chiefs of the country, and how careful the governments were to uphold and strengthen the ancient authority and power of the Ọ̀ọ̀ni of Ifẹ̀," seems to have been demonstrated through this process. But the occasion also gave the Ọ̀ọ̀ni the chance to proffer his own requests to the governor and to challenge the British colonial government to practice what it preached, as the events of the Ọ̀ọ̀ni's third day in Lagos clearly show.

The Ọ̀ọ̀ni Visits the Governor

The day after the epic meeting, the Ọ̀ọ̀ni paid a courtesy visit to the residential home of Governor Macgregor. Since one good turn deserves another, the Ọ̀ọ̀ni took advantage of his visit to present the governor with a list of requests. Under the new dispensation, the colonial presence in Lagos had caused power to shift away from the regional Ọba and traditional rulers to the new Native Authority and the governor. Members of the council in Lagos wielded considerably greater power than ever before. Although recognized as indispensable to the indirect rule system, traditional rulers were nevertheless handicapped by the tradition that forced them to remain in the interior. As the case of Ọ̀ọ̀ni clearly shows, they were ceremonial rulers, and as the status of Ilé-Ifẹ̀ clearly shows, their cities and domains were purely symbolic centers of power. However, in the imagination of the ruling elites and indeed the people, the city of Ilé-Ifẹ̀ was still the seat of power and ritual that remained indispensable to governance. Therefore, it was essential to maintain the city and the Ọ̀ọ̀ni on site so that he could continue to play the role of leader. The Ọ̀ọ̀ni, too, wanted the British to recognize and support his influence in his domain as figurehead of the Yorùbá kings—a role he clearly understood and guarded jealously, even under the new dispensation.

During the Ọ̀ọ̀ni's visit to the governor's residence, Macgregor showed him photographs taken the previous day as proof of the momentous meeting. The delighted and grateful Ọ̀ọ̀ni remarked that it was the first time he had seen his photograph. Then the Ọ̀ọ̀ni tendered his requests. He stated that he had been severely criticized by his people for traveling to Lagos, for he had violated the imperial custom of remaining seated within his domain. The Ọ̀ọ̀ni asserted that he himself had resolved that he was king solely by the governor's authority. To buttress his argument, he reminded the governor of a gift from the British crown—"a knife encased in a sheath on the face of which was the British symbol carved in silver." For the Ọ̀ọ̀ni, "Whenever he looked on this symbol he knew where to look for support and help. The Ọ̀ọ̀ni looked to no one else on the face of the earth besides the British government." This statement is the first indication that the Ọ̀ọ̀ni was feeling helpless against his enemies, especially the Modákẹ́kẹ́ people. In the British, he had found a new avenger and friend. Acknowledging the power of the British presence in the new era, the Ọ̀ọ̀ni undoubtedly expected significant assistance from the British in his quest to return Ilé-Ifẹ̀ to its former glory.

At this moment, "The Ọ̀ọ̀ni got up from his seat and entreated the governor." Embarrassed and shaken on hearing the pleas of a great Yorùbá king, the governor insisted that the Ọ̀ọ̀ni sit down: "A great chief should not rise to speak." The Ọ̀ọ̀ni then declared that he was currently suffering because even though he was regarded as father of the entire Yorùbá country his material possessions were very few. Second, he described to the governor how pacification had greatly reduced the amount of land he had held under the traditional land tenure system: though at one time his lands had extended to the Osua (Ọ̀ṣun) River at Apomu, they now included only the immediate surroundings of Ilé-Ifẹ̀. No one was looking after him in Ilé-Ifẹ̀, the Ọ̀ọ̀ni complained, and he wanted the governor to help reclaim his land "so it would be a source of revenue and a means of livelihood for him."

Responding to the Ọ̀ọ̀ni's pleas, and having no idea of how drastically his realm had been reduced, the governor promised to refer the case to the British resident governor of Ìbàdàn, who would investigate and advise him. No doubt well tutored in methods of conflict resolution, the governor, echoing a Yorùbá proverb that would make sense to the Ọ̀ọ̀ni, remarked, "No chief would decide on the important matter without hearing both sides."[67]

As an immediate solution to the Ọ̀ọ̀ni's isolation and lack of resources, the governor decreed that henceforth the governor would pay the Ọ̀ọ̀ni a handsome stipend of one hundred pounds sterling a year. By the governor's reckoning, the Ọ̀ọ̀ni "would have money more than any chief in the [Yorùbá] country" and would be able to live in a good palace befitting the status of the highest-ranking king in the land. In addition, the governor gave the Ọ̀ọ̀ni a small present to use to buy gifts for his people at home. Besides, the Ọ̀ọ̀ni would use the visit as proof that he—and no one else—could decide cases related to wearing the coveted crown.

Responding to Governor Macgregor's largesse and to his demonstration of the British sense of justice, the Ọ̀ọ̀ni expressed great appreciation, remarking that "he would now be able to thatch his house and lick his fingers after eating, and was full."[68] It was important for the Ọ̀ọ̀ni to demonstrate once again the traditional authority invested in him. Thus, returning to the Ẹlẹ́pẹ́ case, the Ọ̀ọ̀ni asked the governor to "seize his royal shoes, the crown and gown. . . . If it had been in former times, the head of the Ẹlẹ́pẹ́ would have been cut off with the crown on it."

At this point, though, the governor seized the opportunity to learn more about traditional sacred kingship of the Yorùbá, especially the wearing of the sacred crown. The Ọ̀ọ̀ni informed him about the *arè*, the special crown worn just once a year, which required a yearly sacrifice. The Ọ̀ọ̀ni proclaimed: "Anyone who wears a crown that does not belong to him would die within a year except due sacrifices are performed." When the Ọ̀ọ̀ni boasted that he would not be surprised if the Ẹlẹ́pẹ́ died for this sacrilege, the governor expressed hope that the Ẹlẹ́pẹ́'s life would be spared. However, the Ọ̀ọ̀ni stipulated that the Ẹlẹ́pẹ́ would have to pay a fine and send a sheep and a ram to the Ọ̀ọ̀ni to make the necessary sacrifice, as tradition demanded. The Ọ̀ọ̀ni accepted the governor's plea to save the life of the Ẹlẹ́pẹ́ and promised to make the necessary sacrifice on the Ẹlẹ́pẹ́'s behalf. "Sacrifices to the gods and ancestors occur regularly," the Ọ̀ọ̀ni remarked, and added that he himself offered regular sacrifices; in Ìbàdàn, during the first part of his unparalleled journey to Lagos, he had left five sheep behind to provide for sacrifices on his return home to Ilé-Ifẹ̀. In concluding his exchanges with the governor on the themes of the crown, sacrifice, and the fate of the Ẹlẹ́pẹ́, the Ọ̀ọ̀ni asked the governor to place his crown on his head as a special favor, and the governor did.

This last gesture was an important act, symbolizing, for the Ọ̀ọ̀ni, his reinvestiture and confirmation and, for the British governor, the Ọ̀ọ̀ni's kingship, regime, and authority in Yorùbá country. By repositioning himself symbolically, politically, and legally under British indirect rule, the Ọ̀ọ̀ni ended his diplomatic visit stronger than before he took the trip. He was now explicitly declared king of kings of the Yorùbá, and he returned to Ilé-Ifẹ̀ in triumph. As for the governor, the meeting was a powerful way of consolidating British rule by appealing to and reinventing traditional sacred monarchy symbolized in the Yorùbá custom of wearing the sacred crown.

In conclusion, we could argue that the historic visit of Olúbùṣe I to Lagos was in many ways a landmark event in the history of Ilé-Ifẹ̀ and indeed of Yorùbá country, as the region was referred to then. It represented symbolically the Ọ̀ọ̀ni and Ifẹ̀'s encounter with modernity. The Ọ̀ọ̀ni, by heeding the call of the colonial resident officer in Lagos to travel outside his realm, broke with a tradition that forbade him to leave his domain and his palace. Doing so gave the Ọ̀ọ̀ni an opportunity to take his concerns to the new center of colonial power and authority. The encounter provided a glimpse of the function of British indirect rule, for the British government reinforced the Yorùbá traditional kingship system and confirmed the *primus inter pares* status of the Ọ̀ọ̀ni and the ancient city of Ilé-Ifẹ̀. If it achieved no other benefits, the visit raised the status of the ancient city to a higher level among the Yorùbá. One could argue that it was from then on that Ilé-Ifẹ̀ began to recapture its primary status among the Yorùbá city-states. A sacred city that had been politically dormant throughout the existence of the Ọ̀yọ́-Yorùbá Empire centralized in the city of Ọ̀yọ́ in the northeastern part of Yorùbá region began to regain its status in the modern era. What would emerge later in the colonial and postcolonial period was a pan-Yorùbá political dispensation that would draw its unifying symbol primarily from the tradition of Ilé-Ifẹ̀.

The colonial administration was predisposed to a modernizing agenda in which local culture and indigenous social systems would become more Westernized. Yet although modernity and tradition are often perceived to be incompatible, what we see here is a constant dialogue between the two. The governor reminded the Ọ̀ọ̀ni that tradition does not forbid modernization, just as modernization can incorporate tradition.

3

The Sacred Cosmos and Ilé-Ifẹ̀ Religion

Divination, Kingship, and Social Identity

This chapter provides an overview of the ideology and belief system of Ilé-Ifẹ̀ in order to lay a foundation for comprehending the city's sacred identity. According to a common popular saying in Yorùbáland: "Out of the 365 days that make a year, there is only one day in which one form of sacrifice or another is not offered to the gods." In fact, in Ilé-Ifẹ̀ the entire year is taken up with ceremonies, festivals, and rituals, as became clear in the several interviews I conducted with Ilé-Ifẹ̀ priests, diviners, chiefs, men, women, and youth directly involved in Ilé-Ifẹ̀ religious life.

Ifẹ̀ cosmology and society are full of deities, each with its own shrines, temple, and annual festivals. These deities are so numerous that some of them are jointly propitiated in overlapping annual festivals. The gods, god-kings, and goddesses, as well as their shrines and temples, are claimed primarily by specific lineages and clan groups, even when some, such as Ògún, Ọbàtálá, and Ifá, have assumed national status. These lineages have territorial holdings considered to convey the identity of the group, and numerous proverbs and family stories articulate the complex relationship between the gods and these holdings. The central purpose of the rituals and festivals is to reenact a deity's mythology and history, celebrating the significant role the deity has played in the welfare of its devotees and their lineages. The occasion provides an opportunity to sacralize the land and territory over which chiefs and priests preside, to acknowledge the regime of the Ọ̀ọ̀ni, and to make ritual offerings to ensure a peaceful and prosperous year. Ifẹ̀ deities often specialize in one or two spheres of communal life. Thus rituals and sacrifices are directed to the domain that the deity controls: rain, fertility, good harvest, or good health. However, certain festivals are considered universal and of national importance, including the Ọlọ́jọ́ Festival, the festival of Ògún; Ọdún Ifá, which doubles as the agricultural New Yam Festival and as a divination festival of the Ọ̀ọ̀ni and Ilé-Ifẹ̀ diviners; and the Ọdún Edì Festival, which reenacts the redemptive suffering of Mọrèmi, the Ifẹ̀ hero and liberator of the city from Ìgbò invaders. These rituals and festivals are examined in detail in Part Two of this book.

THE RELIGIOUS WORLDVIEW OF ILÉ-IFẸ̀

As constructed and debated in Western discourse, the term *religion* is questionable if not problematic when translated into a Yorùbá context or indeed into any African language. The rough equivalents of *religion* in Yorùbá, *ẹ̀sìn* (that which is worshipped) and *igbàgbọ́* (belief), do not strictly describe what we observe in Yorùbá indigenous religious tradition, which incorporates both spiritual affairs and secular realms. Yorùbá religious ceremonies focus on healing, procreation, human and agricultural fertility, and the quest for long life and wealth. The materiality of the spiritual is an integral part of religion.

What most clearly constitutes religion for the Yorùbá is the address to the supernatural power, whether the *òrìṣà* (gods), the ancestors, or the spirits, for the three blessings of a good life—*ìre owó, ìre ọmọ,* and *ìre àlàáfíà* (wealth, children, and long life). At the center of Yorùbá religion is a concern for a good life on earth that ultimately leads devotees to a good death at the end of time. Even the magical energy *(àṣẹ)* symbolized, for example, in the Ọ̀ọ̀ni's sacred crown *(arè)* is divine, and the Ifẹ̀ people believe that whatever they ask for in its presence will come to pass. The religious actors and actions described above are played out in this world, *ayé*, the central layer of the cosmic sphere, located between heaven *(ọ̀run)* and the underworld *(ilẹ̀)*.

Each of the three layers of the sphere is seen as a separate, autonomous entity, though invisible passageways known only to the gods and spirits connect the three. In Ifá narratives, passage between the three realms is described as a journey, as in "The gods traveled from Ikọ́lé Ọ̀run [the House of Heaven] to Ikọ́lé Ayé [the House of Earth]." Olódùmarè is regarded as king of heaven, the Ọlọ́fin Ọ̀run, a great and mighty king, of whom the earthly king, the Ọlọ́fin Ayé or Ọba Ayé, is but a replica. Ọlọ́run gives an earthly king his *àṣẹ* (sacred power and energy), with which he functions and rules his people. Ifá divination narratives often refer to heaven as the grand calabash *(igbá ńlá)*, a spherical receptacle that harbors the secret of human destiny. The term for "world" *(ayé)* is also used to denote what is called "the grand destiny," or the destiny of humanity as a whole. *Ayé* means both the physical space of the cosmos's middle layer and the life that humans live there. The center of the world is Ilé-Ifẹ̀, which is made up of various sacred places.

Similarly, the world *(ayé)* is anchored by five directional points: front, back, left, right, and center, corresponding to the north, south, west, east, and center ceremonial and ritual spaces in other indigenous religions. In Ifá divination practice, the diviner selects the divining chain (ọ̀pẹ̀lẹ̀) and salutes the ancestors and gods of Ilé-Ifẹ̀; then with the ọ̀pẹ̀lẹ̀ he touches four directional points on the Ifá tray (ọpọ́n Ifá) while reciting the prayer Iwájú ọpọ́n, ẹ̀hìn ọpọ́n, Olùbúlọ́tún-ún, Olùmọ̀ràn lósì, àárín ọpọ́n, ìta ọ̀run (front of Ifá, back of Ifá, right side of Ifá, left side of Ifá, center of Ifá, and center of heaven). With this invocation and directional orientation, the diviner begins his sacred performance.

ÒRÌṢÀ, GODS, AND SPIRITS

The primary players in this complex universe are the òrìṣà (gods). As discussed in the introduction, Yorùbá sources refer to the presence of 401 gods (ọ̀kànlénírínwó òrìṣà) in the universe. However, another tradition refers to the presence of 201 (ọ̀kàn-lélúgba) òrìṣà. These two numbers, when viewed in the context of the religious imagination of the Yorùbá, are not to be taken literally; rather, they suggest the impossibility of counting the deities. As for the final "1" figure, scholars such as Wándé Abímbọ́lá cite it as proof of the inclusivity of Yorùbá religious worldview, which is always willing to add one more deity to the pantheon. This extra deity is most probably the Ọọ̀ni, who is regarded as part of the pantheon and is described as Aláṣẹ, Èkejì Òrìṣà (the Powerful One Whose Power Is Like That of the Deity).[1] A king, though sacred, must seek the protection of the two hundred to four hundred deities to uphold his kingdom.

THE NATURE OF THE ÒRÌṢÀ

In the Yoruba pantheon of deities, the òrìṣà are sometimes grouped by scholars into two categories: those that are intrinsically good and offer immense benefit to their devotees and those that are evil and inflict misery upon their devotees. But such ethical dualism is actually foreign to the nature and character of the òrìṣà, all of whom the Yorùbá see as compassionate, benevolent, and capable of providing the blessings their devotees request of them in rituals and ceremonies. If this were not so, the apparently "evil" òrìṣà such as Èṣù or Ṣọ̀npọ̀nná would not be praised for bestowing the blessings of children on their devotees.[2] At the same time, the òrìṣà are willing to use their power to inflict punishment and to wreak havoc on devotees who violate societal norms. The saying that "two hundred and one gods cannot kill someone who has not offended the gods" is a strong ethical statement about the relationship between punishment and justice in the Yorùbá religious worldview. Ultimately the òrìṣà transcend the dichotomy of good and evil; the Yorùbá believe that the world (ayé) was created in the midst of both (tibi tire l'a dá ilé-ayé).

SACRED SPACE

Ilé-Ifẹ̀ City can be divided into two distinct zones: the palace *(ààfin)* and the outer city or Òde Ifẹ̀. The *ààfin* is located in the center of the city; it is separated from the outer city by a great wall with several gates, the two most important of which are Ẹnu Gbẹ̀du and Ẹnu Ọwá. The gate to the palace precinct, Ẹnu Ọwá (literally, mouth of the Ọba or king), which is the only direct entrance to the king's courtyard, symbolizes the final boundary between the inner and outer city. The two spaces are governed and controlled by sets of chiefs on behalf of the king. The Ọ̀tún Ifẹ̀, eight high chiefs, who are elders elected by the other elders of their particular lineages, govern the affairs of the outer city. Most of them do so from their ceremonial houses *(ilé-oyè)*. Ceremonial homes, like the hogans of the Navajo, double as places of ceremonial activities and places of everyday living, functions that are almost inseparable in Yorùbá culture.[3]

Each high chief takes charge of the quarter *(ọgbọ́n)* under his care, as petty civil cases are brought before him. With the assistance of lower chiefs who serve in his quarter, he adjudicates cases of farm theft (whether theft of animals or the fraudulent seizure of another's property), fighting, accusations of witchcraft, hooliganism, and domestic violence. Cases considered more serious, such as murder and manslaughter, may be referred to the Ọòni's palace. The Òsì Ifẹ̀, the palace chiefs who have responsibility for palace governance, arraign these cases before the Ọòni court.

In both the palace and the Ọ̀tún Ifẹ̀'s places of justice, oath taking ensures that all parties involved speak the truth. Indeed, in rare cases involving serious offenses such as murder, the shrine of Ògún Ladìn in the Ọòni's palace, which consists of a few iron figures and stone blocks, is often used for oath taking, as it is believed that no lie goes unpunished here. Traditionally, iron implements representing Ògún, the quintessential *òrìṣà* and deity of quick justice, were used for oath taking. Today, however, clients before the chief's courts often swear by both the Bible and the Qur'an, and as Islamic sects and evangelical Christian and Pentecostal Charismatic churches make inroads into Ilé-Ifẹ̀'s religious life, traditional morality and ethical precepts face formidable threats from these new religions.

When the Ẹmẹsẹ̀ (the palace servants) took me to see important palace locations and to explain their meaning and functions, they quickly reminded me that the palace is now a place of *prayer*—for good health, wealth, and children—and no longer of curses, as it was before, when people came primarily to seek redress and pronounce curses on those they considered to be evildoers. Littering these shrines are numerous coins and bills that visitors throw as offerings to the god. Undoubtedly, a Christian framework has been superimposed upon an indigenous structure here. Why do the Ẹmẹsẹ̀, custodians of traditions, buy into this new syncretistic theology? They recognize that to keep their clients coming in a modern world dominated and controlled by Christian and Islamic worldviews they must compromise. Confronted by Christian and Muslim accusations that indigenous Ifẹ̀ religion harbors an evil imagination, the people are rapidly changing their perception of the proper role of gods and goddesses in Ilé-Ifẹ̀ City.

ỌJÀ: THE MARKET SPACE

The market *(ọjà)* where the inhabitants of the city buy and sell goods is a significant public space. Three traditional marketplaces—Ọjà Ifẹ̀, Ìta Akọgun, and Ọjà Ayégbajú—are sites not only of secular market activities but also of significant religious meanings and functions. Ajé, goddess of wealth and the market economy, maintains her abode in Ọjà Ifẹ̀. The market calendar indicates when to celebrate the festivals of the gods. Marketing involves both humans and spirits, who mingle freely as both go about their duties. Therefore, market days are auspicious occasions when gods, spirits, and humans are most likely to congregate and to be present for sacrificial and ritual cult activities, as well as for religious and civil activities. Yet the *ọjà* is the most feared public space because the Ifẹ̀—like the rest of the Yorùbá—believe that on market day the newly deceased reveal themselves to their relations as their last rite of passage to the world of the ancestors. Ifẹ̀ Market holds a particular sacredness among the Yorùbá. For example, the eastern Yorùbá group of the Ọ̀wọ̀ tradition believe that upon death the deceased must travel to Ilé-Ifẹ̀ City and thus may pass through Ifẹ̀ Market. Thus, in Ọ̀wọ̀ burial rites, the deceased are admonished, *Ọ̀nà yó r'ufẹ̀ má yà o* (Go on the straight road that leads to Ilé-Ifẹ̀ and don't stray by the wayside).

ILÉ-IFẸ̀ PLACE NAMES

The City of 201 Gods is replete with place names associated with goddesses and gods who cultivate these places and bestow meaning upon them as hierophanies, reminders of sites where their powers were made manifest. Many streets *(ọ̀gbọ́n)* are named for goddesses and gods, such as Ọya, goddess of the whirlwind, and Odùduwà, god-king and founder of the modern ruling dynasty. Lineages as custodians of the traditions of gods and goddesses also bestow their names upon streets and quarters, such as Ìdìta Ilé and Ìdìta Oko, the city and forest homes of Ọbàtálá, god of purity, and Yemòó, his consort. As myth has it, when Ọbàtálá was banished from Ìdìta Ilé, his home place, he moved to Ìdìta Oko to live in the forest.

In one story after another, Ilé-Ifẹ̀'s rivers, groves, outcroppings, hills, and mountains are connected to mythical and legendary figures. Ẹ̀sìnmìrìn River is the site where Mọrèmi sacrificed Olúorogbo, her only son, to save the Ilé-Ifẹ̀ people from perishing at the hands of the invading Ìgbò people.[4] Mọrèmi thus became the savior of the city, and her heroic deeds are still celebrated with great pageantry today. The Ìgbò referred to here must not be confused with the Igbo (Ibo) people of the eastern region of Nigeria; rather, they were probably an invading group from an eastern Yorùbá region, where the term still features in the region's mythic history. For example, in Ilẹ̀-Olúji, Jẹgun Ìgbò was a famous and legendary warrior-king who ruled and was a powerful medicine man.

Ọ̀ṣàrà River marks the abode of a goddess of the same name, whose close relationship with Ọ̀rúnmìlà, god of Ifá divination, unites the devotees of the two deities. Ifá diviners go to the banks of Ọ̀ṣàrà River to begin the annual performance of Ọdún Ifá and the King's New Yam Ceremony. There they mimic the procedure of cultivating yam heaps, symbolizing the tilling and planting of the land and the harvesting of the new yam of which the Ọ̀ọni must first partake. The ceremony indicates the significance of the yam as an elite staple introduced into the Ilé-Ifẹ̀ domestic economy later in history—as opposed to the plantain economy that characterized an earlier Ifẹ̀ era. Ọbá Gẹ̀dẹ̀, Chief of the Plantain, was part of the pre-Odùduwà pantheon. In the ceremony, the river evokes human fertility and the role of Ifá in procuring children to ensure fertility of the fields.

Ifá shrines called òrìgì, conical dirt and cemented mounds on which sacrificial offerings can be laid, are strategically placed outside homes around the city to mark the positions where Ifá or Ọ̀rúnmìlà, god of divination, first established his presence in the city and thus commanded the lineages around it to be devotees of Ifá. To come across an òrìgì is to see the manifestation of Ifá, signifying that members of the compounds and lineages remain ardent devotees of Ifá. These ancient òrìgì are so well regarded that one of them, in the quarter of Mọ̀rẹ̀, whose shrine has been neglected since the residents' conversion to Islam and Christianity, is still remembered in a famous Ifá prayer, Kí awo rere má jẹ́ ní Mọ̀rẹ̀ (May fervent divination never perish in Mọ̀rẹ̀), a supplication for a return to earlier times when the quarter played a central role in Ilé-Ifẹ̀.[5]

SHRINES AND TEMPLES

Shrines and temples are as multiple as the gods are in Ilé-Ifẹ̀. They are primarily the homes of the deities and the sites where they are propitiated. Many gods have simple shrines, some built as the focal points of lineage meeting houses. Major gods, such as Ifá, Ọbàtálá, Olúorogbo, Òrìṣà Akirè, and Odùduwà, occupy temples that are more elaborate. Ifá Temple is the largest in the city.

Because the shrines are the abode of the gods, it is incumbent upon devotees to make them beautiful, just as they would their own houses. The temples of Olúorogbo, Ọbàtálá, and Ìjùgbè contain elaborate murals and drawings. Beyond their aesthetic usefulness, these drawings express the mythic and social meaning of symbols like the snake, snail, dove, and tortoise. In the shrine to Olúorogbo, a scribe

FIGURE 5. The Ifá Temple on Òkè Ìtasè, the sacred hill of Ifá.

who is referred to as Oníwé Ọ̀run (the Holy Scribe/Heavenly Book), beautiful draw-ings depict the god as learned. Shrines display the power of the deity. Their art de-picts women bringing sacrificial offerings and gifts to the gods and sacrificial sym-bols of tortoises, snails, or roosters. The oval tortoise shell, for example, symbolizes the cosmos and the foundation of the world. Similarly, leopards, snakes, and pi-geons symbolize power, evil, and goodness, respectively.

THE SACRED KING

The Ọ̀ọ̀ni, or king, occupies a central place in the mythic history of Ilé-Ifẹ̀ City. In principle, the Ọ̀ọ̀ni, regarded as a descendant and successor of Odùduwà (Àrólé Odùduwà), is a god-king and the spiritual head of the Yorùbá-speaking people. The global explosion of Yorùbá religious culture, especially in the last two decades, has made the incumbent Ọ̀ọ̀ni, Olúbùṣe, a larger-than-life person who wields consid-erable influence in communities the world over, especially in Cuba, Brazil, Trinidad, Jamaica, and the United States.

The king, referred to as Ọlọ́fin Àjàláyé (Divine Ruler of the World), is at the cen-ter of numerous oral narratives in the Ifá corpus. Several ancient events that Ifá nar-rates took place in the king's palace, and just as in the Yorùbá myth of origin, the Ọlọ́fin is portrayed as "god-man." A few years ago, it was common to hear the Ọ̀ọ̀ni referred to as Olúwayé, Ọ̀ọ̀ni Òrìṣà (Lord of the Universe, the Deity King).[6] When I asked one of the Ẹmẹṣẹ̀, the palace servants, why the honorific title of a revered Yorùbá god, Sọ̀npọ̀nná, god of smallpox, had been appropriated for the Ọ̀ọ̀ni, he giggled and remarked, "Ẹ̀yin alákọ̀wé ṣá [Oh, you educated people]! Well, you see, the Ọ̀ọ̀ni is a deity, the last of the òrìṣà." The Ẹmẹṣẹ̀ took the appellation in its lit-eral sense to mean that the Ọ̀ọ̀ni is in charge of the affairs of the world and that in conformity with the Yorùbá myth of origin he is a god on earth. For students of comparative religion, there is no simple explanation of whether the Ọlọ́fin is more god or more human, which is not surprising when we remember that years of New Testament scholarship have never resolved the question in the Synoptic Gospels as to whether Jesus was more divine or human.

That the incumbent Ọ̀ọ̀ni himself is aware of the significance of his status as god and that he has derived political capital from it cannot be denied. Responding to a Jamaican scholar and visitor to Nigeria who once interviewed the Ọ̀ọ̀ni about how he viewed his role in the worldwide expansion of Yorùbá religious traditions, the Ọ̀ọ̀ni answered that he moved with the wind (Atẹ́gùn ni mo ń bá rìn). "Whenever I visit your country [Jamaica] the Jamaicans would say that our Father has come [Bàbá wa ti dé]," the Ọ̀ọ̀ni remarked. The Yorùbá in the New World viewed the Ọ̀ọ̀ni as a god-king, the father of all, and custodian of Yorùbá spiritual tradition.

Several years ago, Ọ̀ọ̀ni Olúbùṣe visited Cuba. He was welcomed by Fidel Cas-tro and especially by Cubans of African descent. Perhaps by coincidence, it rained that day, though it had not rained for months before this visit. President Castro did not miss the opportunity to remark that the Ọ̀ọ̀ni had brought good fortune and that the òrìṣà had brought rain to Havana.[7] In the same vein, revival of the Yorùbá òrìṣà tradition in Trinidad led to major gains for the devotees of Yorùbá tradition. Trinidad instituted an official holiday called Òrìṣà Day. In the United States, pockets of Yorùbá-derived traditions and religious associations are flourishing across the country. The most famous is Ọ̀yọ́túnjí Village in South Carolina, a utopian community created about forty years ago by an African American, Ọba Oseijami Adefunmi I. The village has become a national icon for revitalizing Yorùbá tradition in America. In 1986 all these movements in various parts of the world led to the formation of the Yorùbá Òrìṣà Congress, inaugurated in the city of Ilé-Ifè. The congress is the official forum where scholars and parishioners discuss the status of Yorùbá indigenous religion. These developments around the globe have combined to give Ilé-Ifè City its religious and cultural identity and a prestige unmatched by any other indigenous cities any place in Africa.

KINSHIP, LINEAGE, AND RELIGION

The indigenous social structure of Ifè, under which the aboriginal inhabitants lived, was based on blood relations (mọ̀lẹ́bí). It was made up of lineages whose members regarded themselves as descending from a common ancestor. Each lineage shared a common compound regarded as the ancestral home bequeathed to them through time and without end. Most importantly, however, the power and influence of these lineages were consolidated in myriad myths and rituals of the ancestral deity and in the ceremonial centers: shrines, temples, and lineage halls (àkòdì) that belonged to them. The sacred centers defined the identity of the group. The òrìṣà served "as the nucleus of community among disparate kin groups."[8] Most of the 201 or 401 deities in the Ifè pantheon were lineage deities.

The key kinship groups were connected with national and primordial Ifè deities (òrìṣà afẹ̀wọ̀nrò) and were associated with such deities as Ọbàtálá, Ifá, Ọ̀rànmíyàn, and Ọbamerì. They boasted of large temples, shrines, and territorial space that served as "palaces" of the chief priests who by virtue of their position as heads of the aboriginal groups were referred to as Ọba (kings). Indeed, many titles with the Ọba- prefix indicate high social and religious status in traditional Ilé-Ifè society. In traditional Ilé-Ifè society, myth, ritual, and symbols of the òrìṣà complexes provided the source for kinship groups' social and cultural identity.

As Ilé-Ifè has changed from traditional to modern structures through the intervention of the colonial authority and the new Ifè intelligentsia, Ifè indigenous religions have responded to the changes in different ways. Religious symbols, beliefs, and practices continue to serve as strong markers for kinship groups, despite their conversion to Islam and Christianity. In several cases, the current chief priests bear Muslim and Christian names. Further, the ritual and ceremonial domain has become the arena for dramatizing some of the old conflicts and "unresolved contradictions of the past" embedded in myths of the Yorùbá origin and creation of the world in Ilé-Ifẹ̀.[9]

INITIATION INTO THE CULTS

Membership in religious lineage cults is by birth, and one born into the lineage belongs to it until death. As ọmọ ilé, a child of the "house," one enjoys the rights and privileges of the lineage and its traditions. A newborn baby is initiated into the lineage during his or her naming ceremony. As a young child, he or she watches the elders as they take part in elaborate rituals and festivals of the group. As I saw in the Ọbàtálá Ìdìta house, the children transport the images and the drums of the gods and goddesses from Ìdìta Ilé to Ìdìta Oko. They are responsible for beating the drums and producing the long sticks (ọsán) that members hold during Ìdìta festivals, and they chant in chorus during festivals.

In some instances, outsiders who are deemed qualified are extended the privileges of initiation. Because of the dwindling membership in contemporary Ifẹ̀ cults, most of these cults have become very generous in opening their doors to outsiders, especially to blacks from the Americas. It is not unusual to meet an African American on the streets of New York boasting about being a member of the Ifá or Ọbàtálá group in Ilé-Ifẹ̀, mentioning the date of his initiation and the name of the person who initiated him. One recently told me proudly that he had slept on the same bed with the Àràbà of Ifẹ̀!

There are three stages of initiation into the cult of Ọbàtálá: ògbóni, ọsán, and òru. The ògbóni stage prepares initiates to receive secret knowledge of the tradition that is revealed in the later ọsán and òru stages. Once individuals are fully initiated, they can participate in all the rituals and festivals of the group and are entitled to take one of numerous titles within the cult. The ọsán and òru stages, literarily the afternoon and night initiations, may symbolize the duality that Enrique Florescano has called, in a study of Mesoamerican myth, "the light of day and the darkness of the night, the birth of life and the fatality of death."[10] The initiation carried out in the daytime is softer than the nighttime initiation, which is deeper and more dangerous, intense, and powerful than the daytime ritual. After experiencing both initiations, the devotee is protected from all dangers that may occur at night or during daylight. The ògbóni stage is not to be confused with initiation into the Ògbóni society, a group of elders who, though they no longer have the religious, ritual, and at times political power that they once wielded in traditional Yorùbá society, still exist as a secret cult with religious and ritual functions. Initiation into the Ògbóni society in Ilé-Ifẹ̀ creates a secret inner circle of ritually powerful members within other religious groups.

IFẸ̀ POLITICAL AND RELIGIOUS STRUCTURE

The political and religious structure of Ifẹ̀ is extremely hierarchical. The two sets of traditional political structures that control Ifẹ̀ are the Ọ̀tún Ifẹ̀ ("Right-Hand Chiefs," also called the Àgbà Ifẹ̀, or "Ifẹ̀ Elders") and the Òsì Ifẹ̀, which consists of the seven Mọdéwá or junior palace chiefs. The existence of junior chiefs (Ọmọdé) presumes a hierarchy that includes senior elders who share with the junior chiefs the responsibility for city and palace governance. At the head of this structure is the Ọ̀ọ̀ni himself. The Ọ̀tún Ifẹ̀ are the most senior chiefs and are in charge of the city's affairs, since the king, confined by taboo to the palace, cannot always physically visit to see to the day-to-day affairs of the city. Calling them the Right-Hand Chiefs suggests the prestige and place of honor accorded them in this dual structure. The Ọ̀tún Ifẹ̀ are assigned to the eight quarters into which traditional Ifẹ̀ is divided: Òkèrèwè, Ìlàrẹ́, Ìrẹ́mọ, Ìdìta, Mọ̀rẹ̀, Ìta Akọgun, Ìráyè, and Ìlódè.

Most Ọ̀tún Ifẹ̀ have traditional houses (ilé-oyè) where they live and from which they govern the people of their quarters, just as they have certain shrines assigned to them to protect and propitiate the deities and conduct the festivals in which they play a very significant role. Chief Akọgun, for example, informed me that he plays an active role in the Ọlọ́jọ́, the king's festival and annual propitiation of Ògún, but that he is also one of the custodians of Ọ̀rànmíyàn Shrine, where the deity's staff—one of the historic monuments in the city—is located, not far from his title house. When I asked him what role he played in the civil governance of the city, he remarked that each chief has a god he takes care of and festivals in which he celebrates for the Ifẹ̀ people. The gods in question are national Ifẹ̀ deities whose rituals and ceremonies are incorporated into the town's religious calendar. Unlike the numerous lineage deities that are propitiated by individual lineages and clans, these national gods belong to all Ifẹ̀. The classic examples are Ògún, and Mọrèmi and Ifá, who are celebrated respectively at the Edì Festival and at the Ifá Festival that serves as the King's New Yam Festival (Ẹ̀gbodò Ọ̀ọ̀ni).

The Òsì Ifẹ̀, the second level of chiefly authority, consists mainly of palace chiefs and officials who perform most of their functions in the palace. As a result, they have no need for a title house in town.

A third level of Ifẹ̀ socioreligious structure is the Ìṣòrò (priest-chiefs, i.e., priests who are also chiefs of their lineages), a body that wields considerable ritual and to some extent political power, especially over their own lineages and territorially based clans. In the 1950s, there was confusion about their proper role; consequently, a very spirited debate took place in the city as to whether priests in this third category should command citywide political and civil authority as was the case for chiefs of the first and the second categories. Although Ilé-Ifẹ̀ cultural historians such as Àjàyí Fábùnmi and Chief Lódọkọ̀ Fáṣọgbọ́n argue that the Ìṣòrò constitutes the Òsì Ifẹ̀ and indeed that they supersede the current Òsì Ifẹ̀ in the hierarchical structure,

the then Ọọni Adérẹ̀mí ruled that the Ìṣòrò belonged to an autonomous independent realm and that they were not in charge of civil authority in the city. However,
the debate was more significant than it was initially perceived to be, as it related to
the changing face of religion in Ilé-Ifẹ̀. At a time when increasing modernization
was eroding the authority and rights of the priestly class in the affairs of Ilé-Ifẹ̀, and
when the secular and the sacred realms were increasingly separated, a small but vocal educated elite were very much interested in bringing back the power and honor
of the religious class whose diminishing fortune in civil society intensified with the
increasing evangelization and Islamization of the City of 201 Gods.

PRIEST-CHIEFS AND RELIGIOUS ELITES

According to the Ifẹ̀ local historian and religious activist Chief Fáṣọgbọ́n, originally the traditional Ifẹ̀ priest-chiefs (the Ìṣòrò) had wielded enormous political,
religious, and judicial authority, and the religious and political lives of Ifẹ̀ people
had been inseparable. This state of affairs came to an abrupt end at the turn of the
twentieth century when the British colonial government introduced into the region a system of indirect rule, appointed local elites of less noble birth to manage
the affairs of the newly acquired territories, and exalted the Ọọni into a position
of authority without much political and economic dominance over his own people.
Gradually the kingship began to exercise the limited authority that had traditionally been left to the palace chiefs, who were normally present in the palace as aides
to the Ọọni.

Chief Fáṣọgbọ́n, the most vocal upholder of the status of Ìṣòrò priest-chiefs,
maintained that the numerous taboos kept by the Ìṣòrò threatened the authority
of British rule and made implementing the indirect rule system difficult. Unlike
the palace chiefs, who were duty-bound to remove their caps and to bow before
the Ọọni, the many Ìṣòrò were forbidden to remove the symbol of their priestly
and kingship authority—their coronets—before the Ọọni. On multiple occasions
during my field research, an Ìṣòrò priest described his lineage *oríkì* as *Ọmọ aṣọrò,
kí Ọọni ró gégé* (One who performs rituals while the Ọọni stands at attention!), a
significant reference to the "momentary" submissiveness of the Ọọni, the god-king,
in the midst of an important ritual that an Ìṣòrò priest-chief held on his behalf.
This indicates the significance of power sharing, especially in critical ritual situations. Unlike the palace chiefs, who had the privilege of education in the mission
and public schools, the Ìṣòrò chiefs seldom had that privilege—they were largely
illiterate.

In April 1951, through the initiative of Chief Fáṣọgbọ́n, an umbrella association
of elite Ifẹ̀ priests, Ẹgbẹ́ Ìsowọ́pọ̀ Ìjòyè Ẹ̀sìndálẹ̀ Ilé-Ifẹ̀ (Council of the Traditional
Priests of Ilé-Ifẹ̀), popularly known as the Ìṣòrò, was formed. Fáṣọgbọ́n reported
that the Ọọni was made patron and constitutional head of the council. A letter was

sent to the Ọ̀ọ̀ni on April 25, 1951, informing him of a previous letter, dated April 12, 1951, in which the association had pleaded with the Ifẹ̀ Native Authority to consider the possibility of granting their members "the restoration of their lost seats, and recognitions in the governmental functions of Ilé-Ifẹ̀ like their forbears." Fáṣọgbọ́n argued that the Ìṣòrò priest-chiefs were the second branch of the town's executive body, the Òsì Ifẹ̀, and not the Mọdéwá, the palace chiefs that then currently assumed this role. Ọ̀ọ̀ni Adérẹ̀mí understandably turned down this request and indeed did not mince words in chastising Fáṣọgbọ́n for bringing such a matter before him. The above communication highlights the long-term struggle of the Ìṣòrò priests in contemporary Ilé-Ifẹ̀. A modern nation has evolved in which the Ìṣòrò have increasingly lost their secular power and sacred authority over the affairs of their people, limiting their roles to religious and ritual affairs. By the year 2000, the sacred authority was to be further challenged and curtailed by new forms of religious authority wielded by Muslims and Christians. The last two chapters of the work will explore how modern religion, especially Pentecostal evangelical Christianity, is involved in open battle with òrìṣà tradition in the city.

PRIESTS AND DIVINERS

It is very difficult to classify the numerous guardians of the Ilé-Ifẹ̀ sacred cosmos into strict categories because their functions and roles cut across social and religious boundaries. Most priests not only perform religious and ceremonial functions but also wield considerable political power in their cults. Ifá priests, the most visible in the city, derive their knowledge from the body of Ifá divination orature, which they learn from their mentor priests and pass on to their apprentices. Ifá priests are not shamans, who are possession priests in the classical sense of the term and who gain their knowledge through supernatural power; rather, they are trained in the use of the Ifá technology of the ọ̀pẹ̀lẹ̀, which they cast to determine answers to clients' queries. Ifá is an instrumental form of geomancy and requires deep knowledge of odù divination. Anthropologists have tried to distinguish between the priests of classical shamanism and the nonpossession priests of the Ifá priesthood.[11] The most notable priests are also heads of their lineages and clans (priest-chiefs). Those of the largest lineages are Ọba (kings) in their own right and bear titles with the Ọba- prefix, such as Ọbaléṣùn, Ọbalálẹ̀, Ọbadìo, Ọbaláṣẹ̀, or Ọbaléjùgbẹ̀, but they are still subject to the authority of the Ọ̀ọ̀ni, the de facto king of kings. Each lineage priest-chief presides over the festivals of his own lineage, woven into an elaborate ceremonial calendar that governs the entire year.

The diviners (Babaláwo) are the most visible class of ritual leaders in Ilé-Ifẹ̀. As a powerful elite, they control the course of events pertaining to ritual ceremony. The guild of diviners contains sixteen principal diviners, called Àwọ̀nì (the Ọ̀ọ̀ni's diviners). The first of these sixteen principal priests is the Àràbà, the head, and an Ọba (king) in his own right. With three others, the Àgbọngbọ̀n, Mẹ̀gbọ́n, and Tẹ̀dímọ́lẹ̀, they constitute the four most senior members, and they may embody the entire guild, according to the Ifá saying, *T'ẹ́ẹ bá rí Àràbà, ẹ rí awo, T'ẹ́ẹ bá rí Àg-bọngbọ̀n, na, ẹ rí awo, T'ẹ́ẹ bá rí Mẹ̀gbọ́n, ẹ rí awo, T'ẹ́ẹ bá rí Tẹ̀dímọ́lẹ̀, Awo ti pé* (Once you see in the assembly these principal diviners, the Àràbà, Àgbọngbọ̀n, Mẹ̀g-bọ́n, and Tẹ̀dímọ́lẹ̀, Ifá ceremonials can commence!). This indicates that the presence of any of these four at any important assembly signifies the proper seating of diviners in any ritual ceremony. Each of the major Ilé-Ifẹ̀ quarters is under the guardianship of a principal Ifá priest (Àwọnì) who takes charge of its public and religious affairs on behalf of the king, especially with regard to ritual sacrifice, divination performance, and matters of the general welfare that require divine intervention.

Awo (secrecy) is at the core of divination practice. Ifá divination entails elaborate training and initiation rituals. Learning the sacred knowledge of Ifá is a long process in which one begins with initiation as a novice and gradually qualifies for initiation into the highest order, Awo Olódù. These diviners have entered the sacred forest of Ifá and performed the necessary rites to reveal Ifá's deepest secret. Diviners who remain outside the Awo Olódù circle are ordinary Ifá priests (Babaláwo).

PRAYER, INVOCATION, AND THE POWER OF WITCHES

In his published monograph *Àyajọ́, Ohùn Ẹnu Ifẹ̀* (The Oral Tradition of the Ifẹ̀ People), the late Chief Fábùnmi, the local historian of Ifẹ̀, underscored the religious and social importance of oral poetic narrative that conveys powerful meaning and effect. According to Fábùnmi, sacred incantations and curses affect actions and events.

Diviners, medicine men and women, and *òrìṣà* priests begin the day by invoking the deity in their charge, whether that deity is situated in a shrine, a temple, or the priest's home. The morning session begins with a greeting to the deity and is followed by the recitation of *oríkì* (poetry in praise of the deity). A priest may commend the activities of the day to the deity and pray that he may act properly and be prosperous that day; he will also pray that the Ọòni in the palace may live long and conquer all his enemies. The powerful invocatory language is a fusion of prayer, curses, praise for the gods, and gentle requests for help. I recorded a typical morning invocation session in Bàbá Mòrú's house, on December 24, 1989.

Bàbá Awóyẹlé Mòrú, an uncle of my research assistant, Kẹ́hìndé Elújùlọ, was a medicine man (Olóògùn) who lived close to St. Philip's Vicarage, Ayétòrò. Though he was not regarded as an Awo Olódù, he was very popular and knowledgeable in Ifá and knew how to perform the sixteen cowries divination *(awo Ẹẹ̀rìndínlógún)*. I quote a compelling passage from his early morning invocation:

Àfọṣẹ! Take charge!
Ìránṣẹ́ [messenger]! You take charge!
Èpè [curse]! Take charge!
Ẹ̀fún is the child of Ìdẹ́
Èdì is the child of Òjé!
Ègún is the name of the House of Death.
Èdì is the *harm* of the house.
The front of the house is the name we call *àpèta*.
Ẹ̀báṅtọ́lá, gatekeeper of heaven, our time on earth is not yet near.
Secure a heavy lock on the door of heaven!
Ìdó is the gatekeeper of heaven!
Hardly a day goes by that he does not speak of beheading people.
Anyone who says anything evil about us
Should talk about beheading to the people of heaven and earth.
Our mothers who own the world, we plead for mercy.
Ọrúnmìlà! Àjànà! Take charge of today!
Do not let us lack for anything.
Do not let us be wasted.
Do not let us end today empty-handed.
Because Ojúoró never suffers from lack of water,
May we never suffer before we receive our daily meal,
May we never suffer or thirst!
Ọrúnmìlà! Àjànà! Take charge today!
Ajíkore! Let us encounter bounteous blessings today:
The blessings of money,
The blessings of longevity, prosperity, and peace of mind,
Are what we look for today.

In this invocation, the medicine man calls on divine forces governing the universe to act on his behalf. He cites several mechanisms and tools of his trade, pleading that they be under his command that day. Supernatural forces and agencies, such as witches, are praised and charged with working effectively. The medicine man personifies evil forces such as loss, death, paralysis, and sickness and invokes them in order to appease them. He asks that all these forces be kept under his control through his medicinal and magical power. Nevertheless, they represent a double-edged sword, for he also asks them to act on his behalf to harm those who go against his clients.

The reality of death is quite apparent in these invocations. The medicine man appeals to the gatekeeper of heaven, pleading that his clients need more time to live on earth: they should not be forced by their enemies to return to heaven without fulfilling their mission on earth. The gatekeeper, described as a strong man who speaks of death by beheading or suicide, is enjoined to secure such a heavy lock on the gate of heaven that even he is unable to break it.

Bàbá Mòrú's invocation ends with prayers to his principal deity, Ọrúnmìlà, for the primary blessings of money, children, and long life in which to enjoy one's prosperity on earth. Bàbá Mòrú asked for my name and prayed for me. The medicine man seems to have strong confidence in his ability to manipulate, cajole, and plead with supernatural forces. He often describes the supernatural in metaphors of common natural phenomena. Once the invocation is made, he is ready to begin the day, attending to clients with various forms of complaints such as infertility or manipulation by witchcraft.

In my conversation with him after this prayer session, Bàbá Mòrú focused on a category of supernatural agent often called *àjẹ́*, translated as "witches" in Western scholarship, for lack of a better term. He explained that Westerners, because they are unable to understand this phenomenon, see *àjẹ́* as imaginary beings. However, the Yorùbá believe that they exist and that their presence is a regular occurrence. *Àjẹ́* are generally women who possess innate and extraordinarily dangerous powers and who may form their own secret society (Ẹgbẹ́ Ẹléyẹ) that attempts to control various public and private matters, often in ways that conflict with other individual or group interests. Bàbá Mòrú may have been addressing them when in his invocation he appealed to Àwọn Ìyá (our mothers).

During my second visit to the Bàbá Mòrú's house, I met a woman in her sixties in the doorway coming out of the house. I greeted her, as was the custom in Ilé-Ifẹ̀ tradition, but she did not respond. As I entered the house and sat down, Bàbá Mòrú and I had the following conversation:

> *Bàbá Mòrú:* O mọ̀ ọ́n rìn—you have come at the right time! You had asked about *àjẹ́* (witches) yesterday?
>
> *Olúpọ̀nà:* Yes, Bàbá.
>
> *Bàbá Mòrú:* Did you meet a woman coming down the stairs?
>
> *Olúpọ̀nà:* Yes.
>
> *Bàbá Mòrú:* I am sure she did not greet you. She is one of them.
>
> *Olúpọ̀nà:* But I thought witches are invisible, Bàbá?
>
> *Bàbá Mòrú:* Yes, they are, but we [Bàbá Mòrú and the *àjẹ́*] maintain a very close relationship. This particular woman came to plead with me that I release her wings, which I took yesterday because she will not leave my clients alone. I informed her that unless she releases the soul of my client, whom she wanted to devour, I would not release her wings.[12]

Bàbá Mòrú claimed that medicine men could cure problems caused by the machinations and the power of witches *(Olóògùn ló lè ṣe ọkọ àjẹ́)* and that they worked closely together to ensure equilibrium on earth. He then informed me, "As medicine men, we pray for the ransom of the souls of our clients who are threatened by witches."

Bàbá Mòrú's prayers show the intricate relationship between attributions of benevolence and malevolence in describing supernatural entities. In one sense, there is no intrinsic separation between good and evil. For example, *èpè* (curses) can be employed to fight or to harm a perceived enemy. Deities can be entreated to harm someone whom the petitioner perceives to have wronged him or her. Benevolence and malevolence then become a matter of perspective.

Many scholars comment on the tone of prayers in indigenous religions that seem to "force" supernatural beings to act on their behalf.[13] Oyèékàn Owómóyèlá, a Yorùbá scholar, characterizes prayer as either compulsive or persuasive.[14] To some extent, the priest and devotees are convinced of the appropriateness of their prayer utterances and believe that their requests will be fulfilled by the *òrìṣà*. That conviction is based on a basic principle in Yorùbá cosmology—exchange and reciprocity.

The supernatural realm is governed by a principle similar to the one governing human social relations in the natural world. The gods are at the service of humans, and in return, humans adore, propitiate, and feed the gods. As Trudy Griffin-Pierce remarked about Navajo spirituality, "The language of the prayers expresses reciprocity rather than compulsion. There is a morality of reciprocity expressing the solidarity of interconnected individuals and groups."[15] A Yorùbá proverb demonstrates this principle: *Òrìṣà tí a ké ké tí kò gbó ìké, inú igbó níí gbé* (A deity who is continuously propitiated but fails to return the gesture is thrown into the bush).[16] Devotees' pleas make supernatural beings respond more effectively. The Yorùbá are encouraged to bestow gifts and honor on their deity in return for the ample benefits they receive. The names of Ifè people, such as Òrìṣàkúàdé (the deity brings honor to us), Ifátúnmiṣe (Ifá remakes me), and Ògúnfúnmiṣe (Ògún enables me to achieve greatness), signify the reciprocal relationship to a deity.

A SACRED PEOPLE

Although the history of religion acknowledges and emphasizes the significance of sacred place and time, the phenomenon of a collective sacred people is not common. It is intriguing when a group of people—by the virtue of their location in a sacred city—is set apart from other ethnic groups and given inviolable status. As is evident in historical texts from ancient times, the imagination of the Yorùbá people affirms that Ifè indigenes (often called Onúfè, the people of Ifè) share in the sacredness of the city they inhabit. No matter where they have lived, Ifè indigenes have been given honored status at any gathering, especially gatherings related to ritual or war. Like the biblical Israelites, Ifè indigenes also consider themselves to constitute what Jacob Neusner called "a supernatural community."[17] The popular saying *A kì í f'ọmọ ọrè, b'ọrè* (We do not offer as sacrifice a child of the lineage of Ọrè) describes the taboo that forbade the indigenes of Ifè to be sacrificed to any deity anywhere. Usually, outsiders believed to be sent by the gods to the city were captured and offered as sacrifice.

Evidence of the Ifè as a sacred people can be seen as far away as Ọwò, in the eastern Yorùbá region, at Igbó Lájàá (Lájàá Grove), where archaeological excavations (by Ekpo Eyo and Rowland Abíódún) uncovered remnants of Ifè tradition. During the Igogo Festival of the Olówò and the townspeople, one of the ritual songs warns strangers to depart from the city but exempts Ifè citizens: *Ó mò ón mú omo olufè sebo, Àhòrò Ifè, Ifè méèrè o* (It is forbidden to offer an Ifè indigene for sacrifice).[18] Tradition has it that once, when a "stranger" on his way to the sacrificial place was captured for the annual festival to honor Òròsèn, the victim, after declaring that he was an Ifè indigene, was instantly released by his captors. The Òwò people claim the event generated a song to remind them that Ifè indigenes are sacred and thus taboo as offerings for sacrifice.

RITUAL AND THE FESTIVAL CYCLE

The last day of the ritual and festival cycle of Ilé-Ifè's 201 gods and goddesses is called Enúkòwò. On that day, no deity is propitiated. The Ifá Festival begins its next cycle on the day after Enúkòwò, in the Ìlódè Quarter. The Orè Festival begins in the seventh month of the year, when the rains begin to be heavy. Although a minor deity compared to Ògún, Ifá, and Obàtálá, Orè is nevertheless powerful and at times symbolically represents the totality of Ifè gods and goddesses. The Orè Festival signifies the start of the Ilé-Ifè ritual and festival cycle. It is followed by a series of festivals at five-day intervals (Ìgun Oròórún). Among the minor festivals that fall into this category are those of Ògìyán, Ekùn, Efòn, and Olúwòó, which are connected to the lineages and agricultural life of the people. The only times when lineage members are permitted by their gods and ancestors to eat new yams is after these ceremonies. The Olúwòó Festival ends the Ìgun Oròórún cycle.

In the Olúwòó Festival, women play important roles. Wives married to the lineage are responsible for providing the sacrificial offering, a ram for propitiating the ancestors of their husbands, at the family's ancestral shrine. This is seen as the wives' offering of thanks for the protection the lineage deity provides for them and their children. As the women pick up their drums and go from house to house around the compound, they sing the praise of their husband's lineage, in which they have prospered and given birth to their children. At the end of Olúwòó, the announcement of the grand festival of Ifá is made.

MUSIC, DRUM, AND DANCE

Music is essential to Ilé-Ifè rituals. The music and lyrics of songs accompanied by drums and gongs constitute a central element of worship. Responding to the music, devotees perform the appropriate dances in honor of the gods. Each lineage *òrìsà* has its own songs, as well as its own instrument: Ifá claims the wooden staff or baton; Obàtálá, the *ewó*, or iron gong; Odùduwà, the drums.

The *òṣìrìgì,* or royal music and drum assemblage, is ranked highest in Ifẹ̀ ritual performance. Because it belongs to the Ọ̀ọ̀ni, any appearance by *òṣìrìgì* drummers at a festival, whether for Ifá, Ọbàtálá, or Ògún, indicates that the ceremony has royal significance and that the Ọ̀ọ̀ni has a major role to play in it. Two instances in which the *òṣìrìgì* provides such visibility to lineage festivals are the Ọbàtálá and Ifá divination and festivals. In the former, as the Ìdìta lineage members and devotees of Ọbàtálá return in silence from their pilgrimage to the sacred forest, where they went to pluck the sacred leaves for their god and goddess, the *òṣìrìgì* drummers meet them on their way to Ìdìta Ilé (their home temple), and the devotees, breaking their silence by singing and chanting, dance joyously to the music of the *òṣìrìgì.* Some Ọbàtálá devotees, especially women, remain at home and stand in front of their houses shouting, *Káàbọ̀, Ọba!* (Welcome, oh king) to welcome the Ọbaléṣùn, the chief priest of Ọbàtálá, who leads the procession as he passes by. It is as if the Ọ̀ọ̀ni's *òṣìrìgì* drum gives the procession the status of royalty. In addition, on the morning of the Ifá Festival, the *òṣìrìgì* drummers are in the house of the Àràbà to greet him. The song and music speak favorably about Ifá's status and significance in Ilé-Ifẹ̀ and his importance to the sacred kingship. In both instances, the *òṣìrìgì* invoke the kingship status of the Ọbaléṣùn and Ọba Àràbà in the two lineage traditions of Ọbàtálá and Ifá respectively, though the *òṣìrìgì* actually belongs to the Ọ̀ọ̀ni, the king of kings.

WOMEN AND GENDER RELATIONS

The mythic world of Ifẹ̀ features narratives of numerous goddesses, portrayed variously as wives, mothers, concubines, cultural idols, entrepreneurs, and daughters. Virtually all Ilé-Ifẹ̀ festivals and rituals assign important roles to women. First in the Ilé-Ifẹ̀ festival calendar is the festival of Ọ̀ṣàrà, the goddess often referred to as the consort or confidant of Ọ̀rúnmìlà. She is a powerful goddess whose importance in Ifẹ̀ social and ritual cycles centers on the place of motherhood in Ifẹ̀ gender ideology. One Ifá narrative describes the elevation of Ọ̀ṣàrà to a position of honor. Olókun, goddess of the ocean, and Ọ̀ṣàrà, goddess of the river, were married to the Ọlọ́fin, the king of Ilé-Ifẹ̀. The goddess Olókun was a wealthy and influential woman in the palace and the city.

One year, to celebrate Olókun's annual festival, King Ọlọ́fin invited all the kings to visit and rejoice with him. It happened that the children of Ọ̀ṣàrà quickly devoured all the food prepared for the celebration, leaving little for the honored guests. This greed angered the childless Olókun, who started cursing Ọ̀ṣàrà and her children for such rude behavior. Accusations escalated, leading to open confrontation between the co-wives. Both women promised to quarrel in public after the guests were gone, each boasting that she was greater than the other. Ọ̀ṣàrà, mother of many children, knew to consult her diviner for advice before the showdown. Ifá advised her to prepare plenty of bean cake, to give the bean cake to her children and their

FIGURE 6. Chief Èrí, the priestess of Mọrèmi.

FIGURE 7. Ìyálórìṣà on her way to the palace during the Ọbàtálá Festival.

playmates, and to buy bundles of white cloth. When the appointed day arrived, Ọ̀ṣàrà dressed her children and all their playmates in white wrappers, fed them, and danced with them from her place to the public arena and the palace, showing off her many children and their playmates: "Ọ̀ṣàrà has arrived with the children. The One with many children commands the world" (Ọlọ́mọ, ló layé o, Ọ̀ṣàrà, mà ti kọ́mọ dé o). Olókun, who had adorned herself with stunning garments, beads, and symbols of her affluence and wealth, found that her entourage was outnumbered. The children stole the show. Disgraced, she disappeared from the scene and thus surrendered to her co-wife. Ọ̀ṣàrà, proud Mother-Goddess, was hailed as the greater person. In Ilé-Ifẹ̀ society, the Ọ̀ṣàrà Festival song explicitly indicates the value attached to having many children.

The myth demonstrates that motherhood is an important ideological concept in Ifẹ̀ social and gender relations. It overrides spousal relations because children provide continuity in lineage and clan descent. Children are seen as economic and social capital, essential for honor, prestige, and influence. Wives who bear many children reap greater dividends in a patriarchal system. Celebrating motherhood and featuring a Mother's Day of Ifẹ̀, the festival of Ọ̀ṣàrà is regarded as a national festival.

Although Ilé-Ifẹ̀ has a preponderance of male priests, some female officiates perform similar functions to those performed by men. In the Edì Festival of Mọrèmi, Èrí, a priestess, assumes Mọrèmi's persona and reenacts her role in saving the people of Ifẹ̀. Ọbàtálá, too, has a counterpart in female priests, such as Ìyálájé, a priestess of the marketplace, or Ìyálórìṣà, a priestess of Yemòó, whom I met sitting in her domain outside Ọbàtálá Temple. Many of the 201 deities in the Ifẹ̀ pantheon are female; some are as famous, if not more so, than their male counterparts. Mọrèmi, who saved Ilé-Ifẹ̀ from Ìgbò marauders through her redemptive suffering by sacrificing her only son, Olúorogbo, enjoined the Ifẹ̀ people to her cult. Enshrined in Ọbàtálá Temple, Yemòó, the wife of Ọbàtálá, whose stone image appears in many myths, plays a central role in the Ọbàtálá ceremony.

As a theoretical concept in Ifẹ̀ religion, gender is quite flexible and is not nearly as fixed as it is in Western ideology. For example, a major part of the Ọbàtálá ceremony is the procession of Yemòó to the Ọọ̀ni's palace, bearing gifts of ẹ̀rọ̀ (medicinal water) under her white robes. When I first observed the festival during my research, Yemòó's part was played by Ìyálorìṣà, the female priest. On subsequent years, Yemòó was represented by a male priest dressed as a woman. In general, while gender and sexual division of male and female are basic to the Yorùbá and Ifẹ̀ thought system, many roles in ritual contexts may be assumed by either sex.

PART TWO

4

Myth and Ritual of Sacred Kingship

The Ọlọ́jọ́ Festival of Ògún

The Ọlọ́jọ́ Festival, a complex spectacle and ritual, provides a significant point of entry for understanding ancient Yorùbá myth, history, beliefs, and ceremonial symbols of Ilé-Ifẹ̀. The spectacle captures vividly the religious, social, and cultural core values of this most sacred city of the Yorùbá. It renews the people's belief in the concept of sacred kingship and their understanding of the Ilé-Ifẹ̀ cosmos, where kingship is paramount in the form of the Ọọ̀ni, the god-king who rules Ilé-Ifẹ̀ much as Ajé rules, to a lesser extent, as the goddess of wealth and market economy. It also celebrates wealth and fecundity, political power, and the ethos of war. Significantly, from a phenomenological perspective, the Ọlọ́jọ́ Festival sustains the ritual process the Ifẹ̀ people use to assuage Ògún, Ifẹ̀ hero and quintessential Yorùbá deity of iron and war.

The core narratives of Ọlọ́jọ́ embody the ideology and rituals of Ifẹ̀ kingship through the persona of the deity of war, Ògún, and Ọ̀rànmíyàn, Ifẹ̀ cultural hero, warrior, and king in his own right. All Yorùbá deities are constructed within the Ilé-Ifẹ̀ social order and sacred space. Any attempt to interpret this complex festival using a single approach fails to account for the diverse elements that subtly link the subtexts with the central narratives. In this chapter, I examine the Ọlọ́jọ́ Festival as a narrative of the life of the city, its universe, its social calendar, and its inhabitants. Primarily, Ọlọ́jọ́ serves as a medium of communication by which various segments of society are represented mythologically. It provides a complex framework in which Ifẹ̀ myth and history are reenacted in rituals of renewal and restoration. Within the ceremony, the people of Ilé-Ifẹ̀ attempt to come to terms with social, political, and cultural issues that are at the core of their existence as a culture: myth, history, war, violence, gender, power, kinship, spirituality, and medicine, as well as many gods and spirits in the sacred world. At the center of Ọlọ́jọ́ resides the sacred king, the Ọ̀ọ̀ni, who appropriates Ògún's festival not only as an occasion for the renewal of his own kingship but also as a vehicle for his people's expressions of religious sentiments and devotion. While ritual performances mirror certain ideals of the society they represent, they also depict social contradictions, thereby surreptitiously challenging the social norms that underpin the society. It is indeed a drama of the cosmos *(ayé)*, understood in the Ifẹ̀ worldview as a vastly sophisticated system whereby the forces of good and evil compete to undo each other, much as in the Chinese system of yin and yang. Nothing interprets the divine order of Ifẹ̀ better than the spectacular Ọlọ́jọ́ ritual.

MYTH AND HISTORICAL BACKGROUND

The Ifẹ̀ historian Chief Fáṣọgbọ́n suggests that, historically, Ọlọ́jọ́ commemorates the place of Ògún as a warrior, including his abduction from the throne of Ilé-Ifẹ̀, where he once ruled as Ọ̀ọ̀ni. According to Fáṣọgbọ́n, Ògún's public shrine at Òkè-Mògún in the center of Ilé-Ifẹ̀ designates the place where Ògún descended into the underworld, and this is where he is worshipped. Fáṣọgbọ́n claims that Ọlọ́jọ́ is equally a tribute to Ọ̀rànmíyàn, another warrior, cultural hero, and Ọ̀ọ̀ni, believed to be the direct son of Odùduwà. Although the relationship between the three mythic figures is ambiguous, there are clearly defined beliefs and practices in Ilé-Ifẹ̀ related to them. This chapter will examine the sacred narratives from which the Ilé-Ifẹ̀ people say they derive their knowledge of Ògún and Ọ̀rànmíyàn as spiritual forces and cultural heroes.

The all-powerful Ògún, the quintessential *òrìṣà* or deity, is the focus of the Ọlọ́jọ́ Festival. At the time of creation, Ògún led the other *òrìṣà* from heaven (Ikọ́lé Ọ̀run) to earth (Ikọ́lé Ayé). With his cutlass, he cleared a way for these other gods to walk to the newly created world. Because he cleared the path, Ògún is often called Ọsìn Imọlẹ̀ or Leader of the Gods. As the patron god of iron and steel manufacturers associated with implements of ironwork as well as with farming, hunting, and war, Ògún is regarded as the deity of modern civilization and technological innovation. His leadership and warrior-like persona explain why he is associated with the monarchy, though he is also regarded as one of the Ọ̀ọ̀ni who reigned in Ilé-Ifẹ̀.

Ọ̀rànmíyàn, who, unlike Ògún, is not a universal Yorùbá deity, is also credited with exploits of war. He expanded the Ilé-Ifẹ̀ Kingdom as far east as the kingdom of Benin, where the present ruling monarchy is traced to him.[1] Ọ̀rànmíyàn founded the ancient Ọ̀yọ́ Empire,[2] which ultimately surpassed the medieval Ifẹ̀ civilization, giving birth to modern Yorùbá civilization and culture in West Africa and in the New World.

The myths of Ògún and Ọ̀rànmíyàn situate these two cultural heroes within the context of Ọlọ́jọ́. Unlike the cosmological myth of the Yorùbá world, recounted earlier in this book, the culture-hero myths of Ọ̀ rànmíyàn and Ògún trace human events establishing Yorùbá civilization.

Ògún and Ọ̀ rànmíyàn

Drawing upon an Ifá divination text, Babaláwo Ifátóògùn attributes the power and legitimacy of Ògún to three principal deities in the Yorùbá pantheon.[3] According to this text, heaven's divinities—Ògún, the god of war; Ifá, also called Ọ̀ rúnmílá, the god of divination; and Ọbàtálá, creator and most senior god—decided to come to the world to live. Individually, they went to Olódùmarè, the Supreme God, to inform him about their plans. Ògún was the first to see Olódùmarè. Olódùmarè asked Ògún what he would like to do on earth. Ògún responded that he would be a consultant to men and women who would become traders or "those who work for profit" *(iṣẹ́ ajé)* and prosper thereafter. Olódùmarè blessed Ògún and, according to the Ifá text, stated that he "would be as rich as 'the people of Ayoyaya,' people-who-have-abundance-to-eat[,] the prosperous ones of Benin and the ones of the city of Ìrálè, the white people."[4] He then gave Ògún leave to depart to the world.

Next, Olódùmarè asked Ọbàtálá what he would like to do when he arrived on earth. Ọbàtálá answered that those traders, the men and women that Ògún mentioned, would be created by Ọbàtálá, the fashioning god. Olódùmarè handed Ọbàtálá the instruments, *irin ọnà*, for fashioning humans and objects, and told Ọbàtálá to proceed to the world. There Ọbàtálá used the *irin ọnà* to design *(yá ọnà)* and to mold *(mọ)* human beings.

Ọ̀ rúnmílá (Ifá) was the third god to visit Olódùmarè. When Olódùmarè asked him about his intentions upon reaching the world, Ọ̀ rúnmílá said that the men and women Ògún turned into wealthy people through trade and the men and women Ọbàtálá created should first consult with him about how to use their money wisely and how to enjoy their prosperity on earth. Olódùmarè declared that it was good and that Ọ̀ rúnmílá would prosper on earth. The three deities, Ògún, Ọbàtálá, and Ifá, then shook hands and agreed that since Ògún owned a cutlass he should lead the way to clear a path to the mundane world *(ayé)*. The narrator, Babaláwo Ifátóògùn, concluded, "Ògún leads in everything. He 'owns' and controls smithing and hunting." Whatever profession or job *(iṣẹ́ ajé)* one takes, "Ògún is the architect of it, even any form of travel."

This is an important myth, a rare text in the Ifá corpus, because it gives another deity, Ògún, precedence over Ọ̀ rúnmílá, both in visiting Olódùmarè and in clearing the path to earth. Ifá's hegemonic claim is common in Ifá divination texts. That this story places Ògún as the first of the three principal deities testifies to his strength and leadership. Ògún is considered a "hot" deity among the Yoruba and is described as having a "hot" temper.[5] Through his technological knowledge and control of iron and steel, he is the deity most essential to human life on earth. Ògún's relationship to wealth, or *ajé,* is of particular interest to *òrìṣà* devotees because Ajé, defined as a goddess, is an important figure in the Ọlọ́jọ́ celebration. The narrative introduces the relationship between Ògún and Ajé, a relationship that has been neglected in Yorùbá studies. The myth also suggests that Ọbàtálá's ability to fashion the human form will depend on Ògún's working tools. This relationship will be the subject of chapter 5. The narrative provides the larger context within which to examine the activities and pivotal roles of Ọlọ́jọ́ mythic figures described in the worship of Ògún.

Ọ̀rànmíyàn is a minor focus of the Ọlọ́jọ́ Festival. According to a widely believed story, Odùduwà, founder of the Yorùbá, was the father of Ògún. Ògún went on one of his war expeditions, returning with booty, slaves, money, and the property of the vanquished. All these he handed over to Odùduwà, except for a beautiful woman named Òlóló, whom he kept for himself. Odùduwà's servants mentioned the woman whom Ògún kept, and Odùduwà sent for her. When Odùduwà saw her, he liked her and took her from Ògún. Ògún informed Odùduwà that he (Ògún) had already had intercourse with the woman, which would make it an abomination for his father to take her as a wife. But this information failed to dissuade Odùduwà from taking the woman from Ògún. The woman became pregnant and bore a male child with red and white spotted skin, pigmentation representing the grotesque characteristics of both Ògún and Odùduwà. When Ògún saw the infant, he called it Ọ̀rànmíyàn, translated as "my words are true" or "an abomination." Because of this myth, the people of Ilé-Ifẹ̀ believe that Ọ̀rànmíyàn's red and white pigmentation derives from Ògún and Odùduwà, the two men who had intercourse with Ọ̀rànmíyàn's mother.[6]

This story is often narrated to provide an etiologic explanation for the Lókolóko, the bodyguards of the king, who cover their bodies in white and red spots during the Ọlọ́jọ́ Festival. According to Ilé-Ifẹ̀, the Lókolóko represent Ọ̀rànmíyàn, the great warrior who assisted and protected Odùduwà, the king, in defending the territory of Ifẹ̀. Underpinning this explanation is the desire to provide a strong father-son link between Odùduwà and Ọ̀rànmíyàn as well as between Ògún and Ọ̀rànmíyàn. The two war heroes are the builders of the Yorùbá kingdom of Ilé-Ifẹ̀ that the Ọlọ́jọ́ Festival represents.

Ògún: The One and the Many

Ògún, the central focus of Ọlọ́jọ́, is often called Ògún Ẹ̀rẹ́jà, Ògún of the Market, or Ògúnlade, Ògún the Crowned One, epithets that portray him as central to sacred kingship and to the market economy. Ọlọ́jọ́ propitiates Ògún in all his multiple manifestations. Perhaps the most serious bar to understanding the Yorùbá deities is the use of a standardized Western academic discourse that Diana Eck, in her work on the Hindu pantheon, has called the tendency to consider "singularity or uniqueness" as a special mark of authority and importance.[7] The Yorùbá concept of a Supreme Being has more in common with Hindu and Egyptian religions than with Western monotheistic traditions.[8] Conceptions of Ògún as an abstract force have existed in the Yorùbá imagination since the beginning of time, before the cultural myths incorporated anthropomorphic figures for the tools of highly valued professions, such as guns (hunting), anvils (smithing), hoes (farming), and swords (warfare). Each tool represents a profession and is considered a manifestation of Ògún. The various shrines to Ògún devoted to each manifestation are identified by the symbols of work. Yorùbá gods and deities display human traits—the ability to eat, speak, quarrel, and love. As David P. Silverman observes: "These depictions, whether visual or literary, represented a recognizable conceptualization of what was perhaps originally a more abstract divine power or force. The characteristics possessed by these concretizations were those the Egyptians envisioned the supreme power or force to have."[9] Unlike the deities of ancient Egypt, who were experienced in the form of visual and written images, Yorùbá deities are represented in icons made of iron, rocks, or wood that can be consecrated and that symbolize the deity's power.

THE ỌLỌ́JỌ́ RITUAL

In this section, Ọlọ́jọ́ will be examined as a ritual that connects the myth and history of Ilé-Ifẹ̀ to the contemporary cultural life of the Yorùbá. Broadly speaking, the four-day Ọlọ́jọ́ Festival commemorates Ìlàgún, the great animal sacrifice to Ògún; Òkè-M'ògún Kíní proper, the king's first pilgrimage to Ògún's shrine; and Òkè-M'ògún Kejì, the king's second pilgrimage to Ògún's shrine.[10]

The Ọlọ́jọ́ Festival is celebrated in the ninth or tenth month of the lunar calendar, just at the end of the rainy season and the beginning of the dry season.[11] During the three days of celebration, all markets are closed, perhaps because making a profit from the festival would be considered sacrilegious. Crowds watch in awe as a grand procession of swordsmen and hunters, presided over by the Ọ̀ọ̀ni, advances to Ògún's shrine.

Preparation for the Festival

Consulting with the calendar keepers, the chief priests in charge of the festival ceremony determine the most auspicious time for Ọlọ́jọ́. According to one of the chief priests of Ọlọ́jọ́, the Oṣògún, the date for Ọlọ́jọ́, as opposed to other Ifẹ̀ festivals that are determined by the appearance of the new moon, is determined by the position of the sun, indicating that this is a solar ceremony. Chief Erédùmí, an important Ògún priest, announces the actual date of the Ọlọ́jọ́ Festival to the public. Almost immediately, preparation for the festival begins and lasts for forty days. The shrines of Ògún and the houses of the Ògún priests are decorated with palm fronds (màrìwò) to signal the commencement of the ritual, much as in Christianity candles and fir trees herald the beginning of the Christmas season or palm fronds Palm Sunday.

A week before the commencement of Ọlọ́jọ́, the king begins his own ritual by going into seclusion (Ọba wẹ̀dọ̀) and performing private ceremonies in and around the palace. The most visible preparation is a daily invocation of Ògún and Òràn-míyàn, called *gbàjúre*.[12] Here the various households of the Ògún priests, especially the Akogun, principal custodian of Òrànmíyàn's shrine, and the women, gather in the evening to sing loudly the praises of the two war deities, Ògún and Òrànmíyàn, and to remind them that their festival is fast approaching and that their presence is requested to renew the Ifè cosmos. It is a common practice to call on Ifè deities before a ceremony dedicated to them, as the worship of Odùduwà will illustrate.

The First Day: Ìlàgún

After forty days of preparation, the first major part of Olójó proper begins with the public sacrifice of an animal at Òkè-M'ògún, the most central and public shrine of Ògún in Ilé-Ifè. The key ritual functionaries and chief priests are the Osògún, the Obadìo, the Obawàrà, the Obàlòràn, and the Erédùmí. The main shrine of Ògún at Òkè-M'ògún, Ògún Hill, is located within two hundred yards of the palace entrance. Òkè-M'ògún, which means "Ògún's hierophany," the place where Ògún reveals himself, stands next to a modern town hall. Òkè-M'ògún is a fairly large, walled yard with a main entrance facing the palace. Inside the yard stands the Ògún Shrine, marked by two trees and two carved monoliths of different sizes, referred to as Ògún's Staff and resembling Òpá Òrànmíyàn, the Staff of Òrànmíyàn, one of the mysteries of Ilé-Ifè. Several informants revealed that "Òkè-M'ògún represents the place Ògún disappeared into the earth's crust." Tied to the two trees is the year-old carcass of a dog, as well as dried palm fronds from the previous year's sacred ritual.

Early in the morning of Ìlàgún Day, a search party from the Oba's palace sets out to hunt randomly in the streets of Ilé-Ifè for two dogs that will be sacrificed. Like the victims of war captured on the battlefield, the dogs are tied to a pole and brought to the palace. The manner of capture reflects the persona of Ògún, a violent deity who claims his human victims without warning, be it in hunting, in war, or in accidents on the road. An informant, a member of the search party, explained why the dogs were obtained from a public street—because the sacrifice is a public ritual. "This gift is what the Ifè people give to Ògún every year." In the precolonial period, sacrificial rituals involved human victims. In selecting human sacrificial victims, the priests chose foreigners or those deemed suitable to be captured as slaves. The dog represents a contemporary substitute for the ancient practice of sacrificing the captured "foreigner."

At about 4:00 p.m. the Osògún, or chief priest of Ògún's central shrine at Òkè-M'ògún, and the sacrificer in Olójó go to the palace to begin the ritual sacrifice. The house of the Osògún is decorated with the royal symbol of a crown painted on the yard's pillar. The Osògún is dressed in a red shirt and white wrapper and wears his insignia of office, a badge *(pękę)* that shows his title in the emblem of a crown. Holding his metal staff of office, he proceeds with his entourage to the Ooni's palace, but not before offering sacrifices to Ògún in the private shrine to Ògún at his own palace.

FIGURE 8. Chief Oṣògún in the Ọlọ́jọ́ Festival.

Among his entourage is a boy carrying a leather bag that contains powerful medicinal ingredients and knives for the sacrifice. In a ceremony I witnessed, at one
point an elderly man cautioned the boy to pay attention to what he was carrying,
since "if it [the bag] falls from his shoulder, the elder would look for a replacement,"
an indication that the sacrificial objects might be difficult to replace. At the king's
palace, a number of chiefs led by the Lówà, head of the palace chiefs, await the arrival of the Oṣògún. There they hand over a small pot of medicine as a message
from the Ọ̀ọni that the Oṣògún should proceed to Òkè-M'ògún to make the sacrifice to Ògún. The Oṣògún then offers prayers for the Ọ̀ọni. Holding the small pot,
the Oṣògún invokes Ògún and prays for the Ọ̀ọni as follows: "Kábíyèsí [King],
Death, Aláṣẹ [Owner of Àṣẹ, i.e., sacred power], the Most Powerful One, Whose
Power is Second Only to the God, Èkejì Òrìṣà, may you reign long, may you conquer your enemies. Ògún will assist you in ruling Ilé-Ifẹ̀" (Kábíyèsí, Ikú Bàbá Yèyé;
Aláṣẹ, Èkejì Òrìṣà; Wà á jẹ ẹ́ pé, wà á réyìn odì; Ògún ó bá ọ ṣe Ilé-Ifẹ̀).

In a loud shout, the Oṣògún invokes Ògún, essentially calling attention to
Ògún's power. The Oṣògún then proceeds to Òkè-M'ògún, repeating the call as he
walks quickly while his assistants echo him along the way:

> Ògún gborí, Ọ̀rá gbùrèfee
> Yèsí ló lori ẹ, Ògún ló lorí ẹ
> Orí Ògún fi, orí Ògún fi . . .
>
> Ògún got the head,
> Ọ̀rá got the carcass,
> Who owns the head?
> Ògún owns the head . . .

My informants had difficulty explaining the meaning of these words. The association of Ògún with the thunder god, Ọ̀ràmfẹ̀, is problematic because Ọ̀ràmfẹ̀ has no
direct connection with Olójó. Moreover, different people interpreted differently the
song's reference to "the head" (orí), some describing it as the seat of wisdom or intelligence and others describing it as the most important part of the body, which
Ògún claims as a source of individual essences. As most studies of orí, especially
Rowland Abíọ́dún's seminal essay, have shown, when Ògún kills a victim he severs
the head as a sign of complete victory.

When the Oṣògún's party arrives at Òkè-M'ògún, their first duty is to prepare
the place of sacrifice and adorn Ògún's shrine. From the forest, the Ọbajio, another
Ògún priest, supplies bundles of white palm fronds (màrìwò), used for erecting
Ògún's tent. Yorùbá oral tradition recognizes that the ancient textile design using
finely woven palm fronds represents the cloth of Ògún, a recognition demonstrated
clearly in the phrase màrìwò laṣọ Ògún, literally, "Ògún is attired in palm fronds."
The Oṣògún uses strips of palm fronds and bamboo poles to prepare a tent for Ògún
around the shrine. The deteriorating palm fronds of previous years are removed,

FIGURE 9. The high chiefs in the courtyard of the palace preparing for the Ọlọ́jọ́ Festival.

as well as the carcasses of the previous sacrificial animals, which are taboo for the Ọ̀ni to step on when he visits the shrine.[13]

The sacrifice commences as the Oṣògún calls loudly on Chief Ọbajio, *Ọlọ́rìn, Ọlọ́rìn, Ọlọ́rìn wá à jẹ́* (Club Man, Club Man, Club Man, come and answer me). Emerging with a large club in hand, the Club Man responds, "*Arère, arèsà,* I answer you." With the club held high above his head, in one blow he smashes the head of the dog. In one of the two festivals I witnessed, the Club Man failed to appear. He was nowhere to be found for five minutes after the call to sacrifice, and when he finally showed up, the Oṣògún became very angry with him. Bascom reported a similar occurrence in 1938. The Ọbajio had designated a young man to act as the Club Man. Because of his Christian background, the young man was reluctant to perform the act. Surprisingly, Bascom wrote of another Club Man who was similarly reluctant to perform the clubbing.

In Ifẹ̀, the manner of sacrificing the dog differed substantially from what I had witnessed in the sacrifice to Ògún in other Yorùbá rituals, where a sword was used to cut off the dog's head. What, therefore, is the explanation for the Ifẹ̀ technique? Valerio Valeri observed that sacrificial victims do not have to be alive at the moment of the sacrifice proper.[14] Perhaps the victim was already dead before it was tied to the Ògún trees for the disembowelment. Ògún demands blood and plenty of it. He has been called a deity who prefers to bathe in blood even though there is water at home *(Òlómi sílé fèjè wè)*. With a sharp knife, the dog's stomach is cut open so that the bowel and intestines are visible through the gaping hole and the blood flows out over the stones and entrance to the shrine. This bloody sacrifice shows everyone what the deity is capable of and parallels the manner in which Ògún slaughters human victims—suddenly, swiftly, and violently.

The king's emissary then offers two sacrificial items—red palm oil and a hen—for the Osògún to complete the sacrifice. The hen is sacrificed by having its intestines cut open and is placed over the sacrificed dog. Palm oil is then poured over the dog and the hen, and, with the kola nut, prayers are offered for the king, his subjects, and the entire city.

The sacrificial objects and performance symbolize that the dog is Ògún's favorite food. In sacrificing the dog, the Oòni fulfills a religious obligation and appeals to Ògún to spare human life. In this context, the Yorùbá often pray that God may not give human flesh to Ògún to consume, referring to victims of vehicular accidents, which are believed to be caused by the deity. At first I was unsure why a hen was offered instead of a larger bird such as a rooster, which is more commonly used as sacrifices, even though Yorùbá consider neither hen nor rooster suitable food for Ògún. To my inquiry about the choice of a hen for sacrifice, the Osògún responded, "It is like giving *àdín* [black oil] to Èsù to drink. Èsù, trickster deity and messenger of the gods, abhors *àdín,* but it is offered to him as evil medicine to rile him up so that he will vent his anger on an enemy." In other words, if one wants Èsù to harm an enemy, one presents *àdín* to him as an offering, saying, "Èsù, this offering is what [a named person] asked me to give you." Because *àdín* is tabooed, Èsù considers offering it in the name of that enemy a grave insult and in return unleashes his anger on the enemy. This explanation is not far-fetched in Yorùbá culture. It is supported in the popular Olójó lyrics, *Eni bá ní kí ẹbọ má gbà, á bá ẹbọ lọ* (Whoever would like to prevent this sacrifice from accomplishing its purpose would perish with the sacrifice). The lyrics refer to those perceived as "evil eyes," the king's enemies and persons who may want to disrupt the success of the sacrifice. Moreover, in Yorùbá thought, prayers and curses are intricately linked. To pray for the Oba's success in Olójó, one must curse the Oba's enemies as well.

Having completed these offerings, the Osògún consecrates the sacrifice to Ògún by touching the ground with his sword and touching the animals sacrificed, thus completing the sacrificial preparation for the king's visit to Òkè-M'ògún.

The nature of Ògún's sacrifice and the concept of sacrifice in the context of the Olójó Festival are complex. The Ifè believe that the *ajá* (sacrificial dog) shares a number of traits with Ògún—friendliness, aggressiveness, and, most importantly, unpredictability: in one instant, a seemingly friendly dog can attack its owner or a stranger. In the same way, a Yorùbá proverb describes Ògún's unpredictable violent behavior: *Ojú tí Ògún bá máa fi pani, kì í fi han ni* (Ògún never reveals his eyes to the person he intends to kill).[15] The proverb's image of concealed eyes refers to Ògún's tendency to kill his victims abruptly and without warning.

Though scholars have attempted to interpret the sacrifice ritual in various cultures and societies around the world, only the broadest theories are pertinent to the sacrificial ritual just described.[16] The main theories of sacrifice view it as the offering of gifts to a deity, as communion between human and deity, or as catharsis.[17] I will endeavor to interpret the Ọlọ́jọ́ sacrificial ritual within its social and historical matrix. As Valeri observes, sacrifice is best seen "as a complex ritual process, as a 'symbolic action' that cannot be reduced to any of the elements."[18]

The sacrifice as it takes place in Ilé-Ifẹ̀ provides tantalizing support for Réné Girard's "mimetic" thesis, which argues that a society's awareness of a violence and aggression innate within human beings leads to its seizing a victim for sacrifice.[19] The Oṣògún performs the sacrifice for the king, who symbolizes the actual "sacrificer." The monarchy represents aggression and violence, as the epithets for several Ilé-Ifẹ̀ Ọba suggest. The current Ọba, for example, is described as the Witness of War, Ṣíjúadé Ẹ̀rí Ògún. Often the king must make significant decisions regarding violence and aggression in war, decisions that he defends using the same violent means. The *ajá* is the "perfect" victim because the unpredictably friendly or aggressive disposition that it shares with Ògún makes it properly symbolize the god himself: "The sacrificer now corresponds to the concepts for which the god stands and . . . instantiates it. The sacrificer views himself and is viewed by the audience as a token of which the god is the type."[20] For Girard, "The objective of ritual is the proper reenactment of the surrogate-victim mechanism; its function is to perpetuate or renew the effects of this mechanism, that is, to keep violence outside the community. . . . If the surrogate-victim can interrupt the restructuring process, it must be at the origin of structure."[21] The stray dog captured on the street by the king's emissary for the sacrifice fits well into Girard's idea of the homeless surrogate victim. Dean MacCannell observes: "Ritual, by staging and situating violence, by containing it in a social form within the community, also rules it out of the community, thereby incorporating the most potentially disruptive acts not merely within the framework of order, but by transforming them into the very mechanism which insures order."[22]

The sacrifice to Ògún, then, signifies the transformational nature of the god, suppressed within the very essence of the festival. Ògún's potentially deadly, volatile, and inchoate power is contained within an orderly, judicious display of ritual violence. Ritual directs the path that Ògún takes. After all, Ògún is the same god who at the beginning of time cleared the way with his scythe for all the deities to follow, earning the title "Leader among the Gods" (Ọ̀ṣìn Imọ̀lẹ̀)—a myth that simultaneously expresses the god's various associations with metals, terror, and violence in war.

With the sacrifice complete, it is incumbent upon the Ọ̀ọ̀ni to visit the shrine of

Ògún. The Ọọ̀ni leaves his palace as a warrior, ruler, and king, and, most importantly, as a monarch paying a visit to his superior to seek help for a peaceful region
in Ilé-Ifẹ̀. The Ọọ̀ni carries a ceremonial sword, a symbol of his military power, and
adorns himself with an ordinary crown, called *oríkògbófo*, not the elaborate crown
(*arè*) that he will wear the following day to the same shrine, which will indicate that
he is a lesser god, approaching the deity as a "sacrifice."

In this first grand procession to the shrine, the king presides over warriors,
swordsmen, and hunters shooting their guns. As the chiefs brandish their swords
of office, the entire spectacle becomes a state-orchestrated display of force alluding
to the violence that the monarchy and the gods are capable of, thereby tying in with
the sacrifice that has preceded it. Amid the fanfare of horns, guns, buglers, and
sword-carrying chiefs, the procession moves swiftly to the shrine. The king looks
stern, as if he were going to war. As the Ọọ̀ni reaches the Òkè-M'ògún, the Oṣògún
escorts the Ọọ̀ni's group, including the Lówà, the head of the palace chiefs, and the
Ọbajio. They enter the Ògún's house. The party circle the shrine seven times coun-
terclockwise, each time touching the ground with their swords, and then perform
the sacrifice as an homage to Ògún. The king pays homage to Ògún, *ó ṣe ìba fún
Ògún*. At the end of the rite, the crowd roars, *Kábíyèsí, Ògún yè, mo yè* (Our Royal
Highness, Ògún lives and so do I), greeting both the king and the deity. Standing
on the opposite side of the shrine, the king and the Oṣògún exchange prayerful
wishes, each praying for the other's long life and expressing good wishes for the year
of the sacrifice and for the performance of the sacrifice the following year. The
Oṣògún's words follow:

> *Kábíyèsí,* Aláyé.
> *Èkejì Òrìṣà*
> *Ikú, bàbá yèyé*
> *Eji ayé rà pa ẹ́*
> *Lótùn-ún lósì, Ohun o bá ti wí láyé mà ṣẹ*
> *É è sí Ọlọ́fin méjì*
> *O tójú onílé, tójú àlejò.*

> Your Royal Highness, the Ruler of the World.
> Death, you are our father and our mother [you who have the power of life
>   and death],
> Your power is like that of the gods,
> May the rain of the evil world not fall on you.
> Your words and command will come to pass.
> There is no other Ọlọ́fin [king of kings] like you,
> You care for strangers and indigenes alike.

The prayer recognizes the Ọọ̀ni's sacred kingship and his dominion over Ilé-Ifẹ̀
people and resident aliens as well. The Oṣògún emphasizes the military and political authority of the king symbolized in the ceremonial sword that Ògún, the ar-

chetypal leader and warrior, controls. The Ọba and the Oṣògún strike swords against each other; moving closer, they lock the little fingers of their left hands together as if making a secret pact. The king offers the Oṣògún the traditional token gift for performing the sacrifice. This sword crossing and embrace between the Ọ̀ọni and Oṣògún demonstrates the relationship between kingship and Ògún and the power of rituals in general. It also illustrates the close friendship between the king and the deity, who is in his own right a king among the gods, Ọṣìn Imọlẹ̀. Both Ògún and the Ọ̀ọni reconstitute each other as allies and friends in the ensuing battles of life, which the king constantly confronts in the kingdom.[23] As the protector of his subjects against other warring factions, the king needs the assistance of Ògún to prevail and to maintain a peaceful, prosperous reign in Ilé-Ifẹ̀.

The second phase of the Ìlàgún begins when the Ọ̀ọni walks to the foot of the shrine and sits on a large chair in an open space. The various ranks of Ifẹ̀ chiefs and priests place their ceremonial swords on the ground with the pile of swords that form a temporary shrine of Ògún for a second sacrifice. The Oṣògún places pieces of sacrificial offerings—the dried hind leg of the bush goat *(itan ẹtu),* a dried rat *(eku),* and dried fish *(eja)*—on the swords while invoking Ògún's protection for the chiefs, the users of the swords. These sacrificial objects symbolize the prayerful wishes of the Oṣògún. They are represented as the messengers of the gods—in water, the fish; in the forest, the bush goat; and on land, the rat. The ritual offering conveys the wishes of the chiefs for the deity to become "invisible" to enemies anywhere. The climax of Ìlàgún ritual begins with the "sacrifice" of a second dog, which is killed with a club in the same manner as the first. Its blood is drained over the temporary shrine of the swords. Unlike the first dog, which was offered completely to the deity, the second dog, along with the rest of the sacrificial offerings, is taken to the Oṣògún's house to be eaten by the members of his household and his entourage. To "cool down" Ògún, who is normally a hot-tempered and violent deity, the Oṣògún knocks off the tips of two snail shells and pours the snail liquid onto the outstretched hands of the chiefs and priests, who rub it over their heads and faces. He also pours the liquid on the swords. As Bascom remarks, that liquid represents ẹ̀rọ̀, the antidote to dangerous and "hot" occurrences. Finally, the Oṣògún splits a kola nut and casts a divination to confirm that Ògún has accepted the sacrifice.

At the time Bascom studied the Ọlójọ́ Festival in 1936, Ìlàgún was performed at midnight; however, shortly after Nigerian independence in 1960, when partisan party politics was introduced, serious divisions arose among politicians in Ilé-Ifẹ̀, and the night performance became an excuse for lawlessness and vengeance. As a result, Ọ̀ọni Adérẹ̀mí decreed that the time of Ìlàgún be shifted from night to the late afternoon.

Following Ìlàgún, there is a night vigil, Àìsùn Ògún, during which the people make merry, dance, and sing in praise of the deity. The homes of Ifẹ̀ chiefs connected with the Ògún celebration are filled with visitors during this night.[24] The purpose of the night vigil is to celebrate and sing the praise of the deity, recounting in song his myth-history. In front of the Oṣògún's house stands a shrine to Ògún marking the place in which the Oṣògún offers a sacrifice to Ògún before leaving the house for the rites of Ìlàgún in the afternoon. Members of his group, friends, and household visitors dance around the shrine. Two songs illustrate the perception of Ògún's power. One calls on the deity to save the participants from the evil eye: *Ògún gbà mí o, má jáyé ó ṣe mí* (Ògún save me, do not let the evil world harm me). The other appeals to Ògún's procreative power: *Ọlọ́mọ lèrè àdúgbò. Ògún wá fún mi lọ́mọ.* (Children are the beauty of the lineage. Give us children, Ògún.) Undoubtedly, Ògún's power to give children to his devotees is central to the night's play.

The Second Day

The Ọòni's Pilgrimage to Ògún's Shrine   Judging from the very large crowd that I saw at the ceremonies I witnessed, Ọlọ́jọ́ Day was the climax of this festival. It is also called Òkè-M'ògún Day because it is the day on which the Ọòni performs a second pilgrimage to Ògún's shrine, Òkè-M'ògún, this time wearing his *arè* (sacred crown). From early morning, there was great merriment throughout the city. In the Ọòni's palace, guests and visitors were entertained lavishly. Sitting in a large open hall were foreign dignitaries and visitors from different parts of the country, in-cluding other Ọba and military personnel. I saw the Cuban ambassador to Nigeria and officials from the United States Cultural Center in Lagos.

Four groups of Ifẹ̀ participants in Ọlọ́jọ́ stood out from the crowd. One group consisted of male members of the royal lineage called Ṣòókò, princes, each dressed grandly in a white flowing *agbádá* (traditional outfit) and wearing a large hat with the insignia of a crown. Fringes of thread hung from their hats, concealing their faces as the king's crown veiled his face. The pseudocrowns express the close ties of the Ṣòókò to the king and their divine right to the throne, a sign of their lineage's loyalty to the king. Indeed, before a king is crowned, he must take the title of Ṣòókò as part of the monarchy or pre–kingship investiture rite.

A second group was the guild of medicine men and women (Àwọn Ẹlẹ́sìnjẹ́), which protects the Ọòni and counters all evil forces that may intend to harm him. During this period marked by danger and uncertainty, the Ẹlẹ́sìnjẹ́ openly display the power of their medicine.

The guild also helps ensure that rain does not fall while the Ọlọ́jọ́ is in process, for this would be taboo. The *arè* (sacred crown) attracts rain, making the task of the Ẹlẹ́sìnjẹ́ even more difficult. It was interesting to see the Ẹlẹ́sìnjẹ́'s displays of magical prowess and paraphernalia on Ọlọ́jọ́ Day: one medicine man, wearing trousers and an ordinary undershirt, displayed his medicine staff; another held an animal horn filled with medicine *(àfọ̀ṣe)*; a third whispered incantations and spir-itual sayings, as if to prevent the rain from falling. A most spectacular drama came from an elderly medicine woman, Mama Popo, a nickname referring to the grind-

FIGURE 10. Chief and medicine women in the Ọlọ́jọ́ Festival.

ing of her medicine leaves in a mortar. As priestess, she dressed in white and held a flywhisk *(ìrùkẹ̀rẹ̀)*, a mark of royalty. With an entourage of five men and drummers, she danced around the palace precincts, greeting visitors and the guests of the Ọọni. With her left hand she shook the hands of invited guests, an indication that she belonged to the same secret society as the people she greeted. The lyrics sung by her entourage drew on a powerful Ifá poem narrating Ògún's exploits in myth-history. Various devotees of Ògún also sang in groups, all recounting the power of the deity.

A third group of Ọlọ́jọ́ participants consisted of the palace servants, referred to as Lókolóko in the Ọlọ́jọ́ context. To control the crowd, they carried large whips. They served as the traditional police officers and bodyguards of the Ọọ̀ni. They wore short white pants and carried small pots of protective medicine called *ọpọ́n.* Their bodies were painted in *efun* (white lime) and *osùn* (red camwood), signifying the two colors of the previously discussed myth of the dual paternity of Ọ̀rànmíyàn by Ògún and Odùduwà.

Guilds of hunters and taxi and commercial vehicle drivers, as well as black-smiths, made up a fourth group of Ọlọ́jọ́ participants. Leading the procession, they carried a large banner, "Ifẹ Division Hunters Association," that showed the image of a hunter aiming at an animal in the bush. Professional taxi drivers, too, carried a sign, "Taxi Drivers Association," with the message *Ògún á gbè wá* (May Ògún sup-

FIGURE 11. Medicine men in the Olójó Festival keeping the rain at bay.

FIGURE 12. Lókolóko (palace guards) holding whips made of branches during the Ọlọ́jọ́
Festival.

port us). Contributing to Ọlọ́jọ́ was a large contingency of younger wives in the
households of chiefs (Obìnrin Ilé). They wore costumes *(aṣọ ẹbí)*, while drummers
sang praises to their husbands and lineage. A conspicuous group consisted of the
wives of the royal lineage, bearing signs like *Obìnrin Ilé Olúbùṣe kí Bàbá wa Ṣíjúadé*
(The Women of the Olúbùṣe Household Congratulate Our Father, Ṣíjúadé).

Noble war chiefs and chief priests of the Ọ̀rànmíyàn Shrine, the Akọgun, arrived
at the palace, venerating Ògún with a sword by making ritual signs while swinging
the sword as if in battle. The Akọgun faced the palace gate, indicating that the king
was ready to emerge. By late afternoon, thousands of people filled the palace courtyard, hoping to see the Ọọ̀ni and his ancient *arè* crown. A royal drum, the *òṣírìgì*,
reverberated in the inner courtyard; almost immediately, people stood, welcoming
the king. Wearing the *arè* crown that covered his face, the Ọọ̀ni emerged from the
inner palace with a large entourage. His assistant carried his sword, and a chief held
two pigeons. Once the crowd caught sight of the great crown, they greeted the Ọọ̀ni
with a barrage of prayers asking for good health and abundance, as well as curses
for their enemies, since the *arè* was believed to be powerful enough to induce mis-
fortune. A prominent member of my father's church proclaimed, *Arè á gbè ọ* (May
the *arè* bless and protect you). The Ọọ̀ni acknowledged the greetings of the crowds
by waving and by lifting the flaps of the crown to catch sight of the multitudes. (In

FIGURE 13. The Ọ̀ọ̀ni wearing the *arè* on his way to the Ògún Shrine.

a 1937 photograph Bascom captured the late Ọ̀ọ̀ni Adérẹ̀mí in this same gesture of raising the flaps of his crown.)

Various chiefs, including the Ọ̀tún Ifẹ̀, the Òsì Ifẹ̀, the Mọdéwá, the palace chiefs, and the priestly Ìṣòrò, prostrated themselves in front of the Ọ̀ọ̀ni, acknowledging his authority and divine rule. The chiefs represented a cross section of the ruling class in the community. Bascom noted in 1937 a group of Muslims led by their chief imam who paid the Ọ̀ọ̀ni homage.[25] Generally, the Ọ̀ọ̀ni does not speak if he wears the arè. His emissaries often respond to greetings on his behalf, Ọba kíọ (The king greets you).

Before the Ọ̀ọ̀ni emerged, the anxious masses burst into song, reminding him that it was time to appear, Òde tó o, jẹ́ mi r'arè. The arè is an important symbol of kingship and the focus of the king's pilgrimage to Ògún's shrine. The king's crown maker, Asinde Ọba, told me, "The arè was first worn by Ọbalùfọ̀n Álayémore, regarded as the Ọ̀ọ̀ni, who reigned after Odùduwà." Responsible for crowning a new king, the devotees of Ọbalùfọ̀n, headed by Ọbalara, control the arè.

Here we should describe the meaning and importance of the arè. The arè is a colossal crown regarded as the original crown of Odùduwà. Its multicolored embroidery is stitched with a wool of unparalleled quality, called ṣ́ẹ́ṣ́ẹ́ òwú; in Yorùbá, Ti ṣ́ẹ́ṣ́ẹ́ òwú níí ṣẹ ní àwùjọ òwú (Ṣ́ẹ́ṣ́ẹ́ òwú are the primary wools). Ṣ́ẹ́ṣ́ẹ́ òwú (sacred wool cloth that is specifically made for sacred crowns) signifies the relationship between the royal bearer of the arè and the people of Ilé-Ifẹ̀, who invest their time and effort into crafting this special wool. The crown symbolizes àṣẹ, or spiritual power, the foreordained power to change desire into actuality. Embroidered with white egret and red parrot feathers, it signifies the purity of the sacred monarch. Although the Asinde stated that the embroidery itself lends no power to the arè, its beauty is strongly symbolic in Yorùbá culture, where elaborate adornment is highly prized. To create and to mollify the new arè, elaborate ritual sacrifices of domestic animals— cows, sheep, or pigeons—are performed. The distinctive embroidered image of the medicine patch that is passed from one king to his successor, along with the sacrificial rituals, imbues the arè with power. The Yorùbá believe that when the king wears the arè he is immediately endowed with divine power and whatever he says must come to pass. Thus, when he wears the ancient crown, the Ọ̀ọ̀ni does not utter many words. The Ẹ̀mẹ̀sẹ̀, the palace acolytes, accompany the Ọ̀ọ̀ni as he softly utters incantations—Jẹ́jẹ́ o (Little by little, walk gently) or Ọfẹẹ (Be light), urging the heavy arè to become lighter so that its weight may not be felt. Once the appropriate sacrifices are made, before the Ọ̀ọ̀ni wears the crown on Ọlọ́jọ́ Day, the crown is said to become weightless.

In the ceremony that I witnessed, the Ọ̀ọ̀ni, after a sufficient time to acknowledge the Ifẹ̀ people, entered his open motorcade and was driven to the foot of the Òkè-M'ògún, where he entered the shrine of Ògún. The Oṣ̀ògún collected the king's sword and that of his chief priest. The Oṣ̀ògún entered the inner chamber of Ògún's

FIGURE 14. The Ọ̀ọ̀ni wearing the *arè* during the Ọlọ́jọ́ Festival.

shrine, marking the swords in white chalk and red camwood, the colors of the Lókolóko, to represent a consecration and an acknowledgment of the Ọ̀ọ̀ni's visit to Ògún's home. The swords were returned to their original owners, and the Ọ̀ọ̀ni and Oṣògún struck sword against sword and locked fingers as before. The locking of swords is a metaphor for battle to ensure that the Ọ̀ọ̀ni will triumph against all enemies, symbolizing the ultimate power of the Ọ̀ọ̀ni over all mortals in the kingdom and signifying that the needs of all the people will be met under Ògún's patronage.

The Ọ̀ọ̀ni's Pilgrimage to Ifẹ̀ Market   After visiting the shrine of Ògún, the Ọ̀ọ̀ni made a brief pilgrimage to Ọjà Ifẹ̀ (Ifẹ̀ Market), the traditional abode of the goddess Ajé, whom the Ifẹ̀ people venerate as the goddess of wealth, prosperity, and fecundity. The Ifẹ̀ people believe that the king's visit to Ọjà Ifẹ̀ Market represents a journey to Ajé's agricultural estate or "farm" *(Ọ̀ọ̀ni re oko Ajé)*, metaphorically that of a "subordinate" or a beggar who has no other choice but to plead for what will sustain him in the coming year.

At the market, the Ọ̀ọ̀ni walked up to two flat stones placed on top of each other, which represented Ajé's shrine. The Lọ́wá, head of the palace chiefs, and the Erédùmí, the chief priest of Ọ̀rànmíyàn, placed their feet on the stones to honor and appease the deity on behalf of the king. When the Ọ̀ọ̀ni wears the *arè* to visit Ògún, he is spiritually and magically prepared to venture into Ọjà Ifẹ̀ and to confront the spirits that regulate the Ifẹ̀ universe for him and any malevolent spirits and evil-minded persons who would negate his offering or subvert the prayers and wishes of his subjects.

Ajé: Goddess of Wealth and Prosperity   Ifẹ̀ Market is located about four hundred yards from Ògún's shrine. The Ọọ̀ni's obligatory visit to the market raises an interesting question about Ifẹ̀ cosmology and the place of the gods and goddesses. Ajé certainly is not considered a major deity in Yorùbá religious thought, and she does not retain the power that the goddess Ọ̀ṣun has secured among the deities. Why, then, is the Ọọ̀ni, the god-king, wearing his all-powerful *arè* crown, compelled to visit Ifẹ̀ Market and to greet Ajé, the goddess of prosperity? The Ọọ̀ni's visit must be viewed in the context of Ajé's status in Yorùbá cosmology. The Ifá divination corpus describes a number of narratives showing her relationship with the Ọọ̀ni and the reason she occupies such a pivotal role in the Ọlọ́jọ́ celebration.

I begin with two Ifá narratives about the origin of Ajé. Ajé was the daughter of Olókun Ṣẹ̀níadé, who was the Supreme Goddess of the ocean. Her story began when Ifá asked the goddess Olókun to perform a sacrifice so she could conceive and give birth to a child who would be greater than Olókun herself. Olókun marveled at the Ifá revelation because she was already exalted, wealthy, and prosperous, enjoying abundant treasures in her abode deep on the ocean floor. Nevertheless, she did as Ifá directed: she performed a great sacrifice, offering numerous items in multiples of two hundred. Consequently, she became pregnant and gave birth to a daughter she named Ajé. Before long, Ajé surpassed everyone in prosperity.

This Yorùbá narrative may signify the emergence of trade and commerce across the Atlantic Ocean, represented in the narratives of the goddess Olókun in the fifteenth and sixteenth centuries when Europeans first made contact with West and Central African kingdoms. The Atlantic Ocean trade made possible the ensuing prosperity because without trade and commerce this wealth would have been impossible to attain. The local economy of male-dominated subsistence farming evolved into a larger system of marketing in which women ruled and brought prosperity to their communities. The Ifá narrative may be interpreted as a textual-historical narrative reflecting an economic transformation that took place at a time in which small-scale commerce and trade became linked to the greater overseas trade that transformed local economies.

In another Ifá narrative regarding Ajé, the goddess is credited with the invention of money or cowrie shells, the traditional medium of exchange. The narrative thus explains the change from barter to trade as well as the development of the use of money. According to this narrative, Ajé was planning to buy a slave at Ejìg-bòròmẹ̀kùn Market, the principal market of ancient Ilé-Ifẹ̀. She went to a diviner and after consultation was advised to make a sacrifice concerning the slave she would buy. Ifá predicted that a sacrifice would exalt Ajé's status forever, giving her fame and peace of mind.

After obediently performing the sacrifice, Ajé arrived at Ejìgbòròmẹkùn Market and saw a slave she liked. When she asked his name, he replied, "Owó" (money). Ajé bought him immediately and took him home as her manservant. Owó was so serviceable that even before he was asked to do something he had already done it. Because of his intuitiveness and faithfulness, Ajé summoned all the people around her and instructed them that if they wished to have dealings with her they must first consult with Owó, who would function as an intermediary between her and her clients.

This Ifá legend characterizes the relationship between wealth, prosperity, and money (the medium for becoming prosperous) as well as the eighteenth-century slave trade. The Yorùbá understand money as "male," portraying it as a servant or slave who does the bidding of Ajé. Those who want to acquire riches and prosperity must consult Owó, but anyone who desires wealth must ultimately propitiate Ajé. Without money, one cannot acquire wealth, affluence, or power. Babaláwo Ifátóògùn aptly remarked, "The character of Owó differs from Ajé" (*Ìwà Ajé yàtò sí ti owó*). According to the Babaláwo, Owó signifies toughness and hardship (*Ìwà Owó le*). The goddess Ajé, on the other hand, has a mild, tranquil, loving disposition. Whereas inflexibility, haste, and hotheadedness are characteristic of the desire to obtain wealth, often in the form of money, Ajé herself is associated more with prosperity, serenity, and kindheartedness—attributes more levelheaded or "cooler" than those of Owó.

Still another Ifá narrative credits Ajé with the invention of the savings bank in traditional society. At Ajé's arrival on earth, an unforeseen problem arose. Ajé herself complained to her diviners that despite her riches and wealth she was tired of roaming about and having no permanent abode. According to the Ifá text poetically declaimed by Babaláwo Ifátóògùn, Ajé, daughter of Olókun Sẹ̀níadé, traveled from heaven to earth and on her arrival was asked by Ifá to make a sacrifice of sixteen large pots (*òdù* pots), two hundred pigeons, sixteen cows, two hundred snails, two hundred tortoises, and two hundred cowries in six different places. When she inquired what the purpose of the sacrifice was, she was told that she could have her wish to remain in one place and still be prosperous and famous. Moreover, people on both sides of the Atlantic would continue to seek her out. Ajé replied that this was acceptable to her.

The diviners received the sacrifices from Ajé, and after performing the necessary rituals they asked her to distribute the sacrificial objects among the sixteen large *òdù* pots. After Ajé made the sacrifice, the inhabitants of the world suddenly realized that the practice of carrying around their money on their person was too risky and inconvenient. "Since we do not intend to spend all of our money at the same time, we should keep some in pots and bury the pots until we need money," they concluded.

Babaláwo Ifátóògùn commented that because of the legend of Ajé the people of the world started saving their money in pots. Before Ajé came, there was no reason for saving large collections of cowrie money in pots, because people carried their wealth around with them as ornamentation or in bags.

Local traditions of storing money in pots buried in secret locations initiated the banking system in Yorùbá society. Indeed, it was common during the 1960s to hear of farmers discovering treasures in cowrie pots buried in their farmlands. In traditional Yorùbá society, entrepreneurs used large black pots as vessels for storing money while they were away traveling. The odù pots illustrate a major social and economic transformation that reorganized Yorùbá commerce and financial systems long before modern banking systems were introduced.

Moreover, Ajé's narrative raises an interesting debate that is quite germane to gender discourse: the notion of public space. While men often control the public sphere, women often dominate the marketplace. Jürgen Habermas, for example, maintains that public space is not an arena of market relations but a theater for debate and deliberation.[26] In contrast, Ajé's legend indicates that in Yorùbá culture public and private space are interwoven; market space is an arena feared by African indigenous rulers both because it is not controlled exclusively by men and because it is the arena where the most biting criticisms of the state are made in the gossip of the market women and the open conversations that go on as people meet and conduct business. Market space is a public space at the center of community life where wealth and ideas are created and sought after.

On the basis of the preceding narratives, it is clear that any ruler would want an entrepreneur like Ajé by his side. An odù Ifá titled Òtúrúpòn Obàlùfòn says that when Olófin Odùduwà was about to descend into the world to create the city of Ilé-Ifè, Ajé asked him if she should accompany him. Olófin responded by asking whether she would serve him. Ajé said she would do so faithfully. Consequently, Ajé descended into the world and faithfully served Olófin. Ajé was one of the senior deities who had inhabited Ilé-Ifè since the beginning of time.

This narrative suggests the relationship between Ifè's sacred kingship and the wealth and prosperity symbolized in Ajé. From the beginning of creation, Ajé has played a significant role in Ifè's foundation and political economy. Her abode is in Ojà Ifè, the Ifè Marketplace, where she is enshrined and worshipped annually by the king. In this ritual reenactment, Ajé secures wealth and prosperity for the kings of Ifè and their subjects. The market represents a theater of the mystical Yorùbá world or ayé, reflected in the Yorùbá proverb Ayé lojà ojà layé (The world is a market, and the market is the world).

The king's annual Olójó Festival illustrates Ajé's role in securing prosperity for the political economy and governance of Ilé-Ifè. Wearing his magical arè, the Oòni leads the procession to the market to propitiate Ajé and prays for successful trade, agriculture, and prosperity in his kingdom. Similarly, all the gods of the Yorùbá pantheon, and humans as well, regularly court Ajé's favor in Ilé-Ifẹ̀'s shrines and temples adorned by cowrie shells, the emblems of Ajé's wealth.

In practical terms, Ajé's sovereignty over the Yorùbá market economy links the public realm with the political kingship system. In traditional Yorùbá society, the most important titles for female dignitaries are Ìyálájé, Ìyalọ́jà, and Lọ́bùn. Although primarily representing titles of commerce and economy, these titles are also linked to the imperial political system. Titled women are often viewed as counterparts of the king and other high-ranking sovereigns. As a result, the Ọọ̀ni makes pilgrimages to propitiate Ajé to plead for agricultural productivity of the soil, economic prosperity, and human fecundity in his kingdom.

In addition to its political and economic significance, Ọjà Ifẹ̀ is a particularly sacred site in Ilé-Ifẹ̀ because it serves as the point where the "dead to the world" begin their pilgrimage to the beyond. The people of Ifẹ̀ were well aware of the Ọlọ́jọ́ ritual's connection to this pilgrimage at Ọjà Ifẹ̀. Throughout the festival at the shrine of Ògún and Ajé's marketplace they sang, "Whoever would like to prevent this sacrifice from accomplishing its purpose would perish with the sacrifice" *(Ẹni bá ní kí ẹbọ má gbà, á bá ẹbọ lọ).*

Ancestral Sacrifice   Subsequently, the Erédùmí collected a ram from the king and proceeded to Igbóbodí, the first mausoleum in which early Ifẹ̀ kings were buried. There the Erédùmí sacrificed the ram to the royal ancestors to placate their spirits on behalf of the king, since the Ọọ̀ni himself was forbidden to enter there. Amid the throng's jubilant drumming and singing, the Ọọ̀ni returned to the palace. Standing close to his palace gate, a party of dancers sang to him, rejoicing with him for returning from a good outing and pleading with him to enter the palace to protect his *arè* from harm. When he reached the palace, the sacred *arè* was removed from his head and placed in the Òmìrìn room for safekeeping until next year's ceremony.

The day after the first pilgrimage to Òkè-M'ògún was observed as a day of rest *(ọjọ́ ìsinmi).* Although the day of rest may fall on Sunday, there is no relationship with the traditional Christian practice.

The Fourth Day

On the fourth day of Ọlọ́jọ́, called the Òkè-M'ògún Kejì, the king yet again visited the shrine of Ògún. Unlike his second visit during which he wore the *arè,* on this visit the Ọọ̀ni wore a simple circular crown called *oríkògbófo,* meaning "the head does not go empty," or "the head must be covered." This is a literal reference to the taboo requiring kings to cover their heads, although it also refers to the inner or "spiritual" head *(orí inú)* that allows the king's ancestors and the gods to show favor to him, the prospective subject to become a king, and his "outer" head to wear the crown *(orí adé)*. As on the first visit, the Ọ̀ọ̀ni rode in a motorcade to the Òkè-Mògún shrine. He entered the shrine, repeating the rituals of the previous visit. The Osọ̀gún led the Ọ̀ọ̀ni in a circle around the Ògún Shrine, and they struck each other's swords, exchanged pleasantries, and prayed for the coming year.

After exiting the Ògún Shrine, the Ọ̀ọ̀ni sat on a chair at the foot of Òkè-Mògún while his chiefs bowed to him. In return, the Ọ̀ọ̀ni responded with a raised fist, as if offering a Black Power salute. One onlooker commented, "The Ọ̀ọ̀ni is very modern; he likes ceremonies, and the Ifẹ̀ people, too, love his *afẹfẹyẹ̀yẹ̀* [fun]."[27] His appropriation of an African American symbolic gesture of brotherhood indicated to his followers that he was in touch with the modern global world and thus aware of things that had an impact on their daily lives. After the chiefs bowed to the Ọ̀ọ̀ni, the Àràbà—the chief priest of Ifá—and other Ifá priests took turns greeting the Ọ̀ọ̀ni. The Àràbà knelt down, clapped his hands, murmured Ifá chants, and prayed for the king. At this point, the king's mood changed; instead of offering jubilant greetings, he became prayerful, at times placing his hand on his cheek to indicate mutual recognition of authority between himself and his Ifá priests.

During the last phase of the fourth day's ceremony, the king visited his patrilineal house in the Ìlàré Quarter. On his way, he made brief courtesy calls on the family houses of members of his own royal lineage, who awaited his arrival. From the Òkè-Mògún, he rode in a motorcade through the streets, stopping intermittently to acknowledge the greetings of the people and to accept gifts offered to him. In royal blessing, he touched his people's heads with an *irùkẹ̀rẹ̀*, a horsehair whisk. The Ọ̀ọ̀ni greeted members of specific royal houses related to him, who had decorated their compounds with the royal insignia: a crown and a horsetail flywhisk. They had erected signposts stating the name of their royal household: Ògbórù Olódò, Ògbórù Adéjọkin. Although these houses do not represent the direct descendants of the House of Olúbùṣe, the king's patrilineal line, they share the same royal kinship with the king as co-members of the royal Ògbórù lineage and kinship. The strong relationship between kinship and kingship is symbiotic: the royal houses acknowledge the legitimacy of the incumbent king who rules Ilé-Ifẹ̀ on their behalf, and the king in turn recognizes their right to the throne as equal to his. Through this recognition, history is indirectly constructed and legitimized for the future kingdom. Given the fluidity of Yorùbá kingship and the rules of royal succession, there is pragmatic structure in the king's procession through Ìlàré Quarter. Expediency demands that any royal lineage that wants to participate in future contests for the throne must reaffirm its interest. Since there are four ruling lineages in Ilé-Ifẹ̀, one hundred years may pass before each lineage has its turn to provide a candidate for the throne. Olójó chronicles the royal history of the Yorùbá, providing a "who's who" of personalities in the roster of royal succession.

In the ceremony I witnessed, the Ọ̀ọ̀ni's last destination was the house of his father, Ògbórù Olódò Olúbùṣe, which is built in the style of a palace. At a private ritual in the family house, the elder women honored the king's direct ancestors. In-scribed on top of the veranda pillars were the words "Ògbórù Olódò Royal House," an *arè* crown, and a horsetail flywhisk. Crowds gathered outside, mainly of women wearing uniform outfits made of the same traditional cloth *(aṣọ ẹbí)*, singing praises of the king and his lineage.

At the entrance to the compound, a large ram was tied to an iron gate. Just be-fore the king emerged from his motorcade, the ram was slaughtered so that its blood flowed on the step. Because the ram is the traditional animal sacrificed to the an-cestors, the sacrifice indicated that the central purpose of the visit was to allow the king to offer veneration to his lineage ancestors, especially his father, who had not reigned as an Ọòni. The Ọòni stepped in the blood of the ram as he descended from the front balcony. Welcoming him, the elder women emerged, spontaneously singing in unison, *Wọlé, wọlé, wọlé, Ṣíjúadé, ọmọ Olúbùṣe, ilé bàbá ọmọ kì í b'ọmọ lẹ́rù, wọlé, wọlé, wọlé* (Enter your father's house, a child should not be afraid of com-ing to the father's house. Ṣíjúadé, child of Olúbùṣe, welcome to your father's house). Responding, the king danced to the music and followed them. Embraced by the re-spected Olorìs or "mothers" of the household, the elder women (Ìyá Ilé), and the wives of the deceased Ọba, he entered his father's house. The women who stood outside the house in *aṣọ ẹbí* were the young wives of the house (Obìnrin Ilé), the wives of the male lineage. The special separation of the two age groups indicates the detailed ritual and gender relations of Ọlọ́jọ́. Young wives were considered "out-siders" married to the house and were subordinate to the men or children of the house, but mothers by privilege of seniority were considered "insiders."

These are the women who conduct the ancestral ceremony of the royal house-hold. During the coronation of a new king, his relationship with the creators of the royal house is consummated as he drinks the sacred water, or *Yèyémòólú*, of the palace well. The water is believed to originate from an Olorì, or queen, who was a partner to the Ọba in ancient Ilé-Ifẹ̀. After drinking the water, the new king states that he has "married" *(ṣúlópó)* the wives of his late father, that is, the widows of de-ceased kings. Adopting them as wife-mothers, the new king promises to provide for all their needs. Yorùbá women of age and experience are endowed with "innate" power, and they in turn reassure the king not to fear his father's house, knowing that the king needs their assurance of acceptance. The king needs their consent and goodwill even before he enters his father's own house. He takes his throne and pours liquor, offering schnapps and brandy. He splits open a kola nut, offers a prayer, and bows his head before the women. They, too, pray for him, for a long life and a peace-ful reign. As the scholar Rowland Abíọ́dún has stated, Yoruba women are "openly loved, secretly feared."[28]

In the ceremony that I witnessed, the king, on completing the ritual renewal of the royal house, returned to his motorcade and rode back to the palace. En route, a young man in a wheelchair crossed in front of the motorcade, hoping perhaps to receive prayers and gifts. The king acknowledged his presence and offered him money. Another man lay flat on the road, as if he wanted the motorcade to crush him. But the motorcade halted and again the king offered gifts.

Near the National Museum at Atiba Street, the grand finale of the Ọlọ́jọ́ Festival was commemorated as the Ọbalúfẹ̀ (the Ọ̀ọ̀ni's second in command) visited Igbó Ìja, the hallowed mausoleum of deceased Ilé-Ifẹ̀ kings. The Ọbalúfẹ̀ called on the Yorùbá ancestors, the anointed "sons" of Odùduwà who had departed Ilé-Ifẹ̀ to found new kingdoms of the contemporary Yorùbá nation.[29] The invocation to the founding cultural heroes and the recitation of the primordial founding myth endowed the contemporary political state with the majesty of the sacred. Through this rite, present-day Ilé-Ifẹ̀ reconnects itself with the sovereign and sacred authority of the ancient thrones and with the Yorùbá people, no matter how far they are dispersed. The city-states themselves often perform similar rituals of recounting their origins and renewing ties with the ancient Ilé-Ifẹ̀ celebrations of sovereignty.[30]

Having discussed in detail the ritual process of the Ọlọ́jọ́ Festival and provided a glimpse of the symbolic and ritual images employed, I will interpret key motifs and rituals of Ọlọ́jọ́. The festival may be understood through two often unrelated theoretical discourses: the hermeneutics of the indigenes of Ilé-Ifẹ̀ and the phenomenology and anthropology of ritual.

THE ỌLỌ́JỌ́ FESTIVAL IN THEORY AND PRACTICE

In 1937, the American anthropologist William Bascom became the first outsider to describe in detail the splendor of the Ọlọ́jọ́ Festival, but he did not offer any analysis of his rich data. His account spurred Sandra Barnes in 1980 to ask him to "speculate on some of the meanings of the data" and to "provide the full symbolic range . . . and the full content of the ritual cycle and more analysis of the Ògún materials in light of the whole ideological system."[31]

I would like to examine the Ọlọ́jọ́ performance in a historical and sociocultural context, drawing on ritual theory in particular. Ọlọ́jọ́ is primarily a royal ritual, a genre of ritual that has been the subject of much theoretical and ethnographic research. Royal rituals include performance rites related to the institutions of sacred and divine rulers, such as coronations, funerals, and annual carnivals. They also assert and uphold political power.

The most quoted scholar on royal rituals, Clifford Geertz, has examined the state rituals of Bali's traditional Indonesian monarchy, arguing that the display of pomp and pageantry in these ceremonies upholds the power of the king.[32] Describing Bali as a theocratic state with a ceremonial kingship, Geertz argues that, as a microcosm of the supernatural order, the majesty of the court mirrors the ideal cosmic order.[33] Royal ritual links the cosmic transcendent realm to the political order, thereby legitimizing the latter, and represents an aristocratic appropriation of activities and

ceremonies conducted by commoners in more ordinary contexts. The appropriation explains why royal ritual has a persuasive force over the masses of participants.[34]
Another important study, David McMullen's discussion of the political role of Con-
fucian imperial rituals of Tang China (618–906 AD) that dictate the daily functioning of the state, is also relevant to the Ilé-Ifẹ̀ context.[35] McMullen argues that
in these ceremonies, which address "the cosmic on the one hand, and the social
and moral on the other," "the affirmations of support that surround a traditional
operation of the state cannot always be taken simply at face value, for they very often
disguise other interests."[36] Behind the scenes, rancor, divisiveness, and cutthroat
competition are rife among the agents of the state responsible for formulating and
carrying out imperial ritual activities. The same can be said of the Ilé-Ifẹ̀ kingship
ritual, where the sacred cosmic order is reenacted and relived in the social realm.
Ọlọ́jọ́ brings to the fore the creation of the Ilé-Ifẹ̀ social world where Odùduwà (the
Ọọ̀ni) assumes his superior role as sacred ruler.

Drawing on relevant views of Geertz, Maurice Bloch, and McMullen, as well as
the indigenous hermeneutics of the Ifẹ̀ ritual itself, I provide below a deeper interpretation of Ọlọ́jọ́, emphasizing the relationship of royal ritual to power.

Cosmology and Ọlọ́jọ́ Ritual

From a phenomenological perspective, the central core of Ọlọ́jọ́ is a propitiatory
ritual: sacrifice is offered to the divine powers and cosmological forces to regulate
human activities at the center of the universe, Ilé-Ifẹ̀. The priests eloquently call on
the gods, the spirits of heaven, and the ancestors of the underworld to join in rejuvenating the world of Ilé-Ifẹ̀: *Eégún ayé, èṣìbà òrun, èrò wá o o ká ṣe Ifẹ̀, èrò wá o
ọdún dé.*[37] Ọlọ́jọ́ appeals to three principal gods, spiritual forces, and "correlative"
recipients of ritual offerings:[38] Ògún, god of war and iron; Ajé, goddess of wealth
and prosperity; and Ọ̀rànmíyàn, warlord and cultural hero. Lower-ranking auspicious agents are the ancestral spirits of royalty, the dynasty of primogenitors
and founders of the Yorùbá kingdoms. They represent those who emigrated from
the center to found peripheral states and include the ancestors of the king's own
dynasty, including his royal (deceased) father and grandfather. Other royal ancestors and primogenital ancestors are still lower in status but are revered at the royal
mausoleum.

The ritual that the Ọbalúfẹ̀ performs for the Yorùbá ancestral culture hero has
immensely significant political and cultural effects. Invoking collectively the memory of Odùduwà's sons and daughters who left Ilé-Ifẹ̀ to found new kingdoms, the
Ọbalúfẹ̀ rite incorporates under the cosmic canopy of the sacred city of Ilé-Ifẹ̀ the
far-flung Yorùbá kingdoms. The Ọbalúfẹ̀ extends the dynastic claim of Ilé-Ifẹ̀'s spiritual and cultural hegemony over all Yorùbá-speaking people. The ritual incorporates the Yorùbá diaspora under Ilé-Ifẹ̀'s sovereignty and sanctifies the Ọọ̀ni as
primus inter pares among the Yorùbá Ọba.

The Link between Ritual and Power

While honoring the deities may be the primary purpose that impels Ọlọ́jọ́'s participants to assemble at Òkè-M'ògún and see the great sacrifice, from the commoners' perspective the heart of the performance is the viewing of the *arè* crowning of the Ọ̀ọni and the Ọ̀ọ̀ni's visit to the shrine of Ògún and Ajé's market home. What is the relationship between royal ritual and ordinary participants, as thousands drift to Òkè-M'ògún and the king's palace to celebrate Ọlọ́jọ́? "The crowd in the midst of the hot sun almost made me faint," Bascom confessed.[39] I similarly found that the dense crowds of people made it almost impossible to move from one place to another.[40] Bloch's question, "Why does the royal ritual have the emotional and ideological power to move and organise the participants?" is germane to understanding Ọlọ́jọ́.[41] Going beyond Geertz's explanation of mere splendor and respectability, Bloch proposes that commoners see themselves as an essential part of the ritual celebration. In her article on the Moroccan royal ritual of the prophet's birthday, M. Combs-Schilling similarly points out that every segment of Moroccan society—from village to city—is incorporated into the highly symbolic and performative festival.[42]

In the Ọlọ́jọ́ Festival, the people view the crown—the *arè*—as a spiritual entity and invoke it to ask for good fortune. The wearing of the *arè* transforms the king into a deity, capable of hearing the supplications of his subjects and conveying them to the center of power, the shrine of Ògún. If the Ọ̀ọni delays too long in emerging from the inner palace, the masses become impatient. They burst into song,[43] urging him to come out quickly so they can behold the miraculous *arè*. To ensure that the miracle will occur, they pray that the sacrificial ritual will be protected from any evil glances that might obstruct its power.[44]

Arè á gbè ọ́ (May the *arè* help you) was a greeting I heard from many participants in Ọlọ́jọ́. The sacred crown or *arè* had acquired a spiritual power and authority that could be invoked to bless individuals and groups, to transform evil into good, and to resolve everyday problems in the lives of individuals. Although the *arè* is reserved exclusively for royalty, commoners of the Ifẹ̀ community can invoke its power for personal motives. In so doing, they participate in the divinity of the Ọ̀ọni, the god-king.

The *arè* also has symbolic significance. Why does the Ọ̀ọni adorn himself with such an important symbol of power for only one day of the entire year? Ọlọ́jọ́ is the only mandatory occasion on which the Ọ̀ọni publicly displays his sovereign authority, demonstrating to the nation an important historical truth cloaked in myth. After Odùduwà usurped the royal throne of Ilé-Ifẹ̀, the Ìsòrò priest-kings who had previously ruled the territory were reduced to "token kings," politically marginal but symbolically important in Ilé-Ifẹ̀ mythology. Bloch is accurate in claiming that a proper understanding of royal ritual requires consideration of the politics of royalty.[45] I would add myth and history to his list. As Bloch remarked in his critique of Geertz's one-sided interpretation of Balinese ritual, "Because Geertz insists that royal rituals can be explained only in terms of themselves, he is unable to link their content with the political-economic side of Balinese kingdoms. . . . However, in the end the ritual must have been created by circumstances and human action in social context."[46]

Although it is not known precisely when Ọlọ́jọ́ developed, certain symbols provide clues. Close examination of the *arè* crown reveals a striking resemblance with the *òró*, the officiating "crown" worn by the priest-chiefs (Ìṣòrò) who led the pre-Odùduwà aboriginal groups.[47] Literally, *òró* means something that stands erect, and the priests are called Ìṣòrò because they constitute the priesthood class in charge of the Ilé-Ifẹ̀ ritual calendar. Unlike the customary royal Yorùbá crown worn by the Ọọ̀ni, the priest-chiefs' *òró* is conical—erect when worn but, when lying flat, resembling the miter of the Anglican or Catholic bishop. The Ìṣòrò's titles begin with a prefix Ọba-, indicating that they were rulers and kings of the aboriginal territories before the Odùduwà usurpation. Today they perform merely ritual functions for their lineages, although the Ìṣòrò are still regarded as "Ọba" by their people.

Like the *òró* crown worn on ritual occasions, the *arè* is worn by the Ọọ̀ni on Òkè-Mògún Day, when the Ọọ̀ni assumes the role of a priest-king in visiting the shrines of Ògún and Ajé to solicit assistance on behalf of Ifẹ̀ people. The Ìṣòrò wear the *òró*, which symbolizes the crown of Ilé-Ifẹ̀'s original rulers before Odùduwà's conquest. The Ọọ̀ni wears the *arè*, a "unique" but miraculously powerful crown, a sign of his conquest of the land and the legitimacy of his status as king of all kings, Ọba Àwọn Ọba. The *arè* crown is larger and, unlike the *òró*, bears the *àṣẹ*, symbol of the authority and ultimate power of the Ọọ̀ni. The Ọọ̀ni thus proclaims not only that he is the descendant of Odùduwà but that he has power over Ilé-Ifẹ̀'s original rulers. In this context, the *arè* is a highly potent and "magical" crown. Thus the Ọlọ́jọ́ performance is more than a ritual of abundance and propitiation to Ògún and Ajé; it is in addition a political act.

Local Ritual and Modernity

If Ọlọ́jọ́ is a local Ilé-Ifẹ̀ festival, public reporting about the ritual, especially in the media over the past five years, has transformed its meaning and function so that it now extends far beyond the Ilé-Ifẹ̀ metropolis, as far away as the black Atlantic diaspora, and assumes a larger authority, especially in the developing nation-state of Nigeria. In my study of Oǹdó monarchy rituals, I argued that the Ọdún Ọba ceremony there, like Ọlọ́jọ́ in Ilé-Ifẹ̀, serves as a ritual of a unifying civil religion. The Ọdún Ọba ceremony brings together all the disparate religious factions in Oǹdó society to acknowledge the king's leadership, just as he acknowledges and participates in the religiously diverse pluralistic system. As a de facto "patron of all faith traditions" *(onígbogbo èsìn),* the king rules over all faiths. Although Ọlọ́jọ́ lacks the ritual narrative that supports the performance of Ọdún Ọba, which provides the interpretive framework of Oǹdó civil religion, both ceremonies are powerfully integrative.

At the Ọlọ́jọ́ Festival that he observed in 1937, Bascom reported the presence of Muslim imams, Christians, and representatives of the Ọ̀ràngún of Ìlá, a Yorùbá Ọba and descendant of Odùduwà who had founded the new Ìgbómìnà Kingdom in the northeastern Yorùbá province.[48] In addition, representatives of the major Ilé-Ifẹ̀ civil and religious sectors—the eight senior civil chiefs who govern Ifẹ̀ quarters (Ọ̀tún Ifẹ̀), the warlords, the junior or palace chiefs (Mọdéwá), the chief priests of the prominent òrìṣà cults, Ìṣòrò, and diviners—took turns performing the ritual of submission, taking the oath of allegiance to the Ọ̀ọ̀ni and acknowledging his authority and sovereignty.

Innovations in the performance of Ọlọ́jọ́ have occurred in the context of the nation-state and have reflected Ilé-Ifẹ̀'s increasing pluralism. Since the ascendancy of the current Ọ̀ọ̀ni Olúbùṣe, local Ọlọ́jọ́ festivals have been linked to national, if not global, economic interests. The festival now coincides with what is often called Ifẹ̀ Day, a day dedicated to community development when Ifẹ̀ sons and daughters return to the city to raise funds for development projects, clubs, and community associations in the city and try to outdo each other in their expressions of solidarity and support for their community. Because the arè continues to function as the symbol of Ilé-Ifẹ̀ unity, these social clubs and community organizations have adopted it as their logo. Thus Ọlọ́jọ́'s quasi-religious rituals now function as a civic and social celebration. In a community-sponsored brochure and in the Ifẹ̀ News, paid advertisements congratulated the Ọ̀ọ̀ni on the Ọlọ́jọ́ Festival.

For his part, in 1989, the Ọ̀ọ̀ni distributed pamphlets whose title, "Greetings from the Throne," reflected the transformation Ọlọ́jọ́ had assumed in the last decade of his reign. In the Ọ̀ọ̀ni's own words: "On the occasion of yet another year in the annuals [sic] of our history, another year in the celebration of the Festival of Ọlọ́jọ́, the festival of all festivals, the festival of all Yorùbá, I have the honor to say greetings to all of you."[49] In addition to claiming the great festival for all Yorùbá, Ọbalúfẹ̀'s ritual at the mausoleum of ancient Ifẹ̀ kings was made more meaningful as the Ọ̀ọ̀ni enjoined the Yorùbá to cooperate with the federal government of Nigeria to support the program of transition to a democratic political administration. The Ọ̀ọ̀ni referred to state politics and the abandoned transitional program under the military rule of General Ibrahim Babangida, whose wife, Mariam Babangida, and emissaries were seated in the Ọ̀ọ̀ni's palace during this particular day of Ọlọ́jọ́.

In the same speech, the Ọ̀ọ̀ni established Ọlọ́jọ́ in a national context of inter-ethnic cooperation, religious tolerance, and peaceful coexistence: "Ọlọ́jọ́ is traditionally a period of peace and mutual cooperation among all different classes of the society. Therefore, the message of Ọlọ́jọ́ can be nationally interpreted as meaning mutual cooperation among all ethnic and religious groups of this country. If all of us regardless of religious beliefs, ethnic affiliation, and political groups can with joy

FIGURE 15. A high chief in the Ọlọ́jọ́ Festival. Photo by W. Bascom (1950s).

and happiness proceed to Òkè-M'ògún in Ilé-Ifẹ̀ forgetting all these differences, we can as well live together in Nigeria in peace and tranquility."[50] Linking such rituals to larger interethnic issues and to critical problems of nation building and national unity, the Ọ̀ọ̀ni made nationally relevant what his predecessors had celebrated as a local Ilé-Ifẹ̀ ceremony.[51]

This chapter has described the Ọlọ́jọ́ Festival of Ògún. Leader among the gods, Ògún is the Yorùbá god of iron and war. The spectacular festival renews the people's belief in their sacred king and their understanding of the cosmos in which their god-king (the Ọ̀ọ̀ni, the descendant of Odùduwà) rules Ilé-Ifẹ̀, just as, to a lesser extent, their goddess (Ajé) rules over wealth and the market economy. The ceremony unifies the faithful of all religious factions, who acknowledge the king's rule just as he acknowledges their pluralistic religious systems. Dignitaries of all faiths and stations as well as ordinary folk perform the ritual of submission, swearing the oath of allegiance to their god-king, the king of kings, acknowledging his supreme authority. The spectacle and majesty of the festival reinforce the king's power and lend legitimacy to the king's political order by linking it with the supernatural cosmic realm.

Ọlọ́jọ́ as a civil religious celebration exemplifies the continued relevance of *òrìṣà* tradition in the modern age. It provides a central role to the Ọ̀ọ̀ni in the religious and social order and demonstrates his position as the patron of all the civic religious spheres in his community. Ọlọ́jọ́ also portrays a guiding value of Yoruba religious experience, the quest for good life as described in the sacred blessings of wealth, fecundity, and longevity. The Ọ̀ọ̀ni as the embodiment of the ethos of the community must take his charge seriously in the Ọlọ́jọ́ Festival. The strength of the community in the cosmic order depends on his performance of these sacred rituals.

5

Ìtàpá

*Identity, Ritual, and Power in the Festival
of Ọbàtálá and Yemòó*

Erúwá dájì.
Mo wá ọkọ.
Mo wá aya.
Mo wá, Yemòó, Ìbànìba.
Ọwọ́ párá, ẹsẹ̀ párá.
Àsìngbó, Àsìntọ́.
Àyúnwá ìsìn, àsùnpa ìsìn.
Kí n máa yún, kí n máa wá.
Késẹ̀ mi má sè e.
Kí n sọdún ìí, kí n sẹ̀mìí.
K'áyé rójú, k'óde Ìlú tòrò.
Kí Ṣíjúadé pẹ́ l'ọba!
K'ó sẹ́gun ọ̀tá, kó réhìn odì.
K'àgàn rọbí.
Kí àgàn tọwọ́ àlà bosùn fi pa ọmọ lára.

I greet You, oh great deity.
I seek the husband [Ọbàtálá].
I seek the wife [Yemòó].
I seek Yemòó, the one we worship.
With my hands and with my legs [with my whole body], I salute you.
I will worship you until I am old.
I will propitiate you until I die in old age.
May I come and go home in peace.
May my legs never cease from coming to worship you.
We celebrate this year, and we shall celebrate the next.

May the world have peace, and may our town see prosperity!
May Ṣíjúadé [the Ọ̀ni] reign long!
May he defeat his enemies and overcome all opposition.
May infertile women conceive and give birth to children!

MORNING PRAYER TO ỌBÀTÁLÁ AND YEMÒÓ

Kneeling reverently before stone statues of the divine couple—the deity Ọbàtálá and his spouse, Yemòó—priests and devotees alike recite the Morning Prayer as an invocation in Ìdìta Ilé, the home and temple of Ọbàtálá and Yemòó. Once the prayers are recited, the priests solemnly break open a kola nut to perform a simple divination that will determine the mood of Ọbàtálá and Yemòó and consequently the good or bad that may be in store for their devotees. After this simple invocation, participants may sit and attend to the business of the day, which may include performing various forms of sacrifice to the deities on behalf of clients and supplicants who visit the temple to consult with Ọbàtálá and Yemòó.

As I accompanied the Ọbaléṣùn, Ilé-Ifẹ̀'s chief priest of Ọbàtálá, to the temple to observe the Morning Prayer, I was caught up in the complex rituals performed in honor of the highest-ranking deity in the Yorùbá pantheon—Ọbàtálá.[1] As we saw in the previous chapter, the first of the 201 deities in Ilé-Ifẹ̀ cosmology, Ọbàtálá, was originally designated by the Supreme Being to perform the work of creation at Ilé-Ifẹ̀. However, as he embarked on the great commission, his attention was diverted by the other òrìṣà, who invited him to join them in drinking palm wine. Unfortunately, he got drunk and fell asleep, thus enabling Odùduwà to steal from him the substances essential for creation and to descend into Ilé-Ifẹ̀ to create an incomplete but fairly habitable place. But though Odùduwà became the Ọba (sacred king) in charge of the created world, Ọbàtálá still possessed the àṣe, the sacred energy without which the Ọba cannot function. Their struggle for power, which first resulted in a cosmic battle over control of the world, ended in negotiations that produced a separation between ritual authority and political or state power in the Yorùbá worldview and society. This chapter will explore this division between ritual and state power in the social order of Ilé-Ifẹ̀. The Odùduwà-Ọbàtálá epic, like other epics around the world, describes the paradigmatic structures upon which subsequent Yorùbá cities and towns have been modeled. More importantly, the epic provides a lens for viewing the nature and function of Ọbàtálá and his spouse, Yemòó, in Ilé-Ifẹ̀ and Yorùbá religion. These two deities, who for members of the Ìdìta lineage constitute their life force and the center of their identity, reveal their significance in the daily life of Ilé-Ifẹ̀ as well as in the annual festival that is dedicated to them. As the Morning Prayer shows, Ọbàtálá is never propitiated without

Yemòó, and in rituals, iconography, and myths they are always linked. An examination of this marital relationship thrusts us into the heart of gender dynamics in Ilé-Ifẹ̀ ritual life.

A central concern of this chapter is to show how the Ìdìta people, who claim Ọbàtálá as their deity, define their relationship to the sacred center through ritual performance, including the great annual festival. I will argue that the Ọbàtálá Festival reinforces the Ìdìta people's subethnic and cultural identity through their dramatization and reutilization of the primordial battle between Odùduwà and Ọbàtálá. The festival displays not only Ọbàtálá's defeat but also the subsequent triumph of his ritual power over the conqueror Odùduwà's political authority and military success.[2]

My other objective in this chapter is to unravel the complex mythic and ritual relationship between Ọbàtálá (and, by extension, Yemòó) and the Ìdìta people. Although as a subculture they have been integrated into Ilé-Ifẹ̀, the Ìdìta still maintain a separate close-knit clan identity and a lineage for which Ọbàtálá and Yemòó are tutelary deities. I will examine how the tradition of Ọbàtálá provides the ideological basis for the spatial boundaries maintained by the group, how Ìdìta festivals and ritual processes construct and shape Ìdìta identity, and how the Ìdìta people relate to the polity of the Ilé-Ifẹ̀ sacred center.[3]

RELIGION AND GROUP IDENTITY CONSTRUCTION: THEORETICAL FRAMEWORK

The Ìdìta people, the devotees of Ọbàtálá, constitute a socio-religious entity within the larger Ilé-Ifẹ̀ community. Ìdìta myths, rituals, ceremonies, and worldview provide the basis for processing, constructing, and promoting the group's subcultural identity, in contrast to the powerful pan-Yorùbá ethos cultivated in the myths and rituals surrounding Odùduwà, though paradoxically Ọbàtálá and Odùduwà share the same myth of origin. In examining aspects of the Ìdìta identity-building process, I will borrow from the works of several scholars in the social sciences and cultural studies. Lester Kurtz outlines four ways in which religious traditions in general construct group identities: (1) Through their belief systems (mythology), the group lays out archetypal models of behavior and criteria for evaluating good and evil. (2) The group periodically connects with important reference groups, living or dead, whose association with the members of the community is vital to their existence and survival. These include ancestors or the so-called living dead and religious personages such as the head of the community itself. (3) Through ritual activities, the group constantly interacts and engages with those considered the ultimate transcendent figures, namely, deities and tutelary spirits. (4) The group serves as a sacred canopy and source of stability for individuals in the community, especially when they are faced with socially threatening problems such as illness, death, and loss of material wealth.[4] In a similar manner, several of Hans Mol's studies on the identity model of religion confirm how religion provides identity consolidation (sacralization) through the four mechanisms of objectification, commitment, ritual, and myth.[5] In addition, although the dominance and misuse of cultural studies have lately come under criticism, recent scholarship in this field provides penetrating theoretical insight into the understanding of identity formation, especially as it relates to the theory and politics of identity and difference.[6]

My interest here is in the Ìdìta people's articulation of a group identity, their claim to moral, magical, and ritual power and superiority vis-à-vis the political authority of the sacred kingship and other related figures (diviners, civil chiefs, etc.) who make up Ilé-Ifẹ̀'s secular and spiritual spheres, in the context of a dialectical relationship between subaltern and dominant identities. I intend to address some of the concerns of Lawrence Grossberg, who, echoing a number of cultural theorists, has castigated contemporary identity theorists for sidestepping the conflicting nature of discourses of power by "ignoring the positivity of the subaltern—as the possessor of other knowledges and traditions; as having their own history in which there are power relations defined within the ranks of the subordinated."[7]

In interpreting the identity-forging quest of the Ìdìta people, the devotees of Ọbàtálá, I shall also borrow from Harjot Oberoi's study of the production and reproduction of Sikh cultural identities as these have evolved over time in a specific geographical region. Oberoi considers the following themes of central significance in identity construction: the constitution of the sacred space, taboo behavior, life-cycle rituals, the dynamics of transgression, and the group's definition of the "other." Oberoi observes that rituals constitute a key element in the construction of religious identity.[8] I will examine the ideological, moral, and ritual basis of Ìdìta identity and how this distinct identity is fostered through the festival of Ọbàtálá.

I propose that ritual power, a central focus of the Ìdìta identity construction mechanism, encompasses a large terrain, both secular and sacred. It defines the control over the quintessential àṣẹ, the source of the ultimate power of the Ọ̀ọ̀ni, and it spells out their control over ajé, the source of the town's wealth, prosperity, and fertility. Ideologically, the festival demonstrates (as Madan Sarup has argued) how vital supernatural powers, which are perceived by outsiders as marginal, can be symbolically central in actual life.[9] Because of their conquest by the Odùduwà people, the Ìdìta people have been governed under the new dispensation. Nevertheless, they have maintained a symbolically and morally central place in Ilé-Ifẹ̀'s affairs.

THE NATURE OF THE DEITY

Ọbàtálá is the fashioner god, and his primary responsibility is to mold human beings out of clay according to the àṣẹ, the divine power given him by the Supreme Being.[10] In this manner, Ọbàtálá is regarded as the creator god, the owner of the good clay *(alámọ̀ rere)*. One of his *oríkì* is Ẹ̀ní Ṣojú Ṣemú (The One Who Fashions the Eyes and the Nose). Another name, Adáni Bó Ti Rí, refers to the freedom he enjoys to mold as he pleases. Belief in the fashioning power of the deity is so strong that he is regarded as responsible for creating all varieties of human beings born on earth: beautiful, ugly, deformed, or physically handicapped, all of whom are referred to as *ẹni òrìṣà* (the people and votaries of *òrìṣà*). To him belong the details and the aesthetic design of the human form. Designing the human body, Ọbàtálá pays particular attention to the features of the head or *orí*—the nose, eyes, ears, mouth, and face. A malformed mouth is caused by poor design. Hence, a Yorùbá proverb holds, "One should not laugh at a person with protruding teeth because the deformity is caused by the fashioner god, who made the teeth without covering them with flesh" *(Kì í ṣe ẹ̀bi eléyín ganngan, òrìṣà ló ṣe é tí kò fi awọ bò ó).*[11]

The followers and the enemies of Ọbàtálá have persistently debated possible explanations for deformities among the humans he creates. Ọbàtálá's followers argue that these irregularities were made intentionally to show the power and might of the deity. They hold that Ọbàtálá is a perfect fashioner and that the clay he uses to mold humans is perfect *(alámọ̀ rere).* Ọbàtálá's adversaries argue that the deformities among his creations resulted from Ọbàtálá's drunkenness. The Yorùbá myth of creation holds that he was drunk at the time of creation and thus that he missed the chance to create a complete cosmos. I consider the explanation of deformity as caused by Ọbàtálá's divine mistake to be a theodic narrative that clarifies deformity as a form of imperfection. If deformed persons are seen as votaries of the *òrìṣà*, they are given protection, privileges, and freedom that perfectly functioning humans do not enjoy. In reality, in Ilé-Ifẹ̀ and most Yorùbá cities, albinos *(ààfín)* and those with hunched backs *(abuké)* are treated as sacred beings.[12] Like twins *(ìbejì),* they are accorded respect and honor wherever they go. It is a serious taboo to laugh at their deformity. They are at liberty to enter any marketplace and to help themselves to market wares without paying a *kobo.*[13] Such is the influence of Ọbàtálá over his creations.

Among the pantheon of 201 deities, Ọbàtálá's position is so strong that often the generic term for deity, *òrìṣà,* refers specifically to him.[14] Ọbàtálá is referred to by different epithets that illustrate not only his place in the Yorùbá pantheon but also his mythical and historical context. He is described as Aníyìkáyé, a deity whose honor extends worldwide, like that of the Supreme God, Olódùmarè, and as Bàbá Olú-Ifẹ̀, the guardian father of Ilé-Ifẹ̀'s rulers. Even as an *òrìṣà,* Ọbàtálá is as renowned as the Supreme God himself. As the deity who makes the Ọọ̀ni's rule possible through his *àṣẹ,* his role as a father of Ifẹ̀ rulers is particularly highlighted in the rituals to be examined later in the chapter. Another epithet of mystical importance is the reference to Ọbàtálá as Ọ̀ṣẹ̀rẹ̀ Ìgbò, King of the Ìgbò. In accounts of Odùduwà's migratory legend, the Ìgbò—as we will see in chapter 7—were among the aboriginal groups that immigrants to Ilé-Ifẹ̀ encountered in battle. The festival of Ọbàtálá has been interpreted as a reenactment of such Odùduwà-Ìgbò encounters as well as the festival of the king of the Ìgbò people, who are now incarnated as the Ìdìta people.

My encounters with the devotees of Ọbàtálá led me to identify as a major theme of their repeated portrayals of their deity his truthfulness and high moral character. Never would the Ọbálẹ́ṣùn, chief priest of Ọbàtálá, utter any significant statement in the course of my interaction with him without invoking Ọbàtálá's lofty moral status. Much as an Anglican priest introduces the prologue to a communion service with the phrase "Hear ye, oh Israel, the Lord thy God is one, Thou shalt have no other gods before me," the Ọbálẹ́ṣùn constantly proclaimed, *Ọbàtálá ni Alooo! Èèwọ̀ mọ́ ọn ni, èèwọ̀ danin danin!* (Ọbàtálá says, Listen! It is taboo; it is indeed a great taboo!). The taboo he was referring to was on lying, filthiness, stealing, adultery, drunkenness, or any other behaviors that could tarnish Ọbàtálá's purity. To tell a lie or be deceitful in the shrine of Ọbàtálá is to invoke his wrath. Stories abound about how the deity has punished offenders who break his taboos. His followers wear "pure" white cloth *(aṣọ àlà)* to signify their devotion to truthfulness and their cultivation of a pure ethical character.

Second in rank to the Supreme God, Ọbàtálá bears attributes and honor resembling those of the Supreme God.[15] He is often praised as Òrìṣà Àgbáyé (Universal God), an attribute normally reserved for the Supreme God. Because he ruled the territory before Odùduwà, and is still acknowledged as a king by his devotees, he is still described with epithets of kingship such as Ọbàtarìṣà (God-King or King of the Gods). Since numerous Yorùbá cities, including Ilé-Ifẹ̀, Èjìgbò, Ìlawẹ̀, Ìjàyè, and Popo, claim Ọbàtálá as their founder or have adopted him as a tutelary god, he is often invoked by epithets that describe him as the father, lord, or deity of a city, such as "the Òrìṣà of Ifẹ̀" or "the Òrìṣà of Ògìyán [Ejìgbò]." A central feature of Yorùbá religion and city spirituality is that a particular settlement or township derives sacredness from its relationship to a major deity or cultural hero that played the central role in its foundational myth or history. The town's civil religion and sacred kingship are based on the myth, rituals, and symbols of their particular deity.[16]

However, in Ilé-Ifẹ̀, Ọbàtálá's power is premised on moral right rather than on political authority, which he lost in the primordial battle between himself and Odùduwà's group. As we observed in the last chapter, Ọbàtálá bestows on Odùduwà the *àṣẹ,* the divine power to rule, symbolized in the Ọọ̀ni's *arè* or sacred crown. Ọbàtálá is therefore called Aládé Ṣẹ́ṣẹ́fun (Owner of the Crown of Ṣẹ́ṣẹ́fun Wool), referring to the principal royal wool in the Ọọ̀ni's *arè.*

THE DIVINE COUPLE: ỌBÀTÁLÁ AND YEMÒÓ

The divine couple Ọbàtálá and Yemòó usually appear together as spouses in rituals and iconography, especially in Ilé-Ifẹ̀. They are viewed as complementary to one another and as together representing wholeness. In Ilé-Ifẹ̀ religion, several male

deities are portrayed as being married at one time or another to a female deity. However, Ọbàtálá is *typically* portrayed in relationship to his spouse. One reason for this
is that the divine couple may belong to the category of deities that according to Hilda
Davidson the Scandinavians called "fertility deities of the earth" as opposed to the
"gods of the sovereignty, magic, and warfare" (under which category Ògún, described in chapter 4, would fall).[17] Ifá divination poetry, one of the chief sources
for understanding the nature and character of the gods of Ilé-Ifẹ̀, supports the theory that Ọbàtálá and Yemòó represent a divine primordial couple. One *odù* (divination verse) suggests that at the time of creation in Ilé-Ifẹ̀ male and female deities
lived apart. Yemòó's power and self-discipline elevated her to the status of head of
the female deities. Female deities desired male companions, and through the divination mechanism of Ọ̀rúnmìlà, Yemòó and Ọbàtálá were married. The marriage
bestowed a new status and leadership role on Yemòó as the head of all female deities
and of all women (Olórí Bìnrin). Thus Yemòó became the mother of all people on
earth (Ìyá Ayé Gbogbo). The Ifá story presents the origin of marriage as both a divine and a human institution.[18]

Ọbàtálá and Yemòó may remind us of the archetypal couple Adam and Eve, but
it is important to emphasize that they are a divine couple. Yemòó's status was that
of mother and wife, a model of the ideal Yorùbá woman. But unlike several traditions in which male and female deities were conceived as co-creators of the universe, as in Aztec Nahuatl religion, in Ilé-Ifẹ̀ myth the two individuals became a
couple after creation, marrying here on earth.[19] The following song of Ifá illustrates
vividly the nature and quintessential role of Yemòó:

> *Owó ni o ń wá?*
> *Ni o ò sin*
> *Aya bàbá Àgbà?*
> *Ọmọ ni o ń wá?*
> *Ni o ò sin*
> *Aya bàbá Àgbà?*
> *Ilé ni o ń wa?*
> *Ni o ò sin*
> *Aya bàbá Àgbà?*[20]
>
> Are you seeking money?
> Why not propitiate
> The wife of the great father?
> Are you seeking children?
> Why not propitiate
> The wife of the great father?
> Are you seeking a house?
> Why not propitiate
> The wife of the great father?

These lyrics remind devotees that if they seek the blessings of money, children, and a good life (such as the ownership of a house), Yemòó, the wife of the great god, will answer their prayers. As a goddess she is in no way inferior in essence or function to male gods. As one of the devotees at Ìdìta Ilé, the shrine of Ọbàtálá and Yemòó, informed me, "*Ajé* (money), *ọmọ* (children), and *àṣẹ* (a good life) are at the foot of the *òrìṣà*. The divine pair control all blessings that a devotee's religious quest desires." The stories about them characteristically recount events relating to wealth, procreation, fecundity, children, and marriage.

The marriage of Ọbàtálá and Yemòó is meant to represent the ideal husband-wife relationship in Yorùbá society. A narrative myth suggests why Yemòó plays a central role in the Ọbàtálá Festival and ceremony and why she is revered in several Ifá divination corpuses. According to this myth, when Ọbàtálá took Yemòó as his wife, she stopped drinking water and instead began to show a preference for animal blood, which she drank on a daily basis.[21] It made her a very powerful woman, but having consumed and absorbed the blood, the life force of animals, Yemòó could not conceive. So the couple consulted a diviner-priest, who, after performing Ifá divination, prescribed the necessary sacrifices for her and told her that she needed to have absolute trust in her husband: if she continued to question his comings and goings, she could lose her life. To satisfy Yemòó's new bloodthirsty appetite, Ọbàtálá, too, consulted an Ifá diviner, who made him a magical spoon. Whenever Ọbàtálá went hunting, he could point the spoon at an animal, and the spoon would draw blood from the animal's body. This enabled Ọbàtálá to fetch an ample supply of fresh blood for his wife on a daily basis. Curious to discover the secret of how Ọbàtálá obtained her daily blood, Yemòó made a pinhole at the bottom of Ọbàtálá's hunting bag and filled it with ashes. As Ọbàtálá departed for the forest, the ashes marked his tracks. Yemòó followed behind. When Ọbàtálá reached the hunting forest, which was usually full of game, he waited for hours without any sign of an animal. Then, all of a sudden, he heard movement in the bush close by, and he pointed the magic spoon in that direction, not knowing that Yemòó was hiding there. Yemòó collapsed immediately as blood gushed out of her vagina. Ọbàtálá rushed to the spot and to his dismay discovered Yemòó. He quickly carried her to the Ifá diviner, who reminded Ọbàtálá of Ifá's warning to Yemòó long ago. The Ifá priest prescribed an appropriate sacrifice of five hens to be offered to Ọrúnmìlà each day. Accordingly, the blood stopped gushing out of Yemòó's vagina, and she began menstruating regularly. Later, she conceived and bore several children for Ọbàtálá.[22]

Yemòó's story underscores how important it is in Yorùbá culture for women to become wives and mothers. Her initial childlessness shows her to be an unfortunate woman who reflects the fate of childless women in that culture. Her barrenness is cured when she is struck by the magical spoon: she begins to menstruate, conceives, and bears children. In this myth, then, "the burden of the well-being of

the marital relationship truly falls most heavily on the wife."[23] As a formerly bar-
ren woman who becomes pregnant after years of infertility, she has a story that can
resonate with Ilé-Ifẹ̀ women who are desperate over their gynecological crises, and
such women flock to her shrine. Just as in Ilé-Ifẹ̀ women are blamed for their infertility, in this myth Yemòó's infertility is attributed to her incessant probing into
her husband's private life. Nevertheless, what she ultimately becomes, "the source
of fertility and nourishment," makes her exemplary for women in her accomplishment of one of the three blessings of the òrìṣà—procreation and the joy of children.[24]

Interestingly, Yemòó's drinking of blood is in Yoruba thought a symbol of secret
power. Yemòó abhors the cool water associated with Ọbàtálá, the god of purity. She
prefers to drink the animal blood associated with the dangerous power of witches,
who control the life force that blood symbolizes.

We may read this narrative as a patriarchal story. Wives are expected to be submissive and to restrict their activities to private domestic spaces. Hunting and other
exploits take men to places out of women's reach. The story invokes the negative
stereotype of wives as inquisitive beings who will risk their own safety to discover
their husbands' well-kept secrets. It depicts family social relations in the day-to-day
lives of Yorùbá people. However, it also challenges patriarchal hegemonies. Yemòó
was no ordinary woman. Her iconography depicts her as an obese woman, double
the size of her husband, even if in this story her large size can be maintained only
by a vampirelike practice of drinking blood. When she goes into the forest to track
the movements of her husband, the animals that her husband ordinarily hunts to
obtain blood for her are mysteriously nowhere to be found. Yemòó is admonished
by Ifá to conform to the Yorùbá social realities, to maintain a normal relationship
with her husband. But the diviner-priest's warning indicates that he recognizes her
innate spiritual power and energy.

By crossing the boundary between home and the forest, Yemòó disturbs the flow
of blood, a critical element in this story. As Victor Turner clearly illustrates, blood
represents the life force, but it is capable of multiple meanings, both negative and
positive.[25] Just as animal blood sustains Yemòó, so it propitiates the gods and goddesses during the sacrificial animal celebration of Ọbàtálá. It signals both death for
the animal victims and the menstrual flow, which, though considered polluting and
dangerous, is also life-giving. For Yemòó it is "the basis of her greatest power to
procreate and bring about a new-born to the lineage." The blessings of procreation
and fecundity are traceable to her, the mother of all humans. Like the Hindu goddess Sakti, Yemòó has an "innate female energy" that is "powerful, creative and
somewhat unpredictable."[26] Only with the magical spoon can Yemòó be subdued.
The Yorùbá proverb says, *Olóògùn ló lè ṣe ọkọ àjẹ́* (Only a medicine man can be the
husband of a witch). *Ọko* or "husband" here means the one who controls and do-
mesticates the "other"—not necessarily the female-wife but the subordinate, the
ruled or the domesticated one.

Yemòó, then, like the Hindu goddess Devi, is at once a bloodthirsty deity, a giver of wealth, and a mother who procreates and gives good life.[27] She is a subordinate feminine deity who is "associated with a potentially destructive force that must be restrained" by magical and medicinal means employed by her husband. Her blood-thirsty appetite and "sinister aspects" are subdued by procreation.[28]

TERRITORY, REGION, AND IDENTITY CONSTRUCTION

Throughout the duration of Ọdún Ọbàtálá, which forms the core of this chapter, I was struck by the pattern of movement and the procession of the devotees that ac-companied most of the rituals. The procession began from the divine couple's tem-ple located at Ìdìta Ilé (the home place) and moved through several alleys lined with adjoining houses occupied by people who considered themselves Ọmọ Ìdìta, "chil-dren" of the Ìdìta lineage. It continued through the marketplace where the main shrine of Ajé was located, through Ìta Yemòó (Yemòó's compound) to Ìdìta Oko (village, farm place and forest home of the couple), and back to Ìdìta Ilé. The ritual serves as a means of delineating boundaries, as I once claimed about the Ìwọ́ Pópó ceremony in the sacred festival of Ọ̀sun in Òṣogbo, Nigeria.[29]

Ìdìta group identity is formed and maintained through the symbolic and actual acknowledgment of the vast community called Ará Ìdìta (the Ìdìta people) and their territory.[30] Within this territory are specific sacred precincts such as Ìta Yemòó (Yemòó's Place), the locale of Ọbàtálá's wife and the starting place for some pro-cessions. This is the midway point between Ìdìta Ilé and Ìdìta Oko. While Ìdìta Ilé, the home place and temple, is for the Ìdìta people the "center of the world," Ìdìta Oko invokes their emotions as a place of exile, a place where Ọbàtálá settled when the Odùduwà group and supporters drove him out of Ìdìta Ilé.[31] As Zdzisław Mach has noted, "The land of the ancestors has always been a part of a group's cultural world view, a major component of their symbolic model of the universe. It was fa-miliar, close, and composed of meaningful objects which served as idioms of the conceptual model of identity."[32] In addition, as Anthony Smith has explained, the sacred and special bond between the group and the territory "becomes an essen-tial part of the collective memory and identity of the community."[33]

On the way to Ìdìta Oko, just a few kilometers beyond the area where the Ìdìta sacred bush grows and where the medicinal leaves for the festival are gathered, lies a large area of land. Through the efforts of the Ìdìta people a large piece of this land was carved out to build a community college for the youth of Ìdìta, primarily in re-sponse to modern development. At the time of the school's official registration, to reflect their aspirations and thoughts concerning their land and deity, the Ìdìta people named it Ọbàtálá High School in honor of their god and cultural hero. How-ever, the Ìbàdàn state government objected to this name. The suggestion to call the new school Ọbàtálá High School was in line with previous practices in ancient Ilé-

Ifẹ̀, whereby schools were named after the gods of the lineage of benefactors who donated the land on which the schools were built, as in the case of such older schools as Odùduwà College, Mọrèmi High School, and Olúorogbo, named after Ifẹ̀ gods and goddesses, and even Catholic schools such as Our Lady's and St. John's, named after Christian saints. Now times have changed, and many government bureaucrats are fundamentalist Christians and Muslims who assume that traditional gods have disappeared. But traditions do not die easily, and though the Ìdìta people settled for their lineage name as the official name for their new high school (Ìdìta High School), among themselves they still refer to their school as Ọbàtálá High School.

STAGES OF THE ỌBÀTÁLÁ FESTIVAL

The Ọbàtálá Festival consists of four main ritual performances: (a) Ìwọlé Ọdún (the commencement ceremony), (b) Ìṣúlé (the plucking of the sacred medicinal leaves), (c) Ìpiwọ̀ (the sacrificial rituals), and (d) Ìtàpá (the festival day).

Ìwọlé Ọdún: The Commencement Ceremony

I will group all the ritual activities that are performed in preparation for the beginning of the Ọbàtálá Festival under the name Ìwọlé Ọdún (Entering the Festival). The Ọbàtálá Festival is announced at the end of the Odùduwà Festival when one of the chief priests of Ọbàtálá, Ọbaléṣùn, proclaims that the festival of Ọbàtálá will commence on the seventeenth day. The announcement of the Ọbàtálá Festival officially ends the prohibition against drumming in the city; as the Ifẹ̀ say, *Níjọ́ on làgbá gẹ̀ẹ̀rẹ̀ un na fijọ́ orò ditàdógún nídìta* (The day that the big *agba* drum is sounded is the day we announce in Ìdìta that the festival commences on the seventeenth day). Since it is taboo to sound any drum during the Odùduwà Festival, which is a more somber nightly ritual, only Ọbàtálá's power can reverse this taboo by sounding the drum to set the space for his own festival. The devotees of Ọbàtálá boast of his might with a proverb: *Ìlù tí Oòduà bá tì, òrìṣà ló tó ṣi* (The prohibition Odùduwà places against drumming is lifted only by Ọbàtálá). The reference obviously indicates the rivalry, if not enmity, between the Ọbàtálá and the Odùduwà groups, a rivalry that goes back to the creation myth. That Ọbàtálá is powerful enough to lift the taboo placed by a supposedly more powerful rival accords Ọbàtálá more respect and legitimacy among the deities. Yorùbá descriptions of the Ọbàtálá ritual often mention Odùduwà to demonstrate the opposition, rivalry, and contested power base of the two primordial deities, their two spheres of influence, and, by extension, the two sources of identity.

Ìwọlé Ọdún is a transitional rite of passage that begins with feasting in the temple, a prominent feature of the Ọbàtálá Festival. During one of my many research trips in February 1997, I joined in this ceremony, during which pounded yam with white melon soup (without red oil) was cooked for devotees and visitors like me. With the announcement of the forthcoming ceremony, the shrine of Ọbàtálá was prepared for the beginning of the festival. This first act, called *iyílépadà* (literally, turning the house around), involved ritually cleansing all the paraphernalia of the deity and refurbishing the house for a new beginning. All utensils and materials used in the deity's house were thoroughly washed. Since Ọbàtálá is the embodiment of purity, no dirt could be seen in the temple. To assist in this ritual cleansing, children and the young ones proceeded to a flowing stream located near St. John's College, Ilé-Ifẹ̀, to draw pure, clear water and return to the temple. The water, serving as a prophylactic against evil, was sprinkled on all those who entered the temple to ensure that they were purified.

The next phase was to bring the deities into the temple and to place them in their shrines. This was a spectacular ritual of great significance. To prevent the frequent theft of icons of Yorùbá deities, representations of Ọbàtálá and Yemòó were kept in the National Museum in Ẹnu Ọwá, in a building next to the Ọọ̀ni's palace. In the late afternoon, a number of young men holding *àtòrì* (striped canes) set out for the National Museum, where the Ọbàtálá and Yemòó icons "live" (are safeguarded), to bring them to their Ìdìta Ilé home. This innovation in the ceremony demonstrates how rituals are improvised in response to new developments and changes. As these men walked toward the palace, they gestured at onlookers to go indoors to avoid exposing themselves to the danger of beholding the deities with the naked eye. Passersby who were caught unawares covered their faces. In the museum, two men collected the two icons already wrapped in cloths, and the party headed back to the temple. This time the warning was louder. A few men preceded the party, clearing the way and warning onlookers. As I was later told, the convoy had cast charms on the road *(wọ́n ti ró ọnà)* to prevent evildoers from neutralizing the power of the god and goddess. As they proceeded toward the palace, the young men uttered threats of sudden death to those who defied their warnings to keep indoors.

> *Oròo! Oròo!*
> *A kì í jíẹ̀rẹ̀ wò ó,*
> *Ọni jíẹ̀rẹ̀ wò ó, A kú*
> *Ìgbín wò ó, ó fọ́lójú*
> *Àwòkú ni tòpìpì.*

> Take heed! Take heed!
> If you secretly behold the deities,
> You will secretly die
> Like the snails that beheld
> The forbidden one and lost their sight,
> The *opìpì* snake gazed at the forbidden one
> And died while looking.

FIGURE 16. Ọbàtálá's shrine.

This powerful incantation was both a warning and a curse, particularly as it invoked the images of animals sacred to the two deities. Those who were familiar with the deity took seriously the warnings and ran away to avoid seeing the images of the icons. This ritual was repeated when the deities were returned to the museum. I was informed that in times past the procession would not have been seen at all, since there would have been a curfew in the city to allow the deities to go to the temple unseen. The loud cries and announcements that the òrìṣà procession was in progress indicated the secrecy characteristic of Ọbàtálá rituals in general. Michael Taussig notes that humans who make sounds accompanying rituals of concealment should be seen primarily as "an absent presence that augments the power of the invisible force of spirit."[34] That is, although the Ọbàtálá ritual apparently was concealed by the loud noise of those in the procession, the noise could be heard from far off. This inconsistency presents the paradox of concealment and revelation, the very essence of religion.

Initiatory Ritual   As part of an identity-building mechanism, three initiatory steps are important to Ọbàtálá devotees. The steps are called, in order of importance, ògbóni (initiation into Ọbàtálá's secret cult), iṣòsán (day of initiation), and iṣòru (night of initiation). During the ògbóni stage, a ritual of bonding that should not be confused with the well-known Ògbóni secret society in Yorùbá religion, the devotee is shown the first level of the cult's sacred knowledge and takes secret vows to the symbol of the cult revealed to him in the inner chamber of the temple. At first, there was a controversy as to whether I should be allowed to undergo initiation. After the intervention of a senior colleague from the university and a prominent member of the Ìdìta lineage, the members agreed that although I could not go through the ceremony they would tell me all they could about Ọbàtálá.

Methodologically, approval for initiation would have secured me a privileged position in this field research, allowing me more access than outsiders like the non-indigenous anthropologist William Bascom had been able to obtain. At first, being denied this opportunity to be initiated was a moment of despair for me. But I myself had qualms about being initiated: though I was unafraid to tread where even the initiated feared to tread, I was concerned about the effect of the initiation on my identity as a Christian. Furthermore, those who have undergone the ògbóni stage of initiation exchange ritual greetings of ògbóni-ògborò (an affirmation of a shared secrecy), but I would find it difficult to keep initiation secrets out of my reported research. Although I am not one of the African scholars of religion whom Robin Horton refers to as members of the devout opposition, whose Christian theological upbringing lead them to Christianize African indigenous religious interpretation, I am, nevertheless, the son of an Anglican priest who once ministered in the city of Ilé-Ifè, and the debate made me suddenly aware that I was both an outsider and an insider at Ọbàtálá Shrine.[35] I was surprised that the devotees of Ọbàtálá kept an open gate to outsiders, especially those who weren't even taking part in the rituals but were just there to enjoy the festival. They displayed a tolerance that distinguished them from other devotees, especially those of Odùduwà, who kept all outsiders out of the compound during their rituals. However, I also realized that the deeper meaning and import of the religious experience that noninitiated researchers report often eludes them. To an extent, this has to do with the Yorùbá observation that while natives tread gently on their own ground, foreigners tread roughly *(Ọmọ onílẹ̀ tẹ̀ ẹ́ jẹ́jẹ́, àjòjì tẹ̀ ẹ́ wùrù wùrù)* because they do not know where sacred spots lie.

Although *ògbóni* initiation is not necessarily part of the Ọbàtálá Festival, *ọsán* and *òru* are private initiatory stages that precede the public performances held a few days later. Since these three stages are closed to outsiders, I asked Chief Òrìṣàkúàdé about their meaning and functions in the Ọbàtálá Festival. This chief, the closest to me of all the Ọbàtálá priests, adhered strictly to Ọbàtálá tradition but was thoroughly knowledgeable about the ways of the mission and frequently drew on Christian imagery and metaphors, perhaps because he was aware of my own Anglican background. "The rituals are like baptism and confirmation," he told me. "In *ògbóni*, the devotee is bestowed with honor *[ọ̀wọ̀ ni ti ògbóni]* as a mark of his maturity and a sign that he can keep Ọbàtálá's secrets unrevealed to the uninitiated. The *ọsán* is named because it is done in the afternoon. The *òru* is a step higher than *ọsán* because it is done at night. This is when the deepest secrets are revealed to the devotee and power is given to him." Òrìṣàkúàdé explained that the sacred knowledge of Ọbàtálá consists of esoteric information revealed piecemeal, stage by stage, to the initiate. The *ògbóni* initiation opens the way to obtaining the layers of traditional knowledge that are revealed in the *ọsán* and *òru* stages.

The tradition of Ọbàtálá shares several features of mystery traditions with other religions. Helmut Koester observed seven characteristic features of mystery religions: "(1) a firm organization in each congregation to which all members are subject; (2) membership obtained through rites of initiation; (3) participation in regular meetings in which sacramental ceremonies (such as meals) are celebrated according to fixed rites; (4) obligation to observe certain moral, sometimes ascetic, precepts; (5) mutual support of all members; (6) obedience to the leader of the cult or community; (7) cultivation of traditions that are subject to arcane discipline."[36] In addition, Koester noted that mystery religious traditions are permeated by "secret disciplines" and that information is "frequently transmitted in oral form."[37]

On the basis of these criteria, the rites surrounding Ọbàtálá, especially the preparatory rites associated with the annual festival, constitute a mystery tradition par excellence. The tripartite rites of *ògbóni, ọsán,* and *òru* initiate members into the secret tradition of the groups, during which cult objects and a cult ethos are revealed to novices. Each successive ritual event is concluded with a meal in keeping with strict cooking taboos. Palm products are avoided—especially palm oil for cooking and palm wine intoxicants that could cause members to lose their discretion by divulging well-kept secrets. The Ọbaléṣùn, the chief priest and leader of the group, who was regarded as a king in his own right, was accorded unchallenged authority. As he himself told me, *Èmi ni olórí gbogbo rian* (I am the head of them all). His utterances were law.

What is the probable origin of this mystery tradition? What led to its peculiar nature? Could it be that in the face of persecution and exile members of this "persecuted faith" developed secret rites to cope with threats to their loss of identity? Just as the Jewish people reconstituted Judaism in Jamnia after the destruction of Jerusalem, developing oral traditions and moral and ritual rules as a first line of defense against outsiders, so the Ìdìta people developed the secret traditions and moral rules and precepts of the cult of Ọbàtálá to maintain their features and identity in exile in Ìdìta Oko.[38]

The last of the preparatory ceremonies is called *itàlà,* or hoisting the white banner. In the avenue leading to the temple, a large white banner is hoisted vertically across the road leading to the shrine. It represents a threshold across which everyone coming to the shrine must pass. Its function is to purify all the incoming guests, but it also acts as a warning to visitors with evil intentions. Applying his usual Christian metaphors to explain things, Chief Òrìṣàkúàdé described it as *á wà lábẹ́ àbò* (literally, "to be under divine protection"), referring to the Celestial Independent African Church term for the ritual practice of placing endangered members and properties under the watchful eyes of God. *Ìtàlà* serves the same function that *màrìwò* (palm fronds) perform in the rituals of demarcation for other deities, especially Ògún and Ifá. Whoever crosses into its precinct partakes of the divine essence and purity of these two deities. Often visible in other festivals, the color red constitutes danger or the "forbidden." However, white is the signature of the divine couple, signifying that the devotee has now entered the protection of Ọbàtálá and Yemòó. The grand white banners invoke a sanctity and purity that infuse the entire precinct.[39]

Ìṣúlé: Pilgrimage to the Sacred Forest

The Ọbàtálá Festival proper begins with Ìṣúlé, the pilgrimage to the sacred forest of Ọbàtálá, during which the priests pluck 201 sacred leaves for making prophylactic and healing medicines for the coming year. Because Ọbàtálá priests also serve as medicine men, the ceremony represents the professional aspect of their priestly function. For their medicine and prayers to be efficacious year round, the ritual must be properly performed. Consequently, the pilgrimage was taken very seriously by all involved, as the stern looks on the faces of both priests and devotees indicated.

Early in the morning on the seventh day of the festival, the devotees, each holding a long stick *(iṣán),* formed a processional line. The walk to the sacred forest (Igbó Ogbe, or Grove of Ọbàtálá) was long, about six kilometers from Ìdìta Ilé. On their way out, all the devotees maintained absolute silence. The only sound heard was the flipping of the *ìṣán*, which devotees rattled in the air at passersby to inform them of their presence or to respond to the greetings of neighbors and onlookers who bid them a safe journey. As they proceeded toward their destination, they stood in the middle of a road, claiming the territory that once belonged to them. Motorists and pedestrians were forced to stand still or to follow at a distance while the procession passed. On the day of my visit, recalcitrant motorcyclists—especially fundamentalist Christians and Muslims who were going to or from their places of worship and who dared to challenge the Ọbàtálá devotees—were flogged or severely beaten. Elderly Ọbàtálá devotees, who later heard of this, bemoaned the behavior of these "rebels." One said to me that in earlier days a complete curfew *(ìséde)* would have prevented outsiders from seeing the procession at all. People from the households of the Ọbàtálá priests came out to pray for good health, long life, and many children because the priests were carrying their prayers to the sacred forest. Once the priests entered the forest, they began to select different kinds of medicinal leaves and put them in their pockets. After each had collected 201 leaves, they turned back and slowly proceeded homeward.

As the procession left the sacred forest and descended the hill, Chief Lókòrẹ́, the chief priest of Ọbamerì (Odùduwà and one of the generals at the time of creation and the primal struggle for supremacy), came out of his abode to defile the mission by throwing palm wine at Ọbamerì. This was an important test that Ọbálẹ́ṣùn, representing Ọbàtálá, had to pass. The wine fell on Ọbálẹ́ṣùn's leg, but he was unfazed, responding, "The *òrìṣà* [Ọbàtálá] cannot get intoxicated by his feet" *(Ẹmú ù tẹṣẹ̀ pòrìṣà).* This encounter recalls the primordial battle when, on behalf of his superior (Odùduwà), Ọbamerì tormented Ọbàtálá into submission by laying siege to his home. We recall that Ọbàtálá lost his chance to create the world because the gods lured him into drinking too much palm wine, so that he became drunk and fell asleep. Avoiding being tricked into drunkenness again, Ọbálẹ́ṣùn proceeded on his mission undeterred. The sporadic revival of cultural memories at critical phases of Ifẹ̀ festivals constantly reminds devotees of the history conveyed in myth and ritual. Consequently, throughout centuries of performance, these primordial events remain fresh in the collective consciousness.

By this time, crowds gathered on the street, especially at the junction close to Ọbálẹ́ṣùn's house, where members of their households who had gathered to watch their return welcomed the priests. Women brought out cool water in china bowls and gave it to Ọbálẹ́ṣùn to drink. He drank some of it and passed it on to the others. Some poured water on the ground to cool the earth before they passed by, to ensure the success of the rest of the journey and the ritual process. As the priest moved toward the center of the city, still along the boundary of the Ìdìta Quarter, the Ọ̀ọ̀ni's drummers with the royal drums *(òṣírìgì)* met the procession to usher them into the city center. Several people, especially women of the Ìdìta lineage, shouted, "Ọba *káàbọ̀!* Welcome to the king!" referring to Ọbálẹ́ṣùn. The women were greeting Ọbàtálá. The pilgrimage to the sacred forest was completed and their mission accomplished. It was believed that the procession bearing the sacred leaves brought with it good luck and manifold blessings; after all, a primary purpose for propitiating the deity was to bestow these blessings upon the devotee.

A Yorùbá proverb holds, *Àkíìjẹ́ níí gbé òrìṣà níyì* (It is his silence and unchallenged greetings that bestow honor and sacredness on the *òrìṣà*). The pilgrims and bearers of the sacred leaves were perceived as bearers of Ọbàtálá's message. Their silence gave credence to their power and prestige as priests and medicine men. When they arrived at the temple of Ọbàtálá, each priest took the leaves from his pocket, touched his forehead with the leaves, offered silent, prayerful wishes, and passed the leaves to the Ọbálẹ́ṣùn. The Ọbálẹ́ṣùn then collected all the sacred leaves in a satchel, which he hung from a hook on the ceiling, and prayed for all the devotees present. Touching the forehead with the leaves infuses the leaves with potency, as the Yorùbá believe that "one's inner head [or psyche] enhances the efficacy of medicine" *(orí mú oògùn jẹ́).*

Having gathered the sacred leaves, the priests filed in front of the shrine to thank Ọbàtálá for a successful pilgrimage. They removed the white ceremonial attire from their upper bodies and, led by the Ọbálẹ́ṣùn, danced in circles to celebrate completing the Ọbàtálá Festival's first important ceremony. The priests left the temple, joining the members of their lineage who were waiting outside to dance along the way to their respective homes.

Scholars of pilgrimage traditions have focused largely on the so-called great traditions and have failed to include indigenous religions.[40] But the journey from Ọbàtálá Temple to the forest to gather the 201 leaves has the characteristics of a pilgrimage event, for at the core of pilgrimage is the notion of a sacred journey—whether actual or metaphoric—in which time and space are important, since the leaves must be harvested in a particular forest at a particular time, and since at the end a "spiritual and/or social transformation takes place."[41] Acknowledging the multiple "forms, motivations, and meanings" that pilgrimage traditions take in her study of such centers in Greece, Jill Dubisch remarks that a place of pilgrimage is more powerful and extraordinary than everyday places.[42] She notes that the power experienced by the pilgrims at the pilgrimage site can be accessed and taken home in any form, such as a "feeling of spiritual renewal, . . . healed illness, . . . a physical object," or "a transformation in one's social status."[43] The Ọbàtálá priests will use the sacred leaves to prepare the ingredients for powerful prophylactic medicines. As medicine men and women, Ọbàtálá elders function as healers in their communities. Those who consult them seek cures for all forms of illnesses. The medicine made from the sacred leaves is called *ẹrọ̀* and is given as a first-aid treatment for any kind of ailment. This quintessential medicine is available to most visitors who ask for it. One of the chiefs sent word to me through one of my research consultants, Chief

Ògúndìjo, an instructor at the university, that I must remember to send an empty bottle to the temple to collect the ẹ̀rọ̀ to take to America.

Part of the pilgrimage experience is based on the notion that there is an auspicious time for plucking the leaves—early in the morning when the leaves are said to be "waking up." The Ifẹ̀ people believe that the leaves, like humans, sleep (ewé sunko) and thus that if they are picked at the wrong time they lose their potency and cannot serve their ritual purpose. The pilgrimage ceremony, "the sacred power of both time and space," plays an important role in the efficacy of the ritual.[44]

Like most ancient pilgrimages, the Ọbàtálá pilgrimage represents a test of its participants' will and perseverance. Just as the Muslim pilgrim climbs Mount Arafat or stones the devil at Mina to symbolize an inward jihad, a struggle to follow the way of God (Jihad fil sabil Allah), the chief priest of Ọbàtálá is tested with palm wine, a great taboo of the deity. Overcoming once again the temptation to drink palm wine, he upholds the cardinal taboo of the Ìdìta and proves himself to be the custodian of the moral rectitude of the great god of purity. Thus, after he has successfully completed the pilgrimage, the Ìdìta people meet him and the priests with much celebration. They welcome the priests with the special royal drum in a public event not limited to the Ìdìta kinship group. As several pilgrimage scholars have remarked, the sacred journey, contrary to Turner's findings, does not annul social hierarchy, nor does it eliminate social structure.[45] The Ọbalẹ́ṣùn and the hierarchy of priests maintained their social roles and rank during and after the sacred journey. In the journey both to and from the sacred forest they lined up according to their rank, with the children leading in the front while the elders followed in the back. The roles assigned each priest-chief in both social and ceremonial functions were maintained. The king's drum brought a welcome acknowledgment that the ceremony was not merely a lineage celebration, as many Ilé-Ifẹ̀ festivals are, but a communal celebration.

The Rituals of Sacrifice: Ìpiwọ̀

As we observed in chapter 4, sacrifice is crucial to Ifẹ̀ festivals and rituals. In a major festival like the Ọbàtálá Festival, sacrifice is a central ritual performance to honor the deity. The sacrifice of the Ọbàtálá Festival differs from that of the Ọlọ́jọ́ Festival. All the ceremonies follow a sequence. The sacrifice to Ọbàtálá connects the previous day's ceremony of preparation of the medicinal water to the ritual that will take place on the next day, during which the priests and devotees assert the identity of the Ìdìta kinship group in the Sacred City. In the context of its performance, the sacrifice to Ọbàtálá and Yemòó reinforces Ìdìta ownership of the àṣẹ or sacred power. Like all other aspects of Ọbàtálá rituals, the sacrificial ritual of Ìpiwọ̀ (also called Ìmúwọ̀) is complex. It begins with preparing ritual condiments. Unlike the previous phases that took place in the Ìdìta Ilé (the home shrine), Ìpiwọ̀ takes place in Ìdìta Oko (the forest shrine), about seven kilometers from the home shrine.

According to legend, when Odùduwà and his allies drove Ọbàtálá out of Ilé-Ifẹ̀ and into exile, Ọbàtálá hid in Ìdìta Oko and lived there for decades before he returned home. The ritual, therefore, reenacts the sojourn of Ọbàtálá and Yemòó in the forest through a sacrifice at the place considered to be the most important seat of the òrìṣà's power. The rite of the Ìpiwọ̀ sacrifice reminds the Ìdìta people of the special space that provided a secure sanctuary for their ancestors. The paradigmatic rite is reenacted to relive the Ìdìta lineage's mystic past. The place of the sacrifice represents a ritual center and "frontier outpost" that served as a sacred center while Ọbàtálá and Yemòó were in exile.[46] Because it was seen as an impermanent place of sojourn, its ritual elements are rather simple, lacking any elaborate or permanent temple such as is seen in Ìdìta Ilé.

Training for their journey to the forest and preparing for the great task, two young men practice to carry the sacred icons of Yemòó and Ọbàtálá. Before a novice can carry an icon, he is fully initiated through ritual prayers. An Ifá priest-diviner represents each major deity in Ilé-Ifẹ̀, and the Ọbàtálá diviner performs a kola nut divination to determine the outcome for the young men responsible for the anticipated journey to the shrine of Ọbàtálá. Enemies who may disrupt their journey are cursed by the power of Ifẹ̀ deities (Ọbalùfọ̀n or Olúorogbo) and the earth deity, Ilẹ̀. The diviner then takes a kola nut, splits it into its lobes, and addresses Ọbàtálá and Yemòó: "*Bàbá, obì náà rèé*, Father, here is the kola nut. *Yèyé, obì náà rèé*, Mother, here is the kola nut."

The two bearers of Ọbàtálá and Yemòó are then fully dressed and wrapped in white cloth from the waist down to the knee. The young man in front carries the icon of Yemòó, wife of Ọbàtálá, while the second young man follows with the icon of her husband, Ọbàtálá. Both icon bearers carry the icons vertically on the left shoulder. The icon bearers and the entire entourage, all members of the Ìdìta lineage, pass from the home temple to Ìdìta Oko, while people in the streets flee into hiding so as not to glimpse the images of their gods. As usual, some recalcitrant nonbelievers stand around in defilement of the taboo. During my visit, I saw that one of the Ọbàtálá devotees, a female priest fully robed in white, started to curse the contemptible nonbelievers as the Ọbàtálá priests drove them away or flogged them with canes. *Ọ ráàárò, Ọ ra rálẹ́, Ọ ṣọdúnìí, Ọ ni ṣẹ̀rẹ̀mírìn!* (You see the morning, you are not going to see the night [Literally, you will die before the day dawns]! If you witness the celebration of this year's festival, you will not live to celebrate next year's.) Such curses expressed the increasing frustration of Ọbàtálá's followers with the demonstrated disrespect for an òrìṣà tradition and its declining ritual in the city that once witnessed these celebrations daily.

A somewhat different but related scuffle took place along the way to Ìdìta Oko. A number of young Hausa—Muslim migrants from northern part of the country who lived in a place called Sabo or Foreigners' Quarter—ran into the Ọbàtálá procession and refused to give way or run into the bush as most Ifẹ̀ indigenes did. Consequently, a scuffle ensued between them and the Ọbàtálá people. The Hausa wanted to stone the young Ìdìta boys who were demanding that they comply. The Hausas, probably staunch Muslims who normally disdain traditional rituals and festivals, may have seen the festival as an occasion to challenge social practices that restricted their movement in the city. One young boy pleaded with the intruders to leave the scene and turned back to tell his party that the Hausas did not understand the ritual. The responses from other boys in the party were swift and clear: "Can one disobey their own tradition in their native land?" "The Seriki n'Sabo, the chief leader of the Hausa community in Ilé-Ifè, has warned the Hausa youth to show respect to our Ọbàtálá traditional culture." "What sort of Islam do they practice that it makes them so disrespectful of our tradition?" This last was a loaded question.

In the past, and to some extent until the 1980s, Yorùbá Muslims, Christians, and followers of the indigenous religious tradition were reasonably tolerant of one another. In that climate, religious relations were mediated by a sense of deep cultural and social ties configured in a matrix of exchange. As a Yorùbá who had formerly been a minister of the Nigerian federal government told a *New York Times* reporter in the wake of the religious conflicts in Nigeria in the late 1990s, "Here, nearly every home is part Muslim, part Christian, part pagan *[sic]*. What distinguishes us from the North is not our religion, but the way we interpret it. In the North, Islam is a very serious business."[47] In recent times, radical forms of both Christian and Islamic revivalism have targeted indigenous Yorùbá beliefs for attack. We will see later in the sacrificial ritual a deeper symbolic invasion of tradition, not from outsiders but from young Pentecostal-Charismatic members of the Ìdìta lineage.

Ìdìta Oko and the Sacrificial Ground   Since I had brought my car along, I helped the group carry their great drums to the sacrificial grounds. The evening and night rituals took place in a grove divided into several "chambers," similar to the divisions of the temple in Ìdìta Ilé. The outer section was reserved for the Ọọni's emissaries, called Òmìrìn, who had been sent to present the sacrificial animals—a large and a small goat—and a bottle of gin. In the outer section was posted a sign commanding all strangers to depart, *Àjòjì yóọ́ ṣẹ́ o!* This section was the boundary area where wives who had married into the household and other uninitiated devotees had to wait. A path led to the inner sanctuary of the shrine. Here, as in Ìdìta Ilé, as a sign of respect to Ọbàtálá and Yemòó, women were prohibited from wearing earrings, necklaces, or headgear. Followers were addressed, not by their personal names, but simply as "Children of Ìdìta" (Ọmọ Ìdìta), a custom that provided a sort of communal experience in a hallowed sanctuary. The two great drums and iron percussion instruments *(ẹwọ́)* were placed in the inner sanctuary. A large upturned pot, perforated on top to accommodate the sacrificial offerings, was placed at the end of the space. This area symbolized the navel of the earth or *ojú ilé*, the most central point of the ritual space. The space was large enough to seat several persons, and

FIGURE 17. Ọbàtálá night rituals in Ìdìta Oko (a sacred grove).

large, fully mature banana leaves were laid out on the ground where the priests of Ọbàtálá would sit during the ceremony.

The inner sanctuary was reserved for the priests to dress for the ceremony. Their bodies and faces were dotted with white pigment, and cross marks or "‡" designs were painted on their chests. Each of the priests tied his wrapper from waist to knee and wore a matching cone-shaped cap. The Ọbàtálá chief priest held two horsetail flywhisks *(ìrùkẹ̀rẹ̀)* used in dancing. All the chiefs, including female chiefs, wore badges on their chests bearing their titles.

The First Sacrificial Ritual   The drummers took their positions on the left-hand side of the priests in the inner space while a young boy distributed iron gongs *(ẹwọ́)* to the priests and selected devotees to take part in the percussion. After the priests were seated, all facing the icons of Ọbàtálá and Yemòó, there was a period of deep silence. Suddenly there was a great shout from the outer sanctuary, after which a large goat was ushered in, one of the two goats presented by the Ọ̀ọ̀ni through the emissaries and referred to as *ẹsìn Ọ̀ọ̀ni* (what the Ọ̀ọ̀ni brings to propitiate Ọbàtálá). Meanwhile, the drumming, singing, and beating of the iron gong intensified. The two icon bearers carried the gods gingerly, making a quick circular dance around the center of sacrifice where the great pot stood. Carefully they placed the icons down beside the pot. Ulli Beier reported that a scholar who had observed a simi-

FIGURE 18. Ọbàtálá priests in an Ìdìta ceremony.

lar ceremony in 1955 saw one of the images inadvertently fall down as this special dance was performed, an occurrence that brought great distress to the community and was followed with divinatory inquiry and expensive sacrifices prescribed by the Ifá to appease the deities for such dishonor.[48]

With this segment completed, one of the devotees took the goat by the rope tied around its neck, heaved it vigorously in a circle around the icons, and suddenly smashed it on the ground. Immediately, one of the chiefs took a sharp knife and cut completely through the goat's throat. Blood collected in a container was poured over the icons to anoint them. While this part of the sacrifice was performed, devotees offered vigorous prayers because the sacrifice would ensure that their requests were granted. They then sang in fervent praise of the divine couple:

> T'Olúwa mi l' àṣẹ, tòrìṣà l'àṣẹ,
> T'Ọbaláṣẹ̀, t'òrìṣà l'àṣẹ.

> My Lord's will be done, the gods' will be done,
> The king's will be done, the gods' will be done!

The Quintessential Power of the Òrìṣà: Àṣẹ   The above lyrics set out the foundation and purpose of the sacrifice, affirming the ownership of the *àṣẹ*, or sacred magical power, that bonds the Ọ̀ọ̀ni (Odùduwà) and the Ìdìta (Ọbàtálá) people. The lyrics state that the will of the *òrìṣà* Ọbàtálá will come to pass.

The strength of Ọbàtálá's *àṣẹ* or sacred power is the theme of several discourses among Ọbàtálá devotees. One Ifá narrative states that Odùduwà once invited Ọbàtálá to a great feast and prepared a royal throne for Ọbàtálá, surreptitiously digging underneath it a large grave, which Odùduwà concealed with a thick mat. Ọbàtálá and his children accepted Odùduwà's invitation and went to Odùduwà's house to celebrate together. However, on his way to the feast, Ọbàtálá was secretly informed about Odùduwà's treachery and urged by his followers to return home. Ọbàtálá refused and instead held the symbol of the *àṣẹ* in his left hand and proceeded on the journey to Odùduwà's house. When he reached Odùduwà's house, Ọbàtálá was shown the royal throne. Ọbàtálá pointed the *àṣẹ* toward it, and the grave beneath the mat miraculously filled up. Confidently, Ọbàtálá seated himself on the throne and joined Odùduwà in great merriment and feasting. Upon departing, Ọbàtálá again pointed the *àṣẹ* beneath the throne and ordered the large hole to reappear. Odùduwà was mystified, but he escorted Ọbàtálá and his children out politely. Returning to the throne, Odùduwà sat down incredulously to test it—and down he plunged, throne and all. The devotees of Ọbàtálá boast that this legend explains why no visible image of Odùduwà exists today: his image lies inside the grave. Ọbàtálá's image, however, is in the open, and it is the only deity we can see today.

This oral narrative is one of various myths portraying the contest between Ọbàtálá and Odùduwà. Although this particular story depicts Ọbàtálá's victory over Odùduwà, even more important is its portrayal of the significance of the *òrìṣà*'s *àṣẹ*. As Òrìṣàkúàdé himself acknowledged, "The story indicates that no matter how powerful Odùduwà is, and no matter how flamboyant the Odùduwà Festival becomes, if Ọbàtálá fails to give the new king the *àṣẹ* to rule Ilé-Ifẹ̀, the king cannot be enthroned as the Ọọ̀ni." Reiterating the Yorùbá myth of origin in Ilé-Ifẹ̀, he added, "Olódùmarè gave Ọbàtálá the *àṣẹ* to compensate for the 'blessing' that Odùduwà 'stole at the time of creation,'" a Christian metaphor for the biblical narrative of Jacob and Esau.

I was amazed at how popular this story was and how each group manipulated it to claim superiority over the other. A few weeks before this particular interview with Òrìṣàkúàdé, I was in the Sacred Grove of Odùduwà chatting with Ọbadìo, the chief priest of Odùduwà, and his chiefs. Discussing the status and role of Odùduwà worship in Ilé-Ifẹ̀ today, Ọbadìo referred to the invisibility of Odùduwà as a positive characteristic. "Who can see Odùduwà's [image], let alone steal it away, as they steal the images of other deities [apparently referring to the disappearance by theft of the original icon of Ọbàtálá]?" The person second in command to Ọbadìo responded sarcastically, "Who can steal Jesus, who can see him?" *(A lè jí Jésù, a lè rí i?).*

The great sacrificial festival of Ọbàtálá reaffirms the deity's mystical power and the divinity it shares with both the sacred king, who supplies the sacred animal, and the Ọbalẹ́ṣùn, who is the ruler of the Ìdìta community. Unlike the ritual sacrifice of Ògún, in which the sacrificial animals were taken from public space, here the Ọọni provides the animal to propitiate a deity, without whom he will lack the àṣẹ (vital power) to rule the Ilé-Ifẹ̀ people. Surprisingly, during my visit, school-children, members of the lineage, quietly, almost inaudibly, sang a countercultural song:

> Ti Jesus làṣẹ,
> T'Olúwa làṣẹ.
>
> To Jesus belongs àṣẹ (power),
> To my Lord belongs àṣẹ (power).

These lyrics offered glaring evidence of new fundamentalist, evangelical influence among the youth of Ilé-Ifẹ̀. I was virtually certain that their elders did not hear this Christian affront, which would have been considered repugnant in Ọbàtálá's most sacred space! Not wanting to create commotion, I did not raise the issue with my Ọbàtálá informants.

With the deities soaked and washed in the sacred blood of the animal, gin was poured into the "mouths" of the icons. Finally, some of the blood collected into folded leaves was poured into strategic corners of the open spaces.

The Second Sacrificial Ritual   With the first sacrifice completed, the group moved to the second open space for the sacrifice of a second animal, a kid goat already tied to a stake, as in the case of the Ògún sacrifice. One of the priests took the goat and intoned prayers. The animal was then staked to the ground with two long stakes as it bleated an agonizing cry. The priests began to dance in turn in homage to Ọbàtálá. Holding two ìrùkẹ̀rẹ̀, each of the chiefs danced from one end of the circle to the other, where the Ọbaléṣùn stood. Various songs were rendered, recounting stories of ancestors who had lived in Ìdìta and had performed the rituals before them, of lineage and mythic events, of family valor, and of the meaning and symbolic sig-nificance of their titles and their place in Ilé-Ifẹ̀ myth history. Like the songs of Aus-tralian Aboriginal dreaming reported by Diane Bell, the songs and lyrics to Ọbàtálá infused the lineage with vigor and strength.[49] The acts were rituals of renewal and recollection of the shared identity.

During my visit, the Òmìrìn (emissaries of the Ọọni) were invited to dance in honor of their royal presence. At the climax, when the Ọbaléṣùn took the floor, the beat of the great drums increased in tempo. Dancing in circles, he swung a cutlass and then very deftly severed the head of the goat. He lifted and placed its head be-side the two icons as if to inform the divine couple that the sacrifice was complete.

The final stage occurred with the concluding song, in which the Òmìrìn were asked to greet the Ọọni *(kí Ọọni, Òmìrìn kí Ọọni)*. With this, the king's emissary took leave of the devotees. While the first goat was taken home, hung on a hook from the ceiling of a storeroom, and cooked for a feast the next day, the sacrificed kid goat was left on the ground to putrefy, because it is forbidden for the living to share the animal with the deity.

I asked one of the devotees about how the two sacrificial offering ceremonies differed in their structure and execution. "The first animal was intended for Ọbàtálá and Yemòó, to celebrate their 'birthdays' and eventful lives among the Ìdìta people," he said. "That is why we bathe them in the blood of the animal. The second animal was the *iwọ* sacrificial victim, offered to beg the deity for protection, mercy, and good health for Ilé-Ifẹ̀ people. We do it for the Ọọ̀ni." Thus the second animal is totally sacrificed and given to the gods. No human can partake of such a sacrificial animal. The first goat, which is taken home, poses an interesting question for scholars of religion interested in sacrificial rituals because it exemplifies a communion meal between gods and humans, an often-neglected aspect of such sacrificial rituals. In a critique of theories of sacrifice, especially as espoused by Henri Hubert and Marcel Mauss, Jan van Baal observed that quite often scholars emphasize the process of the preparation and dedication of the animal offering to the deity but leave out the distribution of the sacrificial offering among the celebrants.[50] They make the dedication of the animal to the deity the most essential part of the sacrificial process and interpret the feasting and distribution of food, practices that are common in African and Asian cultures, as a corruption of the true essence of sacrifice. This error, van Baal claims, arose because of the assumption that sacrifice is primarily an "implement in a cunning game of *do-ut-des* with deities and ancestors dull enough to let themselves occasionally be cheated by the presentation of small tidbits."[51]

In several indigenous societies of Africa and Asia, ethnographic evidence suggests that communal feasts and the distribution of the sacrificial food are so common that one would be justified in interpreting a sacrifice as a communal meal joining the gods, spirits, hosts, and the guests—an act of communication both between the sacrificer and his gods, and between him and his fellow man. Two sacrificial layers similarly characterize the Ọbàtálá ceremony. Although both animals are dedicated to Ọbàtálá and Yemòó, the first joins the king and the gods, whereas the second joins the people, marking their sacred pact as members of a mysterious tradition who have taken the sacred vow to keep their lineage and mythic history alive.

Ìtàpá Day: Reenactment of Ọbàtálá's and Odùduwà's Struggle for Supremacy

If Ìpiwọ̀ is a secret and solemn ceremony, the last major event of the Ọbàtálá Festival is very public and spectacular. Its focus is to dramatize the primordial encounter between Odùduwà and Ọbàtálá and the ritual pact between the two forces that hold Ilé-Ifẹ̀ together. This, of course, is done through their archetypal parties: the Ọọ̀ni and the palace, and the Ọbalésùn and the Ìdìta people. Ìtàpá, the climax of the Ọbàtálá Festival, is regarded as Ọbàtálá Day, the equivalent of the Ọlójó Festival of Ògún Day discussed in chapter 4.

In preparation for this ceremony, a grand communal meal of bean cake, *èkuru Ìtàpá*, is cooked and served to all Ìdìta families. We do not know the origin of *èkuru Ìtàpá*, a special meal, but from its idiosyncratic nature (for it is peculiar to the Ìdìta) we can assume that it is a ritual meal for the entire lineage that "served to bond" the Ìdìta, "to define them as a whole, sharing and reenacting a foundation myth that perhaps reflects a historical memory of some elements of the group."[52] It is also a sacred meal shared with the unseen spirits in Ilé-Ifẹ̀. Chief Òrìṣàkúàdé told me the day afterward, "There were numerous spirits who visited them yesterday to partake in the *èkuru* meal." When I asked why I had not seen them, he replied with a smile that only the deeply initiated could see them *(Àwọn tí ó ti wẹjú)*. He said that long ago the *èkuru* would have been sold to anyone attending the meal and the money collected from the sales placed on the shrine of Èṣù, the divine messenger of the gods and the spirit world. "The money is not for humans but for people of the spirit world," Òrìṣàkúàdé commented.

At about 2:30 p.m. that day, I witnessed Ọbàtálá devotees make a procession from the temple to Ìta Yemòó or Yemòó Junction, where the courtyard of Yemòó, Ọbàtálá's wife, was located. Leading the procession, children carried bottles containing a prophylactic medicinal concoction *(èrò)* made from the sacred leaves harvested a few days earlier on their heads. The king's *èrò* was wrapped in white cloth. A girl about nine years old carried a stool, called Yemòó's chair, that would be used during the ceremony. The elders followed the children in the procession. At their destination, the priests dressed as they had done for the Ìpiwọ̀ ceremony: their bodies dotted in white, all holding *irùkẹ̀rẹ̀*, and wearing *pẹkẹ*, chiefs' badges. Several women, including Ìyálórìṣà, Ìyálájé, and other specialists in the rituals, participated in the procession as devotees and title holders.

The procession then went on to the Ọọ̀ni's palace. At the end of it was a small party of men and women of all ages escorting a priestess called Ìyálórìṣà, the most senior woman, who impersonated Yemòó, the wife of Ọbàtálá.[53] The Ìyálórìṣà was dressed completely in white, her body wrapped up in white linens, under which she held the *èrò* prepared for the Ọọ̀ni. It was the duty of a female attendant to walk behind her and grasp her clothing to support her, since the deity would regularly possess her and it was important that she not fall down when possessed. A larger party of priests danced behind her, following the procession.

All eyes focused on Yemòó in this spectacular procession. As she silently and steadily proceeded to the palace, she stopped and sat on her stool on five occasions at the important sacred junctions: the shrine of Obo, the shrine of Ajé, the shrine of Ògún, Ifá Junction at Òkè Ìtasẹ̀, and, finally, the junction in front of the king's palace. At each she was in a trance. Surrounded by the group leading her to the palace, the king's emissaries— Jaàrán, Lọ́wátẹ̀ẹ́, Àgùrò, and Àróde—whispered certain words into her ears. At the fourth stop at Òkè Ìtasẹ̀, a group of Ifá diviners led by the Àràbà of Ifẹ̀ (their chief priest) surrounded her; the Àràbà, holding an *iróké*

Ifá (Ifá bell), rattled it continuously while whispering in her ear, as if he wanted to bring her back into this world from the trance world of the spirits. No one hears the messages that an Àràbà passes on to Yemòó, but from my conversation with the former Àràbà, I was told that Ifá had been pleading with her to make peace with Odùduwà so that their incessant fighting and quarreling would not destroy the world. Another conversation that I had with Chief Ifátóògùn, an Ifá priest, confirmed this meaning: *Ifá fi ọgbọ́n gbé ilé ayé ró* (Ifá uses wisdom to keep the world from collapsing). These words of wisdom were the counsel provided by Ifá, Yorùbá divinatory deity, and the regulator of the universe. I will take up Ifá's place and role in the Ilé-Ifẹ̀ sacred cosmos in chapter 6.

With this counsel, the Ọbàtálá group moved to the front courtyard of the palace, where the Ọ̀ọ̀ni's emissaries awaited the arrival of the procession. The young men from Ọbàtálá's household handed gifts of kola nuts to the palace officials and the Àràbà's group. The party then returned to Ọbàtálá temple.

In the second phase of the ceremony, Ìyálórìṣà walked between the temple and the inner courtyard of the king's palace three times, after which she delivered the king's *ẹ̀rọ̀* to him. This medicinal gift (a bottled liquid) from Ọbàtálá would keep the Ọ̀ọ̀ni healthy and strong throughout the entire year. The *ẹ̀rọ̀* symbolizes Ọbàtálá's own gift of life, offered free to the Ilé-Ifẹ̀ people. To ensure a peaceful reign, the Ọ̀ọ̀ni must keep at bay diseases that could devastate the entire population of Ilé-Ifẹ̀. The entranced Ìyálórìṣà, representing Yemòó, conveyed the *ẹ̀rọ̀* that the Ọ̀ọ̀ni would use to ward off the dreaded smallpox epidemics from the sacred city.

In the late evening, there was a hush in the quarters between the palace and Ọbàtálá Temple. Most participants, who were aware of the ceremonial events, kept their doors locked. The king's emissaries, carrying sacks of gifts on their heads, proceeded to the temple. As they reached the temple, they knelt before the Ọbálẹ̀sùn and offered the Ọ̀ọ̀ni's felicitation and gifts to the deity. The gifts are called *ẹrù Ifẹ̀* (Ifẹ̀'s load). As one priest told me, these are what Ifẹ̀ gives to Ọbàtálá as gifts every year. The obligatory gifts were checked. One priest complained that they were incomplete, apparently referring to the goat that should have accompanied the parcel. The palace official quickly responded that the goat would be added later.

In previous ceremonies, the Ọ̀ọ̀ni would have come in person to propitiate Ọbàtálá and Yemòó, as a penitential "servant" who put on ordinary short pants (*ìbàǹtẹ́*) and walked between the palace and the temple seven times. My guess is that the Ọ̀ọ̀ni was not in town during this current ceremony, for the priests reminisced about his recent visits as they talked among themselves, teasing the messengers and insisting that the messengers do the right thing. One of the priests told me this was why the Ìdìta people were often called *ọmọ aṣorò kí Ọ̀ọ̀ni ró gégé* (descendants of powerful priests who perform rituals while the Ọ̀ọ̀ni stands at attention, in a submissive mood).

The Ìtàpá ceremony was followed by minor sacrificial offerings to various deities connected with Ọbàtálá and Yemòó to appease them and solicit their support in the ensuing battle of life. The festival ended with a grand feast *(àsè Ọbaléṣùn)* provided by the Ọbaléṣùn, after which devotees went back to their normal routines and the daily propitiation of Ọbàtálá and Yemòó at the temple.

From all indications, the Ìyálórìṣà, the incarnation of Yemòó, played a pivotal role in the Ìtàpá celebration, representing Yemòó as wife and mother and, by extension, her central concern for the community's health and healing processes. A parallel exists among Australian Aboriginal cultures, where women play essential roles in maintaining the health of the community through healing rituals and the practice of medicine.[54]

As we observed in the procession to the Ọ̀ọ̀ni's palace, Ìyálórìṣà led the party to the palace to broker a peace settlement between Ọbàtálá and Odùduwà (the Ọ̀ọ̀ni). However, she also held under her robes an *ẹ̀rọ̀*, which she later presented to the king as his own medicinal potion. The ceremony apparently combined several significant and related themes: the drama of Ọbàtálá's confrontation with Odùduwà, as seen in Yemòó's encounter with Odùduwà's emissary, and the subsequent settlement of this dispute. That the pivotal role in Ọbàtálá's ceremony is given to his wife is fascinating. As Diane Bell said of Australian Aboriginal women, "Women, as the ritual nurturers of relationships, seek to maintain and to restore harmony, happiness and thus health."[55] For indigenous peoples and cultures in general, good health entails maintaining harmony between humans, nature, and place. The ritualized display of tension between the factions of Ọbàtálá and Odùduwà led to Yemòó's subsequent peaceful resolution of the conflict. The Ọbàtálá group then presented gifts of kola nut wrapped in leaves to the diviners and the king's emissary as tokens of gratitude for their role in the conflict resolution. For the Ìdìta people, a joyous dance home followed, in which their previous stern looks were replaced with smiles, peaceful songs, and much merriment.

Religious identity is constructed and reinforced in patterns of learned behavior that define what is sacred, what is taboo, who is an outsider, and who is an insider. The Ìdìta people, devotees of Ọbàtálá, constitute a religious minority within the larger Ilé-Ifẹ̀ community. Although the Odùduwà conquered them, they have managed to maintain an image of moral strength in Ilé-Ifẹ̀'s religious and political affairs. Their strong position is achieved through the religious ritual that asserts their control over the *àṣẹ*, the divine magical power that is the ultimate source of the king's authority over Ilé-Ifẹ̀. Odùduwà, the military conqueror, became the divine king in charge of political rule, but Ọbàtálá held the *àṣẹ*, that enabled the conquering king to function.

Ideologically, the Ọbàtálá Festival offers an excellent illustration of how a marginalized group can maintain social control by using the status symbols of religious ritual. Integrated into Ilé-Ifẹ̀'s economy, the Ìdìta maintain a separate but close-knit clan lineage identified with their tutelary deities Ọbàtálá and Yemòó. The struggle for power between the Ọbàtálá worshippers and those of Odùduwà is reflected in the cosmic mythic battle to control the primordial world. The festival relives the defeat and subsequent triumph of Ọbàtálá's ritual power over Odùduwà's military might. Thus claims to moral, magical, and ritual power may at times surpass even the authority of political and military rule. Shared religious traditions provide an identity that guides the social structure and mechanisms of ritual objectification, obligation, mythology, archetypal values of good and evil, and association with community members—including the ancestors, the so-called living dead. Attachment to the ultimate transcendent figures—the deity or deities and the tutelary spirits—reinforces social and individual identity.

6

Ifá

Divination Rituals and the New Yam Festival

In the first three chapters of this book, I alluded to the role of Ifá divination and Ifá priests in various rituals in the sacred city, especially those relating to the resolution of the conflicts between Odùduwà and Ọbàtálá. I will devote this chapter to the place of Ifá divination and the Ifá deity in regulating and managing the spiritual and social affairs of the city and will introduce the myths and rituals of Ọ̀rúnmìlà, also known as Ifá, the Yorùbá god of divination; Ifá divinatory practices; and the religious, ethical, and thought systems espoused in the rich Ifá divination texts, otherwise known as *ẹsẹ Ifá* or Ifá divination poetry. By analyzing certain related festivals of Ifá—Ọdún Ègbodò Ọọ̀ni (the King's New Yam Festival), Ọdún Àgbọnìrègún (the Diviners' New Yam Ceremony), and the annual Ifá Festival, together with the sacred narratives associated with them, I will show how the symbols and rituals of Ifá sanctify the sacred city. Ifá has a pivotal role in maintaining and legitimizing the Ọọ̀ni's sacred kingship and the lineage identity of Ifá devotees, particularly the Àràbà, the chief priest of Ifá, just as the sacred kingship legitimizes Ifá's authority as the spokesperson for the 201 divinities of the Ilé-Ifẹ̀ pantheon.

ENCOUNTERING IFÁ IN THE ÀRÀBÀ'S HOUSE

In 1992, my research assistant, Kẹ́hìndé Elújùlọ, and I decided to begin our conversation about the status of Ifá in Ilé-Ifẹ̀ City with the reigning Àràbà, Ilé-Ifẹ̀'s chief priest of Ifá. The Àràbà is acknowledged the world over as the absolute head of Ifá priests. We entered his house on Òkè Ìtasẹ̀, the Sacred Hill of Ifá, and reintroduced ourselves, having met him on several occasions in the city. Kẹ́hìndé Elújùlọ, an Ilé-Ifẹ̀ indigene, asked if he should consult with Ifá, and, of course, I agreed that he should. Kẹ́hìndé took a *naira* banknote (Nigerian currency) from his pocket, in-audibly said a few words to the *naira* note, touched his head with it, and laid it down on a mat beside the Àràbà, who was sitting next to the *ọpọ́n Ifá* (the Ifá divination tray). Meanwhile, the Àràbà set up his divination paraphernalia, which included his *ọ̀pẹ̀lẹ̀* (the Ifá divination chain, which consists of eight half palm nuts linked to-gether); an *ìrùkẹ̀rẹ̀* (horsetail flywhisk), and the *ọpọ́n Ifá* (divining tray), which was covered with a thin layer of yellowish pollen called *ìyẹ̀rẹ̀ osùn*. The Àràbà brought out his divination bowl or *apẹ̀rẹ̀-Ifá* to show us several *ikin Ifá* or Ifá divination palm nuts, the seeds of the West African oil palm, *Elaensis guineensis*.

The Àràbà began the divination process with a ritual invocation:

> *Àtiwáyé ọjọ*
> *Àtiwọ̀ oòrùn*
> *M'á fi ire pebi*
> *M'á fi ibi pere*
> *Máfòlòlò fọhùn*
> *Iwájú ọpọ́n*
> *Ẹ̀yìn ọpọ́n*
> *Olùbù lọ́tùn-ún*
> *Olùmọ̀ràn lósì*
> *Àárín ọpọ́n*
> *Òde ọ̀run*

> From the dawn of the day,
> To the setting of the sun,
> Never say it is evil when the message is good!
> Never say it is good when the message is evil!
> Never speak deceitfully as a ventriloquist!
> The front of the divining board,
> The back of the divining board,
> The right side of the divining board,
> The all-knowing on the left,
> The center of the divining board,
> The center of heaven.[1]

Holding the divination chain, he touched the *naira* note that Kẹ́hìndé had placed down beside him and further addressed Ifá as follows: "You hear what Kẹ́hìndé has said, Ọ̀rúnmìlà. Kẹ́hìndé's words are secret. You, yourself, are secret *[awo]*, and I myself, the diviner [Babaláwo], I am a novice and an ignorant person *[ọ̀gbẹ̀rì]*. What-ever you decide to do, we will see with our naked eyes. As a fish first sees more clearly in the river; as a toad *[kọ̀nkọ̀]* never refused to hearken to the voice of the river; and as groundnuts were planted in the Ikin's absence but are harvested whenever he goes there."

After the invocation, the Àràbà threw the *ọ̀pẹ̀lẹ̀* on the ground and announced to us that the resulting sign (the pattern produced by the configuration of the chain's palm nuts, convex or concave side facing upwards) was the one called Ìrẹtẹ̀ Ọsẹ́. The Àràbà then recited a few of the *ẹsẹ Ifá* (divination verses) accompanying the Ìrẹtẹ̀ Ọsẹ́ sign:

> Normally, we run to stay alive,
> We do not run to die.
> No one, however wise, can catch water in a cloth.
> No one, however learned, can count the grains of sand on earth.
> No one, however well traveled, can know the length and breadth of the earth.

The Àràbà explained the messages of Ifá by saying that Kẹ́hìndé's matter of inquiry (as yet unspoken except to the *naira*) suggested "intentional disobedience" on his part and that further investigation was necessary to ascertain the truth. "How do we go about knowing the truth?" I asked the Àràbà. Responding to my question, he brought out his *ibò*, a divination apparatus consisting of a pair of cowrie shells tied together and a piece of animal bone, used for further probing a puzzling question to determine definitively and with clarity the sometimes ambiguous messages. "Ọ̀rúnmìlà Àjànà, this boy's message is puzzling! Should we further investigate the matter?" the Àràbà asked Ifá. The Àràbà picked up his *ọ̀pẹ̀lẹ̀* and threw it on the mat. "Yes," Ifá answered positively. The Àràbà picked up his *ọ̀pẹ̀lẹ̀* and threw it again on the mat. Ifá now informed us that the sign of Ọ̀yẹ̀kú had appeared this time. "Ha! Kẹ́hìndé must make a sacrifice." I asked for further explanation, reminding the Àràbà that we were ignorant. Again, the Àràbà recited some Ifá verses to accompany the sign of Ọ̀yẹ̀kú: "It is a long stick that came before we struggled for the wide-open road. Who divined for Ọ̀rúnmìlà when the people on earth wanted to take his voice [to prevent him from speaking]?"

The Àràbà looked at my face, which at this time revealed displeasure at my inability to get a straightforward answer to the question. He sat up straight and explained, "This is the way Ifá speaks; he speaks in parables."

Turning to my research assistant, the Àràbà said, "Kẹ́hìndé, you are struggling for something highly competitive. Ifá said that it will be yours if you make a sacrifice." Kẹ́hìndé paused for a few seconds and said, "Perhaps it has to do with problems at school, but I am not quite sure." I asked if he were struggling with another friend over a girlfriend. Kẹ́hìndé laughed boisterously but refrained from saying yes or no. To end the session, I asked the Àràbà which sacrificial elements were required of us. He suggested that we bring two pigeons, two hens, two kola nuts, palm oil, and fifty *kobo*. I quickly gave the money to his Ojúgbọ̀nà or assistant to arrange to prepare the rituals for sacrifice.

I began this chapter with this description of a divination ritual session because the central part of the annual Ifá Festival and ceremony is the performance of the annual divination for the king, the diviners, and the populace of the city itself. Its purpose is to discern the secrets of heaven pertaining to the destiny of the many humans on earth: the king, the people of the city, the diviners, the Yorùbá people, and the whole world. When Ifá speaks of evil, sacrifices are made to avert disaster that may follow such revelations, but when Ifá speaks of good, there is much merriment among the diviners.

IFÁ IN THEORY AND IN PRACTICE

In traditional and contemporary Yorùbá culture and society, the Ifá divination system occupies a vital role in ordering and regulating the social and moral order. In addition to providing a plausible theory and practice aimed at explaining and controlling events, space, and time, Ifá represents a body of deep knowledge that deals with the past, present, and future all at once. The Babaláwo or diviners memorize Ifá as poetic oral texts and recite them on appropriate occasions, especially during rituals to secure healing and good health for clients.

As a prelude to examining the rituals and ceremonies of Ifá in Ilé-Ifè, it is useful to discuss the practice, logic, and meaning of Ifá. The Ifá divination system of belief and ritual practices derives its authority in Ilé-Ifè from the sacred kingship and the lineage traditions of the diviners. The ritual and ceremonies discussed later in this chapter follow the archetypal format upon which Ifá beliefs and practices throughout Yorùbáland, if not abroad, are based.

The Yorùbá consult Ifá diviners on a wide range of personal, social, and religious matters: for example, before undertaking an important obligation such as marriage, traveling to a distance place, and whenever they are in doubt. They use divination in situations of serious illness, especially when the illness is prolonged. Below, I interpret the symbolic and metaphysical meanings surrounding an Ifá consultation. As in the consultation that my research assistant sought in the Àràbà's house, a client visits a Babaláwo to determine the cause of a problem, typically a physical ailment. The client sits on a mat in front of the diviner while the Babaláwo lays out his divination paraphernalia, which consist of a divinatory chain of linked half nuts and a tray of yellowish pollen. The client takes a coin, touches his forehead with it, and whispers into it his prayer or request, asking Ifá to reveal the secret behind his problem and to find an appropriate solution. He places the coin in front of the diviner, touching his chain with the coin as if conveying the request to it.

The diviner begins the session by invoking Ifá and reciting the words that begin this chapter. Ifá is showered with presents to assist in the process. The diviner requests that Ifá not mislead his client. The invocation also allows the diviner to pay homage to the spirit world, the ancestors, the great diviners before him, and the four directions of the Yorùbá universe as he moves the chain to the front, back, left, right, and center of the tray, acknowledging all the relevant spiritual forces connected to the process. To cast the divination, the diviner holds the chain in the middle and throws it on the mat, making a "U" shape on the floor, so that four nuts fall on each side. The nuts will expose either convex or concave sides, thus displaying sixteen possible forms of the "signature" of Ifá. Each signature stands for an *odù* (divinatory sign or symbol), and each *odù* is linked to several verses of oral poems that interpret it. The diviner then recites the *odù* that appears in the divination castings. The client listens carefully, and after the recitation comments on whether any of the poems is relevant to his illness. At this stage the client may reveal to the diviner the nature of his inquiry. The diviner will interpret the text and, through further questioning, arrive at a definite cause of his client's problem. The diviner will prescribe the appropriate remedy, usually a sacrificial ritual and the use of medicinal herbs.

Although the most frequently employed form of divination involves the use of the *òpèlè* chain, a more prestigious and elaborate form of divination, the *ikin*, involves the use of sixteen palm nuts. The diviner takes the palm nuts from a beautifully carved divination bowl into one hand. He then attempts to grab with his other hand most of the palm nuts in his first hand, leaving one or two. He marks the result of the exercise in the powder in the divination tray. When one palm nut is left in the other hand, the diviner makes two marks, and when two *ikin* are left, he makes one mark. When no palm nuts remain, he makes no mark. This process is done several times until the diviner can make four signs on each side of the tray. Each divination session produces an *odù* divination sign out of the 256 possible signs. The process of reciting the *odù* that appears to the client is similar to the above divinatory session with the *òpèlè*. Below is an example of verses from an *odù* called Èjì Ogbè, which explains how important divination practice is on earth.

> Kò síbi tí aféfé kì í fé ẹ dé
> Kò síbi tí ìjì kì í jà á dé
> A d'ífá fún Òjíṣẹ́ Olódùmarè
> Ẹni tí Olódùmarè rán wá sílé ayé
> Ẹni rán'ni níṣẹ́ là á bèrù
> A kì í bèrù ẹni tá á jẹ fún
> Olówó orí mi kò jé t'Ìkòlé òrun bò wá s'Íkòlé ayé
> Olówó orí mi ò re'bì Kankan
> Tó fi ń ṣe gbogbo ohùn tí ó fé ẹ ṣe
> Ẹni tó bá kọ'tí ikún s'Ífá
> Ènìyànkénìyàn tó ní ẹni wo'fá ò lógbón lórí
> Ẹnikéni tó ní ẹni ń wo'fá n ṣeṣé ibi
> Ó ṣetán tó fé ẹ lọ s'álákéji
> Ojó tó jáde nílé kò jé padà wálé mó
> Ẹbí irú wọn ní í jẹ'ṣé ọwó ọ wọn
> Ẹnikéni ò gbódò sọ pé Ifá ò níí ṣe é
> Ohùn t'Ífá bá sọ níí fún babaláwo lóúnjẹ
> Ẹni tó n'Ífá ń purọ́ ò lérè kankan.

There is no place that the wind does not blow.
There is no place that the hurricane does not blow.
Who divines for the messenger that Olódùmarè the Supreme sends on an errand?
He who sends you on an errand,
He [whom] only you will respect.
Your Master never travels from heaven above.
Your Lord does not go out visiting.
Your Lord stays in one place
and accomplishes everything he wants to bring about.
Whoever refuses to obey the diviners' words,
Whoever says the client's work is not good,
Should be prepared to see Olódùmarè in heaven [i.e., be prepared to die].
When the enemy leaves his house, he will not return home.
The family he leaves behind will have to take charge of his affairs.
No one must doubt the stories of the diviners.
The stories the diviners tell provide for their daily bread.
The enemy who says the diviners are lying will make no progress in life.[2]

In this powerful narrative the heavenly Ifá commands his devotees to take the work of the diviners seriously and spells out consequences for disobedience. Ifá diviners see this passage as proclaiming the authority given to them by Ọrúnmìlà to control, determine, and mediate the affairs of the living. The diviner's role recalls that of the Holy Spirit, who according to Christ's promise would guide the affairs of the world after Christ departed.

The Logic and Meaning of Ifá

African societies recognize two forms of divination: the mechanical and the mystical. The mechanical form involves manipulating divining instruments or objects to arrive at an appropriate answer and treatment for the client. The mystical form centers on possession by a deity and appeal to a deity. In discussing the !Kung or San divination system, Lorna Marshall has argued that mechanical forms of divination fall into the category of magic and "secular" rather than religious forms because they involve no communication with mystical powers.[3] But although Ifá divination is primarily mechanical, the preamble to an Ifá divination session indicates that mystical powers in control of the cosmos are invoked. Ifá divination is also premised on the communication process between the diviner and the spiritual agencies responsible for proper divination performances. William Bascom remarked that the result is influenced by divine guidance.[4] As in the divination process used by the Ainu of Japan, an invocation and prayer to the mystical forces precede the actual mechanical manipulation of the divinatory instrument.[5] The invocation of Ifá provides an important clue to the logic of the divination mechanism. Here we focus on the Ifá divination performance for healing, and our exploration of its three stages—consultation, diagnosis, and sacrifice—must begin with the ritual invocation. It is a poetic ritual prayer addressed to the relevant cosmic powers (the gods, ancestors, spirits) that the diviners know could influence the outcome of the client's diagnosis. The Ifá ritual invocation that I witnessed in 1991 was intoned as follows:

> The front of Ifá,
> The back of Ifá,
> The right side of Ifá,
> The all-knowing on the left,
> The center of Ifá,
> The center of heaven,
> From the dawn of the day
> to the setting of the sun,
> Never say it is good when the message is evil.
> Never say it is evil when the message is good.
> Never speak in a voice of deceit!

These lyrics are the diviner's invocation to Ifá, spoken as a prayer to guide his consultation rightly so that an unequivocal truth may emerge. By his invocations, the diviner symbolically dramatizes the creation of the cosmos, the three layers of the Yorùbá world. At the core of the divination is the idea that the universe and its events are guided by Ifá. He is the regulator of events in the universe (Agbáyégún), and his divination process and activities bring order to a potentially chaotic universe. That spiritual order is symbolized by the regulating grid of the four cardinal points of the universe plus the center, the fifth and the most central point.

The five important axes of power are replicated in the Ifá divination tray, usually carved out of wood, which represents the universe. The circular tray is a replica or "reproduction, on the human scale, of the cosmos [and] of Creation itself. It is an *imago mundi,* an image of the original world order."[6] At times in the course of divination, the Babaláwo may trace these axes in the yellow powder on the Ifá tray, indicating the connection between the four cardinal points and the center. The center of the divining tray, like the center of the world, is the link to the center of heaven, the abode of the Supreme God (Olódùmarè) and the storehouse of sacred knowledge required to discover the "secrets" surrounding the client's ailment, the hidden forces that have produced it. This is analogous to Victor Turner's notion of the center "out there," a place outside the immediate domain of the client, which nevertheless can be accessed through divination.

The act of touching the divining chain or *ọ̀pẹ̀lẹ̀* on the four cardinal points and then the center of the tray captures a complex religious symbolism. By this visually significant act, the tray becomes the earthly sacred center from which the diviner makes present the heavenly center and the ultimate storehouse of Ifá's knowledge.[7] Ifá divination connects the diviner's probing act with the source of the client's being, the *orí* (personal destiny). By this process, divination exposes the client's destiny, the realities that influence his development, and the configuration of sacred powers that governs the world's ceaseless transformations.[8]

Diagnosis and Interpretation of Odù (Divination Texts)

The *odù Ifá,* or divinatory oral narratives, are central to the theory and the control process. These myths, proverbs, and legends express the mythical worldview of the Yorùbá people. The *odù* in Yorùbá imaginations are also personified as supernatural beings transformed into the spoken words of Ifá. They are verbal manifestations of divine power. These spoken words convey the power and imagery of the mythic past. Just as the shaman, to procure a cure for a client, must disclose manifest forces by embodying them and acting them out through music, dance, songs, symbolic gestures, and the supernatural state that conditions his own body and soul, so the diviner recites the appropriate verses that embody the primordial power and events and, in the process of this recitation, recalls plausible events that are similar to the client's own situation.[9] By so doing, he convinces the client that in all likelihood his or her situation will be taken care of by Ifá.

The events and stories are convincing models for the clients to consider. The narratives are archetypes that the diviner can access to assist the client in finding answers to problems. Several of the mythic narratives are stories of knowledgeable diviners in ancient Yorùbá city-states, especially Ilé-Ifẹ̀ (often referred to as Òtù Ifẹ̀ in Ifá poems). In the present divination, the client is faced with the consequences of either rejecting or accepting Ifá's prescription. However, he is left in no doubt about the truth of his own divination session. Because the narratives are archetypical models, and because devotees see the Ifá system as a truthful reflection of their own religious reality, the diviner appropriates the stories and enters into their meaning as he sees fit.

As John Du Bois aptly puts it, in ritual speech, "the role of the ancient diviner-speaker is laminated onto the current diviner, as the role of the ancient client-addressee is laminated onto the current client." The message from Ifá is plausible because of "the ultimate origins of the speech in a distant place and time."[10] The diviner decides which part of the oral narratives comes closest to the client's social world and existential situation. The diviner's role, then, is to interpret the client's situation through the events and meanings the Ifá text conveys and to provide meaning and direction for the client.

The criteria for the direction of the diviner's interpretation are based on the client's assistance and further divining. As the client listens to the texts, he or she determines which part of the story addresses his or her problem and informs the Babaláwo. However, this is considered a partial answer, lacking details. The diviner will then use the *ibò* apparatus to probe further and provide specific details. The diviner provides a set of *ibò* (cowrie shells and animal bone), and the client, after picking it up, whispers a question to it. For example, if the verses in the divination suggest that a witch in the client's lineage is causing a client's illness, to determine whether the witch is from his father's or mother's household the client will whisper to the *ibò*, "Is the witch responsible for my illness from my father's lineage?" He then places the *ibò* back on the divining tray. The diviner touches the tray and chain with the *ibò*, then gives the *ibò* back to the client. He informs the client that the cowrie stands for yes and the bone stands for no. The client picks up the *ibò* and keeps the cowries in one hand and the bone in the other, hidden from the diviners.

The diviner will cast divinations twice and determine which of the two *odù* that appear is the senior of the two, meaning which comes first and carries more weight in the hierarchy of the *odù*. If the first *odù* is superior to the second, the diviner asks the client to show the *ibò* in his right hand. If the *odù* in the second divination performance is superior to the *odù* in the first, he asks the client to produce the *ibò* in his left hand. The type of *ibò* in the left or right hand determines the answer for clients. If the *ibò* in the client's right hand is a piece of bone, the answer to his question is no. However, if the *ibò* is the piece of cowrie, the answer to his question is yes. Through this process, further questions are asked until the diviner determines the precise answers to all the puzzles surrounding the client's problems.

Healing Therapy and Sacrificial Rituals

Once divination is performed to determine the cause of the crisis, especially concerning an illness, a combination of herbs is often prescribed as a cure. The diviner first prescribes and applies herbal medicine and then performs a sacrificial ritual to appease the malevolent spirits identified in the divination process, those suspected of being responsible for the client's illness. The first procedure is carried out with the assistance of the herbal medicine of Òsanyìn, the god of medicine. Pierre Verger, the most authoritative scholar on Yorùbá herbal medicine, has carefully demonstrated that there is a strong causal relationship between the medical herbs administered for illness and their religious and symbolic meanings.[11] What seems different about the Ifá divination process—as compared to other indigenous medicinal systems—is that the preparation of medicine often involves the use of powerful incantations of Ifá oral text without which the medicine would fail to take effect. Spoken incantations infuse the medicine with the power and *àṣẹ* (vital force) that make the medicine work. The Yorùbá believe that one's *orí* plays an important role in medicinal and herbal therapy. The Ifá verses recited often contain references addressed to the client's *orí* to aid in the treatment. "One's *orí*," the Yorùbá say, "enhances the efficacy of medicine" *(Orí mú oògùn jẹ́).*

Sacrificial ritual is the ultimate cure for a client's illness. The diviner prescribes for the client the appropriate sacrifice to the aggrieved supernatural being. Clients may decide to perform the sacrifice on their own or may plead with the diviner to carry out the sacrifice on their behalf. When sacrificial objects are procured and prepared according to the prescription of Ifá, the sacrifice is taken to an auspicious place. This is usually at a crossroads or junction, along a riverbank, in a deep forest, at an open market, and in some other place where supernatural spirits are often found. Èṣù, the bearer of sacrifice, is first offered part of the sacrificial food to ensure its safe delivery to the supernatural realm. The purpose of sacrifice *(ẹbọ)* is to bring about harmony between the social and moral orders and between the earthly and heavenly realms. Disharmony is brought about by problems created by the individual's sins and offenses against the gods, ancestors, or witches. A good number of sacrifices are substitutes and ransoms to buy back clients whom the witches may have vowed to devour or whom the gods may have promised to destroy.

In the sacrificial process, Ifá divination identifies the particular deity or supernatural being that is connected with the affairs of his clients and the issues concerned. The forms of sacrifice appropriate for a remedy are related to the nature of the problem and the personality of the spiritual agent. For example, an issue involving Ṣàngó, god of thunder, may require sacrificing a ram, while one involving Ògún, god of iron, may require sacrificing a dog, and so on. Once a specific sacrifice is determined and prepared, Èṣù, the intermediary between the gods and Ọrúnmìlà, is invoked, fed, and invited to see to that the offering is properly made.

If the propitiatory sacrifice involves offering an animal, the animal is presented to the god with a declaration of the client's intention. For example, a sacrifice to Ògún may include the statement "Ògún, this is your animal [a dog]. My client presents this to you to secure his health back. Keep him and his family safe from destruction." The client then touches the animal's head with his own head. It is assumed either that the evil embedded in the client's head is transferred to the animal or that the client's inner head will enhance the efficacy of the sacrifice.

The sacrificial offerings also involve communal participation. The members of the surrounding community, especially the household and neighbors, must partake of the sacrificial meal and offerings. An *odù* Ifá supports this idea. It refers to a client who performed a sacrifice to an aggrieved deity but did not realize that the neighbors had to partake of the offering to the gods and ancestors. When he came back to the diviner to complain that the sacrifice was not effective, the diviner discovered that the client had failed to give part of the offerings to his neighbors to eat. The text suggests that any sacrifice, whether to avert death or to effect healing, must involve a sacrificial meal shared by immediate neighbors and households of the client. Yorùbá people believe that one of the causes of illness is disputes between neighbors. But once a client feeds his neighbor, the neighbor can no longer effect harm. As the Yorùbá proverb declares, "He who partakes of your salt and pepper can no longer cause evil to befall you." It is assumed that such neighbors bring curses upon themselves if they harm the one who has fed them because Ifá clearly condemns their ingratitude.

Ifá, then, is at the center of the constructs and meanings of Yorùbá cosmology and religious ideas. In addition to determining the cause of illness and its remedy, this complex divination practice and body of knowledge provides explanations and answers to life's difficulties and misfortunes. The festival and ceremony of Ifá in Ilé-Ifè attempts to energize the deity and the diviners to demonstrate the significance of Ifá in the community. Because the Babaláwo lineage derive their authority *(àṣẹ)* to perform divination from the ruling sacred king, the annual Ifá Festival of these diviners (Ọdún Eríwo) immediately follows that of the king (Ọdún Ọòni). The festivals occur when the king, the diviners, and the Ilé-Ifè people celebrate the arrival of the new yam, the end of the old Ifá year and the beginning of a new one.

THE FESTIVAL OF IFÁ

The Ifá Festival is a complex ritual involving celebrations and ceremonies that last for three months. The festival, which relates to the community's personal, collective, and agricultural well-being, renews the communal life of the sacred city, bestowing the blessings of Ifá's abundance upon the diviners and the sacred king and rejuvenating cosmic energy. This communal quest for "blessings of new life" is conveyed on several levels in the ritual festival process. First, the diviners must celebrate the King's New Yam Ceremony (Ègbodò Ọòni) and the King's Ifá Festival (Ọdún Ifá). The King's New Yam Festival expresses the intricate symbolic relationship between sacred kingship and divination practices by demonstrating the political, social, and religious role of Ifá in maintaining kingship and, indirectly, the Ọòni's role in providing authority and legitimacy to divination practices in his domain. Second, the diviners must celebrate their own New Yam and Ifá Festival. The Diviners' New Yam Ceremony (Ègbodò Eríwo) shows how divination and ritual sacralize the lineage identities of the diviners and how the kingship legitimizes their significant role in the sacred city of Ilé-Ifè. For this agricultural society, the Ọòni's symbolic eating of new yam initiates the renewal of life and invokes blessings and authority of Ifá for the sacred king, the diviners' lineage, and the people of Ilé-Ifè for the coming year.

We will see how the first part of the festival centers on the Ọòni. The second part, performed in Òkè Ìtasè, focuses on the Àràbà (the chief priest of Ifá), whose lineage is the custodian of the central Ifá shrine and temple. I will elaborate upon the relationship between the Àràbà and Ọrúnmìlà or Ifá (the deity of divination) in Ifá mythic narrative.

According to Àràbà Awosọpé, an *odù Ifá* called Ogbèyèkú states that once Ọrúnmìlà was on an Ifá journey to the house of Onírèṣáolú (an ancient king). Ọrúnmìlà was asked to perform a sacrifice to ensure a successful journey but was warned that he would see some strange things. Ọrúnmìlà went to Onírèṣáolú's house and returned in peace. Not long after, the Ọlófin sent for Ọrúnmìlà, but he could not go. He then asked his son Àràbà to perform a divination for Ọlófin. Since Ọrúnmìlà was already old, he was very glad to designate Àràbà to perform Ifá for the Ọlófin. As a result, the Àràbà became the head of the Ifá priests.

My informant cautioned that in the past there was only one Àràbà in the entire universe and that this custom of individual towns now appointing an Àràbà was a wrong thing. The head of the Ifá priests in other towns and cities outside Ifè used to be called Olúwo and not Àràbà, a title meant only for the Ifè Òkè Ìtasè diviner. The title Àràbà (literally a giant tree in the forest) connects greatness, massiveness, and incomprehensibility. As a big tree, the Àràbà is believed to be the "king of the forest," perhaps the most massive in Yorùbá's experience.

In Ilé-Ifè, the Àràbà is an Qba in his own right and he is addressed as such by the rest of the diviners. Whereas in other Yorùbá cities the position of Àràbà can come from any lineage, in Ilé-Ifè it is reserved exclusively for the Òkè Ìtasè lineage from which the Àràbà is chosen. As in any socially constructed ritual, the Ifá celebration focuses on this lineage's heritage and honors them as the custodians of Ifá in Ilé-Ifè.

In addition to propitiating the divinities Ifá and Èṣù, the Ifá Festival provides an avenue for the diviners of the lineage of Òkè Ìtasè to reaffirm their identity as the custodians and leaders of Ifá diviners. Both meanings and functions are realized under the purview of the Qòni's sacred kingship.

The King's New Yam Festival

The Diviner's Assistants Visit the Ọ̀ṣàrà River   The king's Ifá sacrificial ceremony begins with the preparation for and public announcement of the festival. It starts with the performance of a ritual of invisibly planting and nurturing the "yam." The acolytes of the sixteen principal diviners, called Ojúgbọ̀nà, take small poles *(èdó)*, symbolic of the poles used to construct the frames that support yam vines, to the bank of the Ọ̀ṣàrà River, one of the sacred rivers in the city. Once at the river, they go through the act of dramatizing the process of planting and harvesting yams. They do this by sticking the poles in the ground to mimic the erecting of the frames and by creating mounds similar to the ones used in yam cultivation.

In this ritual performance, the Ojúgbọ̀nà, who fill the honored role in a diviner's household of acolytes or apprentices, symbolically assist their masters in planting and harvesting farm produce. As members of the priestly class, diviners spend long hours in divination work, making it impossible for them to work on the farm in agricultural production. Singing rapturous songs and dancing, the Ojúgbọ̀nà return to the city, visiting the homes of senior Ifá priests and their own lineage homes, where they are showered with gifts of money and food. This ritual serves as a public announcement that the Ifá Festival will commence in thirteen days.

Gathering Ifá's Sacred Leaves for the King's Divination   In the early morning of the festival's first day, all the Ojúgbọ̀nà assemble in the compound of the Àgbọngbọ̀n, a chief priest second in rank to the overall head of Ifá tradition in Ilé-Ifè, the Àràbà.

The Àgbọngbọ̀n is regarded as the leader of Ilé-Ifẹ̀'s diviners, in contrast to the Àràbà, who is king of the diviners and whose authority and power are derived directly from the sacred kingship and the palace. Jubilantly, the Ojúgbọ̀nà greet the Àgbọngbọ̀n during the New Yam Festival. Holding the royal horsetail flywhisk (ìrùkẹ̀rẹ̀), which is a sacred symbol of Ifá priesthood, they offer prayers and sacrifices to Ọ̀rúnmìlà for guidance during the celebration.

The ìrùkẹ̀rẹ̀ is a symbol of honor, power, and the chiefly status of the diviner. It is also owned by the sacred kings and, in this context, is the symbol of the linkage of the diviner to the royal lineage and power in the city. Further, a material ornament such as the ìrùkẹ̀rẹ̀ becomes a makeshift shrine for propitiating Ifá precisely because it signifies Ifá's authority and power and the sacred identity of its owner. In Ilé-Ifẹ̀, unlike most African communities, where royal power is concentrated entirely in the position of a king, certain clans claim limited royalty, so that royal power permeates a large segment of the society, though the Ọ̀ọ̀ni sits atop the royal pyramid and is accorded supreme authority.

With the ritual completed, the group proceeds to the home of the Àràbà in Òkè Ìtàsẹ̀, where a similar ceremony will take place. The beginnings of both ceremonies are marked by feasting at the respective homes of the Àgbọngbọ̀n and the Àràbà.

Ewé Ifá (Ifá leaves) are some of the most important ingredients for the king's divination ceremony. As in the Ọbàtálá Festival, Ifá diviners proceed in orderly fashion to the sacred forest near Ọ̀sàrà to gather the leaves for the ritual washing of the Ọ̀ọ̀ni's Ifá objects so that these will be renewed and energized for the coming year. One of the diviner's informants told me, "The washing rejuvenates Ifá and renews its strength, just as the Christians ask God to empower an Àlùfáà [a Christian clergyman] or a Wòlíì [a prophet in the Aládúrà African spiritual church] to enable him perform a miracle or heal the sick." We often heard the phrase Kí Ọlọ́run sọ agbára òjíṣẹ́ wọn di ọtun (May God make new the power of his messenger). As I discussed in the earlier part of this work, Ilé-Ifẹ̀ traditionalists freely borrow Christian and Muslim metaphors to convey meanings in their own tradition. Having accepted the reality of Muslim and Christian influences on their own tradition and worldview, they use the new traditions as regular points of reference for making comparative and ontological observations. Many diviners were educated in Christian elementary schools or Muslim Arabic and Islamic schools, and their knowledge of these traditions helps them convey the truth of their own tradition. In addition, when the people of Ilé-Ifẹ̀ encounter "outsiders" such as myself, they often feel the need to explain their faith and tradition using the terminology and vehicle of traditions best known to their interviewers.

During my fieldwork, as the diviners assembled at the base of Òkè Ìtàsẹ̀, Ifá's sacred hill, the Lóòdágbá (the head of the Ojúgbọ̀nà) organized the procession. Just as the Ọbàtálá priests, in their processions, held a long thin stick (àtòrì), the diviners each held an ọ̀rẹ̀rẹ̀ (the iron walking stick). In an order of increasing seniority, with the Àràbà coming last behind all the diviners, they proceeded with drums, music, and dance to the Ọ̀ṣàrà River, where they gathered the leaves. At the Ọ̀ṣàrà Road junction, the Ojúgbọ̀nà branched off to a house referred to as Maliki's compound, where the first òrìgì (Ifá's hierophany) in Ilé-Ifẹ̀ had taken place. The Àràbà and the other diviners continued on to the Ọ̀ṣàrà River.

In a sense, the first portion of Ifá's ceremony is a reenactment of Ifá's primordial journey to Ilé-Ifẹ̀. Maliki's compound, where the Ojúgbọ̀nà went to celebrate the commencement of the festival, was regarded as the first compound in Ilé-Ifẹ̀ where Ifá diviners had lived. In the past, the members of the compound would have been proud of the presence of Ifá in their midst. If the compound was Yorùbá Muslim, the Maliki lineage members would be called "the first fellows and beneficiaries of the prophet's message" (Ajíjọlá Ànábì). However, the story now is different. I was informed that virtually all the members of the lineage had converted to either Islam or Christianity. The remnants of Ifá devotees in the lineage provided the banquet and feast for the Ojúgbọ̀nà only as a courtesy and a remembrance of their ancestral heritage. The Ifá diviners' desire for a renewal of Ifá's power and status in the compound is expressed in the saying, *Kí awo rere má jẹ́ ní Mọ̀rẹ̀* (May fervent divination not perish in the lineage of Maliki in Mọ̀rẹ̀ [the city quarter that has the Maliki shrine and compound at its center]). The prayer expresses the wish that the *orísun* (the place of origin) of Ifá may never perish from the face of the earth. The *orísun* is also significant because it is the site of passage to the world of the ancestors.

While the Ojúgbọ̀nà were busy entertaining themselves in Maliki's compound, the principal diviners went to Ọ̀ṣàrà River, where the Àràbà venerated Ifá. The Àràbà took the sacrificial offerings provided by the Ọ̀ọ̀ni through the palace chiefs and offered them to Ọ̀rúnmìlà. The Àràbà broke the kola nuts in the gift and performed a simple divination to ascertain whether Ọ̀rúnmìlà had accepted the offerings. When an affirmative sign was given, the Àràbà plucked the first sacred leaf and announced very quietly, *Mo fi ewé jìn* (I have plucked the leaf). Afterwards, the other diviners selected varieties of leaves from plants growing along the riverbank, depositing the leaves into the Ifá ceremonial bag *(àpò Ifá)*.

What were the Ifá leaves? What were the criteria for selecting the leaves? A group of Ifá priests with whom I had become acquainted informed me, "There are two hundred types, but the most important are called *ewé ẹ̀rò* [cool, soft prophylactic leaves]." According to Yorùbá nomenclature, "soft" leaves serve to pacify, cool, and calm the patient. Chemical properties in the leaves of such plants as *ewé tẹ̀tẹ̀, rinrin,* and *wọ̀rọ̀wọ́* act as antidotes against poisons, evil spirits, and pain. All medicinal leaves are called *abo ewé,* female leaves—as opposed to *akọ ewé,* male leaves, such as *ẹ̀ṣúrín, àrógbá,* and *ayìn.* Since the purpose of the festival is to bring about harmony and peace with nature and other humans beings, the *abo ewé* leaves were gathered as ingredients for washing the king's sacred instruments used in the Ifá ritual.

Once the Àràbà announced that he had "plucked the leaf," thereby performing the symbolic harvesting of the medicinal leaves for the king's use, the rest of the group was free to collect the leaves. The leaves are regarded as living entities; a sacred pact exists between them and the diviners who use the leaves to benefit the community. With the leaves collected, the diviners left the Ọ̀ṣàrà River and met the Ojúgbọ̀nà at the junction, where they danced and rejoiced on their way to the king's palace, having collected the most important presents for the Ọ̀ọ̀ni's Ifá ceremony.

Washing the King's Ifá Objects   The ritual washing of the king's Ifá objects took place in Ilé-Ìgbò, one of the inner palace chambers designated for holding sacrificial rituals. The ritual washing represented not only an act of renewal but also a mechanism for reenergizing and recharging the sacred instruments so that they would become more effective in performing divination. The leaves collected from the banks of the Ọ̀ṣàrà River were transferred to a great Ifá bowl *(apèrè-Ifá),* where the Àràbà ground them together into a paste. With the paste, he cleansed the tray *(ọpọ́n Ifá),* the palm nuts *(ikin Ifá),* and other instruments belonging to the Ọ̀ọ̀ni. While cleansing them, he continued to recite Ifá verses, and *Ma rí ọ bọ* (May I continue to propitiate you), and pray for his own longevity and the Ọ̀ọ̀ni's long reign in Ilé-Ifẹ̀. The ritual renewed his own identity as the Ọ̀ọ̀ni's chief diviner and reaffirmed the king's existence on earth. Afterwards, to seal the invocation, he offered up sacrifices to Ifá.

Àsùndáná: The Night Vigil at the Palace   The diviners returned to the king's palace with their harvest of sacred Ifá leaves, and that evening the Ifá night vigil began in the palace with the purpose of invoking the spirits, ancestors, and gods to join in propitiating the Ọ̀ọ̀ni's Ifá, using special incantations of Ifá verses or *isokò.* Because of the strength and intensity of the verses, performers and orators had to be "cooled" down by consuming beverages and food with "cooling" properties, such as honey, salt, and bush meat. An informant advised me, "Ordinarily, we cannot rehearse these powerful formulas; recitals must be performed on the appropriate days and time." The verses recited during the night vigil differ from the playful Ifá verses that can be recited at any time. The Ọ̀ọ̀ni visited the group during the night, giving them money and offering them sumptuous food and drink, entertaining the Babaláwo.

   In the early morning of the following day, the priests were obliged to eat a full breakfast supervised by the Àgbọngbọ̀n. Later that day, to propitiate the Ifá of the Ọ̀ọ̀ni, feasting began. The wives of the diviners prepared special dishes for the feast and brought them to the palace, placing them in front of the Àgbọngbọ̀n, who prayed for the group. Once the food from all households was assembled, the Àgbọngbọ̀n threw out morsels to Èṣù, blessed all those assembled, and permitted the priests to feast, beginning with the Àràbà.

   For this agricultural community, the New Yam Festival symbolizes the beginning of a new calendar, the king's sacrifice for fertility and abundance, and the pro-

pitiation of the deities for blessings for himself and his subjects. The king ate from
the new yam to symbolize the renewal of life and the source of sustenance for his
people. At noon, the Àràbà led the diviners to the market stall at the base of Òkè
Ìtasè, where a major Èṣù shrine is located. Kneeling before Èṣù, the god who opens
all doors, the Àràbà invoked this deity and then all the major Ifè deities—gods, goddesses, ancestors, and spirits—urging them to join in the celebration with the king.
In consonance with the Ifè binary ritual structure of night and day, this midafter-
noon ritual of invocation was the counterpart of the previous night's vigil and invocation. It was also an archetypal sacrifice, a ritual model and replica of what the
Babaláwo gives to Èṣù at every sacrificial ritual, and especially before any divination performance.

Èṣù, Ifá, and the King's Sacrifice   The next important ritual of the Ifá of the Ọòni
required that Èṣù be propitiated first, because he is the great messenger who has
the ability to deliver or not deliver the ultimate sacrifice to its appropriate place.
The Babaláwo was emphatic that Èṣù must clear the ritual path toward a successful sacrifice. What is the relationship between Èṣù, Ifá, and the sacred kingship? An
odù Ifá called Ọyèkú Okú Iṣé, which centers on the creation of humans and the
choice of the individual's destiny as he is on the way to the world, provides a plausible explanation. This narrative was told to me by the then Àràbà of Ilé-Ifè, Chief
Awosọpé. It attempts to demonstrate the power of the myth of Èṣù and the need to
propitiate him before the actual sacrifice:

> A number of infants were being transferred from heaven [òrun] to the world [ayé].
> As usual, they had to stop off at the place where they selected their destiny [orí]. Sig-
> nificantly, the *orí* determines a person's entire future identity, fortune, and essence on
> earth. Normally, an individual must decide on different worldly assets: wealth, poverty,
> property, children, and commoner or royal status. After choosing a "head" in the rit-
> ual of *akúnlèyàn* [literally, that which one kneels down to choose], some of the chil-
> dren announced when they would return to heaven. Those who chose to continue on
> to the world chose their *orí*, and a sound like a loud bell rang to confirm the choice.
> As the infants proceeded on their journey, they reached the place of divination where
> the *odù* of Ifá, the messages and secrets of heaven, are stored. They were asked to make
> sacrifices, but they claimed that "the powerful ones of heaven" [Olùgbọ́ Ọ̀run] had
> already given them their destinies and thus that they did not need to offer additional
> sacrifices. The heavenly diviners heeded their words and left them, and the infants
> proceeded on their journey until they reached the River Òsèrè, the river of forgetful-
> ness, at the junction of heaven and earth—the abode of Èṣù.
>
> The infants stopped temporarily at the abode of Èṣù, gatekeeper, customs officer,
> and messenger of the gods. Èṣù stretched out his *àṣẹ* [symbol of authority] over the
> Òsèrè River. At the riverbank, all the newborns held out their destinies in the palms
> of their hands. Èṣù stretched out his rod or *ibọn* toward them, exclaiming, "Ah, you
> babes! You are on your way to the world! Drink of the water and be bold and strong!"

Then Èṣù inquired of them incredulously, "What happened to the destiny you were given in heaven?" But all the destinies had dissolved and disappeared in the water. The infants would have been forced to go to the world empty-handed and to roam about aimlessly without destinies, but instead they decided to turn back to heaven to ask for new destinies.

The people of heaven were surprised to see them. "What have you come back here to do?" they asked. Woefully, the infants explained that at the junction of heaven and earth their destinies had suddenly disappeared into the water. However, the hard-hearted Olódùmarè ordered them to return to the world without destinies. Olódù-marè had never bestowed an orí twice. The infants were advised that when they ar-rived again in the world they should look for Bàbá Atóríṣe—the man who reconstructs a flawed orí or who will help perfect any pieces of destiny that remain with them.

Accordingly, all the infants returned to the world. When they reached the world, they asked for Bàbá Atóríṣe and hurried straight away to the House of Ọ̀rúnmìlà, with whom they consulted Ifá. Ifá informed them that Èṣù had taken away from them all the good things they craved and had put the things in the Òsèrè River. However, if the infants took care to sacrifice regularly, all these things would be returned to them little by little. "There is no such thing as a onetime sacrifice." Ọ̀rúnmìlà spelled out the details of each one's sacrifice according to his needs and circumstances: children, chieftaincy title, wealth, good health, longevity, or honor. Each required the help and essence of different deities and spirits. The children started making sacrifices. They were pleased with good results and offered thanks to Ọ̀rúnmìlà for his counsel and assurance because his words became truth. Thus, whenever Ọ̀rúnmìlà held his annual sacrifice, all the children gathered themselves together to celebrate with him, and dur-ing the Ifá Festival all children greeted him in unison with this celebrated song:

> Ọ̀rúnmìlà tóríṣe, Bàràpàṣè tóríṣe
> Ọ̀rúnmìlà ni mo gbe sí o
> Bàràpàṣè tóríṣe.

> Ọ̀rúnmìlà is the one who renames bad orí.
> To him I give honor and thanks,
> The creator who remakes one's orí.

According to the informant, the reason for Ifá's sacrifice is implicit in these lyrics: each individual has the capacity to choose his or her orí. Never again can Èṣù in-tervene, no obstacle will alter a destiny, and no river that one crosses when travel-ing from heaven to live in this world will affect one's destiny. However, there are numerous alájogun (evil forces) in the world, and the authority by which this world is governed belongs to "our Mothers," a euphemism for the power of witches. Through sacrifice, the diviners are instituted to save the people of earth from evil forces.

The above narrative demonstrates Ifá's ability to tame and control Èṣù's agency in the same way that he intervened to save the children whose good destiny Èṣù had appropriated. As a quintessential deity of divination, Ifá regulates human life and destiny from cradle to grave, because it is only through divination and appropriate sacrifice that humans can counteract Èṣù's role in their lives. It is fascinating how, in the contemporary religious and secular life of the Yorùbá, Èṣù, a word inappropriately translated as "the devil," is blamed for all human errors and mischief. *Iṣé Èṣù ni* (It is Èṣù's doing) is heard in day-to-day Yorùbá parlance to explain why there is evil in the world.[12]

The ambiguous character and double personality of Èṣù is assumed in the narratives. Often described as *ṣòtún-ṣòsì láì nítìjú* (one who belongs to two opposing camps without having any feeling of shame), Èṣù is duplicitous, playing both sides without scruples and acting as both a destroyer and an instigator of events.[13] Since he is regarded as the delight of any place or town (Èṣù Láàlú), the king must appease him and give thanks by offering Èṣù his protection. Like the boundaries between heaven and earth, the shrines of Èṣù are located at auspicious junctions, especially at the entrances to cities and city centers, to ward off any unwelcome visitors. There Èṣù mediates among benevolent and malevolent forces. In another context, the propitiation of the centrally placed shrine of Èṣù at Ẹnu Ọwá (literally, "mouth of the king") represents the archetypal sacrifice. In all the divination rituals that the Babaláwo performs throughout the year, Èṣù must be propitiated before any other sacrificial ritual can take place. Just as the Ọ̀ọ̀ni's Ifá is the archetypal one and its propitiation becomes the model for a town's diviners, so the Ẹnu Ọwá Èṣù is central among all others located in the homes of diviners.

In the context of the festival, Èṣù is situated between the king's palace and the vicinity of Ọrúnmìlà in Òkè Ìtasẹ̀. Passersby must pay tribute to and placate Èṣù to open the gate and ease the way to the temple of Ọrúnmìlà. Èṣù must be willing to convey the king's sacrifice to the potential spiritual and mystical forces that, in turn, help the king administer his city. A stanza in an ordinary Ifá ritual song states, *Eégún ayé, èṣìbá ọrun, è mọ̀ rọ̀ wá ò, k'a ṣe Ifẹ̀, è rọ̀ wá o, ọdún dé* (Èṣù can make and unmake a community and is seen as behind all unusual occurrences in any place). The Ifá priests appeal to his good side as they proceed to offer the new yam to the king in a highly complex ritual.

Offering the New Yam to the Ọ̀ọ̀ni   After the propitiation of Èṣù, and with the ritual path wide open so that the Ọ̀ọ̀ni might commence his own sacrifice, the party of the Àràbà returned to the palace to slice the new yam and present it to Ifá before the king could partake of it. The assembly of Ifá priests invoked Ifá by chanting the *iyẹ̀rẹ̀ Ifá*, Ifá poetic verses. In the invocation, the Àràbà recognized the presence of the other *òrìṣà*, especially Ògún, whose knife the Àràbà used to split the yam into pieces for eating.

A roasted yam was placed in front of the Àràbá; he raised the knife and again invoked Ifá to split the new yam for the king to eat. "Àragbà, Awo Ọrun [Diviner in Heaven], come quickly and cut the yam for us," he intoned. Raising the knife the seventh time, he sliced the yam into several pieces. He touched the Ọ̀ọ̀ni's head with the yam, indicating that the Ọ̀ọ̀ni's inner "head" would grant the Ọ̀ọ̀ni a peaceful reign and a long life, as he could continue to partake in the festival yearly. He then poured red oil on the yam, preparing it for the Ọ̀ọ̀ni. The king tasted it, after which the Àràbà, the rest of the key diviners, and the king's chief lieutenants partook of the sacred yam meal. The way was now open for all in the city to eat new yams or to sell or buy them in Ifẹ̀ market. Finally the Àràbà broke the kola given by the Ọ̀ọ̀ni for the ritual and performed a simple kola nut divination to confirm that Ifá and the gods had accepted the rituals of the new yam.

Animal Sacrifice   The climax of the ritual was the offering of animals donated by the Ọ̀ọ̀ni. As each was picked up, the Àràbà invoked its symbolic *oríkì,* conveying the meaning and function of the object in the context of the particular ritual. For example, a mouse *(eku)* was given to ensure the life of the king, so the Àràbà sang, "The sacrifice takes the 'head' of the mouse and not the head of the Ọ̀ọ̀ni" *(Orí eku ló gbà é má gborí Ọ̀ọ̀ni).* The mouse here served as a redemptive substitute for the Ọ̀ọ̀ni. Next, the Àràbà took a snail and knocked off the bottom of its shell to allow its liquid to pour onto the sacrificial place. The liquid of the snail acted as a coolant that brought peace, tranquility, and a prophylactic against evil. At this stage, the Àràbà sang, "What is the purpose of today's sacrifice? It is to soften and counter the poisons unleashed by the evil ones" *(Kí la fi Ifá òní bọ? Ẹ̀rọ̀, Ẹ̀rọ̀ la fi Ifá òní bọ).* The two motifs of substitution and cooling are important in Ifá's sacrificial ritual.

The climax of the phase of the ritual relating to the king's *orí* and his propitiation of Ifá was the sacrifice of the goat, Ifá's favorite animal. The goat is the appropriate sacrificial animal for divination. In Yorùbá religious ritual, each deity has its own appropriate meat, and the goat belongs to Ifá, just as the dog belongs to Ògún. By offering a goat, the Ọ̀ọ̀ni acknowledged the power and role of Ifá in his reign. The offering of a goat to Ifá was intended to urge him to protect the king. It allowed the *orí* (the "inner head") to carry the Ọ̀ọ̀ni through the next cycle of the year of Ifá. Several *odù Ifá* refer to the importance of the "inner head," as the following *odù* verse clearly shows.

> *Oyè ìhín, oyè ọ̀hún*
> *A dífá fún Olóyègèlè*
> *Ọmọ orí-rere-tó-ń-kù-bí-ọṣẹ-fùlẹ̀-fúlẹ́*
> *Ẹ ò rí i ẹ ò rí orí olóyè*
> *Bíí ti kù*

Honor here, honor there!
Divined for Olóyègèlè, the son of Orí rere [the one with a good *orí*]
Overflowing with happiness, like bubbles of soap washing his head,
Behold the head of the chief [the titled one]
As the *orí,* his "inner being," bubbles over with joy.

The verse alludes to an Ifá narrative about a man named Olóyègèlè who wanted to be king. He consulted a diviner, who advised him to offer sacrifices of a ram, white cloth, money, and a large rooster that had a splendid comb as magnificent as a king's crown. With these objects, the Babaláwo made a medicinal Ifá soap with which the client was to regularly wash his head. When the time came and he contested for a vacant throne, Olóyègèlè was the candidate most favored of candidates by the king-makers and was indeed crowned a king.

The essence of the divination myth centers on the verse "Behold the head of the titled one." The diviner's comment, citing a proverb that "no matter how difficult things are for the rooster, he is able to hold the crown on his head" (Ojú kì í pón àkùkọ gọ̀gọ̀rọ̀ kí ó má lè gbádé baba rẹ̀ borí) conflates the crowned king with the rooster that has a splendid comb. When applied to the king, the proverb suggests that the wearer of the crown can reign for a long time in spite of unforeseen crises. The image of a rooster reflects the power of the Ọ̀ọni. The proverb recognizes the burden of wearing the crown (observance of the duties of the king's office), but sacrifices ameliorate this burden. The king's inner head, the driving force of a human being's life and character, which resides in the spirit world, was propitiated in order to allow his outer head to perform the functions of a king successfully. Once the king's sacrificial offerings were concluded, the Babaláwo prepared to perform a pilgrimage to Ifá Temple on Òkè Ìtasẹ̀ (the Hill of Ifá), near the palace.

Climbing Àgbọnìrègún (Òkè Ìtasẹ̀) Hill and the Pilgrimage to Ifá Temple   On the occasion of my visit, Ifá devotees from all over the world began to arrive in the city in the early afternoon in order to prepare for the night celebration in Ifá Temple. The day officially ended the Ọ̀ọni's Ifá Festival, and the night was when a new Ifá year began, so it was both the end of the old year and the beginning of a new year. The Ọ̀ọni's Ifá was also taken to the temple.

The Àràbà informed me that this was Ifá's own Mount Arafat (Òkè Arafat ti wa nì yẹn), referring to the Muslim pilgrimage to climb Mount Arafat in Mecca.[14] The procession from the palace to Ifá Temple on top of the hill (Òkè Àgbọnìrègún) was the focus of attention here. But this ritual, unlike the rituals of the preceding days, assumed a more international significance because of the visitors from overseas and the participation of Ifá diviners from the rest of Yorùbáland. Devotees of other òrìṣà in Ilé-Ifẹ̀ might also join to celebrate with Ifá diviners. The procession began at about 3:00 p.m. with the song, Olókosẹ́ gbúrére, ìrù la fi káyọ̀ relé (The olókosẹ́ bird received plentiful blessings and uses his long tail to take his joy home), which, by referring to a bird with a long, elegant tail and showy flight display, suggested that the diviners were going home in a joyful mood. But when they arrived at the base of the hill, they sang a more sober song to remind themselves of the sanctity and seriousness of the act to follow, climbing Àgbọnìrègún Hill: "O ye people, think well about this. We are going to the hill of wealth. O ye people, think about these things."

FIGURE 19. Àràbà and Ifá priests on Òkè Ìtasẹ̀, the sacred hill of Ifá.

I was informed that this was a caution to all evil-minded people not to ascend the hill with an impure mind, as they would suffer bad consequences. The Àràbà performed a recitation ritual of *ìsokò* (invocation) three times, and they all climbed the hill. He sang the *ìsokò* twice without any of the priests answering him except in murmurs. On the third oration, all the Babaláwo responded to him. This ritual invocation was performed until the entire group reached the top of the mountain.

One of the most remarkable aspects of the Ifá ceremony relates to its global and modern significance. Over the years, it has become an Ifá fair, an orchestrated performance rather than a merely local ritual. A sizable number of Ifá devotees from Cuba, Brazil, and the United States travel to Ilé-Ifẹ̀ for this ceremony. Because of its international dimension, a local committee of Ifá and *òrìṣà* devotees is put into place to plan the event of the evening. A program is normally printed indicating when various aspects of the night's activities will take place. These include speeches from Ifá guests from abroad and in Nigeria as well as a singing and recitation competition among Ifá representatives from various towns and cities. Prizes and gifts are given to talented Yorùbá groups who impress the assembly the most. In various national and international dignitaries in Ifá cycle are called upon to introduce themselves and speak or perform. It is an occasion to invoke Ifá in prayer for the gathering. In this particular festival, a female diviner from Lagos (whom I later

FIGURE 20. Ifá Children's Choir performing during the Ifá Festival in the Ifá temple on Òkè Ìtasẹ̀.

learned was the daughter of a prominent deceased Ifá leader, the Àjànàkú of Lagos) spoke, holding an *ìrókẹ́* (Ifá bell). An elderly woman who was a devotee of Ṣàngó from Ìbàdàn, whose spectacular drama was performed the following day, also spoke. I recalled that Madam Ìyá Ṣàngó was being carefully watched because she was very prone to being possessed by Ṣàngó and possession in Ifá Temple was taboo (Ifá divination is an instrumental and mechanical cult rather than a possession cult). The town's university vice chancellor, Professor Wándé Abímbọ́lá, an Ifá priest, also spoke, emphasizing the primacy of Ifá among Yorùbá gods. The ceremony involved not only entertainment and formal speeches but rituals, mainly for the local diviners, which were quite dramatic.

All the Ifá priests brought their Ifá paraphernalia to Òkè Ìtasẹ̀ and placed them in a special room in the care of the Àgbọngbọ̀n, second in rank to the Àràbà. The Àgbọngbọ̀n then offered a sacrifice of a goat to propitiate Ifá. We note here that in spite of Ifá's internationalism the local context is equally emphasized and is not lost in the midst of the global spectacle that the Òkè Ìtasẹ̀ ceremony now presents.

The authority of the Àràbà was acknowledged and celebrated in another ritual dance carried out mainly by members of his lineage. Members of his household, especially the women, danced from Òkè Ìtasẹ̀ to the surrounding neighborhood. Three times and on each occasion that they reentered the temple, the assembly in the temple would stop whatever they were doing in honor of the Àràbà and the Òkè Ìtasè Ifá lineage. It was the ultimate acknowledgment of the Àràbà's claim as the chief priest and custodian of Ifá in the world. When they entered the temple, the Àràbà joined them in a dance, and the rest of the people rose to honor him and gave him gifts of money. The songs underlined the importance of the ritual dance. One of them referred to Ifá's most sacred symbol, the palm tree, from which the divination nuts were taken. It also referred to Ifá's most central shrine *(òrìgì)*, located in the temple:

> Igi téérẹ́ lókè yìí o
> Èrìgì àbọlà
> Ọpẹ téérẹ́ lókè yìí
> Èrìgì àbọlà

> A tall tree on this high hill,
> Where a prosperous Ifá shrine is,
> A tall thin palm tree on a hill,
> Where a prosperous Ifá shrine *[èrìgì]* lies.

Lineage members rejoiced that they were the custodians of this rich Ifá heritage in the world. By temporarily stopping their activities to honor it, they acknowledged the Àràbà's authorities on all matters relating to Ifá. The Ifá guild of diviners, over which the Àràbà presided, was also recognized. After various evening rituals and sacrifices, at midnight the assembly performed divination for the king, the Yorùbá kingdoms, and the entire world. The diviners referred to this as *Ifá àgbáyé* (the world's divination consultation). The message was for all. We note the tone of the message here. Ifá was positioned as a deity whose utterances had worldwide application. My informant told me, "The expenses for this event are paid by all towns and cities present, especially by those who are very modern, though even the uncivilized ones send representatives." *Modern* here referred to towns and cities that had embraced the new perception of Ifá's message as universal, that were global in their orientation and aware of Ifá's broader influence in the new age. The messages from the divination were publicly announced to the audience and relayed via radio and television to the public. In the early morning, the group descended the hill and proceeded to the king's palace, where the Ọòni officially gave them audience and discussed the message of the New Year revealed by Ifá in the night's divination process.

Descending the Hill and Visiting the Palace   The group proceeded to the palace to have audience with the Ọòni, who sat on the throne to receive them. The spokesperson for the group was Vice Chancellor Wándé Abímbọ́lá, an Ifá high priest and titled chief, the Àwíṣẹ Ifá Àgbáyé. He reminded the group, and perhaps informed their visitors, that the Ọòni was the last of the 201 deities and that hence his full title was Ọòni-Rìṣà (the Ọòni, the God-King). The acknowledgment of the Ọòni

as a god set the stage for the message. Abímbólá informed the Oòni that the ceremony was ending. The assembly called on their spokesperson to give Ifá's divinatory message to the king. One message asked the Oòni to make sacrifices to avoid
war and devastation in the land of Ilé-Ifè. Another message was sent to all the Yorùbá
Oba to make sacrifices of eggs to Èsù and a goat to Ifá for peace in their kingdoms.
An old man lying flat on his belly pleaded with the Oòni to prevail on the rest of
the Yorùbá Oba to stop disrespecting Ifá messages by refusing to honor him and
make the appropriate sacrifices: "We urge you, Kábíyèsí [Our Lord], to inform the
Oba in the next meeting of the House of Oba [Ìgbìmò Lóbalóba] of these sacrifices
for peace and tranquility in their respective cities and towns."

The Àràbà then took the stage and prayed to Ifá to save the Yorùbá people from
the nonbelievers *(àwon kèfèrí aláìgbàgbó)* among them. In this reference to the *kèfèrí*,
the Àràbà was taking the very concept that Christians and Muslims have often used
to describe the devotee of *òrìsà* and turned it on its head, making it instead refer to
the Muslim and Christian "fundamentalists" who disrupted traditional festivals and
ceremonies and insisted on converting the devotees of the *òrìsà* to their own faiths.
But unlike Christian and Muslim *kèfèrí*, who excluded devotees of other faiths from
their prayers and blessings, the Àràbà was inclusive. He prayed for the devotees of
all religions in the land. It was the Oòni's turn to respond, and he informed the group
that he had a premonition that something unpleasant was about to happen, that indeed it would happen when the rainy season was about to begin. This was in line
with his status as the god-king (Oòni-Rìsà). The Oòni asked the Àràbà to see him
the next day to collect money for sacrifices. He then donated money to the group.
This event completed the festival as vehicles waited outside to take the visitors back
to their places of origin.

With drumming and singing back to their homes, the visitors expressed satis-
faction that Ilé-Ifè City would remain the center of *òrìsà* forever. Ìyá Sàngó, who
had not had the chance to perform during the previous night's vigil, took the open
stage outside the palace. Dressed in her colorful red Sàngó dress and possessed by
the god of thunder, she dashed to the market at the base of Òkè Ìtasè, grabbed a
chicken, pulled off its neck, and drank the blood. *Sàngó, Kábíyèsí Oba Kòso* (Our
Lord, the king who did not hang), the crowd shouted. Not surprisingly, the women
of the market were very happy that Sàngó had manifested itself around them. The
elderly ones among them began to praise the deity, offering prayers for good luck,
good trade, good health, and all the blessings that Sàngó would bring through Ìyá
Sàngó. Ìyá Sàngó's acolyte, a chief priest who introduced himself as the Chief Òtún
Òjè Eégún of Ìbàdàn, took the opportunity to inform the audience, that his own
ancestral festival of Eégún (the ancestral masquerade) began that night in Ìbàdàn;
he extended an invitation to everyone present. One by one and group by group, the
visitors dispersed, leaving the Ifá devotees in Ilé-Ifè to continue the second part of
their own ceremony, the Ègbodò Eríwo (the Diviners' New Yam Festival).

The Diviners' New Yam Festival:
Ọdún Àgbọnìrègún or Ègbodò Eríwo

While the Ègbodò Ọòni addresses the king's physical and spiritual well-being, Ọdún Àgbọnìrègún or Ègbodò Eríwo relates to the well-being of all Ifá priests and their lineages and especially the Àràbà, chief priest of Ifá. It is the occasion when the Àràbà and his lineage are reaffirmed as the legitimate leader and king of the Ifá devotees and the custodians of the Ọòni's Ifá. From a phenomenological perspective, the festival provides the occasion for the diviners to renew their authority to perform divination in the sacred city, an authority derived from the Ọòni's sacred kingship. Ifá's *àṣẹ*, the spiritual and sacred authority, is conferred on them. The transfer of the *àṣẹ*, the divine authority, to the diviners by the Ọòni is portrayed in the following narrative, which was told to me by the Àràbà:

> Ọrúnmìlà has one *àṣẹ*, the divine power and spiritual authority, which he uses to perform divination. One day, the Ọlófin (the Ọòni) called him to perform divination for him. However, the vulture had stolen Ọrúnmìlà's *àṣẹ* and hidden it. A day before Ọrúnmìlà's visit to the house of Ọlófin, he sent to all the diviners to inform them about his predicament. This was a call to duty and Ọrúnmìlà might be disgraced or die if he could not respond to the Ọlófin's call. Upon consulting Ifá, the diviners asked Ọrúnmìlà to prepare *ẹkọ* (cornmeal) and pour red palm oil on it—the favorite meal of the vulture *(igún)*—and place it outside. When the vulture saw the food and wanted to eat it, he vomited up Ọrúnmìlà's *àṣẹ*, and the diviners picked it up to return it to Ọrúnmìlà, who burst into song:

> *Àṣẹ, àṣẹ, Òṣèrè*
> *Ifá gbàṣe lóníí o, Òṣèrè*
> *Àṣẹ, Àṣẹ, Òṣèrè*
>
> Ifá has received the *àṣẹ*, the sacred authority, today.

The above song is what the Àràbà and the diviners sing on their way to the king's palace during the festival of Àgbọnìrègún to confirm the renewal of their authority to serve the Ọòni and the people of Ilé-Ifẹ̀. It is akin to a renewal of one's certificate or license to practice a trade, in this case, Ifá divination.

The Process of the Diviners' Festival   The Ifá ceremony on Òkè Ìtasẹ̀ signals the beginning of Ègbodò Eríwo (the Diviners' New Yam Ceremony). From this day, the diviners' festival is reckoned to be on the eleventh day. The celebration is performed by the Àràbà, the diviners, and their lineages, and it takes place both in the individual homes of the diviners and the Ọòni's palace. Just as in the ceremony of the Ọòni's New Yam Festival, the Ègbodò Eríwo begins with the diviners' visit to Ọṣàrà to pluck the sacred Ifá leaves with which to wash their Ifá sacred objects. Following the ritual bathing of Ifá's instruments, a goat is sacrificed and its blood is poured on the Ifá objects. As the leaves are squeezed in water, the diviner recites the appropriate invocation and ritual formula *(ìsokò)* that make the leaves efficacious. As one diviner informed me, "The *ìsokò* is what we call their *ìpònrí* [inner spiritual identity]." Reciting an *ìsokò* is invoking Ifá verses for peace, tranquility, and quick cure, such as "For what purpose is today's Ifá? It is for tranquility and peaceful life. What do we ask for in today's ritual? We ask for calm and peace as the ritual instruments are washed." The diviners remark that the verses invoke the beings in the medicinal leaves, which in turn act to calm Ifá if he happens to be angry. The leaves must be accorded their rights and identity in the ritual of Ifá. Each leaf is unique and has its own personality and individuality. Thus the diviners must recite the *ìsokò* of each leaf that is used in the ritual worship of Ifá so that the leaves may perform the function for which they are famous. As another Ifá diviner says, "The day Ifá bathes, the same day, he drinks blood."

The following day, the Babaláwo stay in their homes, in their Ifá shrines, and pay homage to Òrúnmìlà and propitiate him. Then they perform divination for the ensuing year *(a dá Ifá Odún)* for themselves, their families, and their neighbors. This is very important because individual diviners must know what Ifá prophesies. Generally, that entails revelation of new taboos and sacrifices to be offered to Òrúnmìlà. One Babaláwo gave the following examples: "Last year, Ifá prohibited me from eating chicken that year. My friend was asked not to go to the shrine of Olúorogbo [an Ifè deity] for six months."

The Àràbà as King and Ferocious Leopard   The most spectacular and colorful part of the Ifá Festival takes place on the sixth day of Ègbodò Eríwo, when the Àràbà assumes the persona of a leopard king and sits on a throne *(l'épo)* in the palace. The city diviners shower him with accolades, acknowledging him as King of all Diviners (Oba Awo) and proclaiming his relationship to the Oòni's sacred kingship.

In the ceremony that I witnessed, the Àràbà, in preparation for his visit to the palace of the Oòni as king and as leopard, was bathed with a special blend of medicinal herbs prepared by medicine men. Then his head was shaved and a "prophylactic medicine" to control his behavior was placed at the top of his head,. The medicine makers rubbed his whole body with special ointment and painted it with red and white spots to make him look like a leopard. Tied around his body was a seamless cloth with an "appendage" resembling a tail. By this time, I was informed that the Àràbà had acquired supernatural power. According to some diviners, "The Àràbà can now display his might and power, and people must surround him and stand by him, otherwise they believe that he could actually turn into a leopard." I was told that the Àràbà might even begin to wail like a child and that his entourage had to be prepared to hold him down.

As the Àràbà returned to the palace, many participants commented in awe: "As I looked back to see the king, the Àràbà had become a leopard"; "He had become a cat, transformed into a mysterious wild being *[ó dèṣe]*"; "Don't you see how his

FIGURE 21. The Àràbà on his way to the palace in the Ifá Festival.

eyes look so red?" "Do they resemble human eyes?" one diviner inquired with alarm. "He can now see beyond us. Spirits appear to him constantly, we have to guide him back to the palace." An often-heard utterance about Àràbà's state of being was "Ẹkùn, Ẹkùn, Ẹkùn—the Leopard, the Leopard, the Leopard."

As the procession advanced from Òkè Ìtasẹ̀ to the palace amid vigorous Ifá drumming and dancing, the diviners greeted the Àràbà as king and as leopard. To control the "wild animal" that the Àràbà purported to be, two hefty men held his white linen robe as he danced to the heavy percussion of the Ifá musical instruments and as the crowd roared, "Ọba, Ọba—Behold the King! Ẹkùn, Ẹkùn, Ẹkùn—the Leopard, the Leopard, the Leopard!" To keep any rain from accidentally falling on him, his entourage covered his head with a flat mat type of umbrella. As in the Ọlọ́jọ́ Festival when the Ọòni wore the arè (the sacred crown), it was believed that the medicine on his body drew rain, but it was taboo for any drop of rain to touch him. Accordingly, local rainmakers were hired to prevent rainfall. In a paradox of nature and culture in conflict, however, rain had to occur on that very day to confirm Ifá's acceptance of the offerings.

The Àràbà descended from Òkè Ìtasẹ̀, his official residence, and danced to the palace. All the Babaláwo carried their Ifá paraphernalia to meet him along the way. In a grand procession, they danced before him. Once in the palace, the Àràbà sat on his throne. Like the king, the Àràbà was said to be on stage in the outer courtyard (Àràbà l'épo or Àgbọnìrègún gúnwà [Àgbọnìrègún is on the throne]). The other diviners sat on mats before him, and each in turn divined for him. The Àgbọngbọ̀n, next in rank to the Àràbà, stood up with the entire group of diviners, walked to the Àràbà, and presented him with kola nuts. The Àràbà first asked the Àgbọngbọ̀n what Ifá had prophesied.

The Àgbọngbọ̀n told the Àràbà that Èjìogbè's sign had appeared on the divination tray, which translated as "good tidings." Ifá had said, "First, the Àràbà will live long to witness more festivals, the diviners will increase in number, and none will die in the coming year." The Àgbọngbọ̀n answered, "Èjìogbè was the most senior of the odù Ifá—there will be peace in the city of Ilé-Ifẹ̀," apparently referring to ethnic warfare between the Ifẹ̀ and their neighbors.

Each of the principal diviners was called by the Àràbà and asked similar questions. Each gave similar answers. In return for these prayerful wishes, the Àràbà prayed for them and their households. For this ceremony, diviners who were already elderly and could not attend the festival sent their sons, who were already practicing Ifá, to take their places. They were given the chance to represent their fathers to declare the prophecy to the Àràbà. Presentation by the younger generation confirmed the importance of lineage identity construction in the Ifẹ̀ ritual cycle. The younger diviners were socialized into their lineage Ifá traditions to ensure continuity.

After the ceremony was over, the diviners returned to their respective homes and the Àràbà returned home to Òkè Ìtasẹ̀, where he would take a full bath to return to his usual self. Individuals I talked to said that bathing to return to normal life was very important. "Water coming from it [the bath] could heal. Those who drink of it will be free of smallpox and other diseases," recounted one informant. "Using the bathwater is particularly good for children, as it protects them from diseases."

After the Ifá ceremony, the diviners went into seclusion for three months, a hiatus called *awo wọlé*. I was told that the importance of the seclusion was underscored by the sudden disappearance of hawks *(àṣá)* from the open sky: they too had to observe seclusion with the diviners. This is powerful imagery: the hawks, the birds of heaven, joining the diviners to observe the taboo. During this period, diviners must not see a dead body or the hair of a newborn. Avoidance of newborn infants and the deceased may indicate the need for diviners themselves, who are in the liminal stage of ceremonial observances, to remain locked into "in-between states" until the festival is over. Since diviners are usually concerned with matters relating to death or birth, it is assumed that a period of rest begins for them, thereby limiting their movement. Several years ago, I interviewed the now-reigning Àràbà—then an ordinary diviner—before he was installed. He informed me that it was his practice to bend over inside his car as his driver drove him to his sawmill to avoid inadvertently seeing a dead body or a newborn.

At the end of seclusion, in the third month after the end of the festival, the diviners shaved their heads and emerged from seclusion. The Àràbà visited the homes of diviners, greeting them with "Happy New Year." The hawks, too, were said to emerge from hiding, wearing new "clothes" (feathers). Like the diviners who became free to perform divination again, the hawks were said to be free to hunt again.

The entire chapter demonstrates the place of Ifá in Ilé-Ifẹ̀ ritual and festival cycle. Ifá as a religious, political, and cultural instrument of regulating order in Ilé-Ifẹ̀ community is enacted in the two-tiered ritual sacrifices described above. Appropriately begun in the king's Ifá Festival, divination and sacrifice are employed to guarantee the health and welfare of the Ọọ̀ni and his subjects. The diviners' central place in the social and religious order is also affirmed. In the same context, the diviners turn to their deity to renew their àṣẹ and enable them to perform their role in the Ilé-Ifẹ̀ kingdom. But in doing so they must demonstrate that they constitute a force to be reckoned with in the scheme of things. When the Àràbà changes, becoming a leopard for all to see, and when he temporarily takes over the Ọọ̀ni's palace and is praised as the king (Ọba) by his followers, he reaffirms not only his kingship among his fellow diviners and subordinates but also his integral role in maintaining the cosmic order in Ilé-Ifẹ̀. With the two sets of rituals completed, Ifá is renewed and ready for another year of divination, sacrifices, and rituals that will ensure the welfare of the community.

7

The Goddess Mọrèmi in the Festival of Edì

Gender, Sacrifice, and the Expulsion of Evil

Whether we are speaking of humans, goddesses, or gods, gender and the role and status of women are central to this work. The study of Ilé-Ifẹ̀ society poses intriguing questions concerning patriarchy, equal opportunity, and gender relations that the prevailing male-centered scholarly discourse surrounding Yorùbá religion has not adequately addressed.

This chapter focuses on the Ifẹ̀ deity Mọrèmi, who has played a major role in the city's history and who continues to do so today, as a recent event illustrates. Ten years ago, the Ọọ̀ni of Ifẹ̀, Ọba Ṣíjúadé Olúbùṣe II, like the Ọọ̀ni before him, began an ambitious project to renovate Ifẹ̀ Palace. As part of a plan to construct a more attractive and better-secured entrance, he ordered workers to create new flower gardens and to install a magnificent statue of Odùduwà in the palace's front courtyard. Inside the palace, in an area open to the public, he ordered the installation of a grand statue of Mọrèmi, Ifẹ̀'s goddess-heroine, whose epic story is of great importance to the city.

The timing of the installation of the Mọrèmi statue was significant. Defeated after incessant battle during the Yorùbá interethnic civil war (1877–93), the Modákẹ́kẹ́, an Ọ̀yọ́-Yorùbá people, migrated to Ilé-Ifẹ̀ as refugees. After being granted a place in the city, they flourished and their population expanded. Historically, the Modákẹ́kẹ́ have challenged their Ifẹ̀ hosts on a wide range of claims, especially concerning land rights. The Ifẹ̀ have been infuriated by these claims to their homeland and the Modákẹ́kẹ́'s refusal to back down from them, with the result of intermittent warfare between the two groups. The last few decades of conflict and uncertainty in Ilé-Ifẹ̀ have fostered much reflection and discussion regarding the Ifẹ̀'s collective memories of past heroic battles and human failures.

One of the recollections that the Ifẹ̀ hold in highest regard is the epic tale of Mọrèmi, the Ifẹ̀ goddess who long ago saved her people through her feminine cunning and wisdom and who fought gallantly to thwart invaders set upon the imminent destruction of the city when groups like the Modákẹ́kẹ́ claimed Ifẹ̀ lands. Mọrèmi thus took on a central role as the city's liberator and deliverer, a role that corresponds to goddess traditions of other Yorùbá communities as well.[1]

This chapter recounts Mọrèmi's epic story and describes the annual Edì Festival celebrating it in order to explore the intersection of gender, sacrifice, and redemption in both. While I raise several questions about the history, meaning, and function of the Mọrèmi myth and the Edì Festival, I argue that discourse about gender relations is significant in understanding two central theological issues: sacrifice and redemptive suffering. Both text and ritual provide a rich context for seeing how the outsider or foreigner to Ilé-Ifẹ̀ becomes the city's adopted scapegoat.[2]

As a commemorative reenactment of Mọrèmi's pivotal role in Ifẹ̀ mythic history, the Edì performance, ritual, and symbolism reinforce the collective memory of the Ilé-Ifẹ̀ people. I will explain why these events are significant for the Ilé-Ifẹ̀ people today and why this goddess tradition continues to occupy a significant place in modern Ilé-Ifẹ̀. My data come primarily from my extensive fieldwork in Ilé-Ifẹ̀, where I have observed the Edì Festival on more than five occasions. An earlier study of the Edì Festival will supplement my current data, allowing discussion of innovations over time in Ifẹ̀'s reconstructions of the Mọrèmi epic and the Edì Festival.[3]

THE MỌRÈMI LEGEND

Although there are many versions of the myth of Mọrèmi, I will begin with the version I collected from the chief priestess of the Edì Festival. The chief priestess, also called Chief Èrí, is regarded as the reincarnation of Mọrèmi. Now deceased, she was in her late seventies when one of my consultants took me to her home. This consultant was Chief Awójẹ̀bi, an Ifá priest who lived nearby in Òkèrèwè. As we drove to Chief Èrí's house, Chief Awójẹ̀bi informed me, "Mama will tell you all you need to hear and explain to you the Edì Festivals you have been watching all these years." On arriving at the house, we glimpsed a magnificent woman dressed appropriately considering her status as a princess of Mọrèmi—or any other Ilé-Ifẹ̀ goddess, for that matter. Wearing an immaculate white *bùbá* and *ìró* (Yorùbá blouse and wrapper) and adorned with colorful necklaces, bangles, and beads *(iyùn)*, Chief Èrí sat regally in her parlor, greeting us in a marked Ifẹ̀ dialect as we entered. We began the conversation with my request, "Mama, please tell me about Goddess Mọrèmi." Here begins the story told by Chief Èrí.

> Mọrèmi was very beautiful and statuesque. She was as tall as the *àjà* or ceiling. Everywhere she went, every able-bodied man immediately desired to marry her. Mọrèmi

had only one child, called Olúorogbo. Following the incessant invasions and ensuing destruction of Ilé-Ifẹ̀, Mọrèmi decided to act instead of helplessly watching marauders destroy Ilé-Ifẹ̀ City yet again. Therefore, she devised a plan to go into enemy territory alone. The Ilé-Ifẹ̀ people were perplexed when she disclosed her plan. After all, she was a woman and no warrior, and they feared she would sacrifice herself in vain. In their opinion, the Ìgbò appeared to be aliens from the spirit world, especially because many Ilé-Ifẹ̀ warriors had perished defending the city against the Ìgbò invaders. However, Mọrèmi remained skeptical of the origins of the invaders, as she herself was no ordinary woman.

Mọrèmi went to the Ẹ̀sìnmìrìn River and vowed that if she were to accomplish her mission in Ìgbò territory to save Ifẹ̀ people from incessant invasion, she would give the river a great gift. The gift could be of great value—whatever the river wanted. Mọrèmi then traveled to Ìgbò territory, where she was captured and taken to the king. At once, her radiant figure caught the king's attention. She told the king she was a suffering woman who needed help, but she failed to disclose her true identity. Mọrèmi became the wife of the king and lived with him for over six months. Before long, she became one of the king's favorites. One day, when the king was spending some time with her and was quite relaxed, she told him that she had an important question to ask him and wondered if he would oblige her with an answer. The king urged her to ask the question, which turned out to be "What was your secret that enabled you to take into slavery such large numbers of people from the ancient city of Ilé-Ifẹ̀?"

Intoxicated with Mọrèmi's beauty, the unsuspecting king revealed the secret weapon of the Ìgbò to her. His invading armies were neither spirits nor ghosts but ordinary people wearing raffia clothing *(ìko)* that allowed them to masquerade as spirits and ghosts. Under her spell, the king divulged more: "If the unwieldy raffia costumes were set on fire, all the Ìgbò would perish at once." Later, safely back in her disguise, Mọrèmi escaped from the Ìgbò palace and the king. She hastened back to Ilé-Ifẹ̀. What a welcome she received, and of course she revealed to the Ifẹ̀ king and his chiefs the Ìgbò secret! Responding to this revelation, the Ifẹ̀ king ordered his people to prepare the native *ògùsọ̀* (torches), dry them, and dip them in palm oil, ready to be lit for action. When the invaders attacked next, the Ifẹ̀ people prepared to light up the *ògùsọ̀* and plunge them into the raffia costumes of the invaders, previously believed to be "ghosts." Not too long afterwards, the Ìgbò invaded, and the Ifẹ̀ did exactly as instructed. They burned some invaders and captured and imprisoned others. These captives are those the Ifẹ̀ people refer to today as the Olúyarè, who live in the Ìrẹ́mọ Quarter—the descendants of the captured Ìgbò. Their leader is known as Ọbàwìnrìn.

Following this great deliverance of Ilé-Ifẹ̀ from the Ìgbò, Mọrèmi returned to thank Ẹ̀sìnmìrìn for her incredible feat and successful conquest. Through divination, she wanted to know what the river demanded. To her terrible dismay, it was ordained that her only son, Olúorogbo, was to be sacrificed to Ẹ̀sìnmìrìn. In keeping with the wishes of the river of the sacrifice requested by Ẹ̀sìnmìrìn, Mọrèmi, in a dreadful moment, threw her precious child, Olúorogbo, into the river.

Thus ends the story told by Chief Èrí, princess and priestess of Mọrèmi.

MYTH, MEMORY, AND THE HEROINE

I know of no better, more powerful, or more solemn narrative in Ifẹ̀ myth and history than Mọrèmi's story. The story itself has formed the plot of plays and provided symbols for artistic creativity. In his award-winning play *Mọrèmi,* the Yorùbá playwright and dramatist Dúró Ládiípọ̀ helped to popularize Mọrèmi nationally and internationally.[4] Wọlé Ṣóyínká, Nobel laureate and celebrated Nigerian scholar, named his firstborn daughter Mọrèmi. The University of Ifẹ̀ (now Ọbáfẹ́mi Awólọ́wọ̀ University) named one of its schools Mọrèmi High School and the central girls' dormitory on campus Mọrèmi Hall. Another school in Ifẹ̀ City is named Olúorogbo High School. Thus, in Ilé-Ifẹ̀ in particular, the Yorùbá find ways to memorialize Mọrèmi's bravery and courage both for themselves and for the next generation.

The Mọrèmi story could be interpreted in many ways. It depicts numerous motifs, themes, and ideas pertinent to the construction of Ilé-Ifẹ̀ identity and the sacred city in the Yorùbá imagination. The story conveys deep religious, cultural, and social meanings extending beyond local space, imagination, and time. Mọrèmi's story displays the role of cultural memory as an avenue for asserting both the power of Mọrèmi's lineage in Òkèrèwè and that of the sacred kingship localized in the palace. For Giambattista Vico, memory was largely the source of human imagination.[5] Michel Foucault's writings on the politics of memory are instructive here. Foucault was deeply interested in how memory functions in the politics of a society, that is, the ways political and social communities use memory to assert their authority.[6] The Mọrèmi narrative and the Edì religious ritual have served historically to assert the authority of the sacred kingship and the Mọrèmi lineage while expressing subterranean conflicts in Ifẹ̀ social and communal life, such as the status of strangers vis-à-vis that of indigenes, gender conflicts, and tension between pre-Odùduwà groups and successive conquerors.

Mọrèmi's story, in which a woman supplicant willingly gives her only child to a god, is not unique in Yorùbá tradition. As young children, my playmates and I were often told stories of Olúrómbí, who sacrificed her only child to a sacred *ìrókò* tree. This story, drawn from Yorùbá folklore, is used to warn children against making promises too difficult to fulfill. Unlike others who vowed to offer up replaceable domestic animals if their wishes were fulfilled, Olúrómbí and Mọrèmi made promises that forced them to offer up their irreplaceable sons. When the time came to fulfill the vow, the *ìrókò* did not hesitate to take Olúrómbí's only child.

Ilé-Ifẹ̀ tradition considers Mọrèmi the most celebrated goddess, perhaps even more celebrated than Yemòó, the wife of Ọbàtálá. Although Mọrèmi is not one of the primordial deities *(òrìṣà afẹ̀wọ̀nrọ̀)* featured in the creation of the city, she has a stronger presence in Ifẹ̀ myths, rituals, and symbol because her story is indispensable to Ifẹ̀ salvation history. Mọrèmi's narrative is second only to the story about the world being created after the great struggle between Odùduwà and Ọbàtálá, an event that is reenacted in the Ọlọjọ and Ọbàtálá festival rituals. As in the creation myths of other world mythologies, creation as recounted by the Yorùbá is an incomplete process. After the act of creation come the challenges of establishing community and living in the created universe. Often portrayed in migration myths of conquest, such challenges include threats of violence, destruction, and intrigue that may destroy the created universe if they are not held in check. Mọrèmi's story seems to fall into this second category of creation story, characterized by chaos and by an intervention that prevents total and imminent destruction. The Ìgbò foreigners' incessant invasions of Ifẹ were destructive events with the potential of ushering the Ifẹ world and cosmos into chaos. But for Mọrèmi's intervention, the Ifẹ and their city would have come to an abrupt end.

Who are the Ìgbò, and what does the Ìgbò invasion represent? Although their name is similar to that of the Igbo people of eastern Nigeria, the Ifẹ-Ìgbò were most likely a different group of people—perhaps one of the pre-Odùduwà groups who lived not too far from the present city. The Ìgbò may symbolize a people that the Odùduwà invaders never completely subjugated or banished at the time of Ilé-Ifẹ's founding. I say this because in the traditional narratives of eastern Yorùbá societies like Ilẹ-Olúji and Ìlàjẹ in Òkìtìpupa in the Nigerian state of Oǹdó (not too far from Ilé-Ifẹ), references abound to rulers or communities bearing the Ìgbò name. For example, a powerful ruler called Jẹgun Ìgbò once reigned in Ilẹ-Olúji. In addition, in the Ìkálẹ riverine area, a group still referred to as Ugbo share traditions with Ilé-Ifẹ.[7] According to the Ìlàjẹ people, the Ugbo were remnants of an Ifẹ aboriginal group who lived in Ilé-Ifẹ before the Odùduwà people came and drove them out. The Ìlàjẹ people state that Ọbàtálá is known as Òrìṣà Onílẹ in Ugbo (the earth deity or the deity of the owner of the land), a fact that supports their connection with Ilé-Ifẹ.[8] The "Ìgbò" in the Mọrèmi myth may therefore stand as a metaphor for a remnant invading group that continued to harass the Ifẹ people long after the Odùduwà people first established their kingdom or usurped it from the original inhabitants.

Ifẹ tradition variously describes Mọrèmi, the heroine of this narrative, as the wife of Odùduwà, as a princess, and as an ordinary citizen of the city. But whatever her status and role, clearly the narratives indicate that Mọrèmi made a great personal sacrifice by offering up her own body—in the traditional wording of the tale, her vagina—and the most important person in her life—her only son—to save her people. Her sacrifice and personal loss saved her community from imminent destruction. Mọrèmi's narrative is concerned with redemptive suffering, a common theme in most world religions, as exemplified in the suffering and death of figures such as Christ in the biblical tradition and the martyrdom of Hussein in the Shi'ite tradition. The martyr undergoes suffering and humiliation for the sake of the living multitudes who benefit from the sacrifice., An oríkì heard quite often during Mọrèmi's magnificent festival describes her as Mọrèmi a f'òbò ṣẹtẹ, the courageous woman who used her vagina to conquer the Ìgbò. In their collective memory, generations of Ifẹ̀ people continue to pass down the story of her sacrifice, in which she offered up an intimate part of her own body to obtain the secrets of the Ìgbò invaders.

Mọrèmi's narrative raises significant questions about gender relations, challenging traditional notions of heroism, especially among the Yorùbá. Mary Beth Rose's insight on the gendering of heroism in sixteenth- and seventeenth-century England may be instructive here.[9] Rose argued that the notion of heroism generally "calls to mind socially or morally elevated protagonists waging war and managing politics: courageous, superior, noteworthy individuals creating or redefining the public sphere."[10] That definition of heroism idealizes masculine qualities and stresses movement, adventure, rescue, rule, exploration, and conquest[11]—qualities primarily associated with the privileged, valued, and separate public sphere traditionally reserved for male activities, as compared to the underprivileged, devalued, and domestic private sphere traditionally reserved for female activities. Rose points out, "Women—or cultural conceptions of the female—are excluded from the questing, striving, and conquering that both form the heroic subject and characterize his actions."[12] On the other hand, Rose argues that female heroism in the early modern period was represented by such qualities as patience, suffering, mildness, humility, chastity, loyalty, and obedience, traits that Rose calls the "heroism of endurance" as opposed to the "heroism of action" more typical of men.

In the light of this gendered typology of heroism, the Mọrèmi narrative is filled with complexity, if not contradictions. Unlike the seventeenth- and eighteenth- century English society that Rose analyzes, Yorùbá society at times blends male and female gender characteristics. As in many Yorùbá narratives concerning female deities, Mọrèmi's heroic identity resembles that of the ideal man, the warrior hero. Like a hunter in search of prey or a warrior in search of enemies, Mọrèmi journeys out beyond the domestic sphere and the community into the unknown. Once there, she cleverly employs tactics and intelligence to discover the Ìgbò secret. Yet at the same time she demonstrates other more traditionally female qualities: a "passive but equally potent dimension of heroic identity . . . that privileges not the active confrontation with danger, but the capacity to endure it, to resist and suffer with patience and fortitude."[13] In the story, the men of Ifẹ̀ consider Mọrèmi's plan to cross the threshold into the public domain—to take the "battle" of liberation into enemy territory— seriously tabooed for women and consequently dangerous. In other versions of the Mọrèmi narrative, the men attempt to dissuade Mọrèmi from leaving. After all, male warriors have tried without success to rescue Ifẹ̀ from the Ìgbò oppressors.

Ifẹ̀'s representation of Mọrèmi's heroism is intriguing. As I mentioned earlier, one of her popular oríkì describes her as the heroine "who conquered rebellion and overcame intrigue with her vagina" (Mọrèmi a f'òbò ṣẹ̀tẹ̀). Such a powerful sexual image employed by men to describe Mọrèmi's suffering and accomplishment raises the question of unequal power relations between men and women. In the mythic narrative, Mọrèmi's redemptive suffering is undertaken for the liberation of Ifẹ̀, but her heroism is represented only by her sexual prowess and her conduct as a seducer—in the words of the myth, she is reduced to her "vagina." The language used, which invokes female symbols and private body imagery, underscores the magnitude of her role in the salvation history of Ilé-Ifẹ̀, though it fails to accord her the glory that would be given to men who have achieved the liberation of their people. In addition, as is consistent with traditional Yorùbá goddess myths and legends, the power of Mọrèmi's creativity and her act of deliverance have been transformed by the use of symbols of motherhood *(ìyá)*. She is constructed, not as a warrior, but as one who shows lovingkindness to her people, to the extent that she would agree to suffer and die for their sake. Thus the depiction of Mọrèmi as a mother provides the subtext for the popular Edì Festival, a theatrical demonstration and reenactment of the Ìgbò's conquest and subsequent defeat in Ilé-Ifẹ̀ myth and history.

Mọrèmi's sacrifice of her only son, Olúorogbo, to Ẹ̀sìnmìrìn represents an aberration from tradition. The Ifẹ̀ never sacrifice an indigene to the gods, a taboo declared in the proverb *A kì í f'ọmọ ọrẹ̀, b'ọrẹ̀* (We never sacrifice the child of a deity to that deity), as I discuss in chapter 3 and in the following chapter on Odùduwà. Unequivocally, the people of Ilé-Ifẹ̀ used nonindigenes as their sacrificial victims. It was forbidden to sacrifice Ifẹ̀ indigenes, who were believed to be sacred beings by virtue of their birth in the City of the 201 Gods. The people of Ilé-Ifẹ̀ consider Mọrèmi's sacrifice of her son as "abnormal" in another sense as well, for a child of any status was considered unsuitable for sacrifice. As one of my informants pointed out, "The male priests of Mọrèmi are called the Yékéré [literarily, this one is too young or small]. This refers to the minor age of Mọrèmi's son, Olúorogbo, who was sacrificed to Ẹ̀sìnmìrìn. That such an utterance became the title of a high priest of the Mọrèmi religious cult indicates the centrality of the sacrifice of Olúorogbo as well as its abnormality."

The story of Mọrèmi is also unusual in that it complicates traditional notions of gender as these intersect with traditional beliefs associated with eldership. In this festival the chief priest, the Yékéré, assumes the part of Olúorogbo, and the chief priestess assumes the part of Mọrèmi, so that he is the son and she is the mother. This power dynamic cuts across the expected power dynamic between male and female elders, in which men take precedence. The tensions that this situation creates are illustrated in a dispute, in one Edì ritual, between the Èrí and the Yékéré, recounted below.

THE EDÌ FESTIVAL

The Edì Festival and its ceremonial performances constitute a complex ritual spectacle that narrates the subjugation and subsequent liberation of the Ifẹ̀ people from the Ìgbò people. The victory that the "Goddess-Mother" delivered to her people signifies the continuing relevance of this goddess in the lives of Ifẹ̀ people today and provides the raison d'être for both the popularity and the controversy surrounding the Edì Festival in Ifẹ̀ history.[14] *Edì*, which literally means "we gather together and tie," refers to the "rubbish of evil" that at the end of the festival individuals will gather for the Teele, a scapegoated figure, to take away into the forbidden forest. As we will soon see, this ritual symbolizes the banishing of evil from the community and the opening of the way for the community's expression of gratitude for their female savior.

Celebration of Lineage and Motherhood: The Fẹrẹkẹtẹ Ritual

The Edì Festival began with the ceremony of Fẹrẹkẹtẹ, which was performed on the festival's eve and involved mainly young unmarried men and women, often those who were engaged to be married.[15] The young men sent firewood to their future fathers-in-law and gave ten yam tubers to their future mothers-in-law. In an agricultural society these were generous gifts, especially at the beginning of harvest season. The firewood was used to make a bonfire and roast the yam tubers given to the mothers-in-law, amid much collective merrymaking within each lineage's quarter. After consuming the yams, the party I witnessed ran up and down, waving the stumps of burnt firewood, to announce the commencement of the Edì Festival. Dressed in a white wrapper, Chief Èrí stood in the middle of the road in her quarter and pronounced the most significant statement of the Edì celebration: *Yọ, yọ, yọ ikú yọ, àrùn yọ, òfò yọ, yọ, yọ, yọ, òfùn yọ* (We expel and cast out all evils, death, sickness, loss, paralysis, etc.). The audience responded to this declaration with *Yèyé ò* (Our Great Mother), an acknowledgment of the power of Mọrèmi, who rules over Ifẹ̀ and on behalf of whom the celebration was staged. Celebrants rubbed their heads (considered among the Yoruba to be a locus of power) with the stumps of charred firewood as a means of cleansing.[16] Then they threw their sticks into the gutter, banishing evil from their "heads," their lives, and their living quarters and thus ushering in the Edì Festival proper.

In Fẹrẹkẹtẹ, merriment and feasting mark a transition from daily life in Ilé-Ifẹ̀ to the more sober atmosphere and mood of the later rituals of Edì. As the Èrí's pronouncement suggests, the central purpose of Edì is the exorcism of evil from the individual, from homes, from quarters, and from the larger community. Like other Ifẹ̀ rituals, this exorcism, begins at the lineage space and the quarters and radiates out to the larger community in which all Ifẹ̀-born participate. Thus it is in Òkèrèwè Quarter, the home of Mọrèmi, that the events begin, before moving to the center of the city, as represented in the palace *(ààfin)*. The expulsion of evil must take place in an open space, and the very name Fẹrẹkẹtẹ (literally "an open space") indicates that the event takes place outdoors. The joy of this first day ushers in the greater Edì.

Fẹrẹkẹtẹ shows that the expulsion of evil from Ifẹ̀ society is clearly connected to family life, marriage, and motherhood, as symbolized in the goddess Mọrèmi and her chief representative, the Èrí, as the binding forces of clans and lineages. When the Èrí named the forces of evil in Yorùbá cosmology (death, loss, theft, paralysis, etc.), it was assumed that Mọrèmi, "the Great Mother," had cleansed the Òkèrèwè Quarter of evil. After the quarter from which the goddess originated was cleansed, the entire city underwent the same cleansing process. Brides and bridegrooms had to acknowledge the power of the mother goddess to achieve stability and prosperity in a conjugal union that would be free of evil.

The Èrí, as the agency through whom evil is banished, had to make herself holy for the task ahead. She could not partake of the new yams and had to deny herself all the rich foods and feasts that others enjoyed during the Fẹrẹkẹtẹ ceremony. In the ceremonies of the following days, she would relive the experience of the goddess Mọrèmi in the mythic history of Ilé-Ifẹ̀ as she and others underwent ordeals and sacrifices for the sake of the community. She would enter into a state of symbolic mourning for Mọrèmi's child and come to embody Mọrèmi's redemptive suffering.

Why is the burden of the ritual cleansing of evil in the sacred city placed on a woman, and especially on the mother of an only child? The answer may be found in the Yorùbá image of womanhood, gender relations, and the sacrificial rituals that will be examined later on.

Ushering Edì into the City

Like most Ifẹ̀ festivals, Edì was preceded by a night vigil *(àìsùn)*. It was festive, with plenty of drinking and dancing. The break of dawn, however, elicited a more sober and quiet mood. For seven days, all drumming in the city was forbidden, to honor the suffering of Mọrèmi, the death of her only child, and the sacrificial victim who would serve as the scapegoat for the community. The first day of Edì was officially designated as "The Bringing of Edì into the City" *(Mímú Edì Wọlé)*. At about 9:00 a.m., the king with his chiefs and palace servants held court in the open courtyard of the palace. Meanwhile, the chief priestess (Èrí) and priest (Yékéré) of Edì and the festival's sacrifice bearer (Teele) gathered at the base of the *ahun* (sacred) tree in the Òkèrèwè Quarter, the lineage home of Mọrèmi. There they conducted a minor ritual of propitiation and animal sacrifice. When they finished, they did not speak. With the Teele at their head, the three proceeded to the palace, murmuring and humming "Hun, hun, hun"—the only sounds they uttered. Their speechlessness initiated the silence and secrecy characterizing most of the following events. Once they had reached the palace, a crowd that had gathered there acknowledged their presence with this chant:

> *Hee O! Mọrèmi Àjànṣorò,*
> *Wun mi l'ewuré yẹle o.*

> Hail to you, Mọrèmi, oh Great Mother, our sacrificial redeemer,
> Grant me the gift of life.

Chief Èrí, Chief Yékéré, and the Teele responded with the joyful, well-known lines:

> Òffà lati rè o
> Òffà lati rè o
> A mí lọ m'Édì wá
> Òffà lati rè o

We have traveled to Òffà to bring Edì home.

This response described the procession as a symbolic pilgrimage from Òffà, an ancient Yorùbá city in Kwara State that the person who had been appointed Teele usually came from. As a foreigner and ritual scapegoat, the Teele would bear the burden of carrying the Ifẹ̀ sacrifice, which represented all the evil being exorcised from the city, into the sacred and forbidden forest for banishment. Indeed, the Edì Festival may be an Òffà festival transported to Ilé-Ifẹ̀, or vice versa (the festivals in many Yorùbá cities originated in other cities). I will explain these motifs in more detail when I examine Ifẹ̀ sacrifice in the context of the Edì Festival. Some narratives describe Mọrèmi herself as an Òffà woman who migrated to Ilé-Ifẹ̀. In any event, the Mọrèmi myth reinforces the connection between strangers and sacrifice that is so common in Ifẹ̀ tradition.

The procession of the Edì party from the Òkèrèwè Quarter to the palace harnessed an outside source of power and moved it to the sacred center of the city. Its wordless murmuring was meant to express solemn mourning for Mọrèmi's ordeal and suffering, and for the sacrifice of her son to the Èṣìnmìrìn River that followed her victory over the Ìgbò. However, one is also tempted to speculate on the meaning of this event in light of other rituals we have discussed in previous chapters. Most Ifẹ̀ festivals and rituals begin with a hunt for a sacrificial victim, who in the past would have been a human being. It is likely that in the past the Teele was himself the victim who would be led in silence to the sacrificial place. As we have seen, the victim of sacrifice was normally a stranger, in conformity with Ifẹ̀'s tradition of not sacrificing an indigene to the gods.

Ìjàkadì: The Wrestling Contest

In Òkè-Igbó, the Edì Festival is believed to have come from Ilé-Ifẹ̀ City, just as in Oǹdó the Òràmfẹ̀ Festival is believed to have come from there. The beginning of the chaos and conflicts that ended the life of plenty the people of Ifẹ̀ had enjoyed before the Ìgbò invasion is historicized and dramatized in the wrestling contest that marks the Edì celebration. By the time the Teele's procession reaches the àdìn (the palace), wrestling contests, watched in amusement by the Ọ̀ọ̀ni, are already under way between a palace chief (Ògúngbẹ́) and an Ẹmẹsẹ̀. A wrestling match begins with an one individual calling on another by name to fight: Pàtẹtẹ̀, mo dáná ẹkẹ síbí o (I have set the fire of wrestling here, and I challenge you to dare scatter it). The challenged person responds by pretending to scatter this fire and fighting with the challenger. The Ṣàárun (the Ọ̀ọ̀ni's personal assistant) and the head of the Ẹmẹsẹ̀ engage in the final wrestling match. We are told that in "the days before," the Ọ̀rúntọ́ (also called Ọbalúfẹ̀—the Ọba and prime minister who was in charge of affairs outside the city walls), the head of the town chiefs (Ọ̀tún Ifẹ̀) and as his name suggests, a king in his own right, would challenge the Ọ̀ọ̀ni to a match. The wrestling contest is another indication that Ilé-Ifẹ̀ originally borrowed the ritual from Ọ̀ffà or vice versa. Wrestling was the main pastime of the Ọ̀ffà people; in fact, the Ọ̀ffà's *oríkì* is *Ìjàkadì l'orò Ọ̀ffà* (The Ọ̀ffà people take pride in wrestling). While the wrestling at the palace may have symbolized the state of chaos and disorder that the Ìgbò's incessant invasions had caused in the city, the wrestling contest that took place between the Ọ̀rúntọ́ and the Ṣàárun, whereby the Ọ̀rúntọ́ was temporarily taken prisoner and brought to the palace, provides a context for understanding the wider mythological meaning of the Edì Festival.

As I argued in previous chapters, Ilé-Ifẹ̀ rituals and festivals displayed the significant lineage identity structure in the city. The mythic struggle between Odùduwà and Ọbàtálá seems to have influenced the pattern and drama of many Ifẹ̀ festivals and ceremonies. The surrendering of the Ọ̀rúntọ́ to the palace chiefs symbolized the subjugation of yet another pre-Odùduwà ruler to the Odùduwà conqueror. At all times in Ifẹ̀ rituals, the Ọ̀ọ̀ni or his aides emerged victorious in the symbolic fights. The climax of the wrestling contest and its meaning in the context of Edì occurred when Chief Ọbaláàyán, representing the Ọ̀ọ̀ni and standing for the royal power, went in a warlike procession to the home of the Ọbalúfẹ̀ (the Ọ̀rúntọ́) to challenge him to a duel. There a mock battle took place in which the Ọbalúfẹ̀ was taken captive to the palace. The Ọbalúfẹ̀ then paid ransom money to gain his freedom. Again, the Ọ̀ọ̀ni's power and ultimate control over his territory was reaffirmed through the humiliation and surrender of the Ifẹ̀ highest-ranking chief, next in rank only to the Ọ̀ọ̀ni himself. It was a metaphor for the Ìgbò drama of invasion of Ifẹ̀ and their subsequent conquest.

Ọmọ Lárère: *The Mystery Bundle*

On the festival's second day, palace officials prepared and carried a magical bundle whose contents no one but the Ẹmẹsẹ̀ themselves really knew. The bundle, which was wrapped in a mat called *fáfẹ̀*, was most likely supposed to represent Mọrèmi's deceased child, Olúorogbo.[17] This is another reversal of tradition characteristic of the ritual events of Edì, because in Ifẹ̀ tradition death at a very young age is not mourned with such honor and respect. This mystery bundle was carried round the town to important shrines, where the Ẹmẹsẹ̀ offered sacrifices and prayed for peace and progress of the city, and was later deposited in the palace. One piece of evidence supporting the idea of *ọmọ lárère* as an effigy of Olúorogbo is the traditional teaching that Mọrèmi, as personified in the Èrí, must be pleased with the way the ritual of the *ọmọ lárère* is conducted: she would want the Ifẹ̀ people to show their

FIGURE 22. Priests during the Olúorogbo ceremony.

gratitude and respect for the sacrifice of her only child. If this interpretation is correct, the silence of the procession and the crowd's subdued responses to it would represent Ifè's collective mourning over the sacrifice of Olúorogbo and their gratitude for Morèmi's silent suffering over losing her only child.

Inasan: The Destructive Fire

The next ritual of the Edì Festival reenacted the Ifè people's use of torches to repel the Ìgbò invaders, a tactic that Morèmi's intelligence from behind enemy lines had made possible. The palace servants, the Ẹ̀mẹsẹ̀, had prepared four long-poled torches (*ògùsò*) made from the chaff of palm kernels, which they carried to the ceremonial ground where the Ọ̀ọ̀ni was. In the festival, the group that represented the Ìgbò people, the Olúyarè, led by their ruler, Ọbàwìnrìn, emerged to pay homage to the Ọ̀ọ̀ni and demonstrate their loyalty to him. As they appeared wearing raffia clothes, just as the Ìgbò had in the past, they took care to avoid the *ògùsò* torches so that their highly flammable raffia clothes would not catch fire and possibly burn them to death. Again, all participants present recited the prayerful chorus of delivery:

> Ikú yọ, àrùn yọ, òfò yọ yọ.
> We expel from our midst death, disease, and loss.

This ritual allowed the Ifẹ̀ community to affirm life and purge evil. Like the Ọlọ́jọ́ Festival, it was an occasion for all the segments of the city represented by the chiefs to pay homage to the Ọ̀ọni and to reaffirm their oath of allegiance. Group by group, the diviners, chief priests, and quarter chiefs performed the *wórí* or salute to roy- alty, a ritual greeting of obeisance to the Ọ̀ọni. Chiefs kneeled before the Ọ̀ọni, touched the earth with their fingertips, and then touched their foreheads and chests three times. This was a ritual of perpetual surrender and homage, an affirmation of the Ọ̀ọni's rule over Ifẹ̀. After paying homage to the Ọ̀ọni, the Olúyarè disappeared, making way for the final ritual cleansing of Ilé-Ifẹ̀, symbolized in the expulsion of all evil from Ilé-Ifẹ̀. The bearer was the Teele.

The Teele: Scapegoating, Sacrifice, and the Expulsion of Evil

The Teele, the scapegoat and bearer of evil from Ilé-Ifẹ̀ to the forbidden bush, was the focus of the next ritual of the Edì Festival. As I discussed earlier in this chap- ter, the Edì Festival is a performance ritual that dramatizes an important moment in the mythic history of the sacred city of Ilé-Ifẹ̀: its defeat by an alien group called the Ìgbò and its subsequent liberation by Mọrèmi, a woman who sacrificed her body for the sake of the city. Edì is also a ritual of expulsion of evil from the city through a sacrifice that must be made by a foreign victim, the Teele.

Teele was a "title" bestowed on a willing foreigner and volunteer. I was fortunate to have met two Teeles. The first one died sometime in the late 1980s, and I en- countered the new one, a younger person, in his second year as Teele in Ifẹ̀. Once made a Teele, the person lived in the palace, was paid a salary, and was accorded the rights and privileges of a freeborn citizen. To be the Teele, the bearer of sac- rifice, was not an enviable position. The former Teele, whom I encountered in his old age, was frail, perhaps because of his annual obligation to bear the "evil load" to the bush. Most Ifẹ̀ indigenes I spoke to were fearful of anyone who had the duty of bearing the evil load on their behalf, yet they recognized how important Edì was in the religious and social life of Ilé-Ifẹ̀. Consequently, the Teele was allowed a great many liberties. He could wake up one day and decide to go to the market to take whatever he liked from the women traders—it was taboo to prevent him from do- ing so. My observation of the Teeles was that they were generally peace-loving men. The old one that I met would go round market stalls with his wife praying for the sellers and buyers, without even exercising his prerogative of taking from traders' wares, and the people themselves would reciprocate his good deeds by bestowing gifts on him.

The current Teele (at the time of my fieldwork in 2002) was a married farmer in his late forties. When I first ran into him, he told me he was just coming back from his farm. He clearly bore the signs of being a foreigner, since his tribal marks and dialect distinguished him from those born in Ifẹ̀. My fortuitous encounter with him took place one afternoon when my research assistant came to my house and wanted

me to meet an important and knowledgeable Ifẹ̀ chief, Ọsundúnrin, who lived some-
where in Òkèrèwè Street. I followed him, and shortly thereafter we ran into a group
of eight men in their late fifties and early sixties, sitting and talking in a family compound. We greeted them and went on our way. But upon our return, not quite twenty
minutes later (Chief Ọsundúnrin was not home), the group of old men stopped us
as we passed by and wanted to know what our mission was. I quickly sensed danger and realized from their cryptic conversation that they most likely belonged to
a secret society. I explained that I was writing a book on Ilé-Ifẹ̀ and had gone in
search of Chief Ọsundúnrin. One of the parties said he recognized me because he
had seen me a week before at the Odùduwà Shrine. He formally introduced himself as a chief and a medicine man. One of his mates, not too satisfied with the modest way the chief had introduced himself to me, interrupted our conversation with
the words *àjísà ògùn* (one with powerful magical "medicine" that is invoked daily).
By this time, I was getting uncomfortable. A diversion occurred when a man and
woman emerged from around a corner and the party, ignoring me, started shouting, "Teele, Teele, Teele!" The august visitors, who were possibly just passing by, were
formally introduced to me as the Teele and his wife. Their sudden appearance dis-
pelled the tension. Having greeted the men with an imitated version of the left-
handed handshake—a further indication that all the men, except the Teele, probably belonged to a secret society—the Teele said to them, "I have come to introduce
my Olorì [wife] to you, my fathers." Since Olorì is normally the title used for the
wife of a king, the Teele was claiming his royal connection by affectionately referring to his wife in this way. After this, we exchanged greetings with the Teele, and
he went his way. "This Teele is a powerful man," one of the people said. "He is very
knowledgeable in traditional medicine."

By this time, the conversation had unexpectedly shifted to the topic of the Teele.
Another man affirmed the view of the earlier speaker: "Ha! Teele is a powerful man
(*ó gbówó*). During the last Edì, the Ẹmẹsẹ̀ had to use powerful incantations to make
him carry the Edì load to the sacred forest." And still another added, *Ẹni gbékú lọ,
gbárùn lọ, ní láti lágbára!* (Whoever takes diseases and death away must be powerful!). These comments made me realize the significance of the sacrificial load the
Teele would soon be carrying. Though light in weight, the load was, by the native
reckoning, a heavy burden for whoever carried it in that it was believed to magically diminish the life force and energy of its bearer. Symbolically concentrating all
the evils in the community into one load made it very heavy indeed. This may partly
explain why in recent years the Edì performance, despite its religious and cultural
significance to Ilé-Ifẹ̀, has faced serious setbacks.[18]

The last phase of the Edì Festival was the ritual of cleansing the city and banishing evil. It was referred to as "carrying Edì out"—the opposite of the first day of
ritual, which was referred to as "bringing Edì home from Ọ̀ffà." In the afternoon of
Ọjọ́ Edì, or Edì Sacrificial Day, a huge crowd gathered at the palace to send off their

loads of misfortunes and to banish any potential evil that might lie in ambush for them in the year to come. The ritual was an occasion when prayers and curses freely mixed—prayers to expunge evil and curses to guard against agents of evil. The Èrí, the Yékéré, and other chiefs involved in the ceremony danced from their various homes to the palace. The Èrí's party was the largest, and her followers sang a song meant emphatically to reinforce her central role in Edì rituals: *Èrí ló l'Edì, Èrí ló l'Edì* (To the Èrí belongs Edì ritual). Indeed, she was the chief sacrificer and ritualist in Edì.

Dressed in white shirt and pants, carrying on his head a bundle of rubbish (dirt, leaves, etc.) put together by the palace Ẹmẹsẹ̀, the Teele stood in the middle of a circle in front of the Ọọni, surrounded by the chief priestess and priest of Edì, the Èrí and Yékéré, and their followers. Perhaps representing Olúorogbo, a little girl joined them in making the rounds as they danced around the Teele, singing the Edì song. I noticed that the ritual perambulation caused a little tension: Chief Yékéré wanted to lead the group, but Chief Èrí prevailed—a dispute that made me recognize why in the procession to the palace her followers had sung "To the Èrí belongs Edì ritual" so emphatically. A few days after the ceremony, I asked the Èrí about the apparent struggle between her and Chief Yékéré. She was surprised that I had noticed it, and she responded: "I am very senior to Yékéré. I am his mother, but because he is a man he behaves that way." After all, Yékéré is said to be the reincarnation of Olúorogbo, and his very name, Yékéré, means "This is too small." Rituals provide avenues for the competition of rivals , even though this competition is not necessarily explicit.

In a frenzied dance, the crowd shouted out prayers: *Gbékú lọ, gbárùn lọ, gbófò lọ!* (Banish death, banish disease, banish loss!). Believing it to be the moment when they could transfer all of their individual and communal evils to Teele's load, they let loose a deluge of prayers and curses. The expulsion of evil required a sacrifice. Someone led a goat with a rope tied around its neck, pulling it along as the Teele left the city. Accompanied by the palace Ẹmẹsẹ̀, the Teele proceeded into the sacred forest of Ìlámájàá (Igbó Ìlámájàá), where the animal was slaughtered and left to rot. The load was dropped beside it.

We must not assume that the Teele is always a willing partner in the ritual process. I was informed that often the year's Teele hesitated to carry the load of evil. It was as if the load by its very nature weighed the Teele down. The palace Ẹmẹsẹ̀ sometimes had to use magical incantations to make the Teele carry it; otherwise, they would have had to carry the repulsive load themselves. The Teele, as the bearer of the sacrifice, had the same status as a sacrificial victim would. No wonder that no Ifẹ̀ indigene could serve in the role of the Teele!

On the return of the sacrificial party, Chief Èrí moved to Mọrèmi's house, where she was secluded for another seven days. According to her, "Once I return from the bush, I will not set my eyes on Olódùmarè [the Supreme God] for a week" *(Mi ò ní fi ojú kan Olódùmarè fún ọ̀sẹ̀ kan).* By this she meant she would not see daylight until the seventh day. On the morning of the seventh day, the Èrí was supposed to go out to the crossroads *(oríta mẹ́ta)* carrying ritually prepared antelope meat *(itan ẹtu)* that she would offer to whoever first approached her. It was believed that whoever took this ritual meat from Èrí would surely die, since it was thought to contain whatever remnant of collective evil the Teele had left behind. As I was puzzled by this last rite of the festival, I asked Chief Èrí and the others present at the interview, "What if the person that first met Chief Èrí refused to take the meat?" *(Tí kò bá gbà ńkọ́?)* The whole party expressed their surprise at my ignorant question. "He or she would surely take the evil meat" *(Kò ní gbà kẹ̀),* they replied. I was stunned by this declaration, but I was informed later that this aspect of Edì is no longer practiced. Modernization has resulted in the abandonment of some of the more magical Ifẹ̀ rituals.

RITUAL LAMPOONING AND LICENSE
IN THE EDÌ FESTIVAL

A letter written by the then Ọ̀ọ̀ni of Ifẹ̀, Ọ̀ọ̀ni Adésọjí Adérẹ̀mí, on November 7, 1952, to a colonial police inspector on a custom of the Edì Festival that had provoked the wrath of the colonial government reveals an aspect of Edì that has important ritual ramifications. The Ọ̀ọ̀ni wrote in part:

> I have had a telephone conversation with you on the question of two men accused of damaging the house of another man in Ìlódè Quarter during the celebration of the Edì Festival recently. I promised to write you a short note on the matter. . . . During the Edì Festival, it is an age-long custom to sing abusive songs in front of the house of anyone known to have stolen another man's property during the year. It is usually done by multitudes of boys and girls running and singing in the street. . . . They go in relays of one or two hundred a set to the offender's compound, carrying rubbish of all kinds and grasses to the gate of the compound. . . . Over the ages, it [the festival] has served as a deterrent to stealing at Ifẹ̀. In those days, natives of Ifẹ̀ never stole anything at Ifẹ̀. All the housebreakings and cases of burglary up to date have been by strangers, not Ifẹ̀ natives. There is no doubt that the custom has prevented stealing by Ifẹ̀ men and women. The number is always two or three in any year. The Native Authority is considering how to control the custom. It is considered an outrage at the present moment, even though it has an age-old sanction.[19]

I have quoted this long passage because of the interpretation it suggests of Edì's cultural and social meanings. The lampooning rite to which the Ọ̀ọ̀ni refers takes place in the evenings throughout the week of the festival—a period of licentious inversion in which participants can express themselves freely without consequences. Like the Òpèpéè ceremony in the Ọ̀ràmfẹ̀ Festival in Oǹdó, it is what Max Gluckman called a "ritual of rebellion."[20] The targets of the lampooning are not only accused thieves but also criminals who have committed grave offences of adultery and murder. In addition, ordinary social boundaries are crossed as sexual desire is freely expressed by both men and women. Sexual matters that are normally experienced and verbalized in private are discussed in public. Edì is a licentious ritual during which public transgression is allowed and expressed and erotic feelings are spoken aloud. Sexual organs (vagina, penis) are ridiculed and sexual acts of copulation are mimicked. Jokes and laughter soften the drama of licentious acts. This supports André Droogers's theories on play as an essential part of religious life cross-culturally.[21]

As I argued when describing the Òràmfè Festival of the Oǹdó people, I propose that this rite is, metaphorically, a way to contain chaos and disorder such as that which Ilé-Ifè faced during the invasion of the Ìgbò.[22] At times like these, when the cosmos needs to be rejuvenated, a ritual to reverse the state of chaos must take place. Just as the Ọòni remarked in his letter, "strangers" are normally the victims of Edì's lampooning, and not indigenes, because strangers are usually the ones who are imagined to be thieves; however, there are times when those ridiculed are indigenes. Just as the Edì sacrifice focuses on the Teele, the stranger par excellence, to carry the burden of evil out of the city to the forest, so the Edì lampooning rite scapegoats strangers as the "other." The moral and social values of Ifè that forbid the offering of indigenes as sacrifice to the gods extend to this situation. Strangers are the proper "food" of the gods, and not indigenes, who are regarded as sacred beings. The stranger symbolizes the communal evil that must be expelled and banished to the forest, outside culture and civilization. In carrying out the ultimate ritual of sacrifice, the Teele plays a similar role, as is shown later in the festival cycle.

SACRIFICE AND REDEMPTION

I would now like to focus on the meaning and context of sacrifice in the core of Edì rituals. Although written with reference to the Christian tradition, Horace Bushnell's book *Vicarious Sacrifice* offers explanations of the phenomenology and theology of sacrifice that are useful for understanding the Yorùbá as well. By "vicarious sacrifice," he means that which is "offered to bear the sins of many" or that which "[bears] our griefs and [carries] our sorrows."[23] It involves "a figure, representing that the party making such sacrifice for another, com[ing] into burden, pain, weariness, or even to the yielding up of life for his sake."[24] Among the Yorùbá, sacrifice similarly involves a form of substitution, such as that of one life for another, or of property, such as a domestic animal, for a human life.

The sacrifice brings about a changed mood in the city. According to Royden Yerkes, in his discussion of ancient Greek and Roman religion and early Judaism, sacrifice always evokes a sadness resulting from the destruction of that which is sacrificed and from the misfortunes that made the sacrifice necessary.[25] The taboo against drumming throughout the Edì Festival, which I referred to earlier, is a reminder of threats to Ilé-Ifè in the past and of the people's present need to perform a sacrifice that will renew the city's vitality and secure the continuing blessings of the ancestors.

Edì is what Arnold van Gennep identified in his classic *Rites of Passage* as a communal rite of passage, a calendrical ritual that involves the society as a whole. It occurs at a period in Ifè ritual calendar when a renewal of the cosmos is warranted. It is the beginning of the dry season, and it follows the Qlójó Festival, the ritual of Ògún, when the Qòni renewed his sacred kingship. As an indication of the auspicious ritual time, all drumming must cease until the completion of the Edì Festival. The music and percussion sounds that accompany most of the sacrificial rituals are not accomplished by drums. The festival is a period of license during which the regular social order is suspended or inverted—what van Gennep called a "liminal" phase. The high and mighty are lampooned, and alleged thieves are publicly reprimanded. People sing obscene songs and make graphic references to genitalia without being accused of obscenity. Further, marginalized figures play very important ritual roles for the sake of the community: the Teele, the foreign-born sacrificer; the Èrí, the female priestess who is the reincarnation of Mọrèmi; the Yékéré, who stands for Olúorogbo, Mọrèmi's son offered as sacrifice; and any nonindigenes who are accused of theft or other crimes in the lampooning rite and whose houses are thus slated for destruction. On the shoulders of the marginalized protagonists in the Edì ritual lie Ifè's salvation and renewal. Through the sacrifice of the Teele, on whose head the "evil" burden is placed, the society undergoes transformation.

Victor Turner's theory on the place and meaning of rituals, especially his transformation theory of sacrifice in human society, throws much light on the Edì sacrificial ritual. According to Turner, periodically occurring rituals involving the society as a whole renew the social structure by addressing and resolving its persisting conflicts through ritualized social dramas that allow for a temporary reclassification of reality, an "antistructure"; these rites and performances invert the social order and disrupt the normal ways of doing things in the society. Once that stage is passed, a new society emerges from the ashes of the old to face the challenges of a new age. Evil is banished so that the cosmos can be renewed. Sacrificial rituals can be employed either to create the antistructure—for example, invoking a shared awe toward the gods that breaks down social boundaries—or to restore structure by reestablishing boundaries and frames.[26] The Edì sacrificial ritual brings about order in a community whose disorder was first portrayed in the lampooning rite that involves throwing rubbish at the houses of suspected thieves. Turner suggests that similar rituals are concerned "with general processes of inclusion and exclusion, of delimiting, of protecting the known against the unknown, and presenting models of symmetry and hierarchy."[27] Turner also raises theological concepts of sacrifice, redemption, and atonement for sin in order to incorporate them into a larger scheme of both personal and societal renewal.[28] The Mọrèmi rituals renew and transform the moral order among those who make the sacrifice. The ritual is about strengthening their social commitment to one another and demonstrating their continued gratitude to Mọrèmi for the agonizing sacrifice she made so they could prosper. Renewal of a social and spiritual contract that keeps the community as a whole in good standing with Mọrèmi and the spiritual forces is at work in this myth. This is the essence and intrinsic value of Edì ritual sacrifice. Individuals, the lineage, the sacred kingship, the city, and community—all are transformed through the sacrificial ritual of Edì.

The role of the Teele in the sacrificial ritual deserves further elaboration, especially as his removal of evil from Ifẹ̀ and his ultimate sacrifice in the sacred forest of Ìlámájàá constitute the climax of the Edì Festival. Here we see the intersection of sacrifice and cultural violence in a manner that reflects the thesis of Réné Girard's classic *Violence and the Sacred*. Girard believed that in the sacrificial process of many societies a surrogate victim is chosen and the violence of the group is transferred to him for expulsion from the community. The scapegoat, Girard observed, is generally a marginalized subject within the group (foreigner, slave, domestic animal) who is not essential to the group. This victim is expelled either by banishment or by killing. Girard observed that in the act of sacrifice the scapegoat is powerless to retaliate and the sacrificial act cannot lead to the revenge that often characterizes violent acts in most cultures. As a result, the spiraling violence that frequently results from revenge killing is put to an end. The outsider, then, pays the ultimate price for ending communal violence.

There are many sacrifices in the Mọrèmi-Edì tradition. First is the redemptive sacrifice of Mọrèmi, the goddess who voluntarily made herself a captive victim of the Ìgbò chief to discover the Ìgbò army's secret and to stop their incessant violence against the Ilé-Ifẹ̀ people. Second is the sacrifice that Mọrèmi made of her son, Olúorogbo, to the Ẹ̀sìnmìrìn River, in order to seal the pact she made with the river. Without the sacrifice of Olúorogbo, the Mọrèmi saga would have been incomplete. Though both Mọrèmi and Olúorogbo are central figures in the narrative, they would be considered marginal characters in the community and hence potential and actual sacrificial victims: a woman and a child in a patriarchal, seniority-conscious society.

The Edì Festival also involves several forms of ritual victimization. First is that of the nonindigenes who are accused of theft and may be seen as the symbol of the society's evil. Theft of one's property leads to loss, which is one of the characteristics of evil *(alájogun)* in Yorùbá society. When the crowd vents its anger on nonindigenes and makes a scapegoat of them, it makes them the symbol of the society's evil. At another level, the Teele, the sacrificial victim par excellence, is an outsider who is made to carry the community's load of evil to the forbidden forest. In the past, when human sacrifice was common, as Michael Walsh has suggested, the Teele was indeed the sacrificial victim, who was killed in the forest because he embodied the bundle of evil he carried. Finally, the innocent passerby takes the magical meat that symbolizes the remnant of evil in the society. By consuming this meat, the passerby ensures his own death, adding his name to the list of surrogate victims in Edì rituals.

In all these instances, the community welfare is at stake rather than individual concerns. As Girard remarked, the elements of dissension scattered throughout the community are embodied in the person of the sacrificial victim and eliminated, at least temporarily, by its sacrifice. What binds the victims together is their marginality. The victims are generally those whose status as "foreigners or enemies, their servile condition, or simply their age prevents [them] from fully integrating themselves into the community."[29]

These issues raise the question of why Mọrèmi, a woman, would be placed in the category of a surrogate victim. I suggest that her marginality may be due less to her gender than to her status as a non-Ifẹ̀ indigene. It is likely that she came from Ọ̀ffà and migrated to Ifẹ̀ either voluntarily or as a refugee of war. References to Ọ̀ffà, which also has a cult of Mọrèmi, abound in the Edì rituals—the wrestling contest and the Ọ̀ffà song are but two examples.

SECRECY AND THE FORBIDDEN

The Mọrèmi epic and the Edì Festival point to the centrality of the cultural idiom of secrecy, the taboo, and the forbidden in Ilé-Ifẹ̀. Secrecy may relate to events, acts, and performances of dramatis personae in narratives and ritual performances. It may also characterize the entire group involved in a religious ritual. The theme of secrecy runs through the entire narrative as well as the public performances. I have pointed out that a taboo is placed on drumming during the period of the festival, an indication of the events' solemnity. Yet the festival also involves expression of that which the community ordinarily forbids and considers taboo, especially the use of "vulgar" words and sexual imagery. As Tony Williams has explored in his essay on the bedroom as a secret space in French nineteenth-century fiction, once a culture defines certain spaces as secret, the forbidden entry takes on the transgressive charge of the "peep show."[30] With reference to the specific narrative and festival events we are dealing with, we may posit that the references to phalluses and vaginas are metaphors for Mọrèmi's encounter and "adulterous" relationship with the Ìgbò king. That the king is a stranger and an enemy complicates matters here. Though theologically we can see Mọrèmi's actions in terms of the suffering she endured for the sake of Ifẹ̀, in popular imagination her deployment of her "bottom power," to use contemporary Nigerian parlance, is what catches the attention of the Ifẹ̀ people. A careful examination of the narrative indicates that in many instances Mọrèmi crosses the sexual/gender boundary to perform her heroic role. Her discovery of a deep Ìgbò secret paved the way for Ifẹ̀'s unmasking of Ìgbò spirit masquerades and their consequent defeat.

In addition, Edì lampooning and licentious rituals provide a way for the Ifẹ̀ to dispel the secrecy surrounding those accused of theft in their community. This is illustrated in several songs sung outside the house of the person being lampooned that begin with the same opening:

> The Ọba (king) asked me not to say it, . . .
> But I will say it.

One aspect of the licentious symbol of inversion is to disobey the Ọba by revealing what he asked them not to reveal—what is hidden and kept secret. After declaring that they will break their silence, the crowd charges into the home of the accused to destroy it.

The nexus of sacrifice and gender offers a viable template for exploring the myth and rituals of Mọrèmi and Edì traditions. Through the myth of Mọrèmi, we can see that gender plays an important role in Yoruba culture, not only in the cultural sphere but in the religious as well.[31] On the basis of interpretations of Mọrèmi's narrative and Edì rituals, we have seen how culture difference and sacrificial scapegoats are constructed in the Ifẹ̀ imagination. Through our imaginative reading of the narrative, we have shown how the Edì ritual can be seen as a theatrical performance of a historical past, during which Ifẹ̀ people struggled with some outsiders for authority and control of Ilé-Ifẹ̀ City. The analysis of the myth also reveals the deep cultural ethos and social structure of the city, the role of lineage in subethnic identity construction, the centrality and importance of the sacred kingship, and, most importantly, how social memory of the past leads to the construction and maintenance of the present.

8

Odùduwà, the God-King

Ilé-Ifẹ̀'s numerous religious rituals and festivals have established the city's primacy as a ceremonial center and as the "epicenter" of Yorùbá religion, culture, and civilization. The founder of the city was Odùduwà (Oòduà), who is also called Ọlọ́fin. The Ifá divination texts, the most in-depth source for Yorùbá epistemology, refer to him as Ọlọ́fin, the honorific title for a god-king. Each year, the people of Ilé-Ifẹ̀ memorialize their founder, Odùduwà, in the great festival of Ọdún Idió. I will argue that Ọdún Odùduwà, or Ọdún Idió, the Odùduwà Festival, and indeed the entire ritual process, is a ritual drama enacted to demonstrate Odùduwà's might and superiority over all mortals and gods in the city he founded. Ọdún Idió is structured to propitiate Odùduwà as the ancestral culture hero and the first god-king of the city.

ODÙDUWÀ: GREAT ANCESTOR AND CULTURE HERO

A cursory examination of the stages of the Odùduwà ritual process reveals that this ancestral festival established a strong relationship between Ilé-Ifẹ̀ cosmology and the city's political and social structure and religion. The symbolic reenactment of traditional ritual reinforces the ideology of the sacred kingship and lineage. Ultimately, through its many sacrificial rituals, the festival provides the chance for the spiritual forces that established the city to return annually to Ilé-Ifẹ̀, allowing continuity between past events, their reenactment, and present reality.

In fact, the rituals and festival celebrations I have examined throughout this work constitute forms of reverence toward the ancestors, allowing devotees to celebrate and commemorate the links between the living descendants, their kinship groups, and their tutelary heroes and deities. In all likelihood, these ancestor-heroes, once deceased, were apotheosized into gods. They were celebrated in rituals performing the linkages among kingship and lineage ties, land, and space. Nevertheless, other festivals differ significantly from the festival of Ọlọ́fin-Odùduwà, also called Idió, because this festival celebrates a greater mythic ancestor whose influence—real or imagined—extends throughout the land of the Yorùbá.

The Odùduwà celebration is filled with both historical and contemporary significance. Among other things, participants in the celebration believe that the great deity Odùduwà is at the center of Ilé-Ifẹ̀'s ritual universe. Thus they "legitimize" the ideology of the Yorùbá and Ifẹ̀ sacred kingship, establishing the relationship between the center (Ilé-Ifẹ̀) and the peripheral states of the Yorùbá kingdoms. Believers demonstrate the almost unchallenged and unrivaled magical power of Odùduwà, defining the relationship between the Ọọ̀ni, the present occupant of Odùduwà's throne, and the great ancestor-god Odùduwà as that between a son-progenitor and an ancestral father. Unlike the Ọlọ́jọ́ Festival, in which the Ọọ̀ni and the Ifẹ̀ people propitiate Ògún, the god of war, who enables land and territory to be conquered, Idió is a solemn ancestral ritual of remembrance and renewal of kinship ties between the great god-king and the Yorùbá people.

The ritual drama and performance of the Odùduwà Festival reflect the imagined mythology, history, and social structure of the city as constructed at the beginning of time. Just as the festival emphasizes the social and ritual differentiation between the Odùduwà lineage group and other lineages in Ilé-Ifẹ̀, so it reinforces civil authority of the Odùduwà lineage and of the Ọ̀tún Ifẹ̀ (the eight powerful civil chiefs in the city), as well as the authority of the ancestral deity who has placed the territory under their control. The conflict between Odùduwà and Ọbàtálá is displayed in the very structure of the festival's ritual drama, in the taboos that surround their performances, and in the physical and open display of the power of the ancestors. The festival redefines the commercial and economic bases of the city and redistributes its wealth in the form of gifts to Odùduwà. In my analysis, I intend to show the interconnection of these various motifs in specific festival rituals, as well as the interconnections of "ideology, economy, and power."[1]

ROYAL ANCESTORS AND THE IDENTITY OF PLACE

All the observable practices and the beliefs espoused by Ilé-Ifẹ̀'s òrìṣà devotees in the entire festival and religious life of Ilé-Ifẹ̀ that I have witnessed point to the motif of ancestor veneration as the cardinal aspect of the celebrations. Undoubtedly, ritual performance and reverence directed to the ancestors is very strong among the Yorùbá people, as it is throughout Africa.[2] It is anchored in burial practices, in a strong belief in life after death, and in the connection between kinship structures and traditions on the one hand and the religious worldview on the other. In her groundbreaking ethnography of ancestor veneration in Mayan society, especially the powerful role it plays in the ideological framework and social structure of ancient and modern Mayan society, Patricia McAnany aptly observes: "Communing with deceased progenitors was not a religious experience divorced from political and economic realities . . . ; rather, it was a practice grounded in pragmatism that drew power from the past, legitimized the current state of affairs . . . and charted a course for the future. Ancestors resided at the critical nexus between past and future, and their presence both materially and symbolically lent weight to the claims of their mere mortal descendants."[3] Although McAnany was not particularly concerned with the details of Mayan ancestor rituals in her study, she did point out the significance of ancestor tradition in understanding "the persistent tension between 'kinship' and 'kingship.'"[4]

The traditions and practices regarding the ancestors that underlie the Idió celebration center primarily on Odùduwà, the royal and deified mythic ancestor of Ilé-Ifè and of the Yorùbá people, who as warrior, founder, creator, and king put his permanent mark on Yorùbá civilization. The Yorùbá as we know them today define themselves as his children.

I am not concerned merely with the veneration of Odùduwà as the Ifè ancestor deity. Rather, I would like to show how Odùduwà ritual and narratives define the sacred character of Ilé-Ifè as the City of the Gods and its central place and space in the religious imagination. The Odùduwà ritual marks and sacralizes two important concepts of place in Ilé-Ifè: (1) the city as the place where Odùduwà lived, reigned, and became immortalized and apotheosized into an ancestor; and (2) the city as a place that provides an eternal sacred canopy for Ifè and for the Yorùbá people as a whole.

The Odún Idió has as its core objective the ritual enactment of the ideology and symbolism of ancestral practice at its highest level, since unlike regular ancestral sacrifices offered to lineage and remote clan ancestors, which are very common in Yorùbá religious tradition and Ilé-Ifè ritual, it is directed to the ultimate mythic ancestor deity from whom the Yorùbá descended. The festival brings to the present the memories of him, whether real or imagined, and honors his deeds on earth, especially in laying the foundation of Ilé-Ifè. It involves reenacting the sacrificial ritual of the foundation of the city. I propose to explore the representations of the power structure in place at the time of Ilé-Ifè's founding and the ancestral ideology and meaning embedded in the Idió Festival, especially as these symbols and meaning affirm Ilé-Ifè as a sacred space.

CONVERSATION WITH THE ỌBADÌO, CHIEF PRIEST OF ODÙDUWÀ

When I asked the Ọbadìo, chief priest of Odùduwà, to tell me about Odùduwà and how he came to the city of Ilé-Ifè, the Ọbadìo began by telling me about the Yorùbá creation myth and the role of Odùduwà as a culture hero, primogenitor of the Yorùbá nation, and founder of the city. The Ọbadìo's version of the myth, though largely the same as the one recounted in chapter 1, differed from it in several intriguing details. The dialogue that follows was part of the conversation between Ọbadìo and me:

Olúpọ̀nà: Bàbá [Father], we would like to know about Odùduwà.

Ọbadìo: Oòduà who descends from the sky above. We knew neither his father nor his mother. He was chosen to come to this world. Olódùmarè sent him on an errand, and he delivered it with thoroughness.

   Gods like Òrìṣà-Ńlá (Ọbàtálá) and Ọ̀ràmfẹ̀ are like prophets *[wòlíì]* who spread the gospel *[ìhìnrere]* of Olódùmarè around the world. Olódùmarè examined Odùduwà and, convinced of his strength and honesty, decided to send him to the earth. He descended to the earth by means of a chain. He gave birth to Olúorogbo, Èsìndálè, and others. When he arrived, the whole world was in chaos, and Olódùmarè decided to destroy the world with water. He made a ship and kept his favorite ones there. He later found a chameleon to test the ground to ensure that the land was dry enough for human habitation. After a while, the chameleon alighted from the ship, and a five-toed guinea fowl spread the soil *[àtẹ̀pẹ́]* that was poured on the water. It was the *àtẹ̀pẹ́* in Èsìndálè's bag that became the solid earth we all walk upon today. When they got out of the ship to tread on the created land, Odùduwà asked Èsìndálè to bring out the objects in his bag, with which they made the earth solid. Once Odùduwà had molded the solid earth, people started arriving, and Odùduwà began to apportion responsibility to them all and assign them living quarters in the city and in places far off. Odùduwà prepared a horse for the Aláàfin [the king of Ọ̀yọ́] and told him to ride on it and to stop whenever the horse slipped in the mud. So when the horse Aláàfin was riding stumbled, he stopped and decided to live there, and it was there that he became Ọbalọ́yọ̀ọ́ [the king of Ọ̀yọ́, the land where the earth slips]. All of these beings departed to their respective homes that Odùduwà assigned to them. They would come back yearly to bring gifts *[ẹ̀sìn]* to their father, Odùduwà. All the other *òrìṣà*—Ọbamerì, Ọ̀ràmfẹ̀, and Ọrè—came with Odùduwà, and they had to answer his call at all times. Ọbàtálá was the only deity who was not on good terms with Odùduwà in heaven. On the way down from heaven, Ọbàtálá got drunk, and Odùduwà then went ahead to do what Ọbàtálá should have done, create the universe. Odùduwà took Ọbàtálá's satchel, which contained the ingredients for creation, and performed the work of creation that Olódùmarè had ordered. When the fight between Odùduwà and Ọbàtálá became deadlocked on earth, God sent Ọ̀ràmfẹ̀ to settle it.

Olúpọ̀nà: What duty did Olódùmarè then give Ọbàtálá?

Ọbadìo: He is the one who breathes into the molded image *[ère]* the breath by which we become human beings.

Olúpọ̀nà: What about the other gods, such as Ògún, Ifá?

  Ọbadìo: Ifá was the "doctor" sent by God to take care of Odùduwà, and Ògún was Odùduwà's son and a brave warrior.

Olúpọ̀nà: Tell us about your title, "Ọbadìo."

  Ọbadìo: Ọlọ́fin [the king] owns the Odùduwà deity to be propitiated [deities are "owned" in the sense that objects consecrated to them are owned]. He only employs me as a laborer [ó gbà mí sí lébìrà ni] to propitiate Odùduwà, his ancestral father, for him.

This conversation with the late Ọbadìo Yusuf Fágbulé (two Ọbadìos have been installed since his demise) was very revealing. Not only did he present another cosmogony, different in many ways from the narrative in chapter 1, but he also clearly defined his own relationship to the Odùduwà tradition and practices of which he was in charge. Odùduwà established the city of Ilé-Ifẹ̀, which by extension covers the entire Yorùbá nation and the whole world. The imaginary world-city defines the bounds within which Odùduwà exercises influence. The myth claims that the land of Ọ̀yọ́ (established as a place where the horse slips, Ọ̀yọ̀ò) was granted to the Aláàfin, a son of Odùduwà. An Odùduwà ritual would later claim that other lands had been given by Odùduwà to his children and that those children had been the principal founders of Yorùbá city-states such as Ẹ̀gbá, Adó (Benin), and Oǹdó.

The act of creating the land of Ilé-Ifẹ̀ takes on a new meaning in this version of the myth because the Ọbadìo emphasizes the very ritual process of turning the small heap of soil *(àtẹ̀pẹ́)* that Odùduwà had brought with him from heaven into an expansive world. Ilé-Ifẹ̀ (the land that is widely spread) belongs to Odùduwà. *Àtẹ̀pẹ́* implies metaphorically "that which we tread on forever," as in the Yorùbá saying, *Àtẹ̀pẹ́ lẹsẹ̀ ń tẹ̀nà* (that we may tread on the earth forever), a prayerful invocation for long life or immortality.

The story reaffirms Odùduwà's relationship to Ọbàtálá and the cause of the enmity between the two gods, which divided Ilé-Ifẹ̀ into two ritual groups, the party of Odùduwà and the party of Ọbàtálá. The distinctions between them are often marked by the taboo against palm wine, to which the devotees of Ọbàtálá adhere. Both the Ọbadìo, the chief priest of Odùduwà, and the Ọbalẹ́ṣùn, the chief priest of Ọbàtálá, presented narratives that privileged their status and standing in the social and ritual order of the city. The priests of the 201 gods in the Ilé-Ifẹ̀ pantheon often define their role as facilitating the propitiation of Ilé-Ifẹ̀ deities, a role that often relates to the sacred kingship. The lineages are custodians of the deities in the sense of being responsible for the upkeep of their shrines. But in most cases, the two roles of custodian and propitiator of the gods have merged together, as the case of Ọbàtálá clearly shows: the Ìdìta lineage claims the deity and also produces the priests who propitiate it.

As the chief priests of Odùduwà claim, the Ọbadìo is the head of the Ìṣòrò priestly class. Just as Odùduwà claims superiority through conquests over all other deities in Ilé-Ifẹ̀, so is the Ọbadìo's leadership undisputed among the Ìṣòrò clan of chiefs. The Ọbadìo described Odùduwà for me as follows.

> Atẹ́rẹrẹ káyé, amosìkalùú
> Agẹgẹrẹ ọ̀gán
> Atúnnìṣe má banijẹ́
> Ẹni béégún jà tó déégún
> Ẹni bá Tata jà lẹ́sẹ̀ omi
> Kó borí Tata
> Oòduà kó bóòrùn jà
> Kó borí Oòrùn mọ́lẹ̀
> Kó báná jà kóo dáná.

> The one whose abode covers the entire world,
> The mighty one of the world,
> He who blesses his devotees and never causes them harm.
> He fought with the ancestral sprits and conquered them.
> He fought with Tata [a river spirit] at the riverbank and conquered it.
> He fought with the sun and conquered it.
> He fought with the fire; he conquered the fire.

This invocation affirms Odùduwà's superiority and power in the city. All the essential forces of nature, along with human and spiritual forces, are subject to him. Water and fire, two essential but powerful and dangerous elements, were conquered by Odùduwà. By implication, no physical or spiritual forces supersede Odùduwà in power. The ancestral god and culture hero is declared spiritual and temporal lord of the Ifẹ̀ universe. Yet the inclination of Odùduwà to fulfill human material needs is reaffirmed. He makes whole and causes no harm or evil to human life. Fertility, long life, and wealth belong to this great ancestor deity, who protects his devotees as they progress along the journey of life. The invocation gives Odùduwà's devotees total confidence in his protective power.

ÀṢẸ: SYMBOLS OF ODÙDUWÀ'S POWER

The Odùduwà Festival is an ancestral ritual characterized by its exclusivity. Odùduwà never shares his glory by being part of other ancestral traditions across the land. It is taboo for priests of Odùduwà and the Ọọ̀ni (king) to take part in or be present at Egúngún, the ancestral lineage masquerades, the symbols of ancestral tradition par excellence in western Yorùbá towns, especially in the core Ọ̀yọ́ regions. Odùduwà abhors tribal marks *(ilà)*, the widespread signs of lineage and clan identity that are common to other Yorùbá ethnic groups. Odùduwà defines himself in opposition to cultural traditions and markers that characterize the majority of the people. An *oríkì* describes the ruler of Ifẹ̀ as *ojúrábẹ:* he who abhors the incision knife (that inscribes the tribal cicatrices). The Ọbadìo claimed, "Those . . . who are very intimate with Odùduwà must not acquire tribal marks. Generally, where people have the marks, not much takes place there."

The *àṣẹ* of Odùduwà—the ritual, magical, and spiritual force symbolizing the deity's power—is given a concrete presence in magical objects that Odùduwà's devotees hold very sacred. One of these is the *ọrún,* a disklike shining object covered with white cloth and held by a devotee. It must never be exposed to the rays of the moon or the sun, and ordinary people are forbidden to gaze at it. A priest of Odùduwà told me, "The *ọrún* is Odùduwà's mace and symbol of authority that is carried before us. It is a very potent object, and it is the instrument we use in weakening the *iwọ̀* or sacrificial animals." No Ọbadìo is ever installed without this object present. The *ọrún* demonstrates Odùduwà's physical power and force to the members of the group. It is what many would call a magical object, which, like Ilé-Ifẹ̀ sacred utterances *(àyájọ́),* can alter the physical form of any sentient being, whether human, animal, plant, or tree. All throughout the sacrificial night, I was warned to keep far away from this object because it might affect me if I came into contact with it or came close to its vital force. When I asked the priests how the ritual objects had come into being, I was told they had come with Odùduwà!

Odùduwà's power is also manifest in the taboo imposed on drumming during the Odùduwà Festival. As in the case of the *ọrún,* I asked, "What function does this taboo play in a festival that is expected to celebrate the deeds of Odùduwà ancestors?" In a city and tradition that values music, dance, and drumming, why did the ritual of Odùduwà forbid these powerful musical forms? The priests again told me that the Supreme God, Olódùmarè, gave the command in relation to Odùduwà's ritual. "We use the taboo to honor the gods because Odùduwà tolerates no noise at all. He is a serious deity! The taboo simply reflects his great power." An *oríkì* of the Odùduwà priesthood lineage supports this position:

> *Ọmọ aṣorò k'Óọ̀ni ro gégẹ́*
> *Ọmọ aṣorò dàlù delẹ*
> *Ibi ọ́n dàlù de*
> *É gbọdọ̀ hu koríko!*

Children [descendants] of those who perform ritual,
While the Ọọ̀ni stands at attention,
Children [descendants] of one who performs rituals while shutting down the drum,
The place where the drum is turned upside down
Will never bring forth grasses!

This *oríkì* of Odùduwà and his priests depicts the drum of Odùduwà as a potent instrument that must be turned upside down to avoid being sounded accidentally and thus causing unwelcome danger. The upside-down drum signifies that drumming is taboo in Odùduwà rituals. The drum of Odùduwà is no ordinary drum! It is so potent that the ground it covers while inverted will never bring forth any living grass. No other drum, not even the *òṣírìgì* drum of the Ọọ̀ni, compares to it. The taboo on drumming, enforced by the order of a superior official, requires that a "lock" be put on the drum, signifying the might and authority of the deity. Odùduwà suspends and "locks up" the ordinary flow and rhythm of life to be able to put things right again in the city. The taboo on drumming marks the liminal period of the Ifẹ̀ ritual calendar when one cycle is ended and a new one begins. The ritual occurs at the end of the year at midnight in utter darkness.

Out of respect for the priest of Odùduwà, the Ọọ̀ni must stand absolutely still while the priests perform the Odùduwà ritual. Although I did not see him physically present in any of the three times that I witnessed this festival, the Lọ́wá, or chief palace administrator, represented him in many ritual performances. The Odùduwà Festival is the collective ancestral ritual of the Ọọ̀ni. It is not like the Ọlọ́jọ́, where the Ọọ̀ni visits his patrilineal house and women of the house propitiate his father and paternal ancestor for him. The Ọọ̀ni here comes as the descendant of Odùduwà to propitiate the collective ancestor of the Ifẹ̀ and all Yorùbá people. To perform this ritual function, the Ọọ̀ni must come as a subdued, submissive individual. The Odùduwà priest claimed that the Ọọ̀ni could not travel outside the palace during the duration of the festival; neither could those connected with the festival go to their farms to work during this period. Because the festival lasts fourteen days, in principle, two ritual weeks *(ìje méjì)* are observed. This double-week ritual cycle is interpreted as a sign of Odùduwà's superiority over all other *òrìṣà,* who have only a one-week ritual cycle.

ODÙDUWÀ AND ILÉ-IFẸ̀'S MORAL ORDER

The Odùduwà Festival is very complex. I will attempt to provide an outline of the festival sequence, presenting both its meaning as explicated by its priests and my own interpretation of it as primarily an ancestral ritual honoring a cultural hero and founder of a city.

The festival takes place in the grove and shrine where Odùduwà's devotees believe he descended into the earth's crust. Except in very few places outside Ilé-Ifẹ̀ where Odùduwà is also viewed as a deity, his cult has not spread to other places, as did the cults of Ògún, Ifá, Ọbàtálá, and several other deities in Yorùbá pantheon. So far, Odùduwà is very much confined to a specific geographical location. As an autochthonous deity, his claim to a pan-Yorùbá ethnicity relies on the fact that his children and their descendants left Ilé-Ifẹ̀ to found other cities. However, Odùduwà himself never left Ilé-Ifẹ̀ except when he was alleged to have traveled to distant places (Ifá claimed, for example, that Odùduwà had made a pilgrimage to Mere Telu, Mecca, in the Middle East, accompanied by his medicine man, Ẹlẹ́sìnjẹ́). But Odùduwà never left Ilé-Ifẹ̀ permanently, as other gods did. For example, the divination texts claim that Ifá, another Ifẹ̀ deity, traveled to many distant places until he made a final trip abroad. This claim would explain his continuous presence in the Yorùbá diaspora communities of the Americas and the Caribbean, as it is thought that he never came back to Ilé-Ifẹ̀.

The Odùduwà Festival reflects the very turbulent conditions in which Odùduwà established his city. Most oral traditions that mention him recognize his readiness to maintain his authority there, given his following of warlords such as Bàbá Ṣìgìdì and Ọbamerì, and his empowerment both by medicine and by his àṣẹ, or powerful magical force. An important resource Odùduwà used for governance and ritual control of events in his city was secrecy. The Odùduwà cult is embedded in deep secrecy *(awo)*, which provides it with the privilege and power it maintains over the Ifẹ̀ people's ritual life. The Ọbadìo, for example, is described as the first among the Àwòrò (priests) of the 201 gods in the city. One oral text says, "It is his command and àṣẹ that must prevail among all the Àwòrò priests" *(Ti Ọbadìo ni ó ṣe láàárín àwọn Àwòrò).* The Odùduwà cult is endogamous, one of the features of traditions that are based on deep secrecy. Membership in Odùduwà's group is not open to outsiders. Although other religious groups may accommodate outsiders, foreigners from outside the city and from overseas—especially members of the diaspora community—Odùduwà forbids outsiders from joining its ranks. It is entirely a ritual kinship and lineage tradition whose priests are responsible for propitiating Odùduwà. Devotees of Odùduwà can be divided into two groups: Ìṣọ̀sán (meaning "the light of the day," in reference to their daytime initiation), a lower-level initiate group, and the stronger Ìṣòru ("the darkness of night," in reference to their nighttime initiation), a more advanced group. For the Yorùbá, *òru*, night, is the time when people do wicked things under the cover of darkness *(òru là ń ṣèkà).* In the ritual context, the nighttime initiation reveals a powerful esoteric knowledge meant only for advanced members of the tradition. As a further sign of their unity and secrecy at Odùduwà Shrine, all members young and old drink palm wine from the same calabash.

Unlike other Ifẹ̀ ritual groups whose female members play central and active ritual roles, that of Odùduwà forbids such roles for women of the lineage. Whereas Ọbàtálá ritual designates specific female roles, however limited, ritual affairs of Odùduwà are purely the business of men. Out of curiosity, I asked the reigning Ọbadìo what status women could attain in Odùduwà's ritual. He told me that no role was forbidden to women. But he was referring to the roles assumed by women who engaged in weeks of hard work organizing feasts to benefit devotees, tourists, civic leaders, and priests. Later we confirmed that women had their own day of propitiating Odùduwà. But the gendered nature of the Odùduwà celebration became apparent when we were told that ordinary women could not enter the compound of Odùduwà. They were forbidden to see the *ẹgánrán,* the musical percussion instrument of the Odùduwà celebration. To keep this taboo from being broken, the door to the Odùduwà compound was marked with a sign at the threshold that separated outsiders and insiders (men and women). Perhaps the cardinal reason for the separation was that the women of the house (Obìnrin Ilé) were considered "outsiders" to the Idió kinship group because they were mainly wives and nursing mothers married to members of the lineage. The Odùduwà devotees justified the taboo by pointing out that women of menstrual age risked missing their periods if they witnessed the powerful incantations sung during the festival.

Because of the many similarities between the Odùduwà tradition and male secret societies, I asked the priests whether there was any connection to the Imalè (house of the gods), an indigenous secret society that preceded the Ògbóni. They informed me that Odùduwà had founded the Imalè. As a further indication of the importance of secrecy in this tradition, the devotees of Odùduwà claimed that images of Odùduwà were hidden in the ground upon which his shrine was built. "Odùduwà's image cannot be stolen," a priest enlightened me. "Just as we cannot steal the image of Jesus," another echoed him. This was apparently a reference to the constant disappearance of *òrìsà* images in Ifè and other Yorùbá cities. Such theft had prompted the priests to safeguard the images of Ọbàtálá and Yemòó in the Ifè Museum and to display them only during the time of their festival. Odùduwà devotees believe that their god is too powerful to be stolen. The daily greeting among them further attests to the strength of their bond. *Mọ́ yẹhùn* (No, do not deviate from the path), they say to each other and reply, *Ẹní yẹhùn tẹ́* (Whoever deviates is disgraced). To deviate from the path by breaking the oath of secrecy is a great taboo that may evoke the wrath of the ancestor. The unity of the Odùduwà group is also maintained by their keeping a taboo about consuming certain foods, including two types of vegetables, *ọ̀yọ́* (an okralike vegetable) and *òdú* (a spinachlike vegetable), which are often associated with Ọ̀yọ́-Yorùbá speaking people.

Odùduwà is very much a chthonic deity, symbolized in his relationship to *ilẹ̀* (the earth). Though as a celestial being he descended by a chain from his abode in the sky, once he got down and created the earth he maintained a strong connection to it. His disappearance was also through the earth's crust. He thus completed the full cycle of celestial, terrestrial, and chthonic realms, the three realms that make up the Yorùbá universe. Unlike other Ifè deities, whose fortunes are tied to one realm, as Òràmfè and Olúorogbo are to the celestial realm, Odùduwà's persona and ultimate strength are derived from the total energy of the universe. When the Ọbadìo or other devotees offer him palm wine libations, they pour them into a small hole dug in the floor, a sign of his connection with the underworld as well as the worlds above.

THE ODÙDUWÀ FESTIVAL

Announcement of the Date

To choose the date for the performance of Odùduwà, the priests consult the phases of the moon in the lunar calendar. The festival must take place in total darkness, when the moon has disappeared completely and the sun is nowhere in sight. The disappearance of the sun and the moon set the stage for the appropriate ritual time for the ultimate sacrifice that will bring about the renewal of the cosmos and the Ifẹ̀ world. The festival enters a liminal period symbolized by the darkness of ritual space and time.

Approximately fifteen days before the new moon in December, the priests of Odùduwà count the days to determine the actual date of the Odùduwà Festival on the Gregorian common calendar. Reconciling the two systems is a difficult task. Recently, the time of the Odùduwà Festival has been set to avoid both Christmas and New Year's Day holidays, so that "the Ọ̀ọ̀ni can have one holiday free to use the drums." The fourteen-day Odùduwà Festival forbids drumming, but the Odùduwà priests prefer to avoid holidays that other religious faiths celebrate with drumming. By conceding this privilege to the Ọ̀ọ̀ni, the priests are indeed thinking of the general public, because December, when the Odùduwà Festival falls, is a festive month for people of all religious beliefs in the city.

After determining the festival date, the priests send word to the Ọ̀ọ̀ni in the palace to inform him officially that they are "about to propitiate Odùduwà, the Ọ̀ọ̀ni's great ancestor." One priest told me, "It is his father's [the Ọ̀ọ̀ni's] ritual and he must not travel out of the city" (*Ọdún Bàbá rẹ̀ ni, tí ó bá ti bẹ̀rẹ̀, Ọ̀ọ̀ni kò gbọ́dọ̀ lọ sí ibikíbi*), a comment that may relate more to the past than to today.

Announcing the coming festival requires a ritual *(ètùtù)* of its own, which is described as bringing *ètùtù*, the propitiatory ritual. To seal this beginning ritual, by the order of Odùduwà himself, a decree prohibits drumming for seven days. This ceremony of prohibition, called *ikàlẹ̀*, marks the beginning of the great festival of Odùduwà.

Preparations

To prepare for the great ancestral Odùduwà Festival, all women of the lineage houses (Obìnrin Ilé) come together to clean the Odùduwà compounds and shrine. These women are the wives and mothers of the priests in the houses of the Idió lineage, especially the four important houses in the lineage of Ọbadìo. They sweep the entire area where the Odùduwà Festival will take place—including the front of the shrine and compounds, the Ọbadìo's lineage house, and the front yard of the grand palace *(ẹnu gbẹ̀ru)* of the Ọ̀ọ̀ni. As the cleaning and purifying take place, the euphoric Obìnrin Ilé sing traditional praises in high voices, in harmony, to Odùduwà, to their husbands, and to their husbands' lineage.

The great all-day, all-night vigil has begun. The women's singing alerts the public that the Odùduwà Festival is about to begin. As Karin Barber remarks, these women have an important role in Yorùbá festivals: to recount through family *oríkì* the myth, legends, and integrity of the lineage. As myth, the *oríkì* preserves cultural and personal memories and reminds hearers of the valor, deeds, and words of the ancestral lineage tradition. Although most women remain passive participants in these ancestral rituals, a few take on pivotal roles in the Odùduwà lineage traditions.

Opening the Ancestral Gate of the Odùduwà Compound

In the early morning of the first day of an Odùduwà Festival that I witnessed, the Ọbàlọràn, an Ọtún Ifẹ̀ and elder chief, had the honor of opening the gate of Odùduwà Shrine. Referring to the Ọbàlọràn as *dáúdù* (first child) of Odùduwà, the Ọbadìo told me that the Ọbàlọràn took precedence over the Ọọni in the context of this festival. According to the Ọbadìo, "If we fail to see the Ọbàlọràn, we can enter the compound, but we cannot approach the shrine of Odùduwà." This remark conformed to the Yorùbá rules of eldership, in which the first son presides over the ancestral rituals and social life of the lineage.

Referring to the sacrificial offerings to Odùduwà as *ẹrù Ifẹ̀* (Ifẹ̀'s load or offerings), the priests said their prayers at the shrine, requesting long life for the Ọọni, peace in the city of Ilé-Ifẹ̀, and prosperity for people of the city, the land of the Yorùbá, and the world.

The annual Odùduwà Festival began with early morning feasting at 5 a.m., a ceremony that my informant the Ọbadìo compared to the early meal (*sàrè*) during the annual Muslim fasting. The meal was called *ẹṣinṣin-kò-bà-lé-e* ("the fly does not land on it," indicating that the meal is so early that flies are still asleep). All the members of the Idió lineage (*eku Idió*) except the Ọbadìo himself gathered in the house of the Apènà Oòduà, an important chief in the Odùduwà cult, to partake of this familiar communal feast. The feast began with a morning invocation prayer for the success of the festival. Returning from the Apènà's house, the priests assembled in the Ọbadìo's lounge to partake in a greater, more elaborate feast.

Feasting and Ritual

Nearly all the people I interviewed mentioned that feasting was an important part of Idió Festival. Throughout the ritual sessions, abundant food and drink were served in the compound and homes of the priests. Feasting in the Odùduwà celebration is not purely ritualistic; it also has political aspects.[5] This is in keeping with the idea, maintained by some scholars, that feasting is not limited to rituals but is a more complex and diverse phenomenon.[6]

All the available evidence suggests that feasting in the Odùduwà ceremony is primarily a ritual event to honor the ancestors. However, feasting has political and economic implications in Ilé-Ifẹ̀ that go beyond mere ritual activity. The foods eaten, especially lamb, are the favorite foods of the gods, and most are gifts brought by the devotees to honor the deity in appreciation for his help the year before. Michael Dietler and Brian Hayden, as well as Barbara Mills, for example, have explained that in the postcolonial period before the modern economy emerged in the 1960s, wealthy market entrepreneurs, known as Ìpànpá, who were business and commercial intermediaries, contributed the animals used for feasting. Gradually, through their shrewd marketing, they and their families gained control of local trade in Ifè markets.[7] Thus the Ìpànpá were able to contribute gifts to Idió to recognize Odùduwà as ancestor and owner of the land upon which they realized great financial gains.

After feasting on sumptuous delicacies at the home of the Ọbadìo, the faithful traveled to Odùduwà Shrine, taking with them the instruments and ingredients needed for the fourteen-day festival. As soon as the festival began, as I mentioned before, an absolute taboo was placed on drumming throughout the city. Not the slightest sound of drumming was tolerated. For the duration of the festival, most of the high priests of Odùduwà resided in the shrine.

Ìwọlé Ọdún

This first ceremony is Ìwọlé Ọdún (Entering the Festival). In the evening of this first day, the Ọọni sent the Lọ́wá, the Ọọni's chief representative, to bring to Odùduwà Shrine all the necessary materials for the Odùduwà sacrifice. Chief Ọbadìo had to call on the Lọ́wá to present the king's gift and sacrificial offering to the priest of Odùduwà, the Ọbadìo, but first he had to be called to come out. Through a ringing chorus, the great assembly reminded the Ọbadìo that it was time for him to make his appearance.

> *Leader:* Lọ́wá, Lọ́wá, we are waiting!
> *Chorus:* Ọwá, we are waiting.
> *Leader:* Lọ́wá, you are welcome.
> *Chorus:* Lọ́wá, we are waiting.

Accompanied by two palace servants, the Lọ́wá brought the sacrificial gifts from the Ọọni. While the Lọ́wá held the sack containing the ingredients of sacrifice, two Ẹmẹsẹ̀ led two white sheep by a rope and followed the Lọ́wá to the Ọbadìo's palace. The Lọ́wá presented the gift on behalf of the Ọọni.

The Odùduwà Compound and the shrine within constitute the largest ritual space in Ilé-Ifè. The large compound and the shrine serve as "a symbol of established power" of the great god, Odùduwà.[8] Although the compound is securely walled and painted in stunning colors befitting the great ancestor god, it harbors no temple or large structure like Ifá's abode on Òkè Ìtasè Hill, only small, modest buildings and a small space where four of the previous Ọbadìo were buried at the

Odùduwà Shrine, the "powerhouse" of the entire compound. The compound has four gates—two located in front of the compound on the west side, one facing north, and another facing south. The front gates are the main entrances to the shrine; all others are closed to the public. Inside the compound are shrines belonging to important Ifè deities who had dealings with Odùduwà during his time. The Ẹlẹ́sìnjẹ́, Odùduwà's trusted medicine man, also has a shrine in the compound, as do Lémásanyìn, Ọbàtálá, Ọ̀ṣun, Ọ̀ràmfẹ̀, and Ọwá Agẹmọ.

Within the compound, worshippers refer to a very large well as ọ̀ṣundió, symbolizing one of the wives of Odùduwà. From this well, devotees draw water for cooking and household use. A well-built hearth and three big cooking pots are also located there. When I first met with the priests of Odùduwà, we sat under a small shelter built like a little house. The priests sat toward the front of the shelter and poured libations into a hole as they prayed to the deity. Perhaps the second most important sacred spot of the central shrine of Odùduwà is a small open space called àtọ̀runbọ̀, which means the place of descent from heaven. Believers say that it is the site Ọ̀ràmfẹ̀ used to descend from and ascend to heaven when he visited Ilé-Ifè.

The Ọbadìo's palace is located at the center of the compound, with small gate entrances leading into the courtyard. It is here that the Ọbadìo sits and holds court with his chiefs—Ọbàlùbọ, Ohùn Ọrun, Akómolẹ́jó, Akirun, and others—conversing and discussing the ensuing festival. As a sign of their unity and solidarity, they drink from the same small calabash.

In the ceremony that I witnessed, as I entered the dimly lit courtyard with my research assistant, Kẹ́hìndé Elújùlọ, perfect silence "greeted" us from every corner. But the members of the Ọbadìo's group greeted each other warmly, shaking hands with their left hand, and each of the chiefs knelt before the Ọbadìo, whom they referred to as Ọba (king).

> Wórí wórí wórí
> Ìre rẹ́ á dọ́run
> Ètùtù rẹ́ á gbà
> Ẹṣin á jòko
> Igba Ọdún àrìmọ̀kà
>
> We greet and salute you!
> Your prayer will ascend to heaven!
> Your propitiation will be acceptable!
> Your horses will eat splendid grasses! [There will be abundance]
> You will live two hundred years on earth! [Live long on earth!]

Those assembled asked the gods for long life, peace, and happiness and requested that the Ọbadìo's years on earth would pass with ease. All the priests were clad in seamless white robes. Clothing the priests was a skilled job, and some of the junior members who helped the others to robe took pride in how proficiently they could

FIGURE 23. Chief priest of Odùduwà in a house prayer ritual.

tie the cloth round the priests' bodies. When these junior members, especially the youngest ones, came into the shrine, they entered through the north gate and shouted in a loud voice, "*Ooooo*." The group around the Ọbadìo knew the people belonging to the group that was arriving and responded:

> *Ọnà yà à à.*
> *Ó yà peregede.*
>
> The road is clear.
> It is very clear and you may enter.

To reaffirm the space in which they were assembled, one or two members called out, *Ilédì?,* and the rest replied in the affirmative, *Ilédì Oòduà* (the court of Odù-duwà). The question was rhetorical in the sense that although it was known to all present that the sacred site was indeed Odùduwà's place of residence, but it was important to reaffirm the assembly's purpose at such an auspicious hour of the day.

Before the ceremony began, members inspected the *ẹgánrán*, the main percussion instrument used in the Odùduwà Shrine, to ensure that it had been ritually prepared for the ceremony. Since Odùduwà had forbidden drumming, the *ẹgánrán* produced the musical voice for the liturgy instead. The *ẹgánrán* was a set of iron gongs that produced exhilarating rhythms of percussive sound when beaten together. Some musicians were especially trained in this art. Every initiated priest of Odùduwà had the responsibility of bringing the *ẹgánrán,* a symbol of the superiority of Odùduwà, out for ritual and ceremonial use. Just as the iron gong *(agogo)* produces the leading tone in a musical assembly, so Odùduwà is the leader of the deities, and thus the *ẹgánrán* must take first place among similar ritual objects of the gods.

The Ritual Drama of the Odùduwà Ceremony

Beginning in the late evening, after everything had been made ready for the celebration, ritual performances concerning the life of Odùduwà in the mythical story of Ilé-Ifè became the focus of activities. The devotees seemed to be reliving the mythic history in chronological sequence. The ritual drama began with a song of homage to the principalities and powers in the Ifè cosmos, inviting them to descend and join the living in renewing the cosmos. The vocalists described themselves as entertainers *(aláré),* announcing that they prayed to the gods to allow them sing well, to remove any impediment from their voices, and to clarify the sound of their voices.

The Ọbadìo himself then led a ritual procession to the shrine of the Odùduwà, followed by one of his chiefs, the Ọbàlùbọ, then the mace bearer, and then the other priests. The Ọbadìo stood facing the shrine directly as one of his lieutenants (also clad in white robes) stood facing him. Then the first phase of the program commenced with ritual dancing and singing. The Ọbadìo himself, who was the featured vocalist, led the ritual opening with great glee.

> *Ègbè kò aláré de o!*
> *Ègbè kò aláré de!*
> *Ègbè kò aláré de o!*
>
> Sing out! The performers have come!
> Sing out! We have come!
> Sing out! The performers have come!

The initial singing and dancing of this night assured us that the ritual performance, though involving moments of great solemnity, would also involve the moments of fun, joking, and play that are so typical of Ifè celebration.

The singers now invoked the ancestral gods and the deities of heaven, asking them to descend and renew Ilé-Ifè's world:

> *Àà Ọdún dé o*
> *Àà Ọdún dé*
> *Eégún ayé éé o o*
> *Èṣibá Ọ̀run*
> *Èrò̩ wá o káṣe fẹ̀*
> *Èrò̩ wá o*
> *Ọdún dé*
> *Àà éé e a a*

> The festival is here!
> Ancestral spirits,
> Gods of heaven,
> Come down, let us rejuvenate Ifè!
> Quickly come down!
> Our festival is here!

In another year, a similar song was performed enthusiastically:

> *Olú Ayé o Èṣìbá Ọ̀run o*
> *Èrò a ó Ṣèbà!*
> *Ohùn ayé, ọ̀run o*
> *Èrọ̀ a tún dé!*

> Lord of the Universe and Divinity of Heaven,
> Descend and hear us perform our homage!
> Voice of the people of the earth and of heaven,
> Descend! We gather here again to make sacrifice!

Just as Odùduwà had relied on supernatural forces to create Ilé-Ifè, so his priests called on them to assist in renewing the Ilé-Ifè cosmos. By tapping into the primordial source of life through praying, ritual chanting, playing the *ẹgánrán,* and dancing, Odùduwà devotees secured an immediate response to their propitiation.

This act of calling supernatural ancestral beings to "descend" may be viewed as an attempt by the priest to invoke the primordial time—what Australian aborigines called the "dreamtime."[9] For the Yorùbá, the sacred primordial time at the beginning of the creation of the world *(ìgbà ìwásè)* is very different from the distant past *(ìgbà láé láé)* and the immediate past *(ìgbà àtijọ́).* This particular way of marking time is very different from Western notions of time. By reaching far back to the "origin" of time, the Yorùbá were here not only renewing their connection with their god-king ancestor but also reaffirming their place in the larger cosmic order.

At the beginning, the music seemed a bit dull, but as time went on, the whole performance became more lively, and before long almost every participant became carried away in its rhythm and melody. Some turned ecstatic in the ritual dance, and a beautiful rhythm was evident, even in the voice of the old priest, the Ọbadìo.

One significant aspect of this festival is that it is invocative, requiring both the priests and the worshippers to call aloud the names of the gods, the priest, the primordial divinities, and the divine ancestors. The Ọbadìo called members of Odùduwà's priestly class, one by one, and they answered dutifully in a call and response manner:

> Ọbadìo: *Ọbàlùbọ! Ọbàlùbọ! Ọbàlùbọ! Wá jẹ́!* [Come and answer us]
> Ọbàlùbọ: *Arère, arẹ̀sà* [I am here].
> Ọbadìo: *Ọṣìnlúbọ! Ọṣìnlúbọ! Ọṣìnlúbọ! Wá jẹ́!*

Ọṣìnlúbọ: *Arère, arẹ̀sà.*

  Ọbadìo: *Ohùn Ọ̀run! Ohùn Ọ̀run! Ohùn Ọ̀run! Wá jé!*

Ohùn Ọ̀run: *Arère, arẹ̀sà.*

After the roll call of Odùduwà's priests, the Ọbadìo called the gods through their respective priests, who were present as the guests of Odùduwà at his feast. Each priest had his own song, and each was called to answer the voice of Odùduwà. For instance, the Lókòrẹ́, the chief priest of the deity Ọbamerì, a warlord and supporter of Odùduwà, was called. But first, Ọbadìo invoked Ọbamerì through Ọbamerì's chief priest, the Lókòrẹ́:

> *Lókòrẹ́! Lókòrẹ́!*
> *Lókòrẹ́! Lókòrẹ́!*
> *Lókòrẹ́! Lókòrẹ́! Wá jé!*

And the Lókòrẹ́ answered the caller:

> *Arère, arẹ̀sà. Arère, arẹ̀sà.*
> *Mo mí bọ̀ á tún Ifẹ̀ ṣe.*
> I am coming to reshape Ifẹ̀ [or make Ifẹ̀ better].

Then Ọbadìo the invocator and lead dancer, led the ritual dance to a song that went as follows:

Leader: Gbogbo Olókòrẹ́ mọ̀-ọ́n jo o Igboróye

Chorus: Gbogbo Olókòrẹ́ mọ̀-ọ́n jo Igboróye

Leader: Gbogbo Olókòrẹ́ dèyìn wá o Igboróye

Chorus: Gbogbo Olókòrẹ́ mọ̀-ọ́n jó Igboróye

Leader: All Lókòrẹ́ are good dancers.

Chorus: All Lókòrẹ́ are good dancers.

  Lead: All Lókòrẹ́ will come back [to remake Ifẹ̀].

Chorus: All Lókòrẹ́ are good dancers.

Having sung the chorus, the *ẹgánrán* players went into action. Accompanied by other chiefs, the Lókòrẹ́ began dancing vigorously. Chief Lókòrẹ́ performed one of the most spectacular dances I had ever witnessed in an Odùduwà celebration. Speaking for the Ọbamerì, Odùduwà's warlord and general marshal, the Lókòrẹ́ answered the call of Odùduwà as his great ancestor and leader and assured Odùduwà that he would always be there to make whole the city of Ilé-Ifẹ̀.

Presently, we entered ritual time. Assured that the ancestors and the gods were indeed present, the Ọbadìo started the sacrificial process. Chief Erédùmí, as the chief sacrificer, responsible for killing the *iwọ* (sacrificial animal), offered the five-toed hen, the tortoise, and kola nuts to Odùduwà. The great crowd sang these words:

Ògungbẹ̀ Ògungbẹ̀
Ògungbẹ̀ Ògungbẹ̀
Án mọ̀ í báhun kù fe.
Ògungbẹ̀ Ògungbẹ̀

No one must cut (kill) the tortoise halfway.

As Erédùmí prepared to cut the tortoise in half, a series of songs were performed in sequence in the vicinity of the shrine, invoking the power of Odùduwà and his priests. These songs evoked fear, laughter, and serious reflection upon the power of the deity. Many of these songs joked about the Ọbadìo and the role he played in dispensing sacrificial gifts brought by the devotees. The songs highlight the role that humor and jokes can have in these rituals and festivals.

I.

Leader: He [the Ọbadìo] gave us what belongs to another person.

Chorus: He gave us another person's belongings.

Leader: He gave us another person's yam.

Chorus: He gave us another person's property.

Leader: He gave us another person's fish.

II.

The Ọba is enjoying.
He is enjoying.
The Ọba is enjoying.
He is enjoying.

III.

The money is not enough.
It is not enough for Olufẹ́'s [Ọ̀ọ̀ni's] ritual.
The money is not enough.

IV.

Ọbadìo: The Ọba is going upstairs [to the sacred precinct].
He is going.
The Ọba is going.
He is going.

V.

Lọ́wá: Let whoever owns a slave protect his slave,
         The Leopard is about to strike.

Chorus: Let whoever owns a slave protect his slave,
         The Leopard is about to strike.

That night, a call was made to the Ọọni through Chief Lọ́wá, his emissary. In the Odùduwà Festival, the Ọọni is the chief celebrant because the festival is performed to his ancestor, Odùduwà. Hence, the Ọọni provides all the things needed to make the sacrifice successful. At one point, the songs informed the Lọ́wá that the gathering was anxiously awaiting him.

Gbogbo ria wọhún wọnà
Á mà á fun rere pè
Lọ́wá, Lọ́wá, a mà, mí wọnà o
Ọwá, an mọ̀ mí wọnà o

We are all waiting!
We are calling you to answer us!
Lọ́wá, we are anxiously waiting!
Ọwá, we are waiting!

The Lọ́wá appeared with the sacrificial objects, and prayers were offered for him, the Ọọni, his chiefs, the Ilé-Ifẹ̀ people, and the whole world. At the second collection of gifts from the Lọ́wá, before the great sacrifice, the Ọbadìo faced the north end of the palace and invoked the spirit of Ọọni to send the Lọ́wá down again. The Lọ́wá replied from behind the curtain that he was on the way. The singing rang out again.

Sing out!
We musicians have arrived!
Sing out, we are here!

Éè [Listen]
Ọba wí éè [the Ọba [Ọọni] has spoken, listen].

The Sacrifice (Ìpiwọ̀)

After midnight, in the dark of night, the rite of animal sacrifice (Ìpiwọ̀) to Odùduwà took place. The group filed out from the shrine in the compound to the outer area near the Ọọni's palace. Tied to an ancient tree, a sheep called *iwọ̀*, given by the Ọọni and dressed in human clothing, awaited the sacrifice. A sheep or lamb is not commonly offered as sacrifice in Ilé-Ifẹ̀, but this passive, calm animal is peculiar to Odùduwà and is seen as an important surrogate for the human sacrificial victim. Human clothing symbolizes the human victims who were used for sacrifices in previous times, as was the custom in many ancient civilizations the world over.

Then the Erédùmí, who emerged suddenly from a hidden spot, sacrificed the sheep. Dressed in attire that was medicinally protected, the Erédùmí had to display the power of a strong sacrificer worthy of Odùduwà, cutting off the head of the animal in one stroke of the sword. To fail to do so was utter abomination. When the moment came to perform this feat, the group sang to empower him.

> *Erédùmí ó mà múdà le!*
> *Ọrùn àgbò mà yi o!*
>
> Erédùmí, hold fast the sword!
> The neck of the lamb is unyielding!

To make this ritual killing possible, the sheep had to be magically weakened. Odù-duwà's symbol of power, his mace *(ọrún)*, was used to make this happen. When it touched the animal, the *ọrún* stilled the animal, and its energy gradually ebbed away. It was no wonder that the Ọbadìo constantly reminded me, *Agbára Odùduwà pọ̀* (Odùduwà is a powerful deity).

The neck of the animal was severed in one stroke. This method of killing is common for animal sacrifice to deities classified as "hot" and "tough," such as Ògún and Odùduwà. The sacrifice signals the mode of sudden and immediate death in battles and wars. Unlike killing by "throat cutting and death through the resulting exsanguination," the ritual of decapitation symbolizes the power and force typical of the deity, power that is privately revealed and relived on this night of sacrifice.[10] With the sacrifice completed, the blood was collected and taken to the shrine of Odùduwà to further revere the ancestor. Once the job was done, the Erédùmí immediately left the gathering.

Immediately after the ritual killing, the Ọbadìo collected the head of the animal in a calabash and proceeded to the inner place of the Odùduwà Shrine to offer the sacrifice. Another priest, following him, took the remainder of the sacrificial elements that had been used to complete the ceremony. The lyrics changed to reflect this event of blood sacrifice.

> *Ọba mà mí mèjè*
> *Ó mèjè*
> *Ọba mà mí mèjè*
> *Áá mèjè.*
>
> The Ọba is drinking blood,
> He is drinking blood.

The Ọbadìo moved slowly from the lower side of the shrine to the small elevated zone where Odùduwà's shrine was located. The cadence of the next tune, sung by his priests and devotees, kept pace with this slow walk.

> *Ọba mà ń gòkè*
> *Ó ń gòkè*
> *Ọba mà nń gòkè*
> *Ó ń gòkè*
>
> The Ọba is ascending,
> He is ascending,

The Ọba is ascending,
He is ascending.

This song suggested that the Ọbadìo, in going to the upper part of the shrine, was metaphorically ascending to a ritual space above the human realm. The shrine was the place of ultimate sacrifice, where the images of Odùduwà, hidden from all but the Ọbadìo, were propitiated on behalf of the Ọọni.

After offering Odùduwà the head of the animal, the Ọbadìo offered other sacrificial elements as well to the ancestral god. Though many other songs were sung in praise of Odùduwà, the Ọọni, and the chief priest, the Ọbadìo, one in particular should be mentioned, the one that confirmed that the sacrifice was efficacious and acceptable to the ancestor god and the spirit world. A song inviting the vulture to eat the sacrifice was followed by this:

> Àrékérekè o o ee.
> Igún fìwọ jẹ.
>
> We have witnessed the truth
> The vulture has devoured the said *iwọ*.

In Yorùbá thought, as in Tibetan thought, vultures carry the sacrifices to the gods. A sacrifice left untouched by vultures is one that the gods reject.

Once the sacrifice was accepted by the gods, it was assumed that the forces that had threatened the city and the cosmos had been destroyed. The cosmos had been regenerated, potential death averted, and life renewed. Lifting the taboo on drumming indicated that the ritual process was complete.

The flow of ritual prayers, jesting, and laughter—and at times, somber reflections upon the sacrificial event—should be put into context. Themes of slavery and stubbornness emerged in the ritual drama of the sacrifice, recalling the past, when human victims, mainly foreigners and slaves, were offered. As was quite typical of Ifẹ festivals in general, the ritual songs were sung in a "non-solemn, informal, often joking manner, characteristic of feast itself."[11] The feasts were a mixture of sacred and secular processes, mingling as ordinary and sacred times intermingle. Besides, play, jest, and merriment can be considered routes to transcendence and the sacred.

Ìtẹ́ni Ọta and Ìwúyè Mọlómù

The next day continued with feasting in the Odùduwà Shrine to celebrate the visits of all the key chiefs in town, as well as the Àwòrò chiefs (Ìṣòrò) and the public. In the Odùduwà tradition, feasting defined the relationship between priestly authorities and political authorities. The ritual hierarchy was reflected in the order of hosts and timing of the feasts. A grand feast arranged for the Ọtún Ifẹ (the senior chiefs and civil leaders) served as a reminder of the role they played in Odùduwà government. While the priests in order of their rank took turns providing food for

the public and visitors, Chief Ọbàlùbọ, who was next in rank to the Ọbadìo, entertained the Ọ̀tún Ifẹ̀, who were next in rank to the Ọọni, reflecting the ranking
order of the political and civil authority of Ilé-Ifẹ̀.

Two groups of people in the Odùduwà household, the Ìṣòru (those who had undergone the nighttime initiation) and the Ìṣọ̀sán (those who had undergone the daytime initiation) held feasts for the groups. The Ìṣòru, the superior level of initiates,
prepared pounded yam, while the Ìṣọ̀sán, the lower initiate group, prepared palm
wine according to their ability.

On the third day of the festival, called the Itá ceremony, the women of the house
honored Odùduwà through the priests. They bought a fat sheep (àgùntàn bòlòjọ̀)
to thank Odùduwà for making them secure as mothers and wives in their husbands'
homes. As the child bearers of the lineage, they thanked, as one priest called him,
"their 'husband' " (Odùduwà). The idea implicit here was that these wives and mothers had been strengthened over the past year by the ancestral god. Ọbadìo Fágbulé,
who had been the reigning Ọbadìo five years earlier, told me that there was no part
of Odùduwà tradition that women did not know about (kò sí nǹkan tí àwọn obìnrin
kì í dá sí) and that "on the day of prayer, all the women in the Ọbadìo's house join
hands to celebrate." Although they did not partake in the esoteric part of the rituals, they were still very knowledgeable about the traditions.

Merrymaking continued unabated on the sixth day of the festival, called Ìtẹ́ní
Ọta or Ìtẹ́ní Oòduà, the special day for the Ọ̀tún Ifẹ̀, the eight senior city chiefs, to
honor Odùduwà. Ìtẹ́ní refers to spreading a mat for someone to sit upon, similar to
"rolling out the red carpet" for the dignitaries, the Ifẹ̀ chiefs. Ìtẹ́ní Ọta honored them
as Odùduwà's assistants in governing the city (àwọn tí ó ń ba ṣe ìjọba rẹ̀). The chiefs
served by the divine grace of Odùduwà, who had created the political structure and
given them the authority to administer the realm for him. Ìtẹ́ní Ọta is a day of prayer
for civil high chiefs and an opportunity to affirm the authority of their position by
relating it to the founding ancestor of Ilé-Ifẹ̀.

The Ìtẹ́ní Ọta was also the festival day for the women of the lineage, when all
married women prepared a feast and brought food to Odùduwà's place, in a ceremony called Ìwúyè Mọlómù. In the past, it was mandatory for all city chiefs (Ọ̀tún
Ifẹ̀) to visit the shrine, and the Odùduwà people feasted and danced for them
(tewa)—after which they went to Chief Ọbàlùbọ's house, where he too provided a
big feast for the high chiefs.

Mímú Ètùtù: Bringing the Sacrificial Blessing to the Palace

Mímú Ètùtù was the seventh day and the midpoint of the festival. It was a day of
prayer and sacrifice, marking the end of the strict prohibition on drumming during the first seven days of the Odùduwà Festival. On this day, festival participants
went to the palace with sacrificial objects, after which drumming was renewed by
Odùduwà's divine command so that other festivals could follow.

Interestingly, this day also marked the beginning of the festival of Ọbàtálá, Odù-duwà's archrival, again an indication of the ritual hierarchy that governed Ilé-Ifẹ̀ by which the Ọbadìo held the first place in Ilé-Ifẹ̀ religious structure. Although he was senior god in the Yorùbá pantheon and was regarded as the most senior of the deities in Ilé-Ifẹ̀, Ọbàtálá was relegated to second place in the hierarchy after the creation of Ilé-Ifẹ̀ City. But according to Ọbàtálá's chiefs, only they and no priests of other deities in Ilé-Ifẹ̀ could remove Odùduwà's taboo on drumming at the intersection of the two festivals. *Ìlù tí Odùduwà tì, Ọbàtálá ló lè ṣí i* (Odùduwà prevents drum-ming, but only Ọbàtálá's priests can remove the taboo), an Ọbàtálá chief claimed, apparently in reference to their own power. In reality, however, Odùduwà's people lifted the drumming taboo themselves.

Palẹ̀mọ́: Ending the Festival

From the eighth day, when the Ọbadìo prepared yet another feast for the Idió people, until the fourteenth day, when the festival ended, the Idió chiefs held feasts by ro-tation. The divination ceremony ending the Odùduwà Festival is called Palẹ̀mọ́ (packing). Celebrants perform whatever sacrifice Ifá recommends before leaving Odùduwà's compound. That sacrifice, called *àrúfín*, the sacrifice accepted by the gods, is a confirmation that previous sacrifices and offerings have been accepted. Thus the devotees sang:

> *Àrúfín ẹbọ àrúdà*
> *Àrúfín ẹbọ àrúdà*
> *Ilé- ire o*
> *Àrúfín ẹbọ Ọ̀ọ̀ni*
>
> Our sacrifice is accepted by the gods!
> It is time to depart.
> A propitious sacrifice is complete.
> The Ọ̀ọ̀ni's sacrifice is accepted by the gods!

REAFFIRMATION OF ODÙDUWÀ'S POWER

The entire Odùduwà ritual recalls the drama, at the time of the creation, of the con-flict between Odùduwà and his rival god of creation, Ọbàtálá, and the victory of Odùduwà over his rivals and enemies, including other aboriginal deities that pre-date his appearance in Ilé-Ifẹ̀. It was also a gathering of Odùduwà warlords and med-icine men who came to Odùduwà's aid in establishing the Ifẹ̀ cosmos. In this re-newal ritual at the end of the Ifẹ̀ ritual calendar, Ifẹ̀ priests honor the primordial power and energy of the creation and bring it into the present. Odùduwà, the an-cestor god, is the only deity who can bring this about.

The festival that I attended began in the big compound of Odùduwà with the convocation of the gods of the land, including the gods of conquered lineages and rivals of the ancestral god, Odùduwà. The Ọbadìo, the chief priest of Odùduwà, informed me that no god in the Ifẹ̀ pantheon was left out of the affairs of Odù-duwà. Indeed, many gods occupied spaces in the form of shrines in the Odùduwà compound.

The roll call of the gods carried out by the Ọbadìo ensured that each god was present. The gods answered the call through their high priests, stating their roles and the assignments they had been given by Odùduwà in rejuvenating the Ifẹ̀ cosmos. Ọ̀ràmfẹ̀, for example, answered that he would descend from Òkè-Ọ̀rà (the first "moun-tain" of the created world, which emerged when the five-toed guinea fowl brought by Odùduwà clawed the earth from the primordial waters) to remake Ifẹ̀. Ọbamerì, the warlord, answered that he would return to help Odùduwà remake Ilé-Ifẹ̀.

The ceremony also conveys Odùduwà's power to conquer all the natural forces that were unleashed against him at the time of the creation. As one of the *oríkì* says, he fought and defeated the sun, fire, and water. Like the deity Huitzilopochtli in the Mesoamerican world, he is hailed in Yorùbáland as "the supreme controller of all the creative forces of nature."[12]

The sacrifice of the *iwọ* is the climax of the Idió Festival. As further evidence of the festival's orientation to the ancestors, a lamb is offered as an animal for the an-cestral spirits. We noted in previous chapters that while a dog is offered to Ògún in Ọlọ́jọ́, and a goat to Ifá in his own festival, it is a lamb that Odùduwà takes. It is, however, a lamb with a difference, because the animal wears human clothes. The his-torical narrative of the ritual may explain why Odùduwà is an esoteric ritual whose cult is kept within the lineage except for Odùduwà's war allies, who are brought in as invited guests to feast, dance, and demonstrate their allegiance to the god-king to help rejuvenate Ilé-Ifẹ̀. The present Ọọ̀ni once reminded me, *Ọba ìlú ò ní jẹ́ kí ìlú òun tú* (The king in charge of the city would not want the city to disintegrate). The preservation and renewal of this sacred city require rituals of sacrifice to the gods and the ancestors, to whom the mysteries of the Ilé-Ifẹ̀ universe were revealed at the time of creation. The festival brings to the forefront the pivotal role of Odù-duwà in Ilé-Ifẹ̀ cosmology.

PART THREE

9

The Changing Face of the City

Royal Narratives and Contested Space in the Palace

This chapter and the next are based on my research in Ilé-Ifẹ̀ in December 2004, a year after I had completed the fieldwork for the book manuscript. The new field research was necessary to inquire into rumors that the Ọ̀ọ̀ni, Okùnadé Ṣíjúadé Olú-bùṣe II, had renounced his sacred status and that evangelical Christian agents were increasingly displacing òrìṣà devotees. I sensed that if the Ọ̀ọ̀ni had, in fact, abandoned the òrìṣà tradition, this would constitute a radical religious change in the heartland of Yorùbá city-states. It would also require me to reassess the status of the ideology and rituals of the Yorùbá sacred kingship that I had described in my previous book, *Kingship, Religion, and Rituals in a Nigerian Community*. My two interviews and meetings with the Ọ̀ọ̀ni and his wife, the Olorì, Morísádé Ṣíjúadé, Yèyélúwa of Ilé-Ifẹ̀, were set up to ascertain the extent to which the sacred kingship was still the pivot of the sacred cosmos that Ilé-Ifẹ̀ represented and also to examine the role of the Olorì in the religious changes that were taking place in the city.

This chapter situates current changes in Ilé-Ifẹ̀ religious life in the context of the history of Yorùbá religion and the comparative history of religions. Ultimately, I argue that their meaning and interpretation are deeply embedded in indigenous Yorùbá traditions. As these religious traditions continue to interact and meet in this space, they convey profound social, historical, and theological meanings.

In December 2004 I interviewed the Ọ̀ọ̀ni, Ọba Okùnadé Ṣíjúadé Olúbùṣe II, face to face in his ààfin. Since becoming king in 1980, Ọ̀ọ̀ni Olúbùṣe, as a million-aire Ọba, has used his wealth, power, and prestige to transform the architecture of the city and rebuild and add to his palace. The Ọ̀ọ̀ni had just returned from Abuja, Nigeria's national capital, where he had been summoned to settle state matters. He knew I was waiting for him, and he sat down briefly to welcome me and to set a date for a more in-depth conversation. Given the opportunity to tell him of my mission, I did not hesitate to express my concerns about the continuing viability of traditional Ifẹ̀ religious practices. I posed a series of questions to the Ọ̀ọ̀ni: Did he remember his grandfather, Ọ̀ọ̀ni Olúbùṣe I? How did he himself understand his status as Aláṣẹ, Èkejì Òrìṣà (Vice-Regent of God)? What did he think about himself as the successor and reincarnation *(àrólé)* of Odùduwà? What did he think about the religious discord in Ilé-Ifẹ̀, about the murmurings among the priestly class that the Ọ̀ọ̀ni was no longer interested in supporting the practices of the *òrìṣà* tradition? What was the current status of Ifẹ̀-Modákẹ́kẹ́ relations? These pointed questions were meant to initiate a discussion about the changing character of the city, especially as the city was striving to maintain its ancient identity in the face of the powerful forces of modernity, recent Christian and Islamic revivalism, and the current discourse on developing Ilé-Ifẹ̀ City. Below I quote excerpts from the interview, which provides a background for discussing the social and cultural drama unfolding in the city today.

After expressing my gratitude to the Ọ̀ọ̀ni for taking time to talk to me, I asked him direct questions about his divine status in Ilé-Ifẹ̀:

> Your Majesty, Kábíyèsí [King], I am happy to speak with you on a number of issues, and I would prefer hearing directly of your more personal reflections on these issues. The first question relates to your role as the Ọ̀ọ̀ni, the Ọba of Ilé-Ifẹ̀, the overall Ọba of all the Ọba in your domain, and the head of the Yorùbá and Ilé-Ifẹ̀ City. How do you view your status and role in Odùduwàland? The second question relates to the Americas and Africans in the diaspora. We have visited a number of places outside Nigeria and talked to people in Brazil, Cuba, and Trinidad, where you are viewed as God.

On hearing this, the Ọ̀ọ̀ni immediately denied his divine status. "There is only one God, and that is the Supreme God on High, Ọlọ́run," he declared, pointing his finger upward toward heaven. His acolytes, the Ẹ̀mẹ̀ṣẹ̀, responded in unison, *Kábíyèsí, Alàṣẹ Èkejì Òrìṣà, Ọmọ Irúnmọlẹ̀* (Your Royal Highness, one whose power is like that of the gods, descendant of the 401 deities of the Yorùbá pantheon). For me, this interjection paradoxically affirmed that the Kábíyèsí spoke nothing but the truth, that his words were law, and that he was indeed perceived to have descended from the gods, contrary to his own claim.

"Kábíyèsí," I continued, "I am interested in the kind of legacy you will leave behind for Yorùbá affairs and for Ilé-Ifẹ̀'s future."

The Ọ̀ọ̀ni realized that the questions I posed deserved deep thought and reflection. He knew that I had just a few more days before returning to the United States and that I had made many trips to the palace trying to meet with him. He asked for more time, and we agreed on December 27, the day before my departure to the United States, as the date for a formal interview. According to custom, the Ọ̀ọ̀ni arranged for a carol service to be held December 24, attended by nine or so local Ọba from surrounding towns and villages. At the service, I was again formally introduced to the Ọ̀ọ̀ni by the provost of Saint Philip's Cathedral, who had been my student at Ọbáfẹ́mi Awólọ́wọ̀ University and was now serving in the church where my late father had worked.

THE Ọ̀Ọ̀NI'S CHRISTIAN CAROL SERVICE

Important local Ifẹ̀ dignitaries attended the Ọ̀ọ̀ni's carol service, as well as several Ọba from surrounding towns and villages and a number of priests from local churches. The Ilé-Ifẹ̀ Baptist Church, Ẹlẹ́yẹlé, took the lead in arranging for this year's service, which was very colorful indeed, with drumming, songs sung by various denominational choirs, biblical lessons, and a sermon. When the provost of the Anglican Cathedral, Reverend Adétunbí, rose to introduce important guests, he mentioned my name as a visiting professor from the United States and as the son of the beloved late archdeacon of St. Philip's Anglican Church, where the provost now served. Overcome with emotion on hearing my name, an elderly Baptist pastor who had ministered in the city when my father was a priest informed the congregation that he and my father had been the first to engage in weekly prayer at the palace during the Ifẹ̀-Modákẹ́kẹ́ crisis in the 1970s. After the service, the elder showed me the place in the palace where they had formerly knelt down together to pray for peace in Ilé-Ifẹ̀. Immediately, I realized that my family was an integral part of Christian evangelical tradition whose expansion into the palace I was now trying to understand. To my great surprise, after the announcement the king departed from his custom of sitting on the royal throne to give felicitations. The Ọ̀ọ̀ni *stood up* to offer thanks. It was then that I realized a new order was in place in the palace. Was the Ọ̀ọ̀ni also among the born-again Ọba now occupying Yorùbá palaces?

EVANGELICAL "BORN-AGAIN" THEATER
UPSTAGES ANCIENT ÒRÌṢÀ TRADITION

The men and women of the Baptist Church Ẹlẹ́yẹlé, where Reverend Mamadelo was a priest, staged a theatrical production to accompany the Ọ̀ọ̀ni's carol service. It was not at all like the usual depictions of Christ's nativity in a manger, nor was it like any biblical play I could remember from my youth. Instead, the dramatic piece was a satire recounting the story of an imaginary town called Ìlú Aríjẹ. It was a morality play intended to depict the downfall of traditional Yorùbá òrìṣà religion and the ascendancy of evangelical Christianity.

The drama began as a large group of actors dressed in the elaborate Yorùbá traditional attire of an "Ọba-king," an "Olorì" (the king's wife), "chiefs," and followers proceeded to center stage, where the carol service was just ending. This colorful procession was led by a very young girl in a traditional òrìṣà dress who carried a ritual stool on her head; just after her was an actor who appeared as one fully possessed, representing Ìyálórìṣà, the priestess who incarnates Yemòó (the wife of Ọbàtálá) in the Ọdún Ìdìta Festival to the deity Ọbàtálá. In the drama, the "king" of Ìlú Aríjẹ welcomed his "subjects" and called on the town's diviner to perform the annual divination to see what the New Year would bring for the town's people. After consultation with an Ifá diviner, the town's Ifá priest announced to the audience, Ifá fọre (Ifá predicts good tidings), indicating that all would be well in the coming year. The "king" or "Ọba" announced the forthcoming national Ayò Festival (Ọdún Ayò), asking for peace among the people. However, the drama took a bizarre twist when two important lineages of the town staged a skirmish. The drama intensified as a mock battle left many actors lying about the stage "dying" and "wounded." A "town crier" went about the terrorized "city" trying to summon people back to the palace in a futile attempt to stop the violence. In despair, the Ọba of Ìlú Aríjẹ asked if Ifá should be consulted again to find the source of rancor in Aríjẹ, to obtain a solution to the crisis, and to bring peace again to the region. However, as art imitated life, the actors rejected the old religion by shouting in prolonged dramatic unison, "No!" In a dramatic final scene, the wife of the king, the Olorì, emerged, holding up a Bible as an instrument of peace. Dismissing their former òrìṣà, the performers readily "accepted" the book and the new religion. Signifying the ascendancy of evangelical Christian ideology, the performance closed with a celebrated Christian hymn, Bíbélì Mímọ́ ti ọrun (Holy Bible of the Heavenly Place). This powerful symbol of Christianity, the Bible, has figured prominently in many accounts of conversion among the Yorùbá.

This "nativity" drama signified a theatrical fusion of the ancient indigenous òrìṣà religion and the recently introduced Christian dispensation. I was so absorbed by the scene that I forgot to take a picture of the performance. The girl carrying the stool on her head resembled the young girl who serves as an Ìyálórìṣà (Yemòó) acolyte in the Ọbàtálá Festival. In that festival (described in chapter 5), Yemòó, in a trancelike state, leads the procession of Ìdìta people to the palace, bearing the sacred ẹ̀rọ̀ (bottled medicinal water) to give to the king. Ifá consultation had always been a regular feature of palace life. Through the divination process, the king's Ifá priests unraveled past, present, and future events and prescribed the appropriate rituals to ensure a peaceful year. But all of these attempts had failed, as the play clearly demonstrated, signifying the weakening structure of òrìṣà religion and the inability of Ifá, the most sacred source of Yorùbá knowledge, to predict and control events accurately. Although such plays are not new in Christian evangelical circles, the Olorì, the wife of the Ọba, took up a new leading role in the drama. This may reflect the new role of the Olorì generally, who throughout Yorùbáland are fast replacing the Ìyálórìṣà priestesses of the ancient Yorùbá tradition as powerful religious leaders. They have emerged as agents of Christian evangelical conversion.

SACRED KINGSHIP: A DYING TRADITION IN ILÉ-IFẸ̀?

Several days after the "nativity" performance, the Ọ̀ọ̀ni instructed his security guards to clear the way for me when I arrived for our tête-à-tête. The impromptu questions I had posed at our first meeting represented a new dimension of my work as much as they reflected a crisis in the city's shifting religious ideology. When I spoke to the Ọ̀ọ̀ni addressing him as a deity, he immediately denied that he was a god, stating that there was only one God, the Supreme God. I wondered if the Ọ̀ọ̀ni's sudden renunciation of his divine status represented a radical departure in thought and practice from Yorùbá religious beliefs and practices. However, without exception, the Ọ̀ọ̀ni's emissaries, the Ẹmẹsẹ̀, continued to reiterate to me their king's divine status. They insisted on calling their king Ọmọ Irúnmọlẹ̀ (Child of the Deities). This, coupled with their Ọ̀ọ̀ni's rejection of his own divinity, further complicated my ability to analyze the extent to which evangelical doctrine was replacing òrìṣà traditions.[1]

As a young man attending church services at St. Philip's Anglican Church, I had listened to my father, the archdeacon, read the prayer for the king (Ọba) from the Anglican Book of Prayer. On numerous occasions as I heard my father's words, I had conjured up the image of the Ọ̀ọ̀ni as King of Kings (Ọba Àwọn Ọba) and Lord of Lords (Olúwa Àwọn Olúwa)—although I knew very well that the liturgy my father read was intended to invoke Jesus Christ himself as King of Kings. Besides, the Yorùbá call the Ọba Èkejì Òrìṣà, one who has godly power. As Pemberton and Afolayan reminded us earlier, "The Ọba's power is like that of the gods" (Kábíyèsí! Ọba aláṣẹ ẹkejì òrìṣà!). The title Ọba is still an appellation and symbol of kingship, authority, and power applicable to the Ọ̀ọ̀ni and Yorùbá Ọba in general.

On the one hand, I wondered to myself, "Did the Ọ̀ọ̀ni actually intend to renounce his own divine status?" And on the other hand, "Were the Ẹmẹsẹ̀ affirming his renunciation or rejecting it in a contradictory manner?" By calling him Ọmọ Irúnmọlẹ̀ (Child of the Deities), the Ẹmẹsẹ̀ suggested that despite his denial of his own divinity in Ilé-Ifẹ̀ and in the Yorùbá imagination the Ọ̀ọ̀ni was actually perceived as a god, the last in the number of the Yorùbá pantheon of deities. Why, then, did the Ọ̀ọ̀ni renounce his divinity? To what extent did this renunciation reflect changes in the sacred city? Had the Ọ̀ọ̀ni converted to radical evangelical Christianity, the type that, along with Islamic sects, had rocked many Yorùbá cities and towns to the extent that some kings had abandoned their own local deities? Did these kings prefer to visit the revival camps of Pentecostal-Charismatic churches and Islamic mosques, seeking their salvation elsewhere? Was the Ọ̀ọ̀ni counting himself among the born-again prophet-kings?

SACRED LINEAGE AND TRADITIONAL RELIGION:
THE KING SPEAKS FROM THE HEART

Given the opportunity to interview the Ọ̀ọ̀ni at his palace in Ilé-Ifẹ̀, I decided to speak to him about the ambiguity of his divine status and the signs of evangelical zeal impinging on òrìṣà traditions. Sitting in a sprawling open-air space in the inner part of the palace not too far from the Ọ̀ọ̀ni's swimming pool, I found myself in the influential company of Ọba Ọlásore of Ìlokò, the Ọba of an Ìjèṣà town who was visiting the Ọ̀ọ̀ni; the late Chief Ọmọ́tọ́ṣọ̀ọ́ Elúyẹmí, Ifẹ̀'s cultural historian and archaeologist; the acolytes and attendants of the Ọ̀ọ̀ni; and the Ọ̀ọ̀ni himself.

Since the Ọ̀ọ̀ni's coronation, I had followed the events of his reign and had observed him closely. In addition, I had become familiar with the archival materials describing the Ọ̀ọ̀ni's grandfather, Olúbùṣe I. In both of them I observed similar personalities and temperaments—both could be described as highly charismatic, affluent, bold, diplomatic, and very generous. I turned to the Ọ̀ọ̀ni and asked, "Did you know your grandfather?"

The Ọ̀ọ̀ni's response was compelling. He began to speak about his grandfather's prediction of his grandson's (the current Ọ̀ọ̀ni's) birth in Ilé-Ifẹ̀ and described his own close encounter with death, a profound experience in which he felt that God had saved him. Hence he believed he should never equate any mortal being, such as himself, with the great immortal God. The Ọ̀ọ̀ni spoke of events before his birth:

> I never knew my grandfather, Olúbùṣe I. He died before I was born, but he left a name for me to bear, that I should be called Saliu [indicating that his grandfather was a Muslim]. My mother knew my grandfather. He predicted to my mother that she would one day marry his son and that the child born by her would wear the crown.

The Ọ̀ọ̀ni's acolytes interjected, *Aláṣẹ òrìṣà. Ọba kí ọ* (The king greets you), and the Ọ̀ọ̀ni continued the story of events before the marriage of his parents:

> But my grandfather [Bàbá Àgbà] was the one my mother really wanted to marry. The story began when my mother was a marriageable young woman. She came to the palace to watch the Ọlọ́jọ́ Festival. She saw the Ọ̀ọ̀ni wearing the colorful arè [crown] and was greatly impressed by him. When she got back home, she told her mother that she had met the Ọ̀ọ̀ni and immediately had fallen in love with him [Ó re òun]. Her mother kept her quiet. "Never let people hear you say that," she said to her daughter. After the festival, my mother went to the farm with her mother, where they normally spent a sojourn of close to three months. When they returned home, they called their Alfa [Muslim cleric] to pray for them and to check on her daughter's future. The Alfa consulted a diviner [a practice associated with popular Islam], and he asked what she had seen lately in the palace. My grandmother remembered that my mother had visited the palace a few months ago, where she had seen Ọ̀ọ̀ni Olúbùṣe I wearing the arè.
>
> So my grandmother talked to Ọwá Erédùmí, the priest of Ọ̀rànmíyàn, who was

her uncle. The Erédùmí normally visited the palace every day, where he paid obei-sance to the Ọòni. My grandmother then asked the Erédùmí to take the young girl (my mother) to the *ààfin* on his next visit to tell Kábíyèsí what the young woman had said. My mother then went to the *ààfin* with the Erédùmí. After he saluted the Ọòni, the Erédùmí introduced the young lady to the Ọòni (my grandfather) and told him what my mother had said: "This was the young lady who came here during the Ọlọ́jọ́ Festival, who told her mother that she loves you!" My grandfather then offered his prediction to her: "You will marry the child whom I bear, and the child born into the marriage will be king." He then asked for a white china bowl, placed cowrie shells in it, and prayed with it. He encouraged her to come regularly to the palace. After three months, my mother met a man who later would become one of my uncles, called Ade-farati (Saaji), and was introduced to him, but she did not like him. The second time she came to the palace, she met my father [the Ọòni's father], who liked her, and they got married. So what my grandfather [Bàbá Àgbà] had said earlier came to pass.

Again, the Ọòni's attendants interrupted, referring to him by praise names: *Kábíyèsí, Aláṣe Èkejì Òrìṣà, Ọmọ Irúnmọlẹ̀*. That was how the Ọòni narrated and interpreted his birth and his relationship and connection to the grandfather he had never known, who had predicted his birth.

I moved to the next section of the interview, asking the Ọòni a question on re-ligious conflict in contemporary Ilé-Ifẹ̀ and Yorùbáland.

> Kábíyèsí, kindly permit me to go into the issue of religion. As I informed you, I have been working to document the history of our indigenous religious *òrìṣà* traditions. I have observed our major traditions, festivals, and ceremonies in Ilé-Ifẹ̀, and I have noticed that these traditions are changing fast. Here in Ilé-Ifẹ̀ City and in Yorùbáland, conflict over various religious beliefs erupts sporadically. Islam and Christianity are becoming increasingly more visible and militant in their encounter with our tradi-tional Yorùbá culture. The model of religious tolerance that you follow is an ideal, which, as I understand it, affirms the long-standing religious pluralism of Yorùbá-land. It is an attitude of "live and let live" in which religion may be pursued as God reveals it. Nothing prevents an Ọba [king] from being a born-again Christian, but an Ọba should never bar his subjects from practicing their own religion. We noticed that religious intolerance is creating widespread tension. Some Ọba claim to be "born again," ceasing to propitiate the community *òrìṣà*, denouncing this tradition from which they obtained their crown. As the most prominent Yorùbá king on the throne of Odùduwà, what do you say to this?

I continued my line of questioning, pressing the issue of participation:

> Kábíyèsí, Your Majesty, in your city of Ilé-Ifẹ̀ we see evidence of much conflict and animosity among *òrìṣà* devotees and Christian denominations. Throughout Yorùbá-land, there is evidence that some Ọba are promoting this conflict by refusing to par-ticipate in the ancient *òrìṣà* tradition of their people. What is your stand on this issue?

The Ọọni responded thoughtfully:

> What I intend to tell you is as follows. Any country that fails to promote its own culture is not a country worth being in. Look at my emissaries [the Ẹmẹṣẹ̀]. Notice that they wear no shoes in the places where the Ọọni sits. That is our custom and tradition.

And yet, I thought to myself, earlier in the Ọọni's presence I had removed my cap, as Yorùbá tradition demands I do to revere his exalted position as god, king, and ruler of Yorùbáland. However, the Ọọni requested that I put my cap back on my head. Some customs were changing, but it was difficult to know which ones. The Ọọni continued to explain his position on some of the city's ancient sacred customs:

> About religion—there is something upon which our kingship is based— *Ó ní ohun tí Ọba jòkó lé lórí.* Whether we like it or not, we must maintain it as the spiritual foundation of the Yorùbá. It is clear to me that we can do nothing without worshipping God. There are different ways each religion worships God. Christians and the Muslims worship the same God. There is only one God. I go to the mosque and the praying ground [the Muslim Yidi]. I go to church, and I participate in the traditions of the *òrìṣà* people— that is, Ọlọ́jọ́. Ọlọ́jọ́ is the main tradition of the Ifẹ̀ people, whether they are Christian, Muslim, or devotees of *òrìṣà.* Ọlọ́jọ́ is Ifẹ̀'s principal religious tradition. The Ọlọ́jọ́ Festival Day is the day I wear the *arè*. All the people come out to see the *arè*. As they see the *arè*, they begin to pray that they may see the *arè* the following year. Their general belief is that through this prayer God will preserve them until the next year's celebration, so it is difficult to erase this belief. If the *"little little"* Ọba claim that they no longer want to participate in this tradition, then they are deceiving themselves. When you are installed as Ọba, there are things you promise to do. Before you can claim to be an Ọba, there are things that you eat that make you an Ọba, and things you swear to do, and that is what is called to be an Ọba, before you can truly call yourself an Ọba. I see nothing wrong in being a Muslim or a Christian in our own tradition.

THE ỌỌNI RENOUNCES HIS DIVINE STATUS: MIRACLE AT ÀPÁPÁ HOUSE

The Ọọni began to tell the story of his narrow escape in his Lagos mansion at Àpápá House. According to the Ọọni, he had been visiting Àpápá House with some forty Yorùbá Ọba and other dignitaries. His second wife, stationed in Lagos, had just gone out to run errands. In addition, the Ọọni's security guards had left to procure their midday meal. The Ọọni and his party carried on, and at some point during the conversation a professor in attendance addressed the Ọọni in the proper parlance as God. In a shocking and unprecedented pronouncement, the god-king abruptly declared, "I am no god." At once, the entire entourage was dumbfounded.

Not quite five minutes after the Ọọni's astounding declaration, a large number of armed robbers brandishing heavy machine guns (AK-47s) made their way into the exterior compound of Àpápá House, attempting to force their way into the interior quarters, where the Ọ̀ọ̀ni was seated with only his entourage for protection. They could hear the thugs attempting to gain entry, fumbling with the somewhat tricky interior door lock that confounded their entry. But before the assailants could force their way inside, quite by coincidence, police sirens started to wail on the street outside. Thinking that the police were coming for them, the would-be assailants fled the palace immediately. The Ọ̀ọ̀ni and dignitaries were astounded but greatly relieved to reflect on their narrow escape.

This brush with death took place almost immediately after the Ọ̀ọ̀ni had told the professor to refrain from addressing him as God. The traumatic experience certainly may have influenced the Ọ̀ọ̀ni's decision to reevaluate his divine status and quite possibly reinforced the notion that the Christian God had intervened to save his life. I confirm this claim because in my conversations with him and the Olorì there was significant evidence that the Ọ̀ọ̀ni's Christian identity trumped his participation in òrìṣà ceremonies and rituals. The Ọ̀ọ̀ni's personal and total surrender to the new dispensation cannot be ignored. Yet he sees as his obligation the duty of an Ọba to keep propitiating Ilé-Ifẹ̀'s ancestral deities. It is just such a cognitive dissonance that characterizes Yorùbá sacred kingship today. I will explain this development further in the next chapter. As the Yorùbá would say, *Àjẹ́ ké lánàá. Ọmọ kú lónìí. Ta ni kò mọ̀ pé ajẹ́ àná ló pa ọmọ je?* (The witch appeared yesterday night and a child died early the next morning. Who doesn't know that it was the witch of yesterday that killed the child?). The Ọ̀ọ̀ni's response referring to his encounter with death came just after my question about his participation in the Christian tradition and the dilemma he faced concerning the increasing neglect of òrìṣà tradition in Ilé-Ifẹ̀.

In my interview with him, perhaps the clearest sign that the Ọ̀ọ̀ni was changing his perspective about his own divinity came when he expressed his views on King Nebuchadnezzar, the Old Testament king of Babylon who willfully disobeyed God. When Nebuchadnezzar compared his own power to that of the Supreme God, he perished because of his arrogance. The Ọ̀ọ̀ni certainly did not want the people to perceive him as an arrogant king, and perhaps the trauma of the almost fatal encounter with armed thugs had convinced him of his vulnerability and mortality.

The Ọ̀ọ̀ni's comments on the state of Ilé-Ifẹ̀ City and his role in maintaining tradition reflect only a minor part of the changing times. As the preeminent Yorùbá Ọba in the Yorùbá kingdom, he was aware that other kings or Ọba took on pivotal roles, serving as unifiers of their communities in a pluralistic society. As a symbol of Ilé-Ifẹ̀ City unity, the Ọ̀ọ̀ni maintained the traditional role of the Ọba, acting in accordance with his title of Custodian of All Religions, Ọba Ónígbogbo Èsìn. He proudly told me that he owned exquisite copies of the Holy Qur'an and the Holy Bible, asking if I wanted to see them. Chief Ọmọ́tọ́ṣọ̀ọ́ Elúyẹmí, who so far had sat quietly listening to the conversations between the Ọ̀ọ̀ni and me, quickly added that the Ọ̀ọ̀ni owned the most excellent divination chain, *ọ̀pẹ̀lẹ̀*, in the palace. Thus the

Ọ̀ọ̀ni and the chief wanted me to know that in keeping with the kings of old the Ọ̀ọ̀ni acknowledged and safeguarded all the various traditions within his kingdom equally.

In 1945, at the close of the World War II, the Allied forces demanded that Japan's 124th emperor, Hirohito, renounce his divinity to signify the Japanese defeat. His coerced renunciation compelled the people of Japan to question their sense of their own status—associated with the emperor's—and broke the spirit of thousands of his soldiers who were still fighting in the name of their emperor-god. Recently, in the Nigerian city of Ilé-Ifẹ̀, in Yorùbáland, something similar happened. The current Ọ̀ọ̀ni, Ọba Okùnadé Ṣíjúadé Olúbùṣe II, suddenly renounced his traditional status as sacred king, the Aláṣẹ, Èkejì Òrìṣà (Vice-Regent of God) of Ilé-Ifẹ̀. Instead, he said, there was only one Supreme God. Unlike Emperor Hirohito, however, the current Ọ̀ọ̀ni renounced his divinity voluntarily.

As we learned in chapter 2, it was this king's grandfather, Ọ̀ọ̀ni Olúbùṣe I, who had embraced the British colonial power in Nigeria a century ago. In an unprecedented move in 1903, Ọ̀ọ̀ni Olúbùṣe I left his palace for the first time to visit British Native Authority Council members in Lagos, then the capital city of Nigeria. At the request of the British, the Ọ̀ọ̀ni Olúbùṣe I agreed to decide a thorny question: Who among the Yorùbá kings was entitled to wear the sacred crown? His trip brought on great panic among the people of Ilé-Ifẹ̀ and other Yorùbá kings. In the end, however, the British acknowledged the Ọ̀ọ̀ni's help by anointing him king of the Yorùbá, king of kings. He was given funds to take care of himself and his palace, and in theory the British "restored" his place in Yorùbá life.

Ultimately, this event proved to be a turning point in Ifẹ̀ and Yorùbá history because it signaled Ilé-Ifẹ̀'s first encounter with modernity. Now, a century later, the current king's renunciation of his divinity indicates a new stage in the Yorùbá negotiation of modernity. This event raises a number of questions. Most importantly, why did the current Ọ̀ọ̀ni renounce his divinity? To what extent does this unprecedented renunciation reflect larger questions about conversion, agency, and modernity in the city of Ilé-Ifẹ̀?

This chapter examines the winds of religious change currently blowing over Yorùbá nations and ethnic groups, particularly changes in the Yorùbá understanding of sacred authority and their causes. Among the forty million Yorùbá in southwestern Nigeria, these changes must be seen in light of an increasing conversion to Pentecostal and Charismatic evangelical Christian movements, the retreat of the gods in indigenous Yorùbá religious practices, and the decline in what I called, in my previous work, Yorùbá "civil religion." I will show that the Yorùbá's initial encounter with modernity—over a century ago—did not destroy the legitimacy of the sacred kingship as more recent religious movements have attempted to do. For these movements, allegiance to the one Supreme God is incompatible with support for the institution of the sacred kingship.

In considering these tensions, I will draw upon my recent field research in Ilé-Ifẹ̀ to examine the continued validity of theories of religious change as discussed by such scholars as Robin Horton, David Laitin, Jean and John Comaroff, Barbara Cooper, and a host of others in an effort to explore the ways that early missionization was tied to particular forms of hybridity. By contrast, the contemporary period has favored a more radical departure from the past, a reordering of the old cosmology and the assertion of new sources of knowledge. Part of this examination will include a consideration of gender in relation to the changes in Ilé-Ifẹ̀, in order to demonstrate the ways that religious change and social change are diverging.

INTERPRETING THE Ọ̀ÒNI'S RENUNCIATION OF THE SACRED KINGSHIP

Today, the contested status of the Ọ̀ọ̀ni's sacred authority illustrates and places the Ọ̀ọ̀ni himself at the center of the confrontation between older and the newer approaches to the negotiation of modernity in Ilé-Ifẹ̀. Bombarded from all sides, he sees that the way he positions himself in the current battle for the soul of the ancient city will, in large part, determine its future. In response to the question, "Why did the Ọ̀ọ̀ni renounce his divine status?" I will suggest that the Ọ̀ọ̀ni, in a psychocultural context, is plunged into a certain cognitive dissonance—a desire to reconcile himself to his own doubts about his divine status.[2] This suggestion could explain some of the concerns the Ọ̀ọ̀ni expressed or implied in his interview with me. However, this suggestion avoids making an incautious or presumptive guess about whether the Ọ̀ọ̀ni's renunciation indicates his definitive conversion to the new Christian movement.

The Ọ̀ọ̀ni's cognitive dissonance can be understood, at least in part, as a conflict between the sacred status accorded to him in indigenous Yorùbá tradition and the strongly pragmatic emphasis of that same tradition—an emphasis that might sanction his renunciation of the sacred kingship if it no longer met his own needs or the needs of his people. In the cosmology of Ilé-Ifẹ̀'s ancient òrìṣà tradition, the position of the Ọ̀ọ̀ni occupies a central role. Unlike the Mesopotamian model of kingship, in which the king is merely a representative of God on earth, the Ọ̀ọ̀ni of Ilé-Ifẹ̀ is God himself (Ọ̀ọ̀ni-Rìṣà), the last of the 201 gods in the Ifẹ̀ pantheon. Yet the arrival of Christian missionary movements in the late nineteenth and early twentieth centuries, and Islamic movements that occurred even earlier, did not bring this sacred kingship to an end.

Rather, the òrìṣà traditions tied to the sacred kingship were recognized and manipulated by the British, as the example of the current Ọ̀ọ̀ni's grandfather shows. Since that time, the sacred kingship has held a certain hegemonic claim on the city as its civil religion. Although Islam and Christianity have been important players in Ilé-Ifẹ̀'s social structure, until recently neither of these two traditions has rivaled the indigenous *òrìṣà* religion in producing the sort of overarching civil religion or hegemonic value system upon which I built my earlier thesis in the book *Kingship, Religion, and Rituals in a Nigerian Community,* and which Laitin also mentions.[3] This civil religion, or sacred canopy, has bound together a pluralistic religious, social, and cultural polity. The Ọòni has been regarded as the "Custodian of All Religions" (Ọba Ónígbogbo Ẹ̀sìn)—including Christianity, Islam, and indigenous religion—and has served as umpire between the two sometimes warring monotheistic traditions brought by missionaries. Irrespective of the personal religion of any particular sacred king, the ideology and rituals of the sacred kingship have helped to maintain significant peace in Ilé-Ifẹ̀.

The sacred kingship has been able to flourish as an institution because of accommodationist attitudes on the part of the earlier missionary movements and indigenous religion alike. The earlier period of religious conversions, particularly in the late nineteenth and early twentieth centuries, saw frequent compromises between indigenous religion and mission Christianity. As Jean and John Comaroff have argued, Christianity and indigenous religious traditions changed each other in their encounters with and negotiations of religious beliefs and practices.[4] Although Christianity and Islam sometimes espoused exclusivist worldviews, they were usually flexible enough to recognize the sacred kingship. At the same time, the pragmatism and dynamism inherent in the Yorùbá approach to religion allowed for *òrìṣà* devotees partially embedded in mission Christianity and Islam to juggle the two religious systems—indigenous *òrìṣà* and monotheistic traditions—by selectively embracing those aspects of the new traditions that they found useful. In this context, Ọlábíyìí Yai has remarked that for the Yorùbá people tradition and custom means *àṣà*—that which we select and use.[5] Some scholars have argued, for example, that the final god in the Yorùbá pantheon—the 201st or 401st god—shows the possibility of adding more gods in response to new situations and needs, while old gods—such as Sònpònná, the god of smallpox—recede into oblivion as the need that they serve disappears. This pragmatic approach to religion among the Yorùbá is expressed in a familiar proverb: "If a god doesn't work, you can cast him into the bush" *(Òrìṣà tí a kẹ́ kẹ́ kẹ́ tí kò gbọ́ iké inú igbó níí gbé).* If a god fails to respond to one's earthly needs—fertility, wealth, longevity, and peace—then one can seek salvation elsewhere.

Given that the Yorùbá find no room for idle gods, I would submit that the Ọòni is ambivalent toward the *òrìṣà* tradition. The efficacy of the indigenous *òrìṣà* tradition and the sacred kingship rooted in that tradition is called into question precisely because of the pull in two different directions from both the devotees of the *òrìṣà* and the devotees of Christianity and Islam. In line with other traditional rulers who have publicly renounced indigenous religion, the Ọòni may have decided to reevaluate his divine status—in his case partly because his near-death experience suggested to him that it was the Christian God, rather than the deities of the indigenous *òrìṣà* tradition, that saved his life. Moreover, because the people of Ilé-Ifẹ̀ have been fighting an intractable civil war with the neighboring Modákẹ́kẹ́ people for the greater part of the Ọọ̀ni's reign, he may have concluded that the indigenous gods are in retreat and are therefore no longer worth propitiating.

Why was the Ọọ̀ni convinced that it was the Christian God who had saved him from the threat of the AK-47-wielding robbers? Given that it was the arrival of the police—who are identified with the deity Ògún because of their protective role—is it possible that Ògún, whom the Ọọ̀ni propitiates in the Ọlọ́jọ́ Festival, was the being who actually saved him? Was this traumatic incident an attempt on the part of the gods to remind the Ọọ̀ni of his presence in the affairs of the sacred king? Given the Ọọ̀ni's full-scale knowledge of Yorùbá religious traditions, could this possibility not have occurred to him? Associated with Islam from birth through his grandfather, raised a Christian, and then initiated into the *òrìṣà* tradition by virtue of his position as the Ọọ̀ni of Ilé-Ifẹ̀, he has had a whole array of religious and moral systems to deal with and respond to on many different levels—from private to public.

CONVERSION AND THE NEW FACE OF MODERNITY IN ILÉ-IFẸ̀

Today, in Ilé-Ifẹ̀ and throughout Yorùbáland, newer Pentecostal, evangelical, and "born-again" Christian movements that first emerged in the 1970s and 1980s are challenging the institution of the sacred kingship and the pluralistic order that has existed for over a century. These movements epitomize a new form of modernity encroaching upon Ilé-Ifẹ̀. Amid hundreds of evangelical Christian programs, revival meetings, open-air services, and nightly vigils taking place in the city, a newly emergent form of discourse is pushing evangelical Christian activities beyond the arena of the churches and private spirituality to public spaces, thereby directly challenging the *òrìṣà*-based civil religion that has been in place. I should add that whereas in the Western world the crisis of modernity often connotes a struggle between religion and secularity, Ilé-Ifẹ̀'s current struggle over the negotiation of modernity concerns which form of religion will control its center and civic life.

This newer negotiation of modernity is driven by generally exclusivist religious movements whose theology subsumes the entire cosmos and its inhabitants under a single divine order, ruled over by a Supreme God. This theology renders implausible the older order, according to which there exists not only the sacred kingship but also a diverse range of spirits and ancestors. As a result, this shift of sacred power and authority—from rulers and principalities that inhabit the living world to a single divine order inhabiting an invisible world (called heaven)—creates significant tension between devotees of the *òrìṣà* and members of the new, predominantly Christian, movements. In short, these new movements challenge existing assumptions about what it means to be human in the cosmos and how civil authority is to be understood. According to these new movements, all kings are simply human beings. Thus no king has any inherent religious or earthly authority that gives him power as head of the community, as the chief priest of the local civil religion. Central to this message is an emphasis on the personal salvation of individual converts. Moreover, unlike indigenous traditions, which were concerned with the temporal domain and a this-worldly proximate salvation, the new movements place significant emphasis on otherworldly salvation and benefits. Kings have become more concerned with their own personal salvation than with the proximate salvation of their people as a whole. Each individual is left to fight for his or her own salvation.

Members of these new Christian movements are targeting the sacred authority of the Ọ̀ọ̀ni, and Ilé-Ifẹ̀ civil religion more generally, because they realize that debunking the legitimacy of the sacred canopy—the guardianship of religious pluralism—will make it possible to destroy all indigenous non-Christian Yorùbá traditions. While this kind of exclusivity is often associated with the European and American missionary enterprises of the nineteenth and twentieth centuries, I have shown that their accommodationist orientation actually tended to support a role for indigenously based Yorùbá civil religion. Rather, native Yorùbá are driving this second, far less tolerant, mode of conversion. Although the new Christian movements are part of a global effort to usher in a universal Christian moral and social order, the conversion tactics employed by native inhabitants of Ilé-Ifẹ̀ are specifically adapted to their local context. These individuals are able to explore and exploit, to their advantage, their knowledge of the indigenous òrìṣà tradition in order to turn that tradition against itself. They draw upon the indigenous tradition's pragmatic orientation—its emphasis on religion's use value—but claim that indigenous beliefs and practices no longer have such use value because they no longer meet people's needs.

Thus these new movements often blame disorderly events—particularly those perceived to be obstruct societal progress—on the continuance of traditional òrìṣà religious practices and ways of life, which are regarded as "pagan." Among these events are pestilence, natural disaster, famine, disease (especially the AIDS epidemic), and military coups, all of which are seen as signs of divine anger and Satan's presence. Paradoxically, whereas indigenous religions have claimed that they were indeed performing rituals, engaging in calendrical ceremonies and holding festivals to explain, predict, and control natural phenomena, the new Christian movements have claimed that destructive natural phenomena and events are caused by the continuation of these very "pagan" rituals and festivals. Evangelical Christianity's desire to trump indigenous religious symbols and practices has effectively devolved into a declaration of hostility and war against indigenous traditions. As the cultured despisers of indigenous practices, these new Christian movements aim at doing away with any forms of local knowledge, language, and ethos, even when they do not have any apparent religious connection. For example, by discouraging the use of vernacular liturgy and local dialects, members of these new movements aim to preach a universal message that is ultimately of global, rather than purely local, reach.

THE AMBITIONS OF NEW RELIGIOUS MOVEMENTS

Several questions present themselves regarding the practical outlook and ambitions of these new movements. To what extent are the older and newer approaches to negotiating modernity intertwined within Ilé-Ifè civil society and the public space? Are the new movements widely regarded as central to the evolution of contemporary African society? Are they more intertwined with governance and the state than the older Yorùbá civil religion?

The impact of these new Christian movements has much to do with the institutionalization of transnational alliances that augment the resource reach of the individual churches and the entire Pentecostal-Charismatic movement. The Pentecostal-Charismatic movement has become central to governance and the public space. Such movements link successfully with the local, regional, and global economic network, resulting in overwhelming growth. They have become a deeply institutionalized form of religion, which, over fifty years of growth, has become embedded in the economy, politics, and infrastructure of the nation-state.

Though the first missionary movement, dating back to the nineteenth century, was foundational to the influence of national leaders of the preindustrial and industrial era, the newer Christian movement is increasingly becoming identified with the building of civil society and the governance of African nation-states, especially in Nigeria. Their social actions and activities are increasingly set in the space formerly reserved for the activities of civil society. For example, in Nigeria, more than 70 percent of public universities founded in the last decade were built and constructed by evangelical Christians. Interestingly, these evangelicals place a significant emphasis on the character of the students at such universities, which is why they insist that, through education, they can refashion the morals of society. They place less emphasis on support of religious studies or seminary curricula than on providing technical training and a practical business education. These universities place a strong focus on producing new technocrats, computer-savvy bankers, and the like. In this sense, they are in fact the vanguard of a new form of education and modernity that seeks to compete with the West on the West's own terms.

Just as in the precolonial and colonial period, the nineteenth- and early twentieth-century missionary movements played a significant role in the emergence of the new elite that still continues to govern Nigeria, the new Christian movements are now competing to produce a new elite that would wrest away the influence that has, up to now, been derived from that earlier missionary legacy. However, the new Christian movements see their ultimate goal less as simply taking the reins of power, with the temptations of corruption that doing so may bring, than as establishing and maintaining a new social and moral order.

To have political legitimacy in Nigeria today, one must be perceived to be a "born-again" Christian, just as in the far northern region (home of the so-called Sharia states), one must be a devout Muslim. Thus religion plays a very significant role even in the so-called "secular" states of Nigeria today: it is central to the goal of building intertwined institutions and governance. We are now witnessing the rapid growth and institutionalization of these new religious movements. The new postcolonial formation connects these Pentecostal-Charismatic movements with the West in a way that did not occur with earlier missionary movements.

We should also point out that some scholars have mythologized religion, emphasizing the religious economy of the state rather than the social construction of faith and spirituality and its impact on civil society and the public space. Although this new movement involves economic networks as well as other aspects of the society and public space (including health, politics, and education), its ultimate goal is to make religion relevant to the affairs of the state and to create foot soldiers who will be responsible for ushering in the new moral order. As such, the community envisioned by these new movements is a religious, economic, and political community. It therefore challenges the hard-won goal of secularization and calls into question the notion that European modernity must leave religion and spirituality out of its idea of progress and the construction of a new society.

While the Comaroffs have provided a useful framework for describing Africans' response to modernity, their theory does not address the condition of this new movement from the 1990s onward.[6] Although they were basically thinking about South Africa, they made a useful case for the link between a growing political economy and the explosion of the church, looking at the social implications and manifestations of the early forms of the Christian movement. The demands of the new movements that are competing with indigenous faith challenge the sacred kingship and traditional religious institutions. While the Comaroffs talk about the public space and social change, they are concerned with presenting a materialist explanation of the impact of this religious movement and exploring the ways that, in different locations, the colonized and the colonizer have mutually shaped each other's worldview.[7]

In the Nigerian context, where the contemporary encounter involves a different form of interaction, we can ask: What is it about this movement that enables new forms of hegemony over the pockets of traditional religious institutions? One may argue that Comaroffian schools of thought, concerned with the political economy of religion and the mutuality of hegemony, cannot adequately address these questions and indeed fail to account for the contemporary explosion of the Pentecostal-Charismatic movement in places such as Nigeria. This movement is very intolerant of the indigenous religious worldview and moral order and seeks to overturn it and implement what its members think is a more plausible answer to the existential questions of daily life.

A DETERMINED OLORÌ WELCOMES
CHRIST INTO THE ILÉ-IFẸ̀ PALACE

We must look at other sources to understand how the renewed forces of Christianity are sweeping into Ilé-Ifẹ̀ in a surge of Christian revival meetings. My encounter with Olorì Yèyélúwa Morísádé Ṣíjúadé provided clues to the changes that were taking place in the palace, to the disappointment and rage of the traditionalists. I was left with the impression that she was very much like the Olorì whom I recalled from the dramatic performance after the Ọ̀ọ̀ni's carol service on December 24, 2004. Yèyélúwa Morísádé Ṣíjúadé seemed to resemble the lead actor in the play who gave the Bible to the king and to the town of Aríjẹ as a way of ending their communal conflict.

Yèyélúwa Morísádé Ṣíjúadé is the Olorì and most senior wife of the Ọ̀ọ̀ni. A native of Ifẹ̀ from a prominent Aládúrà Christian family, the Máyọ̀wá, she had been raised as a staunch Aládúrà Christian, and she claimed that she had never departed from that path. I was informed that she held regular weekly Christian rituals in her own quarters of the palace. She resides in a two-story building, one of the landmarks of the palace. It has its own enclosure and a large space where she runs her own business and attends to her visitors from Ilé-Ifẹ̀ and elsewhere. My participation in a December 23, 2004, carol service in the Olorì's palace chapel set the stage for my interview with her and with the provost of the Anglican Church. Seated in an audience of eighty devotees, I was privileged to attend a service in which the royal choir sang many anthems and over which the chapel priests presided. One could say that it was indeed a national Christian choir, drawn from Anglican, Baptist, and African churches and from all the Christian denominations of the city. They performed a repertoire of various anthems from African American soul music to ethnic Igbo and Yorùbá songs about the birth of Jesus in Bethlehem. The royal children sat respectfully at the front row facing the clergy. A visiting priest read the lessons as various Christian priests offered prayers. During the service, I was not surprised to see that the Olorì Ṣíjúadé was wearing a magnificent headdress and textiles of woven cloth signifying royalty. But she took an inconspicuous seat by the door at the rear of the chapel, like a churchwarden, quietly following the proceedings until she was called to the front to offer words of thanks to the participants. When the Olorì took the microphone to sing praise songs, her zeal electrified the whole chapel.

Her passion signified her belief that God guaranteed Christians and the Elect "victory" over trials and tribulations if they would serve him faithfully.

After the service, the provost of the cathedral introduced me to her formally and commented on the Olorì's belief in the power of prayer and the Christian God who protected the Ọ̀ọ̀ni from physical harm or assault:

> Yèyélúwa, out of her search for God, built this place for prayer. Any time there is a need for prayer and fasting for the Kábíyèsí (the king) and the city, she called us all to the palace for days of fervent prayer. But for her prayers, the Kábíyèsí would be no more.

Olorì Yèyélúwa Morísádé Ṣíjúadé graciously agreed to an interview.[8] In an exquisite section of her palace residence, she held court for over three hours, describing her enthusiasm for the "new" Christian rituals. Our conversation focused on the spacious new royal chapel, which was separate from her quarters and large enough to accommodate throngs of worshippers. In her own quarters of the palace, she had raised funds to construct a quiet chapel for prayer, begun in 1986 and finished in 2004. The Olorì explained that she had built the chapel as a sacred space for prayer in which the Christian God could intercede on behalf of the king and the Ilé-Ifẹ̀ community.

The meeting with the Olorì confirmed all the rumors I had heard that the royal Olorì had initiated and directed the extraordinary construction of a Christian chapel, named Royal Chapel, at the Ọ̀ọ̀ni's palace. The Olorì narrated her story as one of initiating progress and modernity. Christian hegemony was ethically superior to the former palace tradition of òrìṣà religion, she claimed. The interview with Yèyélúwa Ṣíjúadé was one of the most interesting conversations I have had in Ilé-Ifẹ̀. It took place early in the morning when she was just getting up from an all-night private prayer vigil. As I entered her living room, she instructed her attendant to bar anyone from disturbing our conversation. Although our full discussion could form the subject of a book on its own, I will outline here briefly the issues we discussed: religious discord in the city, the Olorì's belief in the efficacy of prayer in the city's quest for peace and progress, and her position on indigenous òrìṣà traditions and the reformation of òrìṣà practices.

INTERVIEW WITH THE OLORÌ

Olúpọ̀nà: Tell me a little bit about this chapel and your role in its construction.

   Olorì: You see, generally, in the palace, we used to have fellowship every morning, and all the Christians come around to participate in it.

Olúpọ̀nà: When did this start? Do you remember? Has it been long?

   Olorì: Long ago, over twenty years ago, we held fellowship in the multipurpose hall in the center of the palace, but as time went on we decided to build a separate place of worship in my compound. As you know, my father was a member of the Christ Apostolic Church; I was born into the Aládúrà faith. I organized my own house fellowship with my workers, sometimes holding morning prayers, sometimes night vigils. Although we had a general hall in the palace, I needed a place to spend my weekdays of prayer without interference, where I could offer my private prayers. I informed Mohammed, who is head of security in this palace, that I wanted to erect a chapel in my residence, in my private quarters. I called a minister of God to lay the foundation; we blessed the land. And I gathered my staff, everybody together to start on build-ing a chapel. Initially, the Kábíyèsí was unaware we were starting con-struction, but the provost and others knew when we had begun. We asked God if he would want us to embark on this, and he told us to go ahead. I called Chief Adégòkè to tell him, "I am building a chapel. I need cement." He replied, "Send your staff to collect money for the cement and construction." So one day the Kábíyèsí drove to my quarters. Seeing the construction, he inquired, "What is happening here?" I explained, "We are building a house of prayer where we can pray. I needed a private place to pray without being disturbed."

Olúpònà: And it would be difficult at that point for the Kábíyèsí, if he disagreed with your plans, to destroy the chapel once construction was under way, correct?

Olorì: The point was that the Ọọ̀ni was not against building it. The plans were still on—he, too, had a plan to build a chapel, but he wanted to build it outside, toward the security gate.[9] That was where the Ọọ̀ni wanted to build a chapel, but I needed a place within my own com-pound where I could stay for three days without going out to allow me to pray fervently to God. I did not want anyone to know about it. So, as we continued, we roofed the chapel with God's efforts. And with the assistance of very many people, we completed the work.

Olúpònà: Is Mohammed Muslim? Is he from the North?

Olorì: Yes, he is from northern Ghana. So, you know, Mohammed brought the fans, saying, "Madam, we have to do it for God." Then one Jonathan—that one believes in nothing anyway but his gun—Jonathan came to me and said, "We have to assist you in what you are doing." Jonathan installed all the lights in the chapel. Then another member of the state security service personnel said, "Mummy, I just want to contribute my own quota," and he brought cement for the foundation. So, then ministers of God gave money here and there. Then the Lord helped me. Some things I sold in America. I contributed my own quarter [money]. Somehow, we completed construction of it. We called ministers of God, and they came here to dedicate the chapel.

It was a challenge to name the chapel. There and then, I said within me, I do not know what name I will call this chapel. Shall I call it, "Royal Christian Chapel," or "Royal Chapel" or "Christ Apostolic Church [CAC] Royal Chapel"? So we prayed, and the Lord said to us, "Name it Christ Apostolic Church Royal Chapel." I called in the Christ Apostolic Church people, saying, "I want a minister of God who has no problem with leading an interdenominational church, who would advise that we worship in our own way. If I say this is the way I want something done, they will allow me to do it my way."

I sent for Professor Imevbore [a prominent CAC leader in the university and the city] who agreed to tell the CAC chairperson in Ifẹ to arrange whatever I wanted. Thus we began our Sunday afternoon fellowship. I only wanted a "powerhouse of prayer," whether a minister was present or not, for anyone to enter to pray fervently to God to yield results. "You need no one to lead you in prayer. Just enter there. The spirit of the Lord will direct you." I selected seven priests. To each I said, "Get seven prayer boxes. Organize your prayer, perhaps a night vigil. Take a day of the week—you don't have to meet anyone there. Come in to pray for Ilé-Ifẹ. Do it for the king, for all of us." That is the way I want it to be.

Subsequently, a woman wanted us to hold Sunday services. But I had my own church to attend in town, and I didn't want us to be accused unfairly of "snatching" others, diverting them from their denominations. Eventually, we held Sunday services, later phased out because of lack of attendance. We held night vigils; Tuesdays, communal prayers; Thursdays, night vigils; Fridays, special prayers; and Sunday, fellowship. Sometimes our vigils lasted even up to seven days. We held revivals as well.

Actually, an intense crisis in 1980 between the Modákẹkẹ and Ifẹ compelled me to build the chapel. At a certain point, as the crisis esca-lated, I declared, "Aha! We need constant prayer in this town, in this palace." Friends joined me in prayer. The Lord created me so that when I pray, I never pray that God should kill the Modákẹkẹ people (our tra-ditional enemies). I believe that all of us are one in the eyes of God Almighty. I always pray that God should touch the heart of each and everyone of us—Ifẹ and Modákẹkẹ alike—so that we will know Christ, and we and they shall know that nothing we brought to this world we are going to take out of it. There is no need for trouble between us.

Olúpònà: I've heard of events that occurred during that crisis that really shook my faith. For example, a young medical student was kidnapped and never found.

Olorì: Yes, that was dreadful. A student informed me about it. We prayed fervently in the chapel that God would spare his life. I was so disappointed and asked how did this thing happen—that a medical student who knew nothing about the crisis was kidnapped. But you know young hooligans, when they have taken Indian hemp [marijuana], they don't know what they are doing anymore. I thank God that the crisis is over. In this chapel, we pray for permanent peace in Ilé-Ifè. We pray for Modákéké, we pray for Ifè, we pray for Òsun State, we pray for the king and for Nigeria. We pray for the government. If there is peace in Nigeria, we will have peace everywhere. If there is peace in this palace, we will have peace in the town. We have no choice; we must pray for peace. Thus we pursued our prayers, we continued to pray. I thank God that the Kábíyèsí had no objection to the chapel. We wanted a place of prayer; we created it.

Olúpònà: A place that is sanctified?

Olorì: Exactly. That was my own aim in building the chapel. The Kábíyèsí, too, comes here whenever we have a prayer meeting, especially early in the morning. So, we continue to offer prayers. There is nothing put before God in this chapel that he fails to answer.

I asked the Olorì to give one or two special instances in which she felt the power of prayers in this chapel was answered by God. The Olorì gave an instance of her workers' quests for obtaining visas.

Olorì: My staff needed visas to travel to the United States of America, and I joined them in prayer during a seven-day vigil. I said to them, "Let your mind be clear; it shall be possible." We went to the chapel, forming a circle to pray. One by one, they went for their visa interviews. Everyone who had prayed to God was answered. Many ministers of God have worshipped here. Many have been transferred to other places on promotion. Students pray for success in securing admissions or employment. God answers prayers here, but everything depends on the individual. It depends on whether one's heart is clean or not.

The Olorì Sìjúadé reflected on the need to focus on God, the source of their prayers, and not on the Kábíyèsí. She mentioned that once she had admonished her workers as follows:

Olorì: I am an Ifẹ̀, both in flesh and in truth. I want it to be known that we
come to this chapel to pray for Ilé-Ifẹ̀ and for no other purpose. We
must feel free to come to the chapel without demanding the Kábíyèsí's
presence. I told my staff, "If we pray very hard, the Lord will touch the
Kábíyèsí's heart, leading him to worship here with us." However, we
ourselves take away the desire of Bàbá [the Ọ̀ọ̀ni] to attend of his own
will. Often, if one problem or another disturbs him, Bàbá arrives at the
chapel at 6:30 a.m. before the staff arrives, before they start making
their demands on him. You know, such requests are intrusions that
diminish the setting of worship. I reminded the staff that Bàbá would
attend prayers if reverence were upheld. I informed them that I wanted
us to maintain an atmosphere of worship in the chapel in this coming
year [2005].

   If we continue to respect the chapel as a place of worship, there will
be a change for good. Freely the Lord gave these things to us; freely we
should offer them. I asked my staff, "Then why are we scaring Bàbá
away? We should try to draw him to God. We must refrain from using
the prayer meeting as a place to request favors. We can choose another
place and day to ask favors of him. Go and see him not at the time he
arrives here to pray." I said that you would see that there would be a
change. I was pleased when they received my directives well. Really,
I thanked all the ministers of God, like Provost Adétunbí, Reverend
Mamadelo, Venerable Bamimosun, and others. You see, the power of
prayer lives in this chapel now.

Olúpọ̀nà: I notice that you were seated at the back of the chapel during the carol
service. Is this where you are usually seated?

Olorì: By custom, I am usually seated in the front of the chapel. But on that
special day of carols, I preferred to remain discreet to avoid distracting
people's attention from the service. If I am in front, children say, "Oh!
We want to see the Olorì." But if I am somewhat secluded, it is difficult for them to identify me. Thus they can concentrate more easily
on what the Lord is telling them. During prayer meetings, I usually sit
in the front row.

Olúpọ̀nà: Can you tell me about other Olorì, the Ọ̀ọ̀ni's other wives? Are you
one of three wives of the king?

Olorì: No, the Ọ̀ọ̀ni has two co-wives here. Ọdún, the second wife—she, too,
is a Christian. In this chapel, customarily she and I say our prayers
together here.

Olúpọ̀nà: Tell me about your own journey in faith—that is what I will call it,
as you were born into a Christ Apostolic Church (CAC) family and

raised in Ilé-Ifẹ̀. When do you think you became a "born-again" Christian? Where were you? Did you really recognize it?

Olorì: As you are aware, I was raised in the Christ Apostolic Church. When I was born, my father, Máyọ̀wá, was seriously ill; my mother visited the mountain Bàbá Àkàndé in Ẹ̀dẹ (Bàbá Àbíyè). My father vowed that if he recovered he would give his life to God. In Ẹléyẹlé, he built a church known as Máyọ̀wá's Church, a Christ Apostolic Church. Our family maintains a devoted affiliation with the CAC.

My parents never chose any other way for my siblings and me except the way of the Lord. Even today, I find it difficult to take any form of medicine. You know that in the Christ Apostolic Church medicine is taboo. You realize that my upbringing reflects my life today. In all these things, the Lord has been with me, the Lord has been faithful to me. I cannot say when I became a "born-again" Christian. It was long ago, perhaps in 1976. I remember during Bàbá Obadare's revival meetings in Ilé-Ifẹ̀ I was part of a proselytizing group talking to people, encouraging them to attend revivals, "You know there is a CAC revival—come, be a part of it." According to CAC custom, I wore no earrings or ornaments then. In the days of our youth, we were brought up to fast on all occasions. All our parents taught us to pray, to fast, to read the Bible, to pray over water, to drink it and bathe with it, and to take water to church. There is no other way of life. I know no other way. My mother was so very kind to everyone; she never held a grudge against anyone. I have to follow her footsteps. If your parents are unpleasant, no way, no way [i.e., there is still no other way; here she paused and sighed before continuing]—you shall surely follow their direction. So, that is what actually made me. So, yes, I have been "born again" for quite some time.

Olúpọ̀nà: What was the role of the Olorì in the palace? Let me ask—the role of Christian Olorì, and as a Christian and an Olorì—Is this a new dispensation?

Olorì: Regarding the role of Olorì, I can speak of myself, but I cannot speak of others. In the palace, I spent my time more in prayer and fasting. Whatever I do, I do in the name of God. Everything I embark upon, I first support myself in some days of prayers asking God whether I should go ahead or not. The Lord keeps me going. This place is like a battleground. I cannot deceive you. I really loathe idol worship [traditional religion]. Even Bàbá [the Ọọni] knows I refuse to attend these festivals—even the Ọlọ́jọ́ Festival, I refuse.

Olúpọ̀nà: You do not attend the Ọlọ́jọ́ Festival?

Olorì: No, no, I do not attend. I stay secluded in my quarters; but for me
to go to Òkè-M'ògún there, I would prefer God to take me. The Òkè-
M'ògún is the thing I pray to God to eradicate. I cannot support it.
All I tell God is that he should open the eyes of those devotees. If they
knew that the worship of the gods was sinful, they would refrain from
it. Pending the time that they will heartily confess, please forgive them
and save them. It is beyond our own power now, because there is no
way I could stop them.

I remember during the Modákékè crisis, I will not deceive you: they
wanted to hold the Olójó Festival. We had not held the festival for a
long time. The Lord told me, "If devotees are allowed to hold the Olójó
Festival, repercussions will be great." The revelation is that if there is
any disobedience to the wish of God on this matter, the effect on Ilé-
Ifè will be serious. We agreed, "We must continue to pray." We gathered
again in the chapel. It is true that we forbade holding the festival. We
had to pray hard to avoid disaster.

A PROPHETESS IN THE OÒNI'S PALACE

Little by little, as Olorì Síjúadé spoke in earnest of her palace chapel project begun
in 1986 (some twenty years ago), she inadvertently revealed to me in the small details of her story the extreme and far-reaching undercurrents of change in power,
authority, sacred knowledge, and sources of religious legitimacy that were sweeping the sacred city of Ilé-Ifè. She seemed rather indifferent to the unprecedented
disruption to the balance of power as religious elites pronounced hegemonic claims
from which to endorse the city's religious ideology and ritual, ancient or otherwise.

The Olorì articulated the agency of an evangelical Christian God, ushering in a
contemporary era fraught with new religious ideologies and elites vying for the
palace center and public space to express political and religious sentiments. Symbolized in palace stories, these encounters created tension and serious conflict between old and new faiths, as well as a changing image of the city as an uncontested
City of 201 Gods.

Olorì Yèyélúwa introduced into the palace a prophetic voice of evangelical prayer
whose repercussions radiated throughout the Yorùbá world. Yet along with the innocent prayer came subversive and contested political scenarios created by this very
prophetic voice. Olorì Yèyélúwa apparently successfully deployed her prophetic
talents to warn that participating in *òrìsà* tradition could bring danger to the city.
She cautioned against performing the Olójó Festival in a particular year because she
claimed that "God had revealed to her" that the consequences of disobeying the
Christian God's instruction would be grave. The occasion of her prophecy coincided

with the Ifè-Modákéké civil war, and it made good sense for the Ifè people to avoid a visit to Òkè-M'ògún because Ògún himself, the god of war, to whom the Olójó Festival is dedicated, was engaged in a real war. During my visit to Ilé-Ifè as the war intermittently erupted, I saw how desolate Ifè had become. In an ominous development, people were referring, in all seriousness, to the Ilé-Ifè Modákéké conflicts as Ógun kìní, Ógun kejì (First War, Second War), as if they were describing the First and Second World Wars.

Why was Olorì Yèyélúwa's prophecy taken so seriously? Did it represent a shift in Ilé-Ifè religious ideology in an era of global evangelical revivalism? In the city, where kings and secular rulers were seeking refuge in the prayer camps of popular evangelical and Charismatic priests, it was certain that Yèyélúwa's prophecy would have plausible meaning. Further, it was during a period of uncertainty and turmoil that individuals began to question the efficacy of the gods they had worshipped through the ages and on whom they had relied for deliverance from the hostility of their Modákéké enemies. This subjective view of the old gods and old tradition in confrontation with emerging new gods and traditions is common to the religious history of Yorùbá, if not to Africa in general. The crisis of the influenza of the 1930s gave impetus to the emergence of the new prophetic voices of the Aládúrà movement, which ultimately trumped the prayers of the Anglican mission churches. Although Aládúrà spirituality was already in vogue in Yorùbáland, the influence of events such as the Modákéké crisis challenged the plausibility and structure of the old tradition.

Subsequently, however, the Òòni unwaveringly performed the Olójó Festival, especially after his subjects insisted that failure to hold the festival would deprive them of viewing the arè, a revered symbol of fertility, wealth, health, and power. More importantly, the Olójó, like the Odún Oba in Ondó, represents the last of Ilé-Ifè's civil faith and the Òòni's own source of legitimacy as Oba over all religious sects and lineages.[10]

The Olorì's carefully articulated opposition to òrìsà differs little from many daily disputes in churches and mosques throughout the land. What differs in the Olorì's encounter with òrìsà is that she is both a palace insider and an outsider. As an Ifè indigene of noble birth, she is an insider to Ilé-Ifè politics and culture. As a royal wife and daughter of a prominent Ilé-Ifè Aládúrà Christian, she is an outsider to òrìsà tradition. Because the palace is a public space, the Olorì's comments provoke deep feelings among devotees of òrìsà. Despite her Christian beliefs, the Olorì remains deeply embedded in palace institutions and structures.

Olorì Yèyélúwa's most egregious confrontation with Ilé-Ifè tradition came when the palace chiefs demanded that she take the mandatory title of Yèyélúwa, which is intended for a "Senior Olorì" or "Elder Consort." The episode surrounding this conflict illustrates how the Olorì handled the assumption of a traditional chieftaincy title that she considered inappropriate given her Aládúrà Christian spirituality. The traditional title of Yèyélúwa secured her status as the chief consort of the king and the senior (female) chief in palace affairs. The Olorì explained how she justified accepting it despite her avowed Christian beliefs:

> When the Ifẹ̀ chiefs approached me to insist that I take this title, they told me that "affairs" must be done traditionally. At first, I resisted by responding that the title defied the will of God and my belief.
>
> But later I had a dream in which a female chief approached me saying, "Olorì, now that you are Yèyélúwa, we must act together." Instantly, I retorted, "No, you know my Christian belief. I cannot act in darkness and light together. If you refuse to accept my way, then I refuse to accept the Yèyélúwa title." When I woke, I told my dream to Chief Elúyẹmí, who assured me that I would be allowed to hold the ceremony according to my Christian faith. Fervently, I began to pray and fast. I asked God to reveal to me whether he wanted me to take this title or not. According to our custom, our Christ Apostolic Church held days of prayer and fasting. A pastor approached me: "Mama, you must refuse the title because the chiefs plan to use 'magic' on you to get you to succumb to their will." But I responded, "The Lord will speak to me on the final day of prayers. Thus I shall know whether the God I serve is greater or lesser than the gods of the chiefs."
>
> Even on the very morning of my installation ceremony, my first daughter came to me: "Mummy, refuse the title. In a dream, I saw vast throngs of troubled people gathering." I said to her, "Don't worry, dear, the Lord will reveal things to us." As we gathered for morning prayers, a minister spoke: "One among us will be installed as chief today—let her go safely, let her return safely [àlọ́re, àbọ̀re]." As the prayer was uttered, the Lord spoke to me, saying, "My daughter, go ahead, accept the title. It will be well with you. Through this title his will shall be revealed to the people."
>
> After this encounter with God, I felt complete peace. God would take control of events today. God would intervene to fight for us. When I returned from morning prayers, I announced to those assembled, "Let us organize our affairs. I shall accept the traditional title. Let us prepare for the ceremony of Yèyélúwa." But my staff was distraught: "Mummy, what is happening?" I replied, "The Lord has told us to receive this title this morning."
>
> As we approached the shrine to attend the ceremony, others were being honored, too, and traditional chiefs were constructing the altar. When I drew near to the entrance, I stopped. Chief Elúyẹmí asked me, "Are you not going to enter the shrine?" I retorted, "No, I am not."

I asked the Olorì if she was referring to the Ògún Ladìn Shrine in the Ọ̀ọ̀ni's palace; she confirmed that she was. The Ògún Ladìn, the shrine to Ògún, is associated with the primordial mythic blacksmith Ladìn and is one of the most revered areas in the palace. It is considered the powerhouse or ilé-àṣẹ of Ilé-Ifẹ̀, and it is believed that any oath taken there occurs in the past and in the present. Today, however, the Ògún Ladìn Shrine is seen more as a place of prayer to the gods, especially to the deity

Ògún. New chiefs take their oaths of office there. Signifying state power, the Ògún Ladìn Shrine has been transformed to accommodate modern trends and values in the city.

The Olorì continued:

> So they brought a chair for me. Holding my Bible, I was seated surrounded by all my children. I said to Chief Elúyẹmí, "Before we start, I would like to read from my Bible." The chief responded, "There is no problem with that. How many Bible passages do you want to read?" I replied, "Thank you, Chief." I read Psalm 24 and Isaiah 6 as prayers for the city of Ilé-Ifẹ̀. I read another passage. After I finished, Chief Elúyẹmí asked me, "Is it okay now?" I declared, "I have finished." Chief Elúyẹmí then asked Chief Erédùmí, the chief of Ògún in charge of the ceremony, to pray, and he prayed in the traditional way. Chief Erédùmí said to me, "Yèyélúwa, may the power of that thing you carry in your hand, that Bible, and the prayer you have prayed bring blessing on the city. During your time as Yèyélúwa, may goodness come to the city of Ilé-Ifẹ̀. You can now pray in the name of Jesus Christ that you worship." After the ceremony, I was asked to climb upon a horse, as social tradition demands, and the chief helped me climb up. I began to sing praise songs to the Lord, that God had revealed his power and allowed his own way to prevail.

I asked Yèyélúwa if they had placed the *akòko* leaves upon her head, a traditional symbol of chieftaincy during coronation. She responded that the leaves were merely a symbol and had nothing to do with traditional rituals.

> Ilé-Ifẹ̀ has really changed. Here in this chapel we pray now. Bàbá, Kábíyèsí, the king himself, no longer opposes evangelical Christian prayer. Bàbá often delights in reminding people that he has a prophetess in the palace. He reminds visiting prophets and priests that we too pray here, that God answers our prayers. I thank God for the way we pray here. God is always answering our prayers for the city, for Bàbá, and for this nation. I am glad we are able to pass this tradition down to our children successfully. And Bàbá, too, he knows that only God is worthy of worship. Bàbá takes no glory for himself. Once Bàbá went to Lagos, and someone said to him, "Kábíyèsí, you are God," but he responded, "You are speaking blasphemy—I am not God."

The above remark takes us full circle to where we began in this chapter—the Ọ̀ọ̀ni's renunciation of his divine status. Furthermore, it points to the agency of Olorì Ṣíjúadé in the unfolding of events in Ilé-Ifẹ̀ Palace and in the city. As she herself recounted:

> When I was a student at the Ẹdẹ Baptist High School, I had three friends. We resolved that nothing could force us to marry into royal families because we knew they worshipped idols. I resolved never in my life to marry a king. But see what the Lord has done. He did it for a purpose. And the purpose of the Lord is fulfilling it. I thank God Almighty that the Lord put me in this place actually to make Christianity stand firm.

THE OLORÌ AS AGENTS OF CHANGE

As Barbara M. Cooper has argued, clashes between indigenous religions and new Christian movements often have a significant gender dimension. In reflecting on the enormous labor of unnamed women whose strength and imagination drive the communities created by these new movements, she quotes Adrian Hastings' claim that women are "Christianity's principal asset in Africa today."[11] Yet while scholars of Yorùbá gender studies such as T. O. Pearce, N. Sudarkasa, B. Awẹ́, Matory, Oyèéwùmí, and Ọlájubù have studied the important role of women in Yorùbá religious and socioeconomic life as agents of historical and social change, the role of women in the public life and power politics of ethno-religious communities, especially the evangelical Christian community, has not been adequately addressed.

Female agency currently plays a decisive role in the encounter between indigenous Yorùbá religion and new Christian movements and the Ọọ̀ni's renunciation of his divine status. In Ilé-Ifẹ̀, women and children make up 70 percent of the membership in the new Christian movements. Moreover, Olorì—senior wives of local kings—are fast becoming catalysts of social change throughout Yorùbáland by encouraging evangelical Christians to occupy Yorùbá palaces,[12] by assuming new political roles in religious theater, and by replacing the òrìṣà priestesses of the Yorùbá tradition as religious leaders and agents of conversion.

The role of Olorì Mori Ṣíjúadé of Ilé-Ifẹ̀ offers a telling example of these larger trends. A native of Ilé-Ifẹ̀ from a prominent Christian Aládúrà family, the Olorì holds weekly Christian rituals in her own quarters of the Ọọ̀ni's palace in Ilé-Ifẹ̀. She has also advanced a new Christian agenda within the palace by radically transforming the Ọọ̀ni's annual Christmas carol service.[13]

This "nativity" drama described earlier in this chapter was a public denunciation of the ancient indigenous òrìṣà religion and a proclamation of the ascendancy of the newly introduced Christian dispensation. Because all of the divination attempts by the king's priests had failed to ensure a peaceful year, the disgraced diviners could be seen as representing the weakening structure of òrìṣà religion and the inability of Ifá, the most sacred source of Yorùbá knowledge, to predict and control events accurately. In this way, the drama played upon the fundamentally pragmatic orientation that drives the Yorùbá approach to religion. The play could also be seen as satirically commenting on the inability of the òrìṣà to save the people of Ilé-Ifẹ̀ from their conflict with the Modákẹ́kẹ́ people. Indeed, the play would suggest that ending that ongoing conflict would require the commitment of the Christian God and the conversion of the Ọọ̀ni. I should also add that at the carol service the Ọọ̀ni's behavior was consistent with his renunciation of his sacred kingship—if not his outright conversion. He presented himself as a mere mortal and worshipper, like any other person, and when addressing the congregation he stood up, rather than sitting on the throne. Finally, he publicly acknowledged the centrality of the Supreme God in ordering the affairs of the universe.

Although such plays are not new in Christian evangelical circles, the Olorì, the wife of the Ọọni, took up new a leading role in the drama. More importantly, her own religion was shown as the model of the truth. The play's emphasis on conversion as the way to peace might have grown from her belief—which she confidently shared with me during our later interview—that her prayers and all-night vigils had prevented Ilé-Ifẹ̀ from seeing more wars. Driven by her conviction that the well-being of the Ilé-Ifẹ̀ depended solely on abandoning previous gods and adopting a Christian God, the Olorì continued to resist the city's religious elites and proponents of indigenous religion and the sacred kingship. Because she saw òrìṣà worship as a hindrance to Ilé-Ifẹ̀'s spiritual and material growth, she had decided that the public and palace domains should be controlled by the agency of the Christian God. Although the ultimate outcome of her undertaking remains to be seen, any account of the future possibilities for Ilé-Ifẹ̀ must reckon with the Ọọni's renunciation of the sacred kingship and his acknowledgment of the Olorì's prophetic gift, powerful interests, and religious influence.

THE ỌỌNI REFLECTS ON THE STATUS OF HIS ROYAL CONSORT

Initially, the Ọọni's remark about a "prophetess in his palace" was sarcastic, but he gradually began to acknowledge the Olorì's prophetic gift, powerful interests, and religious influence. The Ọọni was referring, of course, to his wife, Olorì Yèyélúwa, as a "prophetess" who initiated construction of a palace chapel similar to other Prophetic and Charismatic evangelical churches. Yèyélúwa's construction of a palace chapel presents some intriguing practical and theoretical issues for analysis in the context of gender relations and the meaning and function of power in the newly introduced evangelical Charismatic religion.

Present-day scholars in feminist and gender studies generally accept that gender is socially and culturally constructed.[14] It is now accepted that women are as capable of exercising power as their male counterparts, but when it is "differently exercised from men's power" its importance is often devalued.[15] In addition, women are often said to exercise significantly less power in the public domain than they do in the domestic domain.

Henrietta Moore has challenged the dichotomy often drawn between private and public spheres of influence. Contesting the assumption of Clinton Bennett that women are not "effective social agents in their own right" unless they exercise power in the public domain, she asks, "Is it enough to say that women have power within a specifically female domain, or must we argue that they have power in those areas of social life which have been so often presented as the public, political domain of men?"[16]

Yèyélúwa's narrative engaged several of these issues. She was very mindful of the need to build a chapel in her own quarters for her own purposes. She talked about creating a private space in her quarter for prayer; hence, she requested a Christ Apostolic Church minister from her own denominational affiliation. Yet the construction of the chapel launched her into the public sphere of the palace where ultimately a silent contest raged over control of the sacred sphere. Though her project was motivated as a private religious act, it gradually took on a public character as Yèyélúwa's role in palace religious politics was contested.

During the Ọ̀ọ̀ni's carol service and stage drama, a public affair, the Olorì took a prominent and public role. Standing before kings, chiefs, dignitaries, and me, as well as others gathered to sing Christmas carols, she acted as chief hostess and watched the nativity play of Ìlú Aríjẹ, further thrusting herself into the limelight of palace religious affairs. The play was choreographed to reveal events hitherto concealed from the public, and the drama lent an air of legitimacy to Olorì Yèyélúwa's newly constructed role promoted by the Ọ̀ọ̀ni himself, as he had repeatedly called her "the prophetess in the palace of the Ọ̀ọ̀ni."

The clash between Olorì Yèyélúwa and the Ilé-Ifẹ̀'s religious elites and ritualists centered on two ideologically opposed positions as they struggled for the city's soul in the public and palace domain. The priests of the òrìṣà ceremonial social space demonstrated their ownership and claims to the "collective past" to guarantee the city's well-being.[17] However, Olorì Yèyélúwa believed that the well-being of the city depended solely on abandoning previous gods and adopting a Christian God. Thus she herself decided that the social space should be controlled by the agency of the Christian God. The Olorì perceived òrìṣà worship as a bar to Ilé-Ifẹ̀'s spiritual and material growth.

As noted in earlier chapters, ritual specialists are engaged in year-round propitiation of Ilé-Ifẹ̀ gods and goddesses. The Ọ̀ọ̀ni and the city's political elite use rituals and festivals as tools of cultural hegemony.[18] At the same time, these rituals provide deep-seated religious and cosmological meaning to thousands of devotees who hold to òrìṣà tradition as a source of their being.

Once-popular festivals are no longer performed with the old-time religious fanfare. The gods are in retreat, and the vacuum created by their diminished public presence seems to be filled by Christian ceremonies. Attended by many Ọba and dignitaries, the Ọ̀ọ̀ni's Christian carol service, with its parody of òrìṣà traditions, is fast becoming a major part of the public spectacle in Yorùbá Palace. I read recently about a Yorùbá Ọba in Ògún State, Nigeria, who sponsored a bill to allow traditional Yorùbá Ọba to determine how they would like to be buried when they die. Many Yorùbá Ọba are fighting to avoid their mandatory traditional burial ceremonies, which, according to them, involve "un-Christian idol worshipping"—an attitude shared by the Olorì.

The new Christian push into the public space by the Olorì, and by extension the dominant Christian converts, has significant implications. For the Yorùbá, the Olorì's attitude may reflect a general religious change, in the city and in Yorùbá-land in general, whereby new forms of Christianity and radical Islam are increasingly occupying the public space that once belonged to the òrìṣà. They now enjoy the patronage of the king and the palace chiefs. However, the Ọọ̀ni continues to perform the Ọlọ́jọ́ Festival, which has been the basis of civil religious ritual, and as such he reaffirms his commitment to Ilé-Ifẹ̀'s indigenous spiritual order. More recently, religion is being redefined as a private affair and the òrìṣà devotees are being made to view their tradition as only a lineage tradition, even when it is performed in the vicinity of the palace. By the reckoning of the devotees themselves, it is both public and private. They are performing these rituals for and on behalf of the king. Powerful palace women such as the Olorì, who hitherto have remained silent in a patriarchal tradition, are asserting themselves as the driving force of the new Pentecostal-Charismatic tradition.

We have also examined the central role of the Olorì in religious change in the context of her status as a palace "insider." The Olorì's intervention on the part of the Pentecostal-Charismatic movement may be described as a kind of catalyst that is hastening the eventual change of the religious traditions in Ilé-Ifẹ̀. As an "insider" who is devoutly Christian, the Olorì, as the person closest to the Ọọ̀ni, is in an optimal position to advance her personal convictions and religiosity. As a spiritual agent herself, and a staunch Aládúrà, it is expected that she will have significant influence on the Ọọ̀ni. Consequently, the òrìṣà tradition is being pushed out of public space to the private space of the priests and their devotees—hence the comment that òrìṣà belongs to the lineage ancestral tradition rather than to the larger Ilé-Ifẹ̀ community. This shift from public to private is being accelerated by the rise of the Pentecostal-Charismatic movement and will be very significant in shaping the sacred space of Ilé-Ifẹ̀.

We should not, however, see the òrìṣà devotees as passive in the face of this new threat. Evidence suggests that they are fighting back in a revivalist mode of their own. They are using the mass media—radio, television, and newspapers—to promote what they often call ancestral tradition. They couch the crusade in the language of the revival of a cultural heritage that urgently requires renewal. In addition, the African diasporic community, with its strong interest in òrìṣà tradition, especially in Ilé-Ifẹ̀, is adding yet another dimension to this dynamic religious struggle. The diaspora is engaged in the revival of the òrìṣà traditions abroad, and many of these òrìṣà devotees are shocked at the events taking place in Ilé-Ifẹ̀. How can the place of origin of the òrìṣà become a space where these traditions are neglected?

10

Conclusion

Ancient Òrìṣà and New Evangelicals
Vie for the City of 201 Gods

When I first began investigating the religious culture of Ilé-Ifẹ̀ over twenty years ago, I viewed the city as a ceremonial center similar to the sacred city-states of other ancient civilizations. This view is consistent with that of Paul Wheatley, whose classic work *The Pivot of the Four Quarters* serves as a template for charting an interdisciplinary approach to the study of Ilé-Ifẹ̀. Phenomenological hermeneutics in religious studies, as in anthropological and cultural studies, provides useful theoretical paradigms for interpreting the ethnographic data I collected in Ilé-Ifẹ̀. Having examined various forms of orature, including oral *òrìṣà* traditions, Ifá divination poetry, and *oríkì* praise poetry, I have presented an interpretation of the sacred religious and cultural meaning given to the city.

This book began with a brief introduction to the cosmology of Ilé-Ifẹ̀, according to which Odùduwà, the cultural hero and city founder, created the sacred city through ritual performance and conquest. The cosmogonic myths and other migration narratives of Odùduwà provide a fertile context for understanding the evolving social and political structure. Like other ancient civilizations such as the Aztecs, the powerful new conquerors—Odùduwà and his followers—subsumed aboriginal groups under their rule. Consequently, an indigenous political confederacy evolved in which the priest-kings (little Ọba) and lineage heads (Ìṣòrò) were recognized as rulers, but they remained subordinate to the Ọọ̀ni (the king of kings), the overlord of the theogonic confederacy. Despite challenges from Christian and Islamic evangelism, the Ifẹ̀ ritual calendar, the year-round celebrations, and the ritual and festival cycle continue to provide occasions for renewing the sacred energy of the city that the Ìṣòrò priests ensure on behalf of the Ọọ̀ni. Through propitiation of Ilé-Ifẹ̀'s gods and goddesses, it is assumed that the cosmos is renewed. Life is reenergized for another year.

Ilé-Ifẹ̀'s festivals and rituals are performed and choreographed to highlight the glory of the kingdom and to display the power of the Ọ̀ọ̀ni and the place of the confederacy's Ìṣòrò lineages. Leading the ritual festivals, the Ìṣòrò priest-chiefs reenact their respective lineage histories, recalling the memory of their power over the territories they once controlled. In the modern era, even after these lineages had ceded large chunks of their territories as land grants to the Nigerian state government to establish schools, community hospitals, and other development projects, the lineages and clans still make symbolic claims to these government-controlled institutions, many of which, by virtue of the names they bear, attest to their identity. As I noted in chapter 2, some schools, including the Ọ̀rànmíyàn, Olúorogbo, and Mọrèmi high schools, bear the names of their lineage deities, and it is not unusual for schools named after a deity to take a holiday on the deity's festival day. These institutions, including Ìdìta Community High School, which belongs to the Ọbàtálá lineage, demonstrate how the symbols of the òrìṣà are indelibly etched in the Ilé-Ifẹ̀ cityscape.

Above all, the symbols, the imagined òrìṣà communities, and the civil authority in traditional Ilé-Ifẹ̀ endow the Ọ̀ọ̀ni with the authority of a paramount king who rules the little kings and the city. The Ọ̀ọ̀ni's main festival of Ọlọ́jọ́ is the climax of the Ifẹ̀ ritual cycle uniting the civil and religious divisions of Ilé-Ifẹ̀. As my previous book, *Kingship, Religion, and Rituals in a Nigerian Community,* illustrated, the Òsémàwẹ́'s Ọdún Ọba plays a central role in sustaining the civil religion of Oǹdó, just as the Ọlọ́jọ́ Festival functions in Ilé-Ifẹ̀ as a civil ritual to symbolize the Ọ̀ọ̀ni's power and authority of the sacred canopy that shelters the city's many religious factions. Historically, the Ọ̀ọ̀ni has played this central role in the city. In my conversation with him in December 2004, the present Ọ̀ọ̀ni acknowledged the pivotal place that Ọlọ́jọ́ still holds in Ilé-Ifẹ̀ City.

Nevertheless, at the end of the twentieth century and the beginning of the twenty-first, a departure from the city's ancient past occurred as a new religious ideology took hold of Ilé-Ifẹ̀. To conclude this work, I devoted the last phase of my fieldwork to the palace of the Ọ̀ọ̀ni. In December 2004, I conducted extensive interviews with the Ọ̀ọ̀ni and his senior wife, Olorì Yèyélúwa Morísádé Ṣíjúadé, the details of which I discussed in chapter 9. Today, the advances of Christianity, Islam, and modern secular ideology challenge the plausibility and structure of age-old beliefs, setting the stage for conflict between deeply rooted and newer belief systems in contemporary Ilé-Ifẹ̀.

From Ilé-Ifẹ̀'s inception, the Ọ̀ọ̀ni's palace has always accommodated the religious activities of the city. And today, new cultural and religious beliefs and activities, championed by evangelical, Pentecostal, and fundamentalist Islamic movements, are increasingly practiced at the palace. Consequently, the palace's pluralistic ideology and ethos as a centralizing and unifying force, which had previously survived on the strength of the old structure, are gradually crumbling under the weight of globalization and modern religious ideology. Instead, the palace is emerging as a center disseminating Christian, Islamic, and new religious traditions that now wield authority and influence. However, older traditions are not receding without a fight. Indeed, indigenous religious practitioners are developing strategies for survival.

Paradoxically, indigenous religious practitioners have reframed what was once seen as a purely local tradition as a globally viable religion, which is spreading in much the same way as Christianity and Islam. Ifẹ̀ religion and tradition are drawing significant strength from innovative global encounters, especially with òrìṣà cultures from the African diaspora in the Caribbean and the Americas. In a "reverse" mission, òrìṣà influences from abroad are making inroads into Ilé-Ifẹ̀ City.

In this final chapter, I will further explore several narratives, collected during my 2004 visit to Ilé-Ifẹ̀, to account for shifting religious and cultural events in the palace. The terrain is highly contested, especially as the dynamics of political power have compelled each religious group to exercise hegemony over the affairs of the city and over the crises ensuing from these clashes. Finally, I will predict what the future may hold for òrìṣà traditions in the City of 201 Gods.

Even though Christian and indigenous religions are two formidable traditions at work in the drama of Ilé-Ifẹ̀, it is important to recognize that Islam, including modern radical Islam, plays a role in Ilé-Ifẹ̀'s social and cultural politics as well. During my interview with the Ọ̀ọni, I was struck by his disclosure that he had been born into a Muslim lineage and given a Muslim name, Saliu. As king, he participates in all the city's religious traditions, a reflection of the city's historic religious pluralism. The week of my interview with the Ọ̀ọni, the chief imam of the central mosque, located at the city center, had just celebrated his third anniversary as the leader of the city's Muslim community. Joined by several of his chiefs, the Ọ̀ọni visited the mosque to celebrate with the chief imam. Although violence has often characterized clashes between Christians and Muslims in other parts of Nigeria, in recent times such religious conflicts have not occurred in Ilé-Ifẹ̀. It is fair to say that, except in Yorùbá cities such as Ìlọrin and Òṣogbo, where a large majority of inhabitants are Muslims, Islam in general is not involved in the communal clashes for space and political control that have become daily occurrences in the cities of northern Nigeria. In addition, although this may reflect the fact that Islam is a minority religion in Ilé-Ifẹ̀, it reflects the general observation among scholars that Yorùbá religious traditions have always enjoyed mutual tolerance and respect, at least before the recent period.

THE CITY AND RELATIONS OF POWER

Recent events unfolding in the palace in Ilé-Ifẹ̀ City demonstrate changes in the populace's concept of power, the source of sacred knowledge, and its legitimacy in the sacred city. I have chosen the theory of hegemonic power relations to examine this phase of Ilé-Ifẹ̀'s development because it provides useful avenues for interpreting how religion functions as a source of hegemony and control in society. In ancient times and traditional settings, the religious elites were agents of the òrìṣà tradition, and they maintained a hegemonic claim on the city, providing the framework from which the city's religious ideology and practice were actualized.

The city is entering an era in which new religious elites are increasingly making claims on the public space symbolized by the palace. The encounter between the old and the new, symbolized in the palace narratives that I will discuss below, not only is creating tension and serious conflict between the òrìṣà devotees and the new religious movements but also is leading to changes in the city's image and is transforming power relations among all those involved.

The complexity of the current situation in Ilé-Ifẹ̀ can be illustrated by Foucault's notion of discourse.[1] For a long time, what constituted the dominant discourse in the city (episteme, to use Foucault's language) was òrìṣà tradition. The myths, rituals, and festivals we have discussed in previous chapters provided the context for daily living in the city where religion was a practice and a way of life rather than a formalized belief system or set of doctrines. Whenever we asked the Ìṣòrò (priests) what functions and meanings the year-round festivals and rituals provided in the city, they responded that whenever they performed their sacrifices and prayers the city of Ilé-Ifẹ̀ became peaceful and every sector of life functioned properly *(Tí a bá ti ṣe ètùtù, á tùbà, tùṣẹ ní gbogbo ìlú)*. As Ted Lewellen notes, "The dominant discourse of an age (which, in his early writing, Foucault refers to as an 'episteme') is assimilated by the individual, so that it is virtually impossible to think outside of it; it becomes an aspect of one's very being. Since there is no universal human nature, the discourse of each age in a sense determines what it is to be human."[2] To be human in ancient Ilé-Ifẹ̀ was to assume this worldview and to participate without question in the religious festivals, rituals, and activities of the city.

The current situation in Ilé-Ifẹ̀ requires that we recognize two paradigms operating simultaneously. The first is the hegemony of the indigenous preconquest Yorùbá tradition, which was recognized and even manipulated by the British Council. The council in Lagos insisted that the Ọọ̀ni of Ifẹ̀ travel to Lagos to pronounce on the case of the crown, thereby inadvertently aiding the power structure of the British colonial administration. The second postcolonial paradigm is the new religious ideology symbolized in Christian and Islamic evangelism or revivalism. The tension between preconquest residuals and the postcolonial context is demonstrated in the conflicts and manipulation surrounding the symbols of these traditions in the contemporary period, with adverse effects on the city.

As Islam and Christianity sent out deep roots in the city and indeed in Yorùbá culture and society in general, the òrìṣà indigenous worldview began to retreat. Whereas the first and second generations of Christian and Muslim converts maintained a pluralistic worldview that promoted religious inclusiveness, the third and fourth generations are increasingly adhering to the new religious ideology, which is largely exclusivist in its orientation and totally intolerant of òrìṣà tradition.

As I demonstrated in earlier chapters, one such central discourse is illustrated in the annual performance of the Ọbàtálá Festival, which I witnessed in 2004. At a certain point in this performance of the ritual, devotees of the god and his consort Yemòó invoked and affirmed the power of the deities by chanting vigorously, "It is the will and power of the *òrìṣà* [Our Lord] that will come to pass" *(Tolúwa mi làṣe, t'òrìṣà l'àṣe)*. At the time I carried out my fieldwork in 2002, the dominant *òrìṣà* discourse in the contemporary era was already being eroded, for the children who sat on the other side of a rectangular space were singing softly what could be perceived as an opposing discourse: "It is the will of Jesus my Lord that will be done" *(Ti Jésù l'àṣe, t'olúwa mi làṣe)*. In both sets of lyrics, *Olúwa mi* (My Lord) was the object of their worship, but elderly devotees of the *òrìṣà* called him Ọbàtálá and their children and new converts called him Jesus.

The very fact that the children's song was almost inaudible suggests a conflict between the children's Christian indoctrination and the beliefs of their parents. At the same time, the incident was an ominous sign that the *òrìṣà*'s centrality was being challenged, marginalized, decentered, and jettisoned by the new Christian evangelical onslaught. By birth, the children referred to above belong to *òrìṣà* lineages. Their challenge to *òrìṣà* power and authority is a small matter compared to other challenges taking place in the city. Amid hundreds of Christian evangelical programs in the city—revival meetings, open-air services, and nightly vigils—a new form of discourse is emerging that pushes evangelical Christian activities beyond the domain of the individual or the church and into public spaces, directly challenging the *òrìṣà* tradition. Although the Christian evangelical tradition has existed alongside other traditions for over a century, it has never before been at the city's center of power, where the *òrìṣà* priests remained unchallenged for a long period. Describing this kind of contest over power, Lewellen states, "Power, then, in the sense of control over thought and action, is not merely an incidental aspect of discourse; it is at its center, a part of its essence."[3]

This chapter will focus mainly on how events and narratives in the palace illustrate these fundamental changes in the religious landscape of Ilé-Ifẹ̀. The palace *(ààfin)*, the abode of the Ọ̀ọ̀ni and the center of religious and political activities in the city, is "a site of struggle, a locus of micropolitical contestations" between the old religious traditions and modern religious institutions in Ilé-Ifẹ̀.[4] At the core of this struggle is the very notion of religious power and authority and who wields it on behalf of the people. Whereas kingship has derived its legitimacy from the authority of traditional religious beliefs, cosmology, and meaning systems, the new religious movement has begun to place the Ọ̀ọ̀ni's authority, power, and legitimacy directly under the agency of the Supreme God. This reformulation would inevitably seem to require that the Ọ̀ọ̀ni renounce his godlike status and claim of sacredness. The Ọ̀ọ̀ni has thus been placed between the old and the new frameworks that together characterize modern-day Ilé-Ifẹ̀ religious life.

INFLUENCE OF RELIGION
ON POLITICS IN THE SACRED CITY

Twenty years ago, an American scholar of politics, David Laitin, wrote *Hegemony and Culture: Politics and Religious Change among the Yorùbá*. Laitin's empirical data came principally from his field research in Ilé-Ifẹ̀. Although scholars of Yorùbá culture and politics criticized him for ignoring indigenous Yorùbá practices and focusing mainly on Islam and Christianity, his work is central to the study of contemporary Ilé-Ifẹ̀. What seems important now is what Laitin failed to examine then—the impact and influence of *òrìṣà* indigenous religion at the time he did his research. Laitin began with the common observation that among the Yorùbá people—who are almost equally divided between Islam and Christianity—religious division seems not to have any influence on their political behavior and has not led to the political conflicts that have emerged in other parts of the country. It was this "unnatural toleration," as he describes it, that he set out to investigate using Antonio Gramsci's concept of hegemony.[5] Laitin argues that the Yorùbás "see their attachment to an ancestral city as a key aspect of their identity."[6] This attachment was reinforced by the British indirect rule system, which granted the local chiefs significant authority and power in the new dispensation.

All available data suggest that these notions—that religious affiliation plays no vital role in Yorùbá political activity, that the Yorùbá are incredibly tolerant of religious difference, and that religion constitutes no great divide among the Yorùbá—can no longer be supported. Laitin did not pay much attention to indigenous faith, yet the indigenous religious and political structure supports the hegemonic influence of the ancestral city ideology, as I argue in chapter 2 of this work. Though Islam and Christianity have been important players in Ilé-Ifẹ̀'s social structure, until recently these two traditions produced neither an overarching sacred canopy nor the hegemonic value system on which Laitin built his thesis. Rather, the sacred canopy and value system were derived from the symbols of *òrìṣà* tradition.

How does religion in contemporary Ilé-Ifẹ̀ constitute a source of power that defines how the city space is governed? How is the new Christian ideology embedded in the political power of the city, especially in the evangelical quest to influence the public space of the palace? To answer these questions, we should examine how the definition of power in Western academic discourse differs from that in Yorùbá and Ilé-Ifẹ̀ public space. Generally, in the Western world, sources of power in state formation and maintenance have been economic, social, and political.[7] As Norman Yoffee remarks, "Control over the sources and distribution of subsistence and wealth, the segregation and maintenance of symbols of social interpretation and incorporation, and the ability to impose obedience by force, both on the governmental level and also within local groups, together constitute the main dimensions of power in the earliest states."[8]

Although Yoffee is referring to Western states, the means to power that he describes were also observable in the preconquest state among the Yorùbá, described by some in Yorùbá society as *ayé ìbẹ́rí,* that is, the Age of Execution, when the Ọba were unchallenged. But the Yorùbá have also relied upon another, equally important source of power, namely supernatural, magical, and medicinal knowledge, the invocation and manipulation of which rulers have depended upon to legitimize their reign and to maintain control over their subjects. The Ọọ̀ni of Ifẹ̀, citing the late Chief Ọbáfẹ́mi Awólọ́wọ̀, the Yorùbá leader whom I discussed in chapter 1, invoked a proverb, *Bí owó ò bá jẹ, oògùn á jẹ́* (If money does not do the business, certainly magical medicinal power will do it). While wealth is a significant source of power in Yorùbá worldview and culture, so is magical medicinal power *(oògùn).* For the Yorùbá, legitimacy has traditionally been conferred by ritual performance, invocation of the gods, and deep knowledge of how to manipulate and use ritual power rightly. The showcasing of medicinal magic in festivals and public displays of the king's authority, which I demonstrated in my discussion of the Ọlọ́jọ́ Festival in chapter 5, indicates that it is as effective as wealth and money, although rulers have depended on a combination of both. The Ọọ̀ni himself informed me that before he became king he was a very rich man, a factor that I believe hastened his appointment to the throne of Odùduwà.

What constitutes medicinal and magical power in Ilé-Ifẹ̀ kingship? What are the sources of the power that provides legitimacy to the Ọọ̀ni? As I indicated when describing the Ọbàtálá ceremony, a central part of the festival occurred when Ìyálórìṣà (Yemòó) presented the Ọọ̀ni with Ọbàtálá's gift of ointment to protect him against ailments throughout the ensuing year. The primary duties of the Ìṣòrò priests were to protect the Ọọ̀ni and ensure that his reign was long. According to Yoffee, social power is based on the control of knowledge, ceremonies, and symbols and the "creation and/or adaptation of symbols of cultural commonality" in ways that foster reciprocity between the king, his subordinates, leaders, and elites.[9] In this process, ceremonial buildings provide settings for the enactment of ceremonial roles that are assigned by kingship and that confer honor and prestige on the incumbents.

Yoffee further remarks that the elites and semiautonomous leaders, who maintain these symbols of community, have greater access to the gods and ancestors. Furthermore, they legitimize the order of inequality, incorporate rulers into their ceremonies, and command goods ostensibly on behalf of the entire community but especially for their own ends.[10] The king, as patron of the cultic practices, gives the priests adequate resources and gifts for their ceremonial roles, and they in turn provide legitimacy to his kingship. We will examine how the major roles of the priests and the religious order have been challenged in contemporary Ilé-Ifẹ̀, especially as illustrated in my most recent fieldwork experience in the city.

INTERACTIONS OF TRADITIONAL RELIGION
AND MODERN SECULARISM IN THE SACRED CITY

In chapter 2, I described a critical time in Ifẹ̀ and Yorùbá history as the people of Ilé-Ifẹ̀ encountered modernity at the start of the twentieth century. In an unprecedented move in 1903, Ọ̀ọ̀ni Olúbùṣe I, the grandfather of the incumbent Ọ̀ọ̀ni, left his palace to visit the British governor in Lagos. Normally secluded in the palace, the Ọ̀ọ̀ni dramatically broke with custom by making himself available to British Native Authority Council members in Lagos, where he agreed to decide a thorny question: Who among the Yorùbá kings was entitled to wear the sacred crown? Fearing the worst, the remaining Yorùbá Ọba, including the Aláàfin of Ọ̀yọ́, temporarily left their palaces to stay on the outskirts of the city, performing rituals and consulting their gods to ensure the Ọ̀ọ̀ni's peaceful return to Ilé-Ifẹ̀.

This visit was historic in the sense that the Ọ̀ọ̀ni was suddenly made to recognize the power of the British overlords in the new colonial era. Before this, Ifẹ̀, of course, had been visited by a European explorer and an Anglican missionary: Leo Frobenius and Henry Townsend, respectively. Frobenius, the German art historian, opened the city for research to outside scholars. Townsend brought with him Christian missionaries who attempted to evangelize the Yorùbá. However, the Christians were at that time unsuccessful in establishing a mission post in Ilé-Ifẹ̀ or in gaining converts in the city.

By the time of my fieldwork, however, the city and its priests had developed deep roots in two imported monotheistic traditions, Islam and Christianity, to which many of the priests or their parents converted while at the same time retaining their ancestral traditions and their spiritual and cultural heritage. This realization of apparently conflicting worldviews and dual ideologies prompted the chief priest of Odùduwà to tell me, "Though I am called Yusuf, when I became the Ọbadìo, the chief priest of Odùduwà, I left Yusuf behind me. When I die, I will be buried in this [Odùduwà] compound, and no one will be allowed to carry my body to the outside space for burial." He was referring to the Muslim custom of placing the dead in the outer space of the compound while reciting the Muslim liturgy before the interment. The chief priest continued, "Before my very eyes, they would have selected my successor." The last comment indicates his desire to ensure continuity in the Odùduwà lineage tradition.

I should add that in the course of my fieldwork, when I asked my informants for their names, quite often they gave their Christian or Muslim baptismal names before giving their òrìṣà names, and they saw no contradiction inherent in these dual identities. For example, one of the most powerful chief priests of Ọ̀rànmíyàn was Erédùmí, the sacrificer at the Odùduwà Shrine. Concurrently, he was a Muslim who visited the mosque regularly. Although a staunch traditionalist, Erédùmí died while praying in the mosque.

In my fieldwork, I was impressed by the Ifẹ̀ people's layered responses to modernity and to monotheistic religious traditions. Their repertoire of knowledge, which was derived from multiple sources—mission schools, Islamic traditions, Qur'anic schools, and modern secular traditions—influenced their responses, which others might view as purely indigenous. When people articulate their beliefs, especially to outsiders, their worldview and experiences should be reflected through the prism of their multiple traditions. As Sandra Greene has observed, "Individual African societies need to be studied comprehensively in all their diversity in order to illustrate the range of cultural forms that can exist within a single society, forms that must co-exist peacefully but which can at times clash, producing eruptions of violence."[11]

My recollection of events in Ilé-Ifẹ̀, especially toward the end of my almost twenty years of regular visits to the city, includes memories of tolerance and coexistence and also of a series of clashes between members of indigenous religious groups and their Christian and Muslim cohorts. The responses of the priests in Ilé-Ifẹ̀ to all these events similarly ranged from an acknowledgment of peaceful relations to a sense of conflict with Islam and Christian traditions, as the various chapters in this book clearly show. Although I came across few cases of violent clashes between proponents of indigenous religions and those of Christianity and Islam, I encountered many instances of subtle and peaceful disagreement. In one particular instance, the greatest challenge to òrìṣà tradition arose from the Christian fundamentalist youth within the òrìṣà lineage itself. I would like to problematize this new development within the larger context of Ilé-Ifẹ̀ modernity.

AN EVANGELICAL CHRISTIAN TRADITION ENCOUNTERS ÒRÌṢÀ IN ILÉ-IFẸ̀ CITY

Two major traditions influencing the status and image of Ilé-Ifẹ̀ today are the Christian evangelical tradition, especially the born-again Pentecostal evangelical Christian traditions, and òrìṣà traditional influence in the Americas. Christian evangelicalism is spreading through indigenous Yorùbá states with a message couched in images, imagined or real, of religious battle against what evangelists perceive as the vestiges of "pagan" traditions. Evangelical Christianity is taking a toll on the òrìṣà traditions in the city, the ancient image of the city as the bastion of Yorùbá traditions, and the essential power of the sacred kingship. During the last phase of my research, for example, I stopped at the palace to commiserate with the palace officials (Ẹmẹ̀sẹ̀) over the death of one of their colleagues, Ẹmẹ̀sẹ̀ Èkeje, whose profound friendship and assistance I greatly missed. In the course of my conversation with the palace officials, a former colleague from the university, who was very much aware of my work, drove into the palace, spotted my vehicle, and parked by my side. He emerged from his car carrying a big Bible, greeted me triumphantly, and announced loudly that he was in the palace to attend a Bible study session. Of course, I had been informed by some Ifè priests that Bible classes and Bible revival meetings were held in the palace and that the Ọ̀ọ̀ni himself, favorably referred to by his people as Ọ̀ọ̀ni-Rìṣà (Ọ̀ọ̀ni god) or Olúwayé (Owner of the Universe), attended these prayer meetings. The Ọ̀ọ̀ni also supported the practice of all the religions of his people. However, in the twenty-first century, with the decline of òrìṣà traditions, the Ifè people were undoubtedly torn between the vestiges of òrìṣà traditions and the Christian evangelical zeal sweeping the city. Consequently, there was strong pressure on the Ọ̀ọ̀ni and the palace to abandon the ancient traditions and adopt the new Christian religion wholesale.

The responses of traditional priests to this intense campaign varied from condemnation of Islam and Christianity to pleas for compromise. The Àràbà, the chief priest of Ifá, once prayed to his deity, Ifá, to save his people from "all these kèfèrí [unbelievers]," invoking the derogatory slang with which Muslims and Christians had for over a century described òrìṣà worshippers to condemn the intolerance directed at the òrìṣà devotees. In conversation with me, the current chief priest of Odùduwà, the Ọbadìo, prayed to the irúnmọlẹ̀ (401 gods) to save his people from these "infidels" (àláìgbàgbọ́), enemies of òrìṣà living in the land of Odùduwà. If the onslaught of Christian evangelism represents the negative side of Yorùbá modernity and cultural pluralism from the perspective of òrìṣà devotees, then òrìṣà globalization and the intervention from the Americas, to which I shall now turn, represents a positive—though quite distinct—influence.

VYING FOR THE PALACE AND THE PUBLIC SPACE

As I mentioned in chapter 1, the Ọ̀ọ̀ni's palace (ààfin) is the cultural heart of the city, the most sacred space in Ilé-Ifè. The palace grounds include a public arena referred to as Òkè-Ilé (the upper place and house), reserved exclusively for the Ọ̀ọ̀ni, his subjects, and his people. The Òkè-Ilé represents the center of operations for the traditional city. All rituals and secular activities that concern the welfare of the people and the king must begin and end in this sacred space. As one Ilé-Ifè festival in the yearly cycle of rituals is declared closed at this center, the next begins in the same space. It is no wonder, then, that as Ilé-Ifè confronts modernity and as rival religious bodies compete for influence in the city, the palace itself is the public space where the hegemony of the indigenous institution is being ferociously challenged. As the primary domain of the Ọ̀ọ̀ni, the place where he began and will end his reign, the palace is a microcosm of the sacred city that mirrors its religious tensions and clashes for cultural dominance. But at the same time, the palace reflects the prosperity and material abundance that the city generates.

In theory, the sacred kingship derives its legitimacy, meaning, and function from indigenous òrìṣà tradition. The Ọ̀ọ̀ni is regarded as the last of the 201 gods in the

Ifẹ̀ pantheon. Like the queen of England, who personifies the British people, whose Anglican tradition legitimizes British civil faith, and whose sacred crown is placed on her head in Westminster Abbey, the Ọ̀ọ̀ni has as his symbols of authority the Odùduwà's *arè* (the great crown) and *idà* (the sword of Ọ̀rànmíyàn). These are worn and held, respectively, during the Ọlọ́jọ́ Festival in Ilé-Ifẹ̀. As the Ọ̀ọ̀ni himself admitted to me in an interview, the *òrìṣà* tradition legitimizes the Ọ̀ọ̀ni's and the Ọba's reign and authority over the people. As I discussed in chapter 8, the indigenous institutions and the chief priests fashioned, controlled, and executed the ideology and rituals of kingship, and for centuries they have maintained strong cultural and religious hegemony over the city and its people. However, during the contemporary period, especially in the past twenty years, significant change has taken place in the city. Primarily, the increasingly heterogeneous and pluralistic religious landscape of the city has altered the ideological and spiritual status of the palace and the space hitherto controlled by *òrìṣà* devotees. Devotees themselves recognize that very few people now patronize them, as public loyalty appears to be shifting toward evangelical Christian and Islamic groups. In view of this recent incursion, can Ifẹ̀ civil religion continue to govern the social and cultural religious life of Ilé-Ifẹ̀? Does the increasing militancy of "imported" Christian and Islamic revivalism damage the pluralistic integrity of the ancient city?

Òrìṣà devotees continue to claim control over the space considered traditionally their own—the palace. How will these devotees resist the "foreign" appropriation of their cultural property and rights?[12] As Islam and Christianity have come to dominate the city landscape more and more, they too have laid claim to the *ààfin,* the city's most contentious sacred space. Predictably, Islamic groups have tended to locate their main mosques near the city center, and although Christian groups have mostly tended to locate their places of worship in remote and serene areas far from both the city center and the palace, in this recent dispensation in Ilé-Ifẹ̀ they, like Islamic groups, have been vying for control over the palace, attempting to obtain the political, ideological, and material authority that indigenous religion previously enjoyed. The contest for the soul of the city plays itself out in this sacred space, over the visible icon of the palace.

GLOBAL *ÒRÌṢÀ* DEVOTION AND ILÉ-IFẸ̀ CITY

As a response to the increasing marginalization of *òrìṣà* tradition in Ilé-Ifẹ̀, the involvement of the global *òrìṣà* community in the religious affairs of the city has increased and may ultimately become a formidable strategy for guaranteeing the tradition's survival. The central place and status of Ilé-Ifẹ̀ in global *òrìṣà* devotion have turned the city into a major site of pilgrimage, especially for devotees from the Americas and the Caribbean. Every month *òrìṣà* devotees visit the city to participate in one festival or another. Although the annual Ifá Festival in July (discussed in chapter 7) still attracts the largest number of researchers and students, who visit the city to study the ways of the Yorùbá gods, virtually all the important ceremonies draw participants from abroad. The Ifá Festival is generally the locus of òrìsà activities in Ilé-Ifẹ̀, when hundreds of devotees from all over the world visit the city to climb the sacred hill of Àgbọnìrègún at Òkè Ìtasẹ̀. In the consciousness of some devotees, the hill resembles Mount Arafat in Mecca, and as I mention in chapter 7, I frequently heard people say, Òkè Arafat tiwa nìyẹn (This is our own Mount Arafat). In addition, at a conscious level, the devotees, who may be Muslim as well, confer upon Òkètase the status of the Hajj or Mount Arafat in their own religious imaginations. Such comparative metaphors, derived from other world religions, suggest that òrìsà tradition has taken on global meaning for devotees in Ilé-Ifẹ̀. In addition, several Ifá priestly titles, especially Àràbà Àgbáyé and Àwíṣẹ Àgbáyé, confer international identity through use of the adjective àgbáyé (global), indicating that the jurisdiction of the officeholders extends beyond Ilé-Ifẹ̀ and the land of the Yorùbá to significant portions of the world.

That Ilé-Ifẹ̀ has attained global status is demonstrated in the prominence of city priests, and especially the Àràbà, in the World Congress of Òrìsà Tradition, which meets triannually in such places as Cuba, Brazil, Trinidad and Tobago, the United States, and Nigeria, where the Àràbà takes an essential role in ritual and ceremonial activities. Yorùbás are still amazed by the commitment of the devotees of òrìsà in Brazil, Cuba, Trinidad, and the United States in worshipping the òrìsà of the Yorùbá of West Africa. Earlier, I alluded to the Ọọ̀ni's status among òrìsà devotees around the globe. In 1979 and 1986, his visits to Cuba and to Trinidad and Tobago clearly demonstrated that he was held in the highest esteem as the custodian of òrìsà tradition and even as a god in their religious worldview. Cuba and Trinidad mobilized their state apparatus to honor the sacred king of the Yorùbá. These stories illustrate the changes in the character and identity of the sacred city and highlight the transnational quest to see the city's symbolic significance restored. Òrìsà devotees in Ilé-Ifẹ̀ are beginning to take advantage of this global òrìsà renaissance to discredit disparagers of òrìsà culture.

LOCAL TRADITION, GLOBAL RESPONSES, AND ÒRÌSÀ TRADITION

During my field research in 2004, I witnessed the despair and outrage of Ilé-Ifẹ̀'s indigenous religious intelligentsia, who are gasping for air in a restricted space occupied by apparently hostile forces—conservative evangelical Christian and Muslim revivalists. Ilé-Ifẹ̀'s traditionalists are heeding a call to action, to prevent the last vestiges of their ancestral traditions from disappearing. What, then, are their strategies for survival?

We may begin by discussing the reemergence of the òrìsà tradition, especially as it relates to expanding *òrìṣà* authority, mobilizing resources, and refashioning the identity of the local *òrìṣà* lineage to embrace the global diaspora where *òrìṣà* traditions are vibrant. A vital part of this refashioning process is the zeal of local *òrìṣà* devotees to expand their scope and embrace events at the global level. *Òrìṣà* tradition has also begun to adopt conversion strategies hitherto associated with world religious traditions. Although a number of neo-Yorùbá cultural associations have emerged in the city to buttress the revival of *òrìṣà* traditions, similar events on the city's university campus demonstrated perhaps the strongest responses to the culture war emerging today between *òrìṣà* traditions and Christian evangelical revivalism.

In 1976, in my first year as a junior faculty member (graduate assistant) at the University of Ifẹ̀, Ilé-Ifẹ̀ (now Ọbáfẹ́mi Awólọ́wọ̀ University), Nigeria's premier Yorùbá university, an extraordinary event took place.[13] A group of scholars created an informal *òrìṣà* club—Òrìlé Òrìṣà, or Abode of the Gods. At its core were the influential Yorùbá intellectuals Wọlé Ṣóyínká (the Nobel laureate), Wándé Abímbọ́lá (who would become vice chancellor), Akínṣọlá Akìwọwọ, Bádé Àjùwọ̀n, Ọmọ́tọ́ṣọ́ọ̀ Elúyẹmí, Ọlábíyìí Yai, and the Brazilian-born scholar Pierre Fátúmbí Verger, who, like William Bascom, had been initiated into an Ifá divination tradition. A host of other Yorùbá scholars also participated in the club. Although none practiced *òrìṣà* traditions themselves, they shared the scholarly interest of former influential scholars such as Rowland Abíọ́dún, Babátúndé Lawal, Ṣopé Oyèláràn, and others.

Òrìlé Òrìṣà developed local structures to allow for religious worship intended to rival Christian and Islamic weekly services that were already occupying campus classrooms and lecture halls, taking over campus space beyond the chapel and the mosque normally designated for worship. The Yorùbá intelligentsia organized lectures and seminars on campus to promote scholarly and devotional interest in *òrìṣà* tradition. More importantly, Òrìlé Òrìṣà protagonists maintained close relationships and connections with *òrìṣà* devotees in the city. Òrìlé Òrìṣà quickly became an informal advocacy group that helped local *òrìṣà* devotees to organize themselves and to promote a more cohesive resistance to their marginalization. They gave *òrìṣà* traditions a prestige hitherto denied.

INDIGENOUS IFẸ̀ RELIGION ENCOUNTERS A WESTERN CHRISTIAN SECT

The transformation of Ilé-Ifẹ̀ religion from a strong indigenous tradition that once held sway over the moral, religious, and social life of the people to a somewhat marginal tradition must be placed in a historical and cultural context. Conversions to Islam (beginning in the fifteenth century) and Christianity (beginning in the nineteenth century) in Yorùbáland continue to influence religious ideology in the city to the present day. Although conversion to Islam began much earlier, between the nineteenth and twentieth centuries Yorùbá youth and adults sought out baptism and adopted Christian names, often as a means of obtaining Western education and a "modern" identity. Gradually they began to embrace the ethos of the two introduced world religions, finding indigenous religious traditions less and less plausible.

The new faiths did not recognize the traditional òrìṣà lineage and ancestral heritage. But during this period, despite the exclusivist worldviews of Islam and Christianity, it was not difficult for òrìṣà devotees to juggle the two religious systems (indigenous òrìṣà and monotheistic). The lyrics of a song that is popular to this day reflect this age of religious tolerance and mixing: "We would practice the religion of our ancestors. Christianity and Islam do not forbid us from practicing the religious heritage of our ancestors."[14]

A move to recognize the priestly class as the second branch of Ifẹ̀ social structure began in the 1930s, when Ilé-Ifẹ̀ elites wrote a series of petitions to the Ọọ̀ni Adésọjí Adérẹ̀mí and the district officer. The elites wanted to restore the long-standing tradition in which priests had assumed significant religious and political power in the affairs of the city. One particular member of the Ifẹ̀ elite, who more than anyone else became the rallying figure for this protest, was Chief Fáṣọgbọ́n, a local Ifẹ̀ historian. He argued that the Ìṣòrò chief priests should be designated as Òsì-Ifẹ̀, that is, equal in status to Ọ̀tún-Ifẹ̀ (the secular high chiefs). In the current dispensation, the Òsì Ifẹ̀ are normally the palace chiefs headed by the Lọ́wá and are a part of the political sphere of governance. The priest-chiefs represent a separate layer whose influence in city affairs is based on their moral authority and whose power is defined more by their ritual roles and activities than by civil and political authority. Scholars are unclear about the citywide political role that priests occupied in antiquity. Under the old dispensation in the beginning of the Ifẹ̀ city-state—according to our understanding of Ifẹ̀ cosmology and the evolution of the state—priest-chiefs (Ìṣòrò) were probably religious rulers who presided over the affairs of the lineage-based territories. We can assume that when the ancient Ifẹ̀ federacy was created, the ancient function of the priest-chiefs as minirulers was subsumed under the Ọọ̀ni's rule. It is not clear when and how the transformation took place that removed them from active involvement in Ifẹ̀ civil affairs. Without necessarily winning his case through many years of struggle, Fáṣọgbọ́n provided for the priestly class a more authoritative status and a more visible place in the modern political and social setting of Ilé-Ifẹ̀. His struggle to bring the priestly class into the state's modernizing project never quite materialized, although like the secular chiefs, the priests could have wielded significant judicial and civil authority over their people.[15]

During the 1980s, coinciding with the rapid rise of evangelical Christianity, especially Pentecostal and Charismatic revivalism, that swept the religious landscape of Nigeria, evangelical Christianity laid claim to the most central public space in the city—the palace of the kings. One consequence of this new trend was that the central role of the òrìṣà devotees and the priestly lineages was gradually reduced to performing symbolic functions on state ritual occasions, such as the investiture of chiefs and village heads (Baálè) or the conferral of honorary titles upon foreign visitors to the palace. Though still laden with cultural significance, these rituals became public ceremonies choreographed as spectacles for the enjoyment of the populace and guests. They included sacrifices for maintaining social order and peace in the city, but they had little to do with the maintenance of òrìṣà tradition.

The current battle over the control of public domains of religion in the city is the most difficult that religious elites have ever encountered. Ifè's own modernity is now in crisis, and the question becomes who defines the Ilé-Ifè public civil faith. Whereas in the Western world the crisis of modernity may connote a struggle between religion and secularity, Ilé-Ifè's struggle revolves around which form of religion will control its center and palace. In the past, an òrìṣà-based kingship defined public civil religion through its òrìṣà symbols, rituals, and metaphors, but today religious campaigns, especially of evangelical Christianity, are challenging earlier traditions. Even more significantly, the most central figure in the public faith is the Ọòni, the chief priest of Ilé-Ifè's civil faith. How the Ọòni positions himself in the new dispensation and in the battle between various religious faiths for the soul of the city will determine the future of religion in the ancient city.

AN INTERNATIONAL ÒRÌṢÀ CONGRESS

Out of the grassroots initiatives developed in support of òrìṣà tradition during the last few decades, two significant organizations emerged. One was the annual Ifá Festival in Ilé-Ifè City, discussed in chapter 7, which gradually acquired a wider regional and transnational status as it evolved into a popular event catching the attention of Ifá devotees from the entire Yorùbá region and from abroad, who gathered in the city to celebrate the òrìṣà. The Ifá Festival became an occasion on which to express official views on matters influencing the practice and the state of òrìṣà traditions in Yorùbáland.

The other was the Òrìṣà Congress (officially, the Global Association and Conference of Òrìṣà Tradition), inaugurated in 1977 on the Ilé-Ifè campus. Delegates from Brazil, Cuba, Trinidad, the United States, and other parts of the world attended this landmark conference and began to transform an informal group into a global association that now meets regularly every three years in various parts of the black Atlantic world. The inaugural conference in Ilé-Ifè revealed to the Ilé-Ifè people and to the Yorùbá in general that Yorùbá religion and òrìṣà tradition had spread far beyond the southwestern region of Nigeria. They witnessed firsthand how the New World delegates practiced the tradition, and as Cuban and Brazilian òrìṣà musicians, drummers, and dancers performed, some Nigerian devotees in the audience shed tears of joy upon realizing that their beloved traditions were practiced so far beyond Ilé-Ifè. The more literate Yorùbá, especially university scholars, recognized immediately in the exquisite New World Portuguese and Spanish songs, dance performances, and *bàtá* drumming the precious traditional Yorùbá religious forms that they themselves had all but disowned in Nigeria.

Subsequently, the Òrìṣà Congress met in San Francisco, Havana, Bahia, and Port-au-Prince in Trinidad and Tobago; indeed, it has become a formal, structured congress. Unlike similar ethnic, national, and global associations in other parts of the indigenous world, which have become sensitized to the political and touristic value of culture and identity, the congress has been unable to gain significant political influence from its activities and programs.[16] The reason for this failure is clear. Ilé-Ifè, the place of origin and the focus of this book, though now recognized as the cultural capital of the latest traditional religious movement, is deeply integrated into the structure of Nigeria's nation-state. The state has offered little or no recognition for *òrìṣà* traditions, indigenous cultures, or moral systems.

Several years ago, Nigeria produced a national cultural policy that made not a single reference to its indigenous religious tradition.[17] As a loosely formed transnational organization, the Òrìṣà Congress has no shared symbols or identity markers other than its claim to Yorùbá *òrìṣà* tradition.[18] The Òrìṣà Congress is insufficiently connected to international advocacy groups, consortiums, and scholars whose intervention has helped similar indigenous interest groups fight injustice and benefit from the cultural capital they display to the outside world. Unless the Òrìṣà Congress links its agenda with the global interests of advocacy, universal human rights, indigenous democratic institutions, and environmental protection, it will continue to offer a one-dimensional stage on which to display traditional costumes, music, drumming, and dance. It could establish links with other organizations such as the International Congress of Ethnobotany, for instance, whose members want to preserve indigenous knowledge of ethnobotany, ethnobiology, ethnopharmacology, biodiversity and genetic resources, archaeobotany, traditional medicinal plant sources, indigenous resource management, conservation and development, traditional ecology, biochemistry, environmental protection, mythology, linguistic studies, and other fields. Tapping into these shared interests offers compelling political appeal worldwide. Moreover, when well-educated and professionally trained younger scholars and devotees, such as A. Agboola and Kọ́lá Abímbọ́lá, participate as leaders appealing to diverse disciplines, significant progress will take place.

It is difficult to predict the future of the Yorùbá's indigenous *òrìṣà* traditions, but it seems that diasporic Yorùbá communities are increasingly becoming involved in expanding their own spheres of influence within the African space. This new form of globalization, in which diasporic communities perpetuate rituals and ceremonies that are being stifled within Yorùbáland, offers the tonic that *òrìṣà* devotees in Ilé-Ifè will need in what may be dark days ahead.

NOTES

INTRODUCTION

1. Wándé Abímbọ́lá, Fẹ́mi Taíwò, Rowland Abíọ́dún, and Ọlábíyìí Yai are just a few of the numerous African scholars who are undertaking this project.

2. Abímbọ́lá, *Ifá Divination Poetry*.

3. Unfortunately, a theological approach characterizes some of the classical, pioneering works on Yorùbá religious traditions; see Ìdòwú, *Olódùmarè*; Lucas, *Religion of the Yorùbás*; and Parrinder, *African Traditional Religion* and *Religion in an African City*.

4. Eliade, *Images and Symbols*, 38.

5. I indicated in an earlier work (Olúpọ̀nà, *Kingship, Religion, and Rituals*) that the most efficient entry point into the study of Yorùbá religion is festivals and ritual.

6. Long, *Significations*, 48.

7. Ibid., 75.

8. Olúpọ̀nà, *Kingship, Religion, and Rituals*, 165.

9. I refer here to the "theory of Atlantis" promoted by Leo Frobenius, which denied that the city of Ilé-Ifẹ̀ was the creation of the Yorùbá people.

10. Long, "Postcolonial Meaning of Religion," 166.

11. Ibn al-Kalbi, *Book of Idols*.

12. Henotheism is the belief in one god, though not to the exclusion of belief in others.

13. Wheatley, *Pivot of the Four Quarters*.

14. The gauntlet that Wheatley threw down led not only to the study of sacred centers around the world but also to the assignment of a new meaning to the study of archaic religion in the scholarship of Charles Long and David Carrasco and their students, especially Lindsay Jones and Phil Arnold. Although not a scholar of religion, the cultural historian G. J. Afọlábí Òjó aptly recognized the importance of this new meaning in his work *Yorùbá Culture*.

15. Eliade, *Images and Symbols*, 43.

16. Long, "Postcolonial Meaning of Religion," 92.

17. Carrasco, *City of Sacrifice,* 3–7.

18. Long, "Postcolonial Meaning of Religion," 92.

19. Ibid.

20. Eliade, *Images and Symbols,* 38; Olúpònà, *Kingship, Religion, and Rituals,* 169–70.

21. Eliade, *Images and Symbols,* 39.

22. Ibid., 34.

23. Ibid., 40. Although Eliade uses the term *hell* as the third element, the term betrays his Western religious ideology. The third element in the Yorùbá universe is the underworld or *ilé.*

24. By *magic,* I refer not to practices in European traditions and conceptualizations but instead to spirituality in distinct African forms.

25. Long, "Prolegomenon," 260.

26. Ibid., 261.

27. Eliade, *Images and Symbols,* 39.

28. Ibid.

29. Ibid.

30. Aládúrà is an indigenous Yorùbá Christian movement that began shortly after the Western missionaires established their own churches. It reacted against European domination in the church by founding African churches inspired by African prophets.

31. I never mentioned this behavior to my informants because I feared their reaction. As a priest recites the ritual formula, "The will of the god is supreme" *(Ti Olúwa mi l'àṣẹ; ti òrìṣà l'àṣẹ),* these young children, products of Evangelical schools, quietly hum, "The will of Jesus is supreme" *(Ti Jésù l' àṣẹ).*

32. Gross, *Feminism and Religion,* 85.

33. The first wave of missionizing occurred between the fifteenth and nineteenth centuries. During this period, the Yorùbá converted to the two world religions without necessarily destroying their indigenous culture, faith, and spirituality.

1. ILÉ-IFÈ IN TIME AND SPACE

1. Rappaport, *Ecology, Meaning, and Religion,* 209.

2. Eliade, *Sacred and the Profane,* 22.

3. J. Smith, *To Take Place,* 14–15; Rappaport, *Ecology, Meaning, and Religion,* 210.

4. Sole and Woods, "Protection of Indigenous Sacred Sites."

5. J. Smith, *To Take Place,* 26–29.

6. Kunin, *God's Place,* 11.

7. Ibid., 21, 22.

8. J. Hubert, "Sacred Beliefs," 11.

9. Kunin, *God's Place,* 21.

10. Olúpònà, *Kingship, Religion, and Rituals.*

11. Wheatley, *Pivot of the Four Quarters,* 9, 225, 226.

12. Carrasco, *Religions of Mesoamerica,* 14.

13. Ibid., xviii.

14. Ibid., 1–2.

15. Eck, "City as Sacred Center," 1–2.

16. All these quotes are from ibid., 2.

17. Lane, *Landscapes of the Sacred,* ix.

18. Ibid.

19. Ibid., x.

20. This phrase "cultured despisers" was coined by Friedrich D. E. Schleiermacher in his work *On Religion* (originally published in 1799).

21. Cooney and Grogan, *Irish Prehistory,* 33.

22. J. Smith, *To Take Place,* 48.

23. Theodoratus and La Pena, "Wintu Sacred Geography," 21.

24. Òjó, *Yorùbá Culture,* 194.

25. Ibid.

26. Lalèyê, *La conception de la personne,* 73.

27. Ibid.

28. Livingston, *Anatomy of the Sacred,* 56.

29. The legend of Oníbodè Lálúpọn in Ìbàdàn is a classic example of the larger-than-life persona of gatekeepers, but that is outside the purview of this book.

30. Translated into English by Wọlé Ṣóyínká.

31. J. Smith, *To Take Place,* 25–30.

32. Laurence, "Ritual, Landscape," 120.

33. Werblowsky, "Introduction," 11.

34. Ìdòwú, *Olódùmarè,* 11–12.

35. Ibid., 15.

36. Scully, *Homer,* 4.

37. Ibid., 72–73.

38. Another version of the Ìdànrè myth of origin claims that Ọlọ́fin was indeed the same as Odùduwà and that he lived in the mountain for decades.

39. Ọwá, a synonym for Ọba, or king, is more commonly used in eastern Yorùbá towns than in western towns.[0]

40. Friedland and Hecht, "Politics of Sacred Place," 26–28.

41. Ibid., 21.

42. Ben-Israel, "Hallowed Land," 282.

43. Ibid., 279.

44. Kunin, *God's Place,* 26.

45. Ibid., 26, 27.

46. Swain and Trompf, *Religions of Oceania,* 24.

47. Akínjógbìn, *Dahomey and Its Neighbours,* 14–17.

48. Akìwọwọ, *Àjọbí and Àjọgbé.*

49. Ògúnde's song, "In Praise of Chief Awólọ́wọ̀," was written in the 1960s after Nigeria gained its independence.

50. Trager, *Yoruba Hometowns.*

51. Translation adapted from Babáyẹmí, *Content Analysis,* 97–102.

52. See Ọláníyan, "Modakeke Question," and Ṣóyínká-Airewele, "When Neutrality Is Taboo."

53. Ọláníyan, "Modakeke Question," 269.

54. Ibid.

55. Ibid., 269–76.

56. My friend Jimi Badà, now a judge in Ọṣun State High Court and the son of a prominent Ifẹ̀ lawyer and chief, married a Modákẹ́kẹ́.

57. Thornton, "South Africa," 12.

58. Werbner, *Memory and the Postcolony*, 1.

59. Traditionally, *iṣákọ́lẹ̀* signifies the farm tribute a tenant paid to an overlord; Report of the Meeting of the Presidential Conflict Reconciliation Committee on Ifẹ̀/Modakeke, Ifẹ̀ North Local Government Communities, June 2000, 11–12. When the Ọ̀ọ̀ni visited Lagos in 1903 to settle the dispute between two Yorùbá Ọba about the sacred crown, the Ọba of Ẹ̀pẹ́, whose judgment the Ọ̀ọ̀ni did not favor, asked the Ọ̀ọ̀ni if the Ẹlẹ́pẹ́ was not considered a "Son of Odùduwà."

60. Wale Folarin, "Osun Approves Beaded Crown for Modakeke Ruler," *Nigerian Compass,* July 15, 2009, www.compassnewspaper.com/NG/index.php?option=com_content&view=article&id=22572:osun-approves-beaded-crown-for-modakeke-ruler&catid=43:news&Itemid=799.

61. Gewurtz and Errington, "Toward an Ethnographically Grounded Study."

2. THE IMAGINED SACRED CITY

1. Pacheco Pareira's *Esmeraldo de situ orbis,* 130–47.

2. Excerpted in Hodgkin, *Nigerian Perspectives*, 124.

3. Ibid.

4. Ibid.

5. Ibid., 124–25.

6. For discussions on the passage's historicity, see Bradbury, *Benin Kingdom*, 19–23, 35–46; Ryder, "Reconsideration." On the authenticity of the ambassadors, see Ryder, *Benin and the Europeans*, 1–23; on the likelihood of the gift of the cross, see Willett, *Ife in the History*, 153–65.

7. Frobenius, *Voice of Africa,* 93.

8. Senghor, "Lessons of Leo Frobenius," vii.

9. Frobenius, *Voice of Africa,* 32, 84.

10. Ibid., 32.

11. Around 360 BCE, Plato first described an ancient, exotic kingdom catastrophically buried beneath the sea as a punishment from the angry gods.

12. Frobenius, *Voice of Africa,* 88–89.

13. Ibid., 263, 262.

14. Ibid., 90.

15. Ibid.

16. Ibid., 92.

17. Ibid., 95.

18. Ibid., 96.

19. Ibid., 98. (I might note that Frobenius paid just six pounds to purchase this priceless object.)

20. Ibid., 84.

21. Ibid., 88.

22. Ibid.

23. Johnson, *History of the Yorùbás*, 3–4.

24. Johnson (*History of the Yorùbás*, 4) reminds us of the similarities with the story of Gideon, Josiah, and the Abiezrites in the Bible (Judges 6:25–32).

25. Ibid., 3.

26. Hodgkin, *Nigerian Perspectives*, 81.

27. R. Smith, *Kingdoms of the Yorùbá*, 9.

28. I intend to discuss this in my next work, *Yorùbá Thought and Culture: Insight from Ifá Divination Poetry*.

29. Ìṣọ̀lá, "Religious Politics."

30. Egharevba, *Short History of Benin*, 2, 9.

31. At the time of my writing, a new controversy has surfaced between the Ọba of Benin and the Ọ̀ọ̀ni of Ilé-Ifẹ̀. The Ọba of Benin claims that Benin has no connection whatsoever with Ilé-Ifẹ̀ and that the founder of Ilé-Ifẹ̀ was in fact a Benin slave.

32. Bolle, "Myth," 6360.

33. See Ajayi and Smith, *Yorùbá Warfare*; Ayandele, *Missionary Impact on Modern Nigeria*; Peel, *Ijeshas and Nigerians*; Law, *Oyo Empire*.

34. David Hinderer to CMS office, May 14, 1875, Original Papers—Missionaries, Rev David Hinderer, 1849–1876, 1880, CA2/049, Yorùbá Mission, Church Missionary Society Papers, Church Missionary Society Archive, University of Birmingham, Birmingham, UK (hereafter CMSA).

35. Ibid.

36. Peel's *Ijeshas and Nigerians* and my *Kingship, Religion, and Rituals* contain the "stories" of the establishment of Christianity in the Ìjẹ̀ṣà and Oǹdó districts, respectively.

37. Hinderer to CMS office, May 14, 1975.

38. Another CMS missionary who attempted to sway the indigenous beliefs of Ifẹ̀ was the Reverend Charles Phillips, the Apostle of Oǹdó Christianity. A full account of Bishop Charles Phillips's mission work in Oǹdó and Yorùbáland is yet to be written. However, Omotoye's PhD thesis, "Charles Phillips," is a good beginning.

39. Hinderer to CMS office, May 14, 1875.

40. Ibid.

41. Ibid.

42. Charles Phillips, journal entry, August 19, 1877, Original Papers—Missionaries, Charles Phillips, 1852–1858, CA2/077, CMSA.

43. Olúpọ̀nà, *Kingship, Religion, and Rituals*.

44. Ibid.; Eames, "Oǹdó Women's War."

45. Matthew John Luke, journal entry, November 21, 1888, Original Papers—Missionaries, Matthew John Luke, 1877–1879, CA2/064, CMSA.

46. Willett, "Archaeology," 119.

47. Ibid., 123.

48. Willett, *Ife in the History*, 15, quotes from 25.

49. Ibid.

50. Ibid., 15.

51. Willett, "Archaeology," 120.

52. Willett, *Ife in the History*, 27.

53. Ibid., 29.

54. Willett, "Archaeology," 125.

55. Willett, *Ife in the History*, 49.

56. Willett, "Archaeology," 128.

57. Bascom to Herskovits, June 1951, William Bascom Papers, Carton 21, Bancroft Library, University of California at Berkeley (hereafter BL).

58. William Bascom, pers. comm., n.d., William Bascom Papers, Carton 21, BL.

59. Bascom, *Yoruba of Southwestern Nigeria*, 26.

60. William Bascom, Ilé-Ifè fieldnotes, 1937–38. William Bascom Papers, Carton 21, BL.

61. Bascom, *Yoruba of Southwestern Nigeria*, 1.

62. Ibid., 70-97.

63. William Bascom, notes from "Forms of Folklore," presented paper, 1963, William Bascom Papers, Carton 21, BL.

64. Bascom, "Oba's Ear," 149.

65. Bascom, notes for "Oba's Ear," William Bascom's Papers, Carton 21, BL.

66. The details of the account that follows, including quotations from official correspondence, are taken from the *Colonial Government Gazette* (Lagos, Nigeria), February 1903, 165–70, National Archives, Ibadan, CSE/1/1285, No. 1881/1902/3.

67. The Yorùbá proverb says: *A gbọ́ ẹjọ́ ẹnikan dá, àgbà òṣikà ni.*

68. This refers to remaking the roof of his palace and having abundant food to eat.

3. THE SACRED COSMOS AND ILÉ-IFÈ RELIGION

1. Pemberton and Afọláyan, *Yorùbá Sacred Kingship*, 1.

2. Children born through the favor of Èṣù are often named Èṣùbiyi (Èṣù provides this child) or Èṣùtosin (Èṣù is worthy of worship).

3. Griffin-Pierce, *Earth Is My Mother*, 65.

4. The myth of Mọrèmi and the festival of Edì are described in chapter 7 in this book.

5. It is a reference to a nostalgia for a paradise lost: sorrow for the demise of an important Ifá center. The prayer resembles the biblical text, "Pray for the peace of Jerusalem, and all those who love it shall prosper" (Ps. 122:6).

6. Another name for Olúwayé is Sònpònná or Ọbalúayé.

7. Private conversation with the Ọòni Olúbùṣe, December 2005.

8. Skoggard, *Indigenous Dynamic*, 21.

9. Ibid., 3.

10. Florescano, *Myth of Quetzalcoatl*, 1.

11. Griffin-Pierce, *Earth Is My Mother*, 32; Lessa and Vogt, *Reader in Comparative Religion*.

12. In Ilé-Ifè's imagination, witches are thought to fly at night with wings.

13. Reichard, *Prayer.*

14. Oyèékàn Owómóyèlá, pers. comm., January 1991.

15. Griffin-Pierce, *Earth Is My Mother,* 340.

16. Owómóyèlá, pers. comm., January 1991.

17. Neusner, "Being Israel," 39.

18. Rowland Abíódún, private conversation, January 2005.

4. MYTH AND RITUAL OF SACRED KINGSHIP

1. Egharevba, *Short History of Benin.*

2. Ifè indigenes cite Òrànmíyàn as the link between Òyó and Ilé-Ifè. The ritual investiture of an Aláàfin (the Oba of Òyó) required a sword of authority, Idà Òrànmíyàn, brought from Ilé-Ifè.

3. Babaláwo Ifátóògùn is an Ifà diviner from Ilobu who teaches at Obáfémi Awólówò University, Ilé-Ifè, Nigeria.

4. The Ifà texts speak in metaphors and make numerous references to archetypal figures and cultural heroes. Some of the characters are given "nicknames" that bear profound ethical and moral injunctions. The above is an important text because it refers to the city of Benin, a city culturally linked to Ilé-Ifè, and to the presence of the Europeans in this city, apparently during the period of the European trade with Benin, when Benin City became quite prosperous.

5. Ògún also administers justice, and his judgments generally involve harsh punishment of evildoers. However, he bestows manifold benevolence and blessings upon his faithful devotees. Ògún is considered to be "a hot" deity because he deals primarily with energy and forceful motion, as opposed to "cooler" deities like Obàtálá, whose colors are white and who is associated with calm and a deliberate slowness.

6. Like most myths, the story is apparently sacred and out of the ordinary because it conveys what happened at the time of the world's creation. I am intrigued that my consultant repeatedly referred to the Virgin Birth while telling me the story, apparently to convince me about the story's plausibility. A recurring issue in my field research in Ilé-Ifè was that the òrìsà devotees constantly used Christian and Islamic metaphors, images, and stories to explain their worldview to outsiders.

7. Eck, *Banaras,* xv.

8. *Ìjálá,* the poetry of Yoruba hunters, speaks of seven manifestations of Ògún in the Yorùbá pantheon.

9. Silverman, "Divinity and Deities," 16.

10. The first, second, and fourth days are the ritual days. On the third day no major ritual is performed.

11. For the purpose of this research, in 1993 and 1995 I attended two Olójó ceremonies. My descriptions are based on these festivals as I observed them upon these two occasions. I provide additional information from the study of the same festival reported by William Bascom in 1938 and by the Ifè historian Chief Fásogbón, who has also written about the festival.

12. I am intrigued by this rite of invocation because in the towns of Ondó and Ilè-Olúji a local form of a bugle-like instrument called the *upe,* made from a kind of gourd, is sounded

for about fifteen days before the Ògún Festival. The purpose is the same as in the *gbàjúre* ritual.

13. Bascom, "'Secret Societies.'"

14. Valeri, *Kingship and Sacrifice*, 337.

15. *Ojú* (the eyes) refers to the blade of the sword that Ògún uses to kill his victims. Rowland Abíódún, pers. comm., January 1995.

16. See H. Hubert and Mauss, *Sacrifice;* Girard, *Violence and the Sacred;* Valeri, *Kingship and Sacrifice.*

17. Valeri, *Kingship and Sacrifice*, 62.

18. Ibid., 70.

19. C. Bell, *Ritual,* 16.

20. Valeri, *Kingship and Sacrifice,* 71.

21. Girard, *Violence and the Sacred,* 98.

22. MacCannell, *Empty Meeting Grounds,* 264.

23. Bird, *Sticks, Stones,* 215.

24. I spent the larger part of the night with the Oṣògún, where those who took part in the evening ceremony congregated for the night vigil.

25. During my first period of field research in Ilé-Ifẹ̀, when my late father was the Anglican archdeacon of Ilé-Ifẹ̀, he led a group of Anglican priests, all dressed in white cassocks, on the day before Ọlójó, to greet Ọòni Adérẹ́mí in the palace. My father described Ọlójó to me as the Ọòni's festival, Ọdún Ọòni, an acknowledgment of the monarchy of the Ọòni in religiously pluralistic Ilé-Ifẹ̀.

26. Habermas, *Structural Transformation.*

27. The Yorùbá word *afẹfẹyẹyẹ* is a slang term meaning flamboyant celebration.

28. Rowland Abíódún gave a lecture with this title, on Yorùbá women and the arts, at Smith College in February 1991.

29. This list includes the Ọba who founded the ancient Yorùbá cities of Oǹdó, Ọ̀yọ́, Ketu, Ọ̀wọ̀, Sabe, Benin, and Popo.

30. Pemberton and Afọláyan, *Yorùbá Sacred Kingship.*

31. Sandra Barnes to William Bascom, June 28, 1980, William Bascom Collection, Bancroft Library, University of California, Berkeley.

32. Geertz, *Negara.*

33. C. Bell, *Ritual,* 86; Geertz, *Negara.*

34. Bloch, "Ritual of the Royal Bath."

35. McMullen, "Bureaucrats and Cosmology," 184.

36. Ibid., 187, 188.

37. The lyrics say: "The earthly masquerade *[eégún ayé]* and the heavenly spirits *[èsìbà ọrun]* descend and let us 'make' *[se]* Ifẹ̀, descend! Our festival is here."

38. McMullen, "Bureaucrats and Cosmology," 202. I use the term *correlative recipient* in the same context as McMullen to refer to a divinity or deceased exemplar who is loosely associated with the main recipients.

39. William Bascom, field notes from research in Ilé-Ifẹ̀ in 1937, William Bascom's Papers.

40. A police guard saw my zoom camera and assumed that I was a reporter working for

a foreign newspaper. He took it upon himself to escort me around the palace and the shrine while clearing the crowd away for me as we moved from place to place.

41. Bloch, "Ritual of the Royal Bath," 295.

42. Combs-Schilling, *Sacred Performances*.

43. The lyrics, *Òde tó ojẹ́ mi rí arè*, are translated, "It is time to come out! Time for the outing. Let me behold the *arè* crown."

44. The lyrics of the song say, *Ẹni bá ní kí ẹbọ má gbà, á bá ẹbọ lọ, àṣẹ fíń o, ẹbọ Ọòni* (Whoever would prevent the sacrifice from being accomplished will perish with the sacrifice. The Ọòni's sacrifice will be accomplished).

45. Bloch, "Ritual of the Royal Bath," 295.

46. Ibid., 296.

47. Rowland Abíọ́dún, pers. comm., July 1998.

48. Pemberton and Afọláyan, *Yorùbá Sacred Kingship*.

49. Olúbùṣe II, "Greetings from the Throne," 4.

50. Ibid.

51. Similarly, Java's Indonesian performances and the local ritual investiture of the sultan responded to the demands of the nation-state and global contingencies of modernity.

5. ÌTÀPÁ

1. The Ọbàtálá religious community is headed by one of two chief priests chosen in rotation from two lineages. At the time of my research, the Ọbálẹ́ṣùn was the chief priest in charge. After his reign, Chief Priest Ọbalálẹ̀ from the other lineage will head the community.

2. It is interesting that Ọbàtálá festivals in many Yorùbá towns reflect similar motifs of the defeat, imprisonment, and subsequent rehabilitation of Ọbàtálá. Like Ilé-Ifẹ̀ myth and ritual, the sacred kingship plays a similar role of conceding some amount of authority to this deity. See Beier, "Year of Sacred Festival."

3. Mol, *Identity and Religion*.

4. Kurtz, *Gods in the Global Village*.

5. See, e.g., Mol, *Faith and Fragility*, 2, as well as *Identity and the Sacred* and *Identity and Religion*.

6. For a critique of identity theory in cultural studies, see Grossberg, "Identity and Cultural Studies," 90. My own interest lies, not in the new theories' focus on subaltern, marginalized, or dominated identities (90), or on oppressed or minority groups, significant as these may be, or on their construction as a subject standing outside and against a well-established structure of power (87), but in their relevance to a study of power relations in the Ilé-Ifẹ̀ sacred center.

7. Ibid., 92.

8. Oberoi, *Construction of Religious Boundaries*, 63.

9. Sarup, *Identity, Culture*.

10. As mentioned in chapter 1, Ọbàtálá gave up his claim to the leadership of the created world.

11. Daramola and Jeje, *Awọn asa ati òrìṣà ilé Yorùbá*.

12. Ọbàtálá is often called Ọ̀rọ̀ Ọkọ Àfín (the Spirit-Husband of the Albino).

13. A *kobo* is the smallest unit of Nigerian money.

14. A similar phenomenon may be seen in Hinduism when Shiva is referred to simply as "god." See Eck, *Banaras.*

15. Some of the attributes of Ọbàtálá are cited in Adeoye's *Ìgbàgbọ́ àti ẹ̀sìn Yorùbá,* while others were communicated to me by Babaláwo Ifátóògùn and several of Ọbàtálá's devotees.

16. Olúpọ̀nà, *Kingship, Religion, and Rituals.*

17. Davidson, "Hooded Men," 105.

18. Adeoye, *Ìgbàgbọ́ àti ẹ̀sìn Yorùbá,* 120.

19. Shelton, "Preliminary Notes," 157.

20. Adeoye, *Ìgbàgbọ́ àti ẹ̀sìn Yorùbá,* 122–23.

21. Note that although Yemòó and Ògún are both deities who are revered in blood, in mythological narratives, Ògún bathes in human blood, while Yemòó prefers to bathe in animal blood.

22. Elebuibon, *Adventures of Ọbàtálá,* 12.

23. McGee, "In Quest of Saubhagya," 160. Attitudes toward women in Hindu society as depicted by McGee are in several respects similar to those in Yorùbá society.

24. Erndl, *Victory to the Mother,* 6.

25. V. Turner, *Ritual Process.*

26. McGee, "In Quest of Saubhagya," 155.

27. Babb, *Divine Hierarchy,* 221. According to Babb, Devi could manifest as Kali (the destroyer), Lakshmi (the giver of happiness and wealth), or Mate (the mother or giver of life).

28. Ibid., 229.

29. Olúpọ̀nà, "To Praise."

30. See Mach, *Symbols, Conflict,* 173.

31. Eliade, *Sacred and the Profane.*

32. Mach, *Symbols, Conflict,* 177.

33. A. Smith, *Ethnic Origins of Nations,* 29.

34. Taussig, "Transgression," 357.

35. Horton, "On the Rationality."

36. Koester, *History, Culture,* 198.

37. Ibid.

38. Koester, "Writings and the Spirit."

39. Douglas, *Purity and Danger.*

40. On the great traditions of pilgrimage, see, e.g., Dubisch, *In a Different Place;* V. Turner and Turner, *Image and Pilgrimage;* Morinis, *Pilgrimage.*

41. Dubisch, *In a Different Place,* 35.

42. Ibid., 46.

43. Ibid., 35.

44. Ibid., 38.

45. V. Turner and Turner, *Image and Pilgrimage;* Eickelman, *Moroccan Islam;* Dubisch, *In a Different Place.*

46. Niditch, *Ancient Israelite Religion,* 105.

47. Cohen, "Anger," 3.

48. Beier, "Year of Sacred Festival."

49. D. Bell, *Daughters of the Dreaming.*

50. Hubert and Mauss, *Sacrifice;* Van Baal, "Offering, Sacrifice, and Gift," 169.

51. Van Baal, "Offering, Sacrifice, and Gift," 162.

52. Niditch, *Ancient Israelite Religion,* 105.

53. The role of Yemòó is sometimes played by a man, who, of course, is dressed as a woman. Several scholars have reported that during the period of their own research the role of Yemòó was played by a man (Stevens, "Orisha-nla Festival"). This practice shows how flexible gender roles can be in Yorùbá society.

54. D. Bell, *Daughters of the Dreaming,* 145.

55. Ibid., 146.

6. IFÁ

1. Every Ifá divination performance begins with this recited poem, which I collected from Ilé-Ifè diviners in 1991. The *odù Ifá* recitations, which I have been collecting independently of this work, will form the basis of my next book, *Yorùbá Culture and Religion: Insights from Ifá Divination Poetry.*

2. Adeoye, *Ìgbàgbọ́ àti ẹ̀sìn Yorùbá,* 175–76.

3. Marshall, "!Kung Bushman Religious Beliefs."

4. Bascom, *Ifá Divination,* 70.

5. Coon, *Hunting Peoples,* 372.

6. Livingston, *Anatomy of the Sacred,* 56.

7. Pedya, "Divinity as Place," 85.

8. Sullivan, *Icanchu's Drum,* 346.

9. On shamanism, see ibid., 459.

10. Du Bois, "Meaning without Intention," 56.

11. Verger, *Flux et reflux.*

12. Rowland Abíọ́dún, pers. comm., December 1995.

13. Abíọ́dún, "Ifá Art Objects," 437.

14. The Àràbà's reference to Òkè Arafat was characteristic of a tendency among Ilé-Ifè devotees of *òrìṣà* to compare events and situations in the *òrìṣà* tradition to those of either Islam or Christianity: first as a way of conveying to "outsiders" in their own terms what is otherwise obscure in local tradition, and second as a way explicating *òrìṣà* cosmology beliefs and rituals to the many *òrìṣà* devotees who participate as well in either the Islamic or the Christian tradition. Such comparisons can universalize the otherwise local message of the Ifá cult.

7. THE GODDESS MỌRÈMI IN THE FESTIVAL OF EDÌ

1. My articles "Yoruba Goddesses" and "Òrìṣà Ọṣun" emphasize this new line of research about the Yorùbá goddess tradition. See also Murphy and Sanford, *Ọṣun across the Waters.*

2. See Girard, *Violence and the Sacred.*

3. Walsh, "Edi Festival."

4. Dúró Ládíípọ̀, "Mọrèmi: An Historical Play," in *Three Nigerian Plays,* ed. Ulli Beier (London: Longmans, 1967), 1–34.

5. Vico, *New Science.*

6. Foucault, "Politics."

7. Awolalu, *Yorùbá Beliefs,* 21, 26.

8. Ibid.

9. Rose, *Gender and Heroism.*

10. Ibid., xi.

11. Ibid.

12. Ibid.

13. Ibid., xii.

14. The similarity between Mọrèmi's narrative and the story of Delilah and Samson in the Bible is striking.

15. Fẹrẹkẹtẹ is performed in the Òkèrèwè quarter of Ilé-Ifẹ̀, presided over by Chief Èrí, the priestess and reincarnation of Mọrèmi. Although a national festival in Ilé-Ifẹ̀, Edì is the lineage ritual of people of Òkèrèwè. This is in conformity with the ritual pattern in Ilé-Ifẹ̀ in which most festivals belong to specific lineages, yet are celebrated by all.

16. On the head as a locus of power, see Abíọ́dún, "Ori Divinity"; Lawal, "Ori."

17. Walsh, "Edi Festival."

18. During a visit to Ilé-Ifẹ̀ last year, I was informed that the festival had not been performed for two years. The Ọ̀ọni discouraged its performance because of the burden it placed on the king himself and on the Teele, and also because of the increasing influence of Pentecostal churches and Islam on palace officials.

19. Ọ̀ọni Adésọjí Adérẹ̀mí to British Colonial Police Inspector, November 7, 1952, Ife Papers, National Archives, Ìbàdàn, Nigeria, IFE D.V. 1/1/40.

20. Gluckman, "Ritual of Rebellion." On the Òpèpèé ceremony, see Olúpọ̀nà, *African Traditional Religions.*

21. Droogers and van Harskamp, *Playful Religion.* Droogers was influenced by Huizinga's *Homo Ludens.*

22. See Olúpọ̀nà, *African Traditional Religions.*

23. Bushnell, *Vicarious Sacrifice,* 39.

24. Ibid., 40.

25. Yerkes, *Sacrifice,* 2.

26. V. Turner, "Sacrifice as Quintessential Process," 209–13.

27. Ibid., 210.

28. Ibid., 213.

29. Girard, *Violence and the Sacred,* 12.

30. Williams, "Thresholds of Desire," 49.

31. Ever since Oyèérónkẹ́ Oyèéwùmí published her well-known work *The Invention of Women: Making an African Sense of Western Gender Discourses,* there have been spirited and sometimes contentious debates about her central thesis concerning African gender discourse in Western and African scholarship. The book was the impetus for a very lively conference organized by Stephan Miescher and Catherine Cole at the University of California, Santa Barbara, "Africa after Gender? An Exploration of New Epistemologies for African Studies,"

April 20–22, 2001. I was thrust into the controversy earlier, in December 1999, when I held a major international conference, "Yorùbá Òrìṣà Traditions in the Global Context," at Florida International University in Miami. At that conference, J. Lorand Matory criticized Oyěéwùmí's analysis of gender in traditional Yorùbá society and expressed some concerns about the apparent silence of Yorùbá scholars on what he thought was Oyèéwùmí's misrepresentation of Yorùbá tradition. Matory's counterargument to support the significance of gender in precolonial Yorùbá society, "Is There Gender in Yoruba Culture?", appears in the proceedings of the conference, *Òrìṣà Devotion as World Religion: The Globalization of Yorùbá Religious Culture,* edited by myself and Terry Rey.

In a presentation at the African Studies Association (ASA) meeting in Houston in 2001 that became the article "Gender in Yoruba Religious Change," J. D. Y. Peel indicated that nineteenth-century Church Missionary Society (CMS) archival materials on Yorùbá religion fail to support Oyèéwùmí's thesis. Oyèéwùmí argued that no gender distinctions were made in precolonial, pre-Christian Ọ̀yọ́ Yorùbá society and that "gender was not an organizing principle in Yorùbá society prior to colonialism" (Oyèéwùmí, *Invention of Women,* xi). She claimed that whatever gender references exist today are products of Western feminist scholarship in which gender discourse constitutes a central category. In addition, Oyèéwùmí questioned the wisdom of trivializing African agency and epistemology in Western scholarly discourse on African traditional societies.

My contribution to the debate in this work represents not so much an intervention, though I personally think that gender dynamics are fluid, as a detour that will allow me to recast the issue in a different way in the context of Ifẹ̀ materials. I have concerned myself principally with religion and gender discourse and adopt an interdisciplinary, phenomenological, and hermeneutic approach, in contrast to the anthropological and sociological methods that have characterized this discussion so far. The history of religions is concerned primarily with meaning as it is embedded in the historical and mythic texts or orature, ritual performance, and traditions, which at times are studied cross-culturally and comparatively. It deals with the phenomenology of archetypes, similarities, and differences in structures of meanings, and the development of religious ideas and practices.

8. ODÙDUWÀ, THE GOD-KING

1. McAnany, *Living with the Ancestors,* 6.
2. Ibid.; Fortes, "Some Reflections"; Goody, *Death, Property;* Olúpọ̀nà, "To Praise."
3. McAnany, *Living with the Ancestors,* 1.
4. Ibid., 9.
5. Mills, *Identity, Feasting,* 3; Dietler and Hayden, *Feasts.*
6. Mills, *Identity, Feasting,* 11.
7. Ibid.; Dietler and Hayden, *Feasts.*
8. Florescano, *Myth of Quetzalcoatl,* 189.
9. Masuzawa, *In Search of Dreamtime,* 167.
10. Levy, *Mesocosm,* 327.
11. Ibid., 330.
12. Florescano, *Myth of Quetzalcoatl,* 191.

9. THE CHANGING FACE OF THE CITY

1. A clearer situation occurred several years ago when the Ṣaàrun, a senior Ẹmẹṣẹ̀, told me that òrìṣà worship was the main responsibility of Ifẹ̀ lineages *(oro ite bàbá won mi)* and that they should not expect the palace to continue to bear the burden of providing the money for sacrifices. Incidentally, the Ṣaàrun is regarded as a devout Muslim who has performed the Hajj.

2. As first described by Leon Festinger in *A Theory of Cognitive Dissonance,* cognitive dissonance is the uncomfortable tension that comes from holding two conflicting thoughts at the same time. The theory of cognitive dissonance states that contradicting cognitions serve as a driving force that compels the mind to acquire or invent new thoughts or beliefs, or to modify existing beliefs, so as to reduce the amount of dissonance (conflict) between cognitions.

3. Olúpọ̀nà, *Kingship, Religion, and Rituals;* Laitin, *Hegemony and Culture.*

4. The Catholic enculturation movement that followed the Second Vatican Council preached that Christ and culture were inseparable. A careful study of Yorùbá religion and society at this time would reveal that the religious encounters involved kinds of compromise and mediation that are no longer practiced. The earlier mode of conversion did not privilege Christianity. See Comaroff and Comaroff, *Of Revelation and Revolution.*

5. Yai, "Path Is Open."

6. Comaroff and Comaroff, *Of Revelation and Revolution.*

7. The Comaroffs' *Of Revelation and Revolution* was written in 1991; currently, they have in their newer publications explained the formation of new religious publics (see the introduction to Comaroff and Comaroff, *Civil Society*). The essays in this important new collection explore the diverse, unexpected, and controversial ways in which the idea of civil society has recently entered populist politics and public debate throughout Africa.

8. I had a three-hour interview with Olorì Morísádé Ṣíjúadé, Yèyélúwa of Ilé-Ifẹ̀, Nigeria, on December 23, 2004, at her residence in the Ọ̀ọ̀ni's palace.

9. It is becoming customary for traditional Ọba to build chapels and mosques in their palaces reflecting the religious tastes of the king.

10. On the Ọdún Ọba in Ọndó, see Olúpọ̀nà, *Kingship, Religion, and Rituals.*

11. Hastings, "Were Women a Special Case?" 124.

12. Nigerian daily newspapers frequently tell stories about the wives of Ọba playing very active roles in promoting Christian revival meetings. Several of them serve as goodwill ambassadors and emissaries of their husband-kings, giving testimonies in revival meetings for the Christian God in their respective towns and cities.

13. The notion of female agency in connection with the Ilé-Ifẹ̀ Ọ̀ọ̀ni's palace provides a fascinating comparison to another culture. According to Ọlábíyìí Yai, "Path Is Open," a similar situation arose in the nineteenth-century Dahomean kingdom in Benin. After many attempts to convert the Dahomean kings failed, the missionaries started using the kings' women or ladies (called Christian wives). These women, imported from the coastal forts of Whydah, were sent to the capital, Abomey. These Christian wives were responsible for building churches in palaces that had indeed been the center of indigenous religion. The Christian wives were vodou Malatus, born to French slave owners, and were then baptized and regarded

as Christian. The interesting thing about this situation was that the name given to the Supreme God (Mawu) was in fact the choice of these female Christian wives. For a long time, Mawu competed with another name for God in the Egun tradition. In the indigenous tradition, Mawu-Lisa was the name for the Supreme God, but in the Christian tradition this name was degendered or masculinized. In the indigenous tradition, Mawu was the wife of Lisa. The Supreme God in Porto Novo is Jiwayewhe, which means "the sky spirit."

14. Moore, *Feminism and Anthropology;* Oyèéwùmí, *African Women and Feminism.*

15. Bennett, *In Search of the Sacred,* 159.

16. Moore, *Feminism and Anthropology,* 39; Bennett, *In Search of the Sacred,* 159.

17. Tavarez, "Colonial Evangelisation," 228.

18. Curcio-Nagey, *Great Festivals,* 3.

10. CONCLUSION

1. Foucault, *Archaeology of Knowledge;* Lewellen, *Anthropology of Globalization.*

2. Lewellen, *Anthropology of Globalization,* 73.

3. Ibid., 73.

4. Ferguson, *Expectations of Modernity,* 192.

5. Laitin, *Hegemony and Culture,* 9.

6. Ibid., 17.

7. Yoffee, *Myths,* 34–35; Runciman, "Origins of States"; Mann, *Sources of Social Power.*

8. Yoffee, *Myths,* 34.

9. Ibid., 37.

10. Ibid.

11. Greene, *Sacred Sites,* 7.

12. It is possible to frame this counterclaim as a form of infringement on the *òrìṣà*'s cultural property in the same way that intellectual property groups make counterclaims to rights that they consider stolen from them.

13. In Nigeria graduate students are considered to be junior faculty members by the university.

14. A commonly popular song in festivals and ceremonies in Yorùbáland.

15. Although the Ọ̀tún Ifẹ̀ preside over their royal court in their respective domains, the Lówá and other chiefs do so within the Ọọ̀ni's palace. The priest-chiefs have no such power or authority, except within their lineages.

16. Lewellen, *Anthropology of Globalization,* 205.

17. Prior to this, in 1977, Nigeria sponsored a world event called the FESTAC (African Festival of Arts and Culture), organized under the presidency of the Nigerian head of state, General Yakubu Gowon, which highlighted Nigerian and African culture. In the four-week duration of the festival, conservative Christian evangelical groups consistently blamed indigenous religion for the evils and satanic influences that they claim Nigeria now harbors.

18. Such as common kinship, language, ritual, and custom; see Lewellen, *Anthropology of Globalization,* 207.

Abímbọlá, Wándé. *Ifá Divination Poetry.* New York: NOK Publishers, 1977.

Abíọdún, Rowland. "Ifá Art Objects: An Interpretation Based on Oral Traditions." In *Yorùbá Oral Tradition,* edited by Wándé Abímbọlá, 421–69. Ilé-Ifẹ̀: Department of African Languages and Literatures, University of Ilé-Ifẹ̀, 1975.

———. "Orí Divinity: Its Worship, Symbolism and Artistic Manifestation." In *Proceedings of the World Conference on Òrìṣà Tradition,* 484–515. Ilé-Ifẹ̀: Department of African Languages and Literature, University of Ilé-Ifẹ̀, 1981.

Adeoye, C. L. *Ìgbàgbọ́ àti ẹ̀sìn Yorùbá.* Ìbàdàn, Nigeria: Evans Brothers, 1985.

Ajayi, J. F. A., and R. S. Smith. *Yorùbá Warfare in the Nineteenth Century.* Cambridge: Cambridge University Press, 1964.

Akínjógbìn, I. A. *Dahomey and Its Neighbours, 1708-1818.* Cambridge: Cambridge University Press, 1967.

———. "The Out-Lying Towns of Ife." In *The Cradle of a Race: Ife from the Beginning to 1980,* edited by I. A. Akínjógbìn, 217–41. Port Harcourt, Nigeria: Sunray Publications, 1992.

Akìwọwọ, Akínṣọlá. *Àjọbí and Ajogbé: Variations on the Theme of Sociation.* Ilé-Ifẹ̀: University of Ifẹ̀ Press, 1983.

Awẹ́, Bọ́lánlé, ed. *Nigerian Women in Historical Perspective.* Ibadan: Bookcraft, 1992.

Awolalu, J. O. *Yorùbá Beliefs and Sacrificial Rites.* London: Longman, 1979.

Ayandele, E. A. *The Missionary Impact on Modern Nigeria, 1842–1914: A Political and Social Analysis.* London: Longman, 1966.

Babáyẹmí, S. O. *Content Analysis of Oríkì Orílẹ̀.* Ìbàdàn, Nigeria: Institute of African Studies, University of Ìbàdàn, 198-?

Babb, L. A. *The Divine Hierarchy: Popular Hinduism in Central India.* New York: Columbia University Press, 1975.

Barber, Karin. *I Could Speak until Tomorrow: Oríkì, Women, and the Past in a Yorùbá Town.* Washington, DC: Smithsonian Institution Press, 1991.

Bascom, William Russell. *Ifá Divination: Communication between Gods and Men in West Africa.* Bloomington: Indiana University Press, 1969.

———. "Oba's Ear: A Yorùbá Myth in Cuba and Brazil." *Research in African Literature* 7, no. 2 (1976): 149–65.

———. "'Secret Societies': Religious Cult-Groups and Kinship Units among the West African Yorùbá: A Study in Social Organization." PhD diss., University of Chicago, 1939.

———. *The Yoruba of Southwestern Nigeria.* New York: Holt, Rinehart and Winston, 1969.

Beier, Ulli. "A Year of Sacred Festival in One Yoruba Town." *Nigeria Magazine,* special issue, 1959, 92.

Bell, C. M. *Ritual: Perspectives and Dimensions.* New York: Oxford University Press, 1997.

———. *Ritual Theory, Ritual Practice.* New York: Oxford University Press, 1992.

Bell, Diane. *Daughters of the Dreaming.* Minneapolis: University of Minnesota Press, 1993.

Ben-Israel, Hedva. "Hallowed Land in the Theory and Practice of Modern Nationalism." In *Sacred Space: Shrine, City, Land,* edited by Benjamin Z. Kedar and R. J. Z. Werblowsky, 278–94. New York: New York University Press, 1998.

Bennett, Clinton. *In Search of the Sacred: Anthropology and the Study of Religions.* London: Cassell, 1996.

Biobaku, S. O., ed. *Sources of Yorùbá History.* Oxford: Clarendon Press, 1973.

Bird, Stephanie Rose. *Sticks, Stones, Roots and Bones: Hoodoo, Mojo and Conjuring with Herbs.* St. Paul, MN: Llewellyn Publications, 2004.

Bloch, Maurice. "The Ritual of the Royal Bath in Madagascar: The Dissolution of Death, Birth and Fertility into Authority." In *Rituals of Royalty: Power and Ceremonial in Traditional Societies,* edited by David Cannadine and S. R. F. Price, 271–97. Cambridge: Cambridge University Press, 1987.

Bolle, Kees. "Myth: An Overview." In *Encyclopedia of Religion,* vol. 9, edited by Lindsay Jones, 6360–71. Detroit: Macmillan Reference USA, 2005.

Bradbury, Robert E. *The Benin Kingdom and the Edo-Speaking Peoples of South-Western Nigeria.* London: International African Institute, 1970.

Bushnell, Horace. *The Vicarious Sacrifice: Grounded in Principles of Universal Obligation.* Hicksville, NY: Regina Press, 1975.

Callaghy, T. M. "Politics and Vision in Africa." In *Political Domination in Africa: Reflections on the Limits of Power,* edited by Patrick Chabal, 30–51. Cambridge: Cambridge University Press, 1986.

Carrasco, David. *City of Sacrifice: The Aztec Empire and the Role of Violence in Civilization.* Boston: Beacon Press, 1999.

———. *Religions of Mesoamerica: Cosmovision and Ceremonial Centers.* San Francisco: Harper and Row, 1990.

Cohen, Roger. "Anger Is Shaking a Dead Nigerian Town to Its Foundation." *New York Times,* July 15, 1998, 3.

Comaroff, Jean, and John L. Comaroff. *Civil Society and the Political Imagination in Africa: Critical Perspectives.* Chicago: University of Chicago Press, 1999.

Combs-Schilling, M. E. *Sacred Performances: Islam, Sexuality, and Sacrifice.* New York: Columbia University Press, 1989.

Coon, C. S. *The Hunting Peoples.* Boston: Little, Brown, 1971.

Cooney, Gabriel, and Eoin Grogan. *Irish Prehistory: A Social Perspective.* Dublin: Wordwell, 1994.

Cooper, B. M. *Evangelical Christians in the Muslim Sahel.* Bloomington: Indiana University Press, 2006.

Curcio-Nagy, L. A. *The Great Festivals of Colonial Mexico City: Performing Power and Identity.* Albuquerque: University of New Mexico Press, 2004.

Daramola, Oludaisi, and Adelbayo Jeje. *Awọn asa ati òrìṣà ilé Yorùbá.* Ìbàdàn, Nigeria: Onibonoje Press, 1967.

Davidson, Hilda E. "Hooded Men in Celtic and Germanic Tradition." In *Polytheistic Systems,* edited by Glenys Davies, 105–24. Edinburgh: Edinburgh University Press, 1989.

Dietler, Michael, and Brian Hayden. *Feasts: Archaeological and Ethnographic Perspectives on Food, Politics, and Power.* Washington, DC: Smithsonian Institution Press, 2001.

Douglas, Mary. *Purity and Danger: An Analysis of Concepts of Pollution and Taboo.* London: Routledge and Paul, 1966.

Drewal, H. J., J. Pemberton, R. Abíọ́dún, and A. Wardwell. *Yorùbá: Nine Centuries of African Art and Thought.* New York: Center for African Art / H. N. Abrams, 1989.

Droogers, A. F., and Anton van Harskamp, eds. *Playful Religion: Challenges for the Study of Religion.* Delft, Netherlands: Eburon, 2006.

Du Bois, John W. "Meaning without Intention: Lessons from Divination." In *Responsibility and Evidence in Oral Discourse,* edited by J. H. Hill, and J. T. Irvine, 48–71. Cambridge: Cambridge University Press, 1993.

Dubisch, Jill. *In a Different Place: Pilgrimage, Gender, and Politics at a Greek Island Shrine.* Princeton: Princeton University Press, 1995.

Eames, E. A. "The Oǹdó Women's War: The Politics of Women's Wealth in a Yorùbá Town." PhD diss., Harvard University, 1992.

Eck, D. L. *Banaras, City of Light.* New York: Columbia University Press, 1999.

———. "The City as a Sacred Center." In *The City as a Sacred Center: Essays on Six Asian Contexts,* edited by B. L. Smith and H. B. Reynolds, 1–11. New York: Brill, 1987.

Egharevba, J. U. *A Short History of Benin.* 3rd ed. Ìbàdàn, Nigeria: Ìbàdàn University Press, 1960.

Eickelman, D. F. *Moroccan Islam: Tradition and Society in a Pilgrimage Center.* Austin: University of Texas Press, 1976.

Elebuibon, Yemi. *The Adventures of Ọbàtálá.* Òṣogbo, Nigeria: A. P. I. Production, 1989.

Eliade, Mircea. *Images and Symbols: Studies in Religious Symbolism.* New York: Sheed and Ward, 1961.

———. *The Sacred and the Profane: The Nature of Religion.* San Diego: Harcourt Brace Jovanovich, 1959.

Erndl, K. M. *Victory to the Mother: The Hindu Goddess of Northwest India in Myth, Ritual, and Symbol.* New York: Oxford University Press, 1993.

Fábùnmi, Àjàyí. *Àyajọ́, Ohùn Ẹnu Ifẹ̀.* Ibadan: Onibonoje Press, 1972.

Fágúnwà, D. O. *Forest of a Thousand Demons: A Hunter's Saga.* Translated by Wọlé Ṣóyínká. London: Nelson, 1982.

Ferguson, James. *Expectations of Modernity: Myths and Meanings of Urban Life on the Zambian Copperbelt.* Berkeley: University of California Press, 1999.

Festinger, Leon. *A Theory of Cognitive Dissonance.* Stanford: Stanford University Press, 1957.

Florescano, Enrique. *The Myth of Quetzalcoatl.* Baltimore: Johns Hopkins University Press, 1999.

Folarin, Wale. "Osun Approves Beaded Crown for Modakeke Ruler." *Nigerian Compass,* July 15,

2009, www.compassnewspaper.com/NG/index.php?option=com_content&view=article&id=22572:osun-approves-beaded-crown-for-modakeke-ruler&catid=43:news&Itemid=799.

Fortes, Meyer. "Some Reflections on Ancestor Worship in Africa." In *African Systems of Thought,* edited by Meyer Fortes and Germaine Dieterlen, 122–44. London: Oxford University Press, 1965.

Foucault, Michel. *The Archaeology of Knowledge and the Discourse on Language.* New York: Pantheon Books, 1972.

———. "Politics and the Study of Discourse." *Ideology and Consciousness* 3 (1978): 7–26.

Friedland, Roger, and R. D. Hecht. "The Politics of Sacred Place: Jerusalem's Temple Mount Al-Haram Al Sharif." In *Sacred Places and Profane Spaces: Essays in the Geographics of Judaism, Christianity, and Islam,* edited by J. S. Scott and P. Simpson-Housley, 21–61. New York: Greenwood Press, 1991.

Frobenius, Leo. *The Voice of Africa: Being an Account of the Travels of the German Inner African Exploration Expedition in the Years 1910–1912.* London: Hutchinson, 1913.

Geertz, Clifford. *Negara: The Theatre State in Nineteenth-Century Bali.* Princeton: Princeton University Press, 1980.

Gewertz, Deborah, and Frederick Errington. "Toward an Ethnographically Grounded Study of Modernity in Papua New Guinea." In *Globalization and Culture Change in the Pacific Islands,* edited by V. S. Lockwood, 273–84. Upper Saddle River, NJ: Pearson/Prentice Hall, 2004.

Girard, Réné. *Violence and the Sacred.* Baltimore: Johns Hopkins University Press, 1977.

Gluckman, Max. "Ritual of Rebellion in South-East Africa." In *Order and Rebellion in Tribal Africa: Collected Essays,* edited by Max Gluckman, 110–36. London: Cohen and West, 1963.

Goody, Jack. *Death, Property and the Ancestors: A Study of the Mortuary Customs of the Lodagaa of West Africa.* Stanford: Stanford University Press, 1962.

Greene, Sandra E. *Sacred Sites and the Colonial Encounter: A History of Meaning and Memory in Ghana.* Bloomington: Indiana University Press, 2002.

Griffin-Pierce, Trudy. *Earth Is My Mother, Sky Is My Father: Space, Time, and Astronomy in Navajo Sandpainting.* Albuquerque: University of New Mexico Press, 1992.

Gross, R. M. *Feminism and Religion: An Introduction.* Boston: Beacon Press, 1996.

Grossberg, Lawrence. "Identity and Cultural Studies: Is That All There Is?" In *Questions of Cultural Identity,* edited by Stuart Hall and Paul du Gay, 87–107. Thousand Oaks, CA: Sage Publications, 1996.

Haberland, Eike, ed. *Leo Frobenius: An Anthology.* English ed. Wiesbaden: F. Steiner, 1973.

Habermas, Jürgen. *The Structural Transformation of the Public Sphere: An Inquiry into a Category of Bourgeois Society.* Translated by Thomas Burger. Cambridge: MIT Press, 1989.

Hastings, Adrian. "Were Women a Special Case?" In *Women and Missions: Past and Present: Anthropological and Historical Perceptions,* edited by Fiona Bowie, Deborah Kirkwood, and Shirley Ardener, 109–44. Providence, RI: Berg, 1993.

Hodgkin, T. L. *Nigerian Perspectives: An Historical Anthology.* 2nd ed. London: Oxford University Press, 1975.

Horton, Robin. "On the Rationality of Conversion. Part II." *Africa: Journal of the International African Institute* 45, no. 4 (1975): 373–99.

Hubert, Henri, and Marcel Mauss. *Sacrifice: Its Nature and Function.* Chicago: University of Chicago Press, 1964.

Hubert, Jane. "Sacred Beliefs and Beliefs of Sacredness." In *Sacred Sites, Sacred Places,* edited by D. L. Carmichael, 9–19. London: Routledge, 1994.

Huizinga, Johan. *Homo ludens: Proeve eener bepaling van het spel-element der cultuur.* Haarlem, Netherlands: H. D. Tjeenk Willink, 1938.

Ibn al-Kalbi, Hisham. *The Book of Idols: Being a Translation from the Arabic of the Kitāb Al-Asnām.* Edited by N. A. Faris. Princeton: Princeton University Press, 1972.

Ìdòwú, E. B. *Olódùmarè: God in Yorùbá Belief.* Plainview, NY: Original Publications, 1995.

Ìṣọ̀lá, Akínwùmí. "Religious Politics and the Myth of Sango." In *African Traditional Religions in Contemporary Society,* edited by J. K. Olúpọ̀nà, 93–100. New York: Paragon House, 1991.

Johnson, Samuel D. *The History of the Yorùbás from the Earliest Times to the Beginning of the British Protectorate.* Edited by Obadiah Johnson. London: G. Routledge and Sons, 1921.

Koester, Helmut. *History, Culture, and Religion of the Hellenistic Age.* Vol. 2 of *Introduction to the New Testament.* Philadelphia: Fortress Press, 1982.

———. "Writings and the Spirit: Authority and Politics in Ancient Christianity." *Harvard Theological Review* 84, no. 4 (1991): 353–72.

Kunin, S. D. *God's Place in the World: Sacred Space and Sacred Place in Judaism.* London: Cassell, 1998.

Kurtz, Lester R. *Gods in the Global Village: The World's Religions in Sociological Perspective.* Thousand Oaks, CA: Pine Forge Press, 1995.

Laitin, D. D. *Hegemony and Culture: Politics and Religious Change among the Yorùbá.* Chicago: University of Chicago Press, 1986.

Lalèyê, I. P. *La conception de la personne dans la pensée traditionnelle Yorùbá: Approche phénoménologique.* Berne: Herbert Lang, 1970.

Lane, Belden C. *Landscapes of the Sacred: Geography and Narrative in American Spirituality.* Baltimore: Johns Hopkins University Press, 2002.

Laurence, Ray. "Ritual, Landscape, and the Destruction of Place in the Roman Imagination." In *Approaches to the Study of Ritual: Italy and the Ancient Mediterranean: Being a Series of Seminars Given at the Institute of Classical Studies School of Advanced Study, University of London,* edited by John B. Wilkinson, 111–22. London: Accordia Research Centre, 1996.

Law, Robin. *The Oyo Empire, c. 1600–c. 1836: A West African Imperialism in the Era of the Atlantic Slave Trade.* Oxford: Clarendon Press, 1977.

Lawal, Babátúndé. "Ori: The Significance of the Head in Yorùbá Sculpture." *Journal of Anthropological Research* 41, no. 1 (1985): 91–103.

Lessa, W. A., and E. Z. Vogt, eds. *Reader in Comparative Religion: An Anthropological Approach.* Evanston, IL: Row, Peterson, 1958.

Levy, R. I. *Mesocosm: Hinduism and the Organization of a Traditional Newar City in Nepal.* Berkeley: University of California Press, 1990.

Lewellen, T. C. *The Anthropology of Globalization: Cultural Anthropology Enters the 21st Century.* Westport, CT: Bergin and Garvey, 2002.

Livingston, J. C. *Anatomy of the Sacred: An Introduction to Religion.* New York: Macmillan, 1989.

Long, Charles H. "A Postcolonial Meaning of Religion: Some Reflections from the Indigenous World." In *Beyond Primitivism: Indigenous Religious Traditions and Modernity,* edited by J. K. Olúpọ̀nà, 89–98. New York: Routledge, 2004.

———. "Prolegomenon to a Religious Hermeneutic." *History of Religions* 6, no. 3 (1967): 254–64.

———. *Significations: Signs, Symbols and Images in the Interpretation of Religion.* Aurora, CO: Davies Group, 1999.

Lucas, J. O. *The Religion of the Yorùbás, Being an Account of the Religious Beliefs and Practices of the Yorùbá Peoples of Southern Nigeria, Especially in Relation to the Religion of Ancient Egypt.* Lagos: C. M. S. Bookshop, 1948.

MacCannell, Dean. *Empty Meeting Grounds: The Tourist Papers.* London: Routledge, 1992.

MacDonald, M. N., ed. *Experiences of Place.* Cambridge, MA: Center for the Study of World Religions, Harvard Divinity School, 2003.

Mach, Zdzisław. *Symbols, Conflict, and Identity: Essays in Political Anthropology.* Albany: State University of New York Press, 1993.

Mann, Michael. *The Sources of Social Power.* Cambridge: Cambridge University Press, 1986.

Marshall, Lorna. "!Kung Bushman Religious Beliefs." *Africa* 32, no. 3 (1962): 221–52.

Masuzawa, Tomoko. *In Search of Dreamtime: The Quest for the Origin of Religion.* Chicago: University of Chicago Press, 1993.

McAnany, P. A. *Living with the Ancestors: Kinship and Kingship in Ancient Maya Society.* Austin: University of Texas Press, 1995.

McGee, Mary. "In Quest of Saubhagya: The Roles and Goals of Women as Depicted in Marathi Stories of Votive Devotions." In *Images of Women in Maharashtrian Literature and Religion,* edited by Anne Feldhaus, 147–70. Albany: State University of New York Press, 1996.

McMullen, David. "Bureaucrats and Cosmology: The Ritual Code of T'ang China." In *Rituals of Royalty: Power and Ceremonial in Traditional Societies,* edited by David Cannadine and S. R. F. Price, 181–236. Cambridge: Cambridge University Press, 1987.

Mills, Barbara J., ed. *Identity, Feasting, and the Archaeology of the Greater Southwest.* Boulder: University Press of Colorado, 2004.

Mol, Hans. *Faith and Fragility: Religion and Identity in Canada.* Burlington, ON: Trinity Press, 1985.

———. *Identity and Religion: International, Cross-Cultural Approaches.* Beverly Hills, CA: Sage Publications, 1978.

———. *Identity and the Sacred: A Sketch for a New Social-Scientific Theory of Religion.* New York: Free Press, 1977.

Moore, H. L. *Feminism and Anthropology.* Cambridge: Polity Press, 1988.

Morinis, E. A. *Pilgrimage in the Hindu Tradition: A Case Study of West Bengal.* Delhi: Oxford University Press, 1984.

Murphy, Joseph M., and Mei-Mei Sanford, eds. *Ọṣun across the Waters: A Yoruba Goddess in Africa and the Americas.* Bloomington: Indiana University Press, 2001.

Neusner, Jacob. "Being Israel: Religion and Ethnicity in Judaism." In *The Religion Factor: An Introduction to How Religion Matters,* edited by W. S. Green and Jacob Neusner, 32–44. Louisville, KY: Westminster John Knox Press, 1996.

Niditch, Susan. *Ancient Israelite Religion*. New York: Oxford University Press, 1997.

Oberoi, Harjot. *The Construction of Religious Boundaries: Culture, Identity, and Diversity in the Sikh Tradition*. Chicago: University of Chicago Press, 1994.

Òjó, G. J. Afọlábí. *Yoruba Culture: A Geographical Analysis*. London: University of London Press, 1967.

Ọláníyan, Richard A. "The Modakeke Question in Ife Politics and Diplomacy." In *The Cradle of a Race: Ife from the Beginning to 1980*, edited by I. A. Akínjógbìn, 266–86. Port-Harcourt, Nigeria: Sunray Publications, 1992.

Olúbùṣe II, HRM Okùnadé Ṣíjúadé. "Greetings from the Throne." Publicly distributed pamphlet, November 1989.

Olúpọ̀nà, J. K., ed. *African Traditional Religions in Contemporary Society*. New York: Paragon House, 1991.

——. *Kingship, Religion, and Rituals in a Nigerian Community: A Phenomenological Study of Ondó Yorùbá Festivals*. Stockholm: Almqvist and Wiksell International, 1991.

——. "Òrìṣà Ọ̀ṣun: Yoruba Sacred Kingship and Civil Religion in Òṣogbo." In *Ọ̀ṣun across the Waters: A Yoruba Goddess in Africa and the Americas*, edited by Joseph M. Murphy and Mei-Mei Sanford, 46–67. Bloomington: Indian University Press, 2001.

——. "To Praise and to Reprimand: Ancestors and Spirituality in African Society and Culture." In *Ancestors in Post-Contact Religion: Roots, Ruptures, and Modernity's Memory*, edited by S. J. Friesen, 50–71. Cambridge, MA: Harvard University Press, 2001.

——. "Yoruba Goddesses and Sovereignty in South-Western Nigeria." In *Goddesses Who Rule*, edited by Elizabeth Benard and Beverly Moon, 119-132. Oxford: Oxford University Press, 2000.

Olúpọ̀nà, J. K., and Terry Rey, eds. *Òrìṣà Devotion as World Religion: The Globalization of Yorùbá Religious Culture*. Madison: University of Wisconsin Press, 2008.

Ọmọ́sini, Olufẹ́mi. "Ife: the Years of Recovery (1894–1930)." In *The Cradle of a Race: Ife from the Beginning to 1980*, edited by I. A. Akínjógbìn, 171–91. Port-Harcourt, Nigeria: Sunray Publications, 1992.

Omotoye, R. "Charles Phillips and His Contribution to the Church's Political and Economic Development of Eastern Yorùbá." PhD diss., University of Ìbàdàn, 2000.

Oyèéwùmí, Oyèérónkẹ́. *African Women and Feminism: Reflecting on the Politics of Sisterhood*. Trenton, NJ: Africa World Press, 2003.

——. *The Invention of Women: Making an African Sense of Western Gender Discourses*. Minneapolis: University of Minnesota Press, 1997.

Pacheco Pareira, Duarte. *Esmeraldo de situ orbis*. Edited and translated by G. H. T. Kimble. London: Hakluyt Society, 1937.

Parrinder, E. G. *African Traditional Religion*. London: Hutchinson's University Library, 1954.

——. *Religion in an African City*. London: Oxford University Press, 1953.

Pearce, T. O. "Cultural Production and Reproductive Issues: The Significance of the Charismatic Movement in Nigeria." In *Religion and Sexuality in Cross-Cultural Perspective*, edited by S. Ellingson and M. Green, 21–50. New York: Routledge, 2002.

Pedya, Haviva. "The Divinity as Place and Time and the Holy Place in Jewish Mysticism." In *Sacred Space: Shrine, City, Land*, edited by Benjamin Z. Kedar and R. J. Z. Werblowsky, 84-111. New York: New York University Press, 1998.

Peel, J. D. Y. "Gender in Yoruba Religious Change." *Journal of Religion in Africa* 32, no. 2 (May 2002): 136–66.

———. *Ijeshas and Nigerians: The Incorporation of a Yorùbá Kingdom, 1890s-1970s.* Cambridge: Cambridge University Press, 1983.

Pemberton, John, III, and F. S. Afọláyan. *Yorùbá Sacred Kingship: "A Power Like That of the Gods."* Washington, DC: Smithsonian Institution Press, 1996.

Rappaport, R. A. *Ecology, Meaning, and Religion.* Richmond, CA: North Atlantic Books, 1979.

Reichard, G. A. *Prayer: The Compulsive Word.* New York: J. J. Augustin, 1944.

Rose, M. B. *Gender and Heroism in Early Modern English Literature.* Chicago: University of Chicago Press, 2002.

Runciman, W. G. "Origins of States: The Case of Archaic Greece." *Comparative Studies in Society and History* 24, no. 3 (1982): 351–77.

Ryder, A. F. C. 1969. *Benin and the Europeans, 1485-1897.* Harlow: Longmans.

———. "A Reconsideration of the Ifè-Benin Relationship." *Journal of African History* 6, no. 1 (1965): 25–37.

Sarup, Madan. *Identity, Culture, and the Postmodern World.* Edited by Tasneem Raja. Athens: University of Georgia Press, 1996.

Schleiermacher, F. E. D. *On Religion: Speeches to Its Cultured Despisers.* New York: Harper, 1958.

Scully, Stephen. *Homer and the Sacred City.* Ithaca: Cornell University Press, 1990.

Senghor, Léopold. "The Lessons of Leo Frobenius." In *Leo Frobenius, 1873-1973: An Anthology,* edited by Eike Haberland, vii–xiii. Wiesbaden: F. Steiner, 1973.

Shelton, Anthony. "Preliminary Notes on Some Structural Parallels in the Symbolic and Relational Classifications of Nahuatl and Huichol Deities." In *Polytheistic Systems,* edited by Glenys Davies, 151–83. Edinburgh: Edinburgh University Press, 1989.

Silverman, D. P. "Divinity and Deities in Ancient Egypt." In *Religion in Ancient Egypt: Gods, Myths, and Personal Practice,* edited by B. E. Shafer, J. Baines, L. H. Lesko, and D. P. Silverman, 1–87. Ithaca: Cornell University Press, 1991.

Skoggard, I. A. *The Indigenous Dynamic in Taiwan's Postwar Development: The Religious and Historical Roots of Entrepreneurship.* Armonk, NY: M. E. Sharpe, 1996.

Smith, Anthony D. *The Ethnic Origins of Nations.* Oxford: B. Blackwell, 1986.

Smith, Jonathan Z. *To Take Place: Toward Theory in Ritual.* Chicago: University of Chicago Press, 1987.

Smith, R. S. *Kingdoms of the Yorùbá.* 3rd ed. Madison: University of Wisconsin Press, 1988.

Sole, Tony, and Kirsty Woods. "Protection of Indigenous Sacred Sites: The New Zealand Experience." In *Aboriginal Involvement in Park and Protected Areas,* edited by Jim Birckhead, Terry De Lacey, and Laurajane Smith, 339–51. Canberra: Aboriginal Studies Press, 1992.

Ṣóyínká-Airewele, Peyi. "When Neutrality Is Taboo: Reconstituting Institutional Identity and Peace-Building Paradigms in Africa—the Nigerian Ife/Modakeke Case." *African and Asian Studies* 2, no. 3 (2003): 259–305.

Stevens, Phillips. "Orisha-nla Festival." *Nigeria Magazine,* September 1966, 184–99.

Sudarkasa, Niara. *Where Women Work: Yoruba Traders in the Market Place and in the Home.* Ann Arbor: University of Michigan Press, 1973.

Sullivan, L. E. *Icanchu's Drum: An Orientation to Meaning in South American Religions.* New York: Macmillan, 1988.

Swain, Tony, and G. W. Trompf. *The Religions of Oceania*. London: Routledge, 1995.

Taussig, Michael. "Transgression." In *Critical Terms for Religious Studies*, edited by M. C. Taylor, 349–62. Chicago: University of Chicago Press, 1998.

Tavarez, David. "Colonial Evangelisation and Native Resistance: The Interplay of Native Political Autonomy and Ritual Practices in Villa Alta (New Spain), 1700–1704." In *Interpreting Colonialism*, edited by B. R. Wells and P. Stewart, 209–30. Oxford: Voltaire Foundation, 2004.

Theodoratus, Dorothea, and Frank La Pena. "Wintu Sacred Geography of Northern California." In *Sacred Sites, Sacred Places*, edited by David L. Carmichael, Jane Hubert, Brian Reeves, and Audhild Schanche, 20–31. London: Routledge, 1994.

Thornton, Robert. "South Africa: Countries, Boundaries, Enemies and Friends." *Anthropology Today* 10, no. 6 (1994): 7–15.

Trager, Lillian. *Yoruba Hometowns: Community, Identity, and Development in Nigeria*. Boulder, CO: Lynne Rienner, 2001.

Turner, V. W. *The Ritual Process: Structure and Anti-structure*. Chicago: Aldine, 1969.

———. "Sacrifice as Quintessential Process: Prophylaxis or Abandonment?" *History of Religions* 16, no. 3 (1977): 189–215.

Turner, V. W., and E. L. B. Turner. *Image and Pilgrimage in Christian Culture Anthropological Perspectives*. New York: Columbia University Press, 1978.

Valeri, Valerio. *Kingship and Sacrifice: Ritual and Society in Ancient Hawaii*. Chicago: University of Chicago Press, 1985.

van Baal, Jan. "Offering, Sacrifice, and Gift." *Numen* 23 (1976): 161–78.

van Gennep, Arnold. *The Rites of Passage*. Chicago: University of Chicago Press, 1960.

Verger, Pierre. *Flux et reflux de la traite des nègres entre le Golfe de Bénin et Bahia de Todos os Santos, du XVIIe au XIXe siècle*. Paris: Mouton, 1968.

Vico, Giambattista. *The New Science*. Translated by T. G. Bergin and M. H. Fisch. 3rd ed. Garden City, NY: Doubleday, 1961.

Walsh, Michael J. "The Edi Festival at Ile-Ife." *African Affairs* 47, no. 189 (1948): 231–38.

Werblowsky, R. J. Z. "Introduction: Mindscape and Landscape." In *Sacred Space: Shrine, City, Land*, edited by Benjamin Z. Kedar and R. J. Z. Werblowsky, 9–17. New York: New York University Press, 1998.

Werbner, R. P., ed. *Memory and the Postcolony: African Anthropology and the Critique of Power*. London: Zed Books, 1998.

Wheatley, Paul. *The Pivot of the Four Quarters: A Preliminary Enquiry into the Origins and Character of the Ancient Chinese City*. Chicago: Aldine, 1971.

Wilkinson, John B., ed. *Approaches to the Study of Ritual: Italy and the Ancient Mediterranean*. London: Accordia Research Centre, 1996.

Willett, Frank. "Archaelogy." In *Sources of Yoruba History*, edited by Saburi O. Biobaku, 111–39. Oxford: Clarendon Press, 1973.

———. *Ife in the History of West African Sculpture*. London: Thames and Hudson, 1967.

Williams, Tony. "Thresholds of Desire and Domestic Space in Nineteenth-Century French Fiction." In *Secret Spaces, Forbidden Places: Rethinking Culture*, edited by Fran Lloyd, and Catherine O'Brien, 39–50. New York: Berghahn Books, 2000.

Yai, Ọlábíyìí Babalola. "The Path Is Open: The Herskovits Legacy in African Oral Narrative

Analysis and Beyond." Working Paper, Program of African Studies, Northwestern University, 1999.

Yerkes, R. K. *Sacrifice in Greek and Roman Religions and Early Judaism*. New York: Scribner, 1952.

Yoffee, Norman. *Myths of the Archaic State: Evolution of the Earliest Cities, States, and Civilizations*. Cambridge: Cambridge University Press, 2005.

INDEX

Àààfín/Òkè-Ilé, 39, 89, 148, 210, 212, 251, 257, 286, 291, 292

Abẹ̀òkúta, 11, 43

Abewéelá, Ọ̀ọ̀ni, 46, 49

Abímbọ́lá, Kọ́lá, 297

Abímbọ́lá, Wándé, 2, 3, 88, 195, 196, 294

Abíọ́dún, Rowland, xv, 2, 3, 68, 103, 136, 294

Accra, 73

Action Group Party, 41, 42–43

Adefunmi I, Ọba Oseijami, 94

Adérẹ̀mí, Ọ̀ọ̀ni Adésọjí, 47, 48, 70, 97–98, 123, 129, 218, 295

Adétunbí, Reverend (provost of Anglican Cathedral), 253

Adó (Benin), 228

Adó-Èkìtì, 41, 67

Afọláyan, Fúnṣọ, 3

Agbáyégún, 31

Àgbọngbọ̀n (Ifá chief priest in Ilé-Ifẹ̀), 185

Àgbọnìrègún (founder of Ifá), 57

Àgbọnìrègún Hill, 193, 293

Àìsùn Ògún, 143

Ajagun, Ọ̀ọ̀ni Adémilúyì, 47

Àjàlá (custodian of destiny), 33

Àjànàkú of Lagos, 195

Ajé (goddess of wealth and prosperity), 13, 33, 67; and banking, 132–33; and cowrie shells, 131–32; in Ifá narratives, 131; and kingship, 133–34; and market economy, 33; and ọjà

(market), 90; and Ọlọ́jọ́ Festival, 131; and owó (money), 132

àjọbí (principles of kinship and religious association), 41

Àjùwọ̀n, Bádé, 294

Àkàrìgbò of Ṣágámù (now Ìjẹ̀bú Rẹ́mọ), 41, 78–84

Akínjọ́gbìn, Adéagbo, 41, 46

Akínwùmí, Ìṣọ̀lá, 60

Akìwọwọ, Akínṣọlá, 41, 294

Akogun (war chief and chief priest of the Ọ̀rànmíyàn Shrine), 96, 116, 127

Aláàfin of Ọ̀yọ́, 41, 78, 81, 227, 289

Aláké of Abẹ̀okúta, 78, 81

Aláyémore, Ọ̀ọ̀ni Ọbalùfọ̀n, 129

Àlùfáà (a Christian clergyman), 186

alùkan (royal drum), 45

Americas, the, 284, 292

ancestor-heroes. See Mọrèmi, Odùduwà (Oòduà), and Ọ̀rànmíyàn

ancestral veneration, 225; comparison between Yorùbá and Mayan society, 226

ancient: Greek and Roman religion, 219; Romans, 35

anthropology, traditional, 2

Apènà Oòduà, 235

approach(es): holistic, 2; interdisciplinary, 3

Apter, Andrew, 2, 3

Àràbà (chief priest of Ifá), 13, 15, 39, 98, 135,

TEXT
10/12.5 Minion Pro

DISPLAY
Minion Pro

CARTOGRAPHER
Bill Nelson

COMPOSITOR
Integrated Composition Systems

PRINTER AND BINDER
IBT Global

9 780520 265561